BROADMAN COMMENTS 1995-96
52 Ready-To-Teach
Bible Study Lessons

BROADMAN COMMENTS 1995-96

52 Ready-To-Teach Bible Study Lessons

ROBERT J. DEAN
J. B. FOWLER, JR.
JAMES E. TAULMAN

Based on the International Sunday School Lessons
Each Plan Includes These Sections : ❀ Studying the Bible
❀ Applying the Bible ❀ Teaching the Bible

BROADMAN
&HOLMAN
PUBLISHERS

Nashville, Tennessee

4217-34
ISBN: 0-8054-1733-6

The Outlines of the International Sunday School Lessons, Uniform Series, are
copyrighted by the Committee on the Uniform Series and are used by
permission.

Dewey Decimal Classification: 268.61
Subject Heading: SUNDAY SCHOOL LESSONS—COMMENTARIES

ISSN: 0068-2721

POSTMASTER: Send address change to *Broadman Comments*,
Customer Service Center, 127 Ninth Avenue, North
Nashville, Tennessee 37234

Library of Congress Catalog Card Number: 45-437
Printed in the United States of America

WRITERS

STUDYING THE BIBLE
Donald F. Ackland has written the biblical interpretation portion of *Broadman Comments* since 1970.

APPLYING THE LESSON
J. B. Fowler, Jr. is a freelance writer from San Antonio, Texas. He has recently retired as editor of *Baptist New Mexican*, Albuquerque, New Mexico.

TEACHING THE CLASS
James E. Taulman is Biblical Studies Designer for *The Adult Teacher* in the Bible Teaching–Reaching Division of the Sunday School Board, Nashville, Tennessee.

ABBREVIATIONS AND TRANSLATIONS

KJV   *King James Version*

NASB   From the *New American Standard Bible*. © The Lockman Foundation, 1960, 1962, 1963, 1968, 1971, 1972, 1973, 1975, 1977. Used by permission.

NIV   From the Holy Bible, *New International Version*. Copyright © 1973, 1978, 1984 by International Bible Society. Used by permission.

NEB   From *The New English Bible*. Copyright © The Delegates of the Oxford University Press and the Syndics of the Cambridge University Press, 1961, 1970. Reprinted by permission.

NRSV   From the *New Revised Standard Version Bible*. Copyright © 1989, by the Division of Christian Education of the National Council of Churches of Christ in the United States of America, and used by permission.

Contents

FIRST QUARTER:
The Story of Christian Beginnings (The Acts)

UNIT I: BEGINNINGS IN JERUSALEM
Sept. 3 — The Promise of the Spirit's Power 2
Sept. 10 — The Holy Spirit's Coming in Power 10
Sept. 17 — Healing and Preaching 18
Sept. 24 — Obedient to the Spirit 26

UNIT II: WITNESSING IN JUDEA AND SAMARIA
Oct. 1 — Chosen to Serve 33
Oct. 8 — Philip: Witness to Outcasts 41
Oct. 15 — Saul Becomes a Disciple 48
Oct. 22 — Gentiles Receive the Spirit 56
Oct. 29 — The Church at Antioch 64

UNIT III: SPREADING THE GOSPEL INTO ALL THE WORLD
Nov. 5 — Mission to Gentiles 71
Nov. 12 — The Jerusalem Conference 79
Nov. 19 — A Gospel Unhindered by Geography 86
Nov. 26 — Power of the Gospel 94

SECOND QUARTER:
God's Promise of Deliverance

UNIT I: THE COMING OF A NEW DAY
Dec. 3 — A Time of Comfort 104
Dec. 10 — A Time of Encouragement 112
Dec. 17 — A Time of Joy 120
Dec. 24 — A Time of Righteousness and Peace 127
Dec. 31 — A Time of Sharing Good News 134

UNIT II: THE MINISTRY OF THE SUFFERING SERVANT
Jan. 7 — The Servant's Call 142
Jan. 14 — The Servant's Mission 149
Jan. 21 — The Servant's Steadfast Endurance 156
Jan. 28 — The Servant's Victory 163

GOD'S LOVE FOR ALL PEOPLE
Feb. 4 — Jonah Flees from God 172
Feb. 11 — God Shows Mercy 180
Feb. 18 — The Loyalty of Ruth 187
Feb. 25 — The Kindness of Boaz 195

THIRD QUARTER: Teachings of Jesus

UNIT I: TEACHINGS ABOUT THE KINGDOM OF HEAVEN
Mar. 3   — Parable of the Sower 204
Mar. 10 — Parable of the Unforgiving Servant 212
Mar. 17 — Parable of the Vineyard Workers 219
Mar. 24 — The Parable of the Three Servants............ 227
Mar. 31 — The Parable of the Great Feast 234

UNIT II: TEACHING ABOUT GOD
April 7   — The Living Lord 241
April 14 — The Living God.......................... 248
April 21 — The Good Shepherd 255
April 28 — The True Vine........................... 263

UNIT III: TEACHINGS ABOUT LIVING
May 5   — Teachings About Happiness 270
May 12 — Teaching About Loving Your Enemies 277
May 19 — Teaching About Riches and Anxiety 284
May 26 — Teaching About Prayer 294

FOURTH QUARTER:
A Practical Religion (James)

June 2   — Faith and Faithfulness...................... 300
June 9   — Faith and Relationships..................... 307
June 16 — Faith and Action 315
June 23 — Faith and Wisdom........................ 322
June 30 — Faith and Righteousness 330

God Is With Us (Psalms)

UNIT I: PRAISING GOD
July 7   — Praising God as Creator and Sustainer 338
July 14 — Praising God for Mighty Acts 346
July 21 — Praising God for Deliverance 354
July 28 — Praising God Who Knows and Cares 361

UNIT II: RESPONDING TO GOD
Aug. 4   — Trust in God............................. 368
Aug. 11 — Obey God's Laws 376
Aug. 18 — Repent and Confess 384
Aug. 25 — Worship and Witness 392

Alternative lesson for January 21st

Jan. 21 — Sexual Purity 399

Index 406

The Story of Christian Beginnings (The Acts)

INTRODUCTION

The New Testament contains four Gospels to tell the story of Jesus' coming, life, death, and resurrection; however, it contains only one book to tell the story of the early Christians. The Book of Acts tells the exciting account of how God's Spirit led the believers to spread the good news. This particular study of Acts gives attention to beginnings in Jerusalem, to the spread of the gospel to Gentiles, and to the missionary work of Paul.

Unit I, "Beginnings in Jerusalem," which is based on Acts 1–5, tells of the earliest days of the church in Jerusalem. It includes the promise of the Spirit, the coming of the Spirit at Pentecost, the healing and preaching of the apostles, and their obedient testimony regardless of threats.

Unit II, "Witnessing in Judea and Samaria," which is based on Acts 6–12, tells of the spread of the good news to Gentiles. It includes the selection of the seven, the witness of Philip in Samaria and to the Ethiopian, the conversion of Saul of Tarsus, Peter's witness to Cornelius, and the church at Antioch.

Unit III, "Spreading the Gospel into All the World," which is based on Acts 13–19, tells of missionary work associated with Paul. It includes the missionary journey of Barnabas and Saul, the Jerusalem Conference, the missionary work of Paul in Macedonia, and the evidence of the gospel's power at Ephesus.

The Promise of the Spirit's Power

Basic Passage: Acts 1
Focal Passage: Acts 1:1–14

A cts 1 binds together the two volumes of Luke's work: the Gospel of Luke and the Book of Acts. Chapter 1 provides a brief summary of the Gospel, with emphasis on the appearances of the risen Lord. Also in this chapter are the main themes that run through the Book of Acts. Stress is placed on the promise of the coming of the Spirit, whose power would enable the believers to launch a worldwide witness. We call the book the Acts of the Apostles; a more apt title would be the Acts of the Holy Spirit.

▶ ▶ ▶ ▶ ▶ ▶ ▶ ▶ **Study Aim:** *To explain the relationship between Jesus' promise of the Spirit's power and His commission for worldwide witness*

STUDYING THE BIBLE

LESSON OUTLINE
  I. Prologue to the Book of Acts (1:1–2)
  II. The Risen Lord's Instructions (1:3–8)
    1. His appearances and instructions (v. 3)
    2. Promise of the Spirit (vv. 4–5)
    3. Commissioned to worldwide witness (vv. 6–8)
  III. Other Events Before Pentecost (1:9–26)
    1. The ascension (vv. 9–11)
    2. Prayer in the upper room (vv. 12–14)
    3. Selection of a twelfth apostle (vv. 15–26)

Following a brief prologue (vv. 1–2), Luke described the instructions of the risen Lord to the apostles. After His resurrection, the Lord appeared to them over a period of forty days (v. 3). He told them to wait in Jerusalem for the promise of the Holy Spirit (vv. 4–5). When the apostles asked if this was the time for Israel's restoration, Christ told them not to be concerned about times and seasons, but to concentrate on being His witnesses both near and far (vv. 6–8). After Christ's ascension, angels promised the apostles that the Lord would return (vv. 9–11). The apostles and other believers gathered in the upper room and prayed with one accord (vv. 12–14). Matthias was chosen to be an apostle to fill out the number to twelve.

I. Prologue to the Book of Acts (Acts 1:1–2)

1 The former treatise have I made, O Theophilus, of all that Jesus began to do and teach,

2 Until the day in which he was taken up, after that he

through the Holy Ghost had given commandments unto the apostles whom he had chosen.

Luke began both his books with a short prologue. Luke intended these works to be a two-volume work. One evidence of this is that both works were dedicated to someone named Theophilus (thih AHF ih luhs). Also Luke began the second volume with a brief summary of the contents of the Gospel. The Gospel told "all that Jesus began to do and teach." Verses 1–2 do not spell out what will be in the Book of Acts; however, the word "began" in verse 1 implies a continuation of the Lord's work. In other words, the Gospel of Luke tells what Jesus began to do and teach; the Book of Acts tells what He continued to do and teach by the work of His Spirit.

II. The Risen Lord's Instructions (Acts 1:3–8)

1. His appearances and instructions (v. 3)

3 To whom also he shewed himself alive after his passion by many infallible proofs, being seen of them forty days, and speaking of the things pertaining to the kingdom of God.

The risen Lord appeared to His followers over a period of forty days. He was not with them continuously. Instead, He appeared at various times and places. During those forty days, Jesus was trying to teach them several important lessons.

For one thing, the Lord was showing them the reality of His resurrection. In spite of all that Jesus had said before His death and resurrection, the apostles were not expecting Him to be raised from the dead. When the women first brought word of His resurrection, the apostles did not believe them (Luke 24:11). Only after they saw Jesus alive were they convinced.

Another purpose of Jesus during the forty days was to open the disciples' minds to the truths of the Scriptures about the kingdom of God. The Gospel records how the Lord used the Scriptures to teach them of Him. Jesus emphasized His death and resurrection and their mission to all nations (Luke 24:44–48).

2. Promise of the Spirit (vv. 4–5)

4 And, being assembled together with them, commanded them that they should not depart from Jerusalem, but wait for the promise of the Father, which, saith he, ye have heard of me.

5 For John truly baptized with water; but ye shall be baptized with the Holy Ghost not many days hence.

The risen Lord had another purpose during the forty days. He was preparing His followers for the coming of the Holy Spirit. During His earthly ministry, they could see Him, hear Him, and touch Him. During the forty days, they also were able to see, hear, and touch Him when He appeared to them. Most of the time, however, He was not visible among them. But they knew that, at any moment, the risen Lord might suddenly be with them. Jesus was preparing them for a time when He would no longer be available to see, hear, and touch. However, He wanted them to realize He would continue to be with them by His Spirit. During the forty days, Jesus told them to remain in

Jerusalem and wait for the fulfillment of the promise of the coming of the Holy Spirit (Luke 24:49; Acts 1:4–5).

3. Commissioned to worldwide witness (vv. 6–8)

6 When they therefore were come together, they asked of him, saying, Lord, wilt thou at this time restore again the kingdom to Israel?

7 And he said unto them, It is not for you to know the times or the seasons, which the Father hath put in his own power.

8 But ye shall receive power, after that the Holy Ghost is come upon you: and ye shall be witnesses unto me both in Jerusalem, and in all Judaea, and in Samaria, and unto the uttermost part of the earth.

The disciples knew that Old Testament prophets foretold the restoration of Israel in the last days. They asked Jesus if this promise was about to be fulfilled. Their question provided the Lord with an excellent teaching opportunity.

First, Jesus told His followers not to be concerned about times and seasons of divine fulfillment. This was not something for them to seek to know. Acts 1:9 reminds us of the words of Jesus about the time of His future coming. He made clear that no one but God knows the time (Matt. 24:36; Mark 13:32).

Second, Jesus emphasized what His followers were to do as they awaited the Lord's return. The risen Lord commissioned His followers to be His witnesses near and far. He promised the Spirit to guide and empower them as witnesses. Jesus taught that the Holy Spirit was to glorify Him, not to call attention to Himself (John 16:14). The Spirit is the Spirit of the Lord calling people to Christ, transforming them into His likeness, and sending them forth as His witnesses. The apostles were eyewitnesses of Jesus; although we have not been with Him as they were, we too can bear witness to Him.

The risen Lord commissioned His followers to be witnesses to the ends of the earth. For the first believers, this meant to begin in Jerusalem and Judea. Jesus also included the half-breed Samaritans, whom the Jews detested. And He spoke of going to the uttermost part of the earth. The Book of Acts tells of the struggle of the early Jewish believers to move from verse 6 to verse 8. They were interested in the restoration of Israel. Jesus wanted them to go to all kinds of people in all nations.

III. Other Events Before Pentecost (Acts 1:9–26)

1. The ascension (vv. 9–11)

9 And when he had spoken these things, while they beheld, he was taken up; and a cloud received him out of their sight.

10 And while they looked steadfastly toward heaven as he went up, behold, two men stood by them in white apparel;

11 Which also said, Ye men of Galilee, why stand ye gazing up into heaven? this same Jesus, which is taken up from you into heaven, shall so come in like manner as ye have seen him go into heaven.

The Gospel of Luke closes with the ascension (24:51). Acts 1:9–11 enlarges on the description of that event. The ascension showed the disciples that this was the end of their relationship with Jesus as One whom they could see, hear, and touch. They realized that a new kind of relationship with Him was soon to begin. This helped them take seriously His words about waiting for the coming of the Spirit. God used the ascension as a sign of Christ's future coming. As His followers stood looking into heaven, two angels assured them that the Lord would return as they had seen Him go. When the words of the angels are taken in context with verses 6–8, the angels were telling them that the way to be ready for the Lord's return was to be obedient to His commission and other commands.

2. Prayer in the upper room (vv. 12–14)

12 Then returned they unto Jerusalem from the mount called Olivet, which is from Jerusalem a Sabbath day's journey.

13 And when they were come in, they went up into an upper room, where abode both Peter, and James, and John, and Andrew, Philip, and Thomas, Bartholomew, and Matthew, James the son of Alphaeus [al FEE uhs], and Simon Zelotes [zih LOH teez], and Judas the brother of James.

14 These all continued with one accord in prayer and supplication, with the women, and Mary the mother of Jesus, and with his brethren.

Jesus ascended from the Mount of Olives. The reference to a Sabbath day's journey doesn't necessarily mean that the event took place on a Sabbath. The Jews had defined a distance that someone could walk on the Sabbath without it being called work. The distance was about three-fourths of a mile.

The names of the apostles are the same as in Luke 6:13–16, except for the deletion of Judas Iscariot. Verse 14 shows that others were present. Verse 15 says about 120 were present. The reference to "the women" probably included the women who helped Jesus during His ministry, those who witnessed His crucifixion, and those who went early to the tomb (Luke 8:2; 23:55; 24:10).

During Jesus' earthly life, His family often didn't understand what He did. Even Mary, who knew the miracle of His conception, at times received from Jesus a mild rebuke (John 2:3–4). His brothers didn't even believe in Him (John 7:5). On one occasion, when His family came to get Him, Jesus spoke of His larger family of faith (Mark 3:31–35). Now His mother and brothers met with others of that larger family. One of those who saw the risen Lord was James, Jesus' half brother (1 Cor. 15:7). James later became a leader in the Jerusalem church (Acts 12:17; 15:13; 21:18).

This group of believers met in an upper room to wait for the promised Spirit. As they waited, they prayed. They were in one accord as they waited and prayed.

3. Selection of a twelfth apostle (vv. 15–26). One item of business was handled during those days. Peter quoted Scripture that predicted the ruin of Judas Iscariot and the need to replace him. In order to be qualified to become an apostle, one had to have been with Jesus and to have been an eyewitness of the risen Lord. Two qualified candidates were named. Using an Old Testament method of seeking the Lord's will, the choice fell on Matthias.

APPLYING THE BIBLE

1. The reality of the resurrection. The visitor to Paris can see Napoleon's huge, red granite tomb in the Hotel des Invalides. It is 13 feet long, 6 1/2 feet wide, and 14 1/2 feet high. In it are the remains of the "Little Corporal" who was brought to his knees by the Duke of Wellington at Waterloo in 1815. Once master of all Europe, Napoleon "was cursed as a despot, blessed as the embodiment of progress and order," as Lowell Thomas put it. However, Napoleon, who rewrote history by conquering Europe, has not conquered the grave. But Jesus Christ, the humblest of men, was nailed to His cross on Friday and raised from the dead on Easter morning.[1]

The reality of the resurrection is the bedrock of Christian teachings (v. 3). Without His resurrection there would be no salvation from sin and no outpouring of the Holy Spirit upon His people.

2. The "baptism" of the Holy Spirit. In his book *The Holy Spirit in Today's World*, W. A. Criswell writes that the baptism of the Holy Spirit is a term widely used but greatly abused. He says that some groups build whole systems of theology on the term and teach that it is some kind of second work of grace. They teach salvation comes first and, later, as some second work of grace, comes the baptism of the Holy Spirit.

Criswell rightly points out that the baptism of the Holy Spirit to which Jesus refers in verse 5 of our lesson today, is that act in which the Holy Spirit places believers in Christ, making them a part of his body which is His church.[2]

The word translated "baptized" (v. 3) means "to place." It is not, as so many erroneously claim, a second act of grace, but that initial act in which we are placed into Christ Himself. The infilling of the Holy Spirit is often confused with "the baptism."

3. Everything but the power.—George Duncan, well known in earlier years as one of the great Keswick preachers, told about visiting a home in England. It was an old stone building that had been renovated. Everything was shining and new, with all kinds of electrical appliances: an electric stove, electric lights, and an electric iron. But Duncan was amazed to discover that the lady of the house was using an old oil stove, oil lamps, and the house smelled of burning oil. When Duncan asked about the newly renovated house and electrical appliances and why they were not being used, he was told not to forget there was a war on. "We have everything except the power," the lady of the house said.

Before the outpouring of the Holy Spirit the apostles had everything but the power. But Jesus promised they would receive power after the Holy Spirit had been poured out upon them (v. 8).

That "promise of the Father," to which Jesus referred in the Gospels, was fulfilled on the day of Pentecost.

4. Commissioned. Christians should be missionary people. We believe in the Great Commission (Matt. 28:19–20). Jesus said in His Great Commission that we should begin with "Jerusalem"—the homeland. American Christians have been commissioned to share the good news with more than 250 million Americans—at least 167 million of whom do not know Jesus as their Savior. This means that two out of three Americans are unsaved. And the number of lost people in America increases by 2 million each year. Only four nations in the world have a greater population than America.

Conclusion: America is one of the greatest mission fields in the world. But our mission commission does not end here at home. We are also to take the gospel to the "uttermost part of the earth" (v. 8).[3]

5. The last instruction of Jesus to His disciples. Before Jesus ascended, He gave His disciples one parting commandment: "They should not depart from Jerusalem, but wait for the promise of the Father" (v. 4; Luke 24:49). The disciples knew what Jesus meant and verse 14 shows their obedience: "These all continued with one accord in prayer and supplication."

Nothing is more important than prayer. Jesus knew that, and the disciples quickly learned it.

Veteran mountain climber George Adam Clark tells about climbing a dangerous peak in the Alps when a sudden gust of wind threatened to blow him and his guide off the mountain. Above the gale of the wind, Clark heard his guide calling out, "On your knees, sir, on your knees. It is not safe to be on this mountain in this wind except on your knees."[4]

As the church tries to minister to our kind of world, it can only do so on its knees. And we never stand taller with God or people than when we are on our knees in prayer.

TEACHING THE BIBLE

▶ *Main Idea:* Jesus promised the Holy Spirit to His disciples and commissioned them to be worldwide witnesses.
▶ *Suggested Teaching Aim:* To lead adults to explain the relationship between Jesus' promise of the Spirit's power and His commission for worldwide witness.

A TEACHING OUTLINE

1. Give a quiz to introduce the Book of Acts.
2. Use various teaching techniques to examine the Scripture passage.
3. Determine what steps the class and members need to take to claim Jesus' power to be worldwide witnesses.

Introduce the Bible Study

Share "Everything but the power" from "Applying the Bible."

Search for Biblical Truth

IN ADVANCE, make a quarter poster on which you list the unit headings, the Scriptures being studied, and the dates. Place this on the wall for the whole quarter and use it to introduce each lesson.

Use the following quiz to introduce the study of Acts. Read the questions aloud and ask members to share their opinions:

(1) Who wrote the Book of Acts? (Probably Luke, but we can't be absolutely certain because the Bible does not say.)

(2) What other book in the Bible did this same author write? (Gospel of Luke.)

(3) To whom are both books dedicated? (Theophilus.)

(4) What other book in the Bible is like Acts in its structure and approach? (No other book is like Acts.)

Point out that Acts begins with the ascension of Jesus and ends with Paul's imprisonment in Rome. The time span is approximately thirty years. Lecture briefly on verses 1–3 to set the context of Jesus' statements about the Holy Spirit.

Ask members to open their Bibles to Acts 1:4 and find a command Jesus gave the disciples. (Stay in Jerusalem and wait for the Holy Spirit.)

Read aloud verses 6–8. Ask half the class to listen for the disciples' question (Will you restore the kingdom?) and the other half to listen for Jesus' answer (You shall receive power). Point out Jesus' refusal to give information about the end times; instead, He told them to be faithful in their witnessing after they had received the Holy Spirit.

Use a map of the first-century world to show the divisions of verse 8. Ask: Why was obeying this Scripture difficult for Jesus' hearers? (They were Jews and had a difficult time associating with Samaritans and Gentiles.)

Ask members to read silently verses 9–11 and then turn to a person near them and discuss: Why was this event significant? (Many possible responses, but it brought an end to Jesus' appearances and prepared the way for the Holy Spirit.) Call for responses and list these on a chalkboard or a large sheet of paper.

Ask members to read verses 12–14. Summarize the comments on these verses in "Studying the Bible."

Give the Truth a Personal Focus

Ask members to identify specific groups that would correspond with the groups mentioned in verse 8. Ask: How can we take the gospel to these groups? (By relying on the same Holy Spirit.) Why is it hard to reach out to all people with the gospel? What do we need to do as a class to prepare ourselves for worldwide witnessing? as individuals?

Close in prayer of commitment for the Holy Spirit to use you even as He used the early disciples.

1. Adapted from J. B. Fowler, Jr., *Illustrated Sermons for Special Occasions* (Nashville: Broadman Press, 1988), 107.

2. W. A. Criswell, *The Holy Spirit in Today's World* (Grand Rapids: Zondervan Publishing House, 1966), 93.

3. *Pulpit Helps*, June 1990.

4. J. Ralph Grant, *Letters to the Seven Churches and Other Sermons* (Grand Rapids, Mich.: Baker Book House, 1962), 104.

The Holy Spirit's Coming in Power

Basic Passage: Acts 2
Focal Passages: Acts 2:1–4, 14a, 29–33, 37–39, 44–45

T he coming of the Spirit at Pentecost marked a new era in the life of God's people. The power and presence of God came upon them to equip them for God's work. This is not the first mention of the Holy Spirit, for the Spirit is none other than the Spirit of the eternal God. However, at Pentecost the Spirit of God came with new power because the Son of God had completed His mission.

▶ ▶ ▶ ▶ ▶ ▶ ▶ ▶ **Study Aim:** *To explain the significance of the Spirit's coming at Pentecost*

STUDYING THE BIBLE

LESSON OUTLINE
I. Coming of the Holy Spirit (2:1–13)
  1. Signs of the Spirit's coming (vv. 1–4)
  2. Witnessing in other tongues (vv. 5–13)
II. Peter's Sermon (2:14–41)
  1. Fulfillment of Joel's prophecy (vv. 14–21)
  2. Exaltation of Jesus Christ (vv. 22–6)
  3. Conviction, invitation, and response (vv. 37–41)
III. The Common Life of the Believers (2:42–47)

On the Day of Pentecost, special signs marked the coming of the Spirit (vv. 1–4). Believers bore testimony in the many languages of the people gathered in Jerusalem (vv. 5–13). Peter interpreted this as fulfillment of Joel 2:28–32 (vv. 14–21). Peter pointed to the life, death, resurrection, and exaltation of Christ as fulfillment of Scripture (vv. 22–36). When the people were convicted, Peter told them what to do; and about three thousand received his word and were baptized (vv. 37–41). The believers shared together in study, fellowship, and praying; and they shared their possessions with the needy among them (vv. 42–47).

I. Coming of the Holy Spirit (Acts 2:1–13)
1. Signs of the Spirit's coming (vv. 1–4)

1 And when the day of Pentecost was fully come, they were all with one accord in one place.

2 And suddenly there came a sound from heaven as of a rushing mighty wind, and it filled all the house where they were sitting.

3 And there appeared unto them cloven tongues like as of

fire, and it sat upon each of them.

4 And they were all filled with the Holy Ghost, and began to speak with other tongues, as the Spirit gave them utterance.

Pentecost, which means "fiftieth" in Greek, came fifty days after Passover. When Pentecost came, the believers were continuing what they had been doing in Acts 1:14. Suddenly the Spirit came. Three parallel signs marked His coming: (1) They heard what sounded like a powerful wind sweeping through the house. (2) They saw what looked like tongues of fire that came to rest on each of them. (3) They began to speak "with other tongues."

Not all Bible students agree about the tongues at Pentecost. Some think that the tongues were ecstatic speech as described by Paul in 1 Corinthians 14. However, the verses that follow support the view that the tongues at Pentecost were the languages of the people gathered in Jerusalem. Verse 6 says, "Every man heard them speak in his own language."

2. Witnessing in other tongues (vv. 5–13). In the first century, Jews lived all over the known world. Many Jews returned to Jerusalem for festivals like Pentecost. As the Spirit-filled believers began to speak, a crowd gathered. Jews from many nations were amazed to hear the believers speaking in their own languages. They wondered what was happening. Some of the crowd accused the believers of being drunk.

II. Peter's Sermon (Acts 2:14–41)
1. Fulfillment of Joel's prophecy (vv. 14–21)

14 But Peter, standing up with the eleven, lifted up his voice.

Peter, who had often been the spokesman for the twelve during the life of Jesus, did the same here. Remember that this was the same Peter who had denied the Lord not many days earlier. Now he boldly proclaimed the Lord.

Although only he and the eleven are mentioned in verse 14, his later words show that all 120 had been filled with the Spirit and had been witnessing in other tongues. Peter denied that they were drunk (v. 15). Instead he said these Spirit-filled witnesses fulfilled the prophecy of Joel, who had spoken of the Spirit poured out on both men and women (vv. 16–21; see v. 18). He also quoted the important promise of God through Joel, "Whosoever shall call on the name of the Lord shall be saved" (v. 21).

2. Exaltation of Jesus Christ (vv. 22–36). The heart of Peter's sermon focused on Jesus Christ: His life (v. 22), His death (v. 23), and His resurrection (v. 24). Peter supported this by quoting Psalm 16:8–11 (vv. 25–28).

29 Men and brethren, let me freely speak unto you of the patriarch David, that he is both dead and buried, and his sepulchre is with us unto this day.

30 Therefore being a prophet, and knowing that God had sworn with an oath to him, that of the fruit of his loins, according to the flesh, he would raise up Christ to sit on his

throne;

31 He seeing this before spake of the resurrection of Christ, that his soul was not left in hell, neither his flesh did see corruption.

32 This Jesus hath God raised up, whereof we all are witnesses.

Peter called David both a "patriarch" and a "prophet." The "oath" in verse 30 refers to God's promise to establish an eternal kingdom with one of David's descendants (2 Sam. 7:12–13). Peter interpreted Psalm 16 in light of that promise. David expressed the hope that God would not abandon his body to the decay of the grave. Peter said that this was not fulfilled for David himself, who died and whose tomb was well known at the time. Instead, God used David to prophesy of the One who fulfilled the promise of King of an eternal kingdom. Jesus, the son of David and Son of God, was raised from the dead.

The word "hell" in verse 31 translates the Greek word *hades*. The word sometimes referred to a place where the dead are punished; at times it referred to the grave. That is its meaning here. David was not in a place of punishment, but his body was decaying in the grave. Peter supported his proclamation of the resurrection of Christ not only by quoting Scripture but also by bearing personal testimony. He and the other apostles were witnesses of the fact that God had raised Jesus from the dead.

33 Therefore being by the right hand of God exalted, and having received of the Father the promise of the Holy Ghost, he hath shed forth this, which ye now see and hear.

The crucified, risen Lord had been exalted to the right hand of God. The Father had given to the Son the promise of the Holy Spirit, which was now poured out on the believers. Peter told his audience that this was what they saw and heard.

Verse 33 clearly relates the coming of the Spirit at Pentecost to the death and resurrection of Jesus Christ. The successful completion of the Son's redemptive mission endued the eternal Spirit of God with new power. The Lord's abiding presence through His Spirit empowered His people to tell the good news.

The exaltation of Christ to God's right hand was in fulfillment of Psalm 110:1 (vv. 34–35). Building on this, Peter said, "God hath made that same Jesus, whom ye have crucified, both Lord and Christ" (v. 36).

3. Conviction, invitation, and response (vv. 37–41)

37 Now when they heard this, they were pricked in their heart, and said unto Peter and to the rest of the apostles, Men and brethren, what shall we do?

38 Then Peter said unto them, Repent, and be baptized every one of you in the name of Jesus Christ for the remission of sins, and ye shall receive the gift of the Holy Ghost.

Those who heard Peter were convicted in their hearts, no doubt by the convicting power of the Spirit (see John 16:8–11). They asked, "What shall we do?" Peter told them what to do. They needed to repent and to be baptized. They would receive forgiveness of sins and the gift of the Spirit.

Did Peter mean to say that baptism is essential for forgiveness? Two factors argue against this. (1) The word translated "for" can be translated "on the basis of." The same word is in Matthew 12:41, which describes the people of Nineveh repenting "at the preaching of Jonas." They did not repent with the result that Jonah preached, but because of Jonah's preaching. (2) Other references to forgiveness link it to repentance, with no mention of baptism (Luke 24:47; Acts 3:19; 5:31). Believers are baptized not to receive forgiveness but because they have been forgiven.

This does not mean that baptism is unimportant. The people asked what they should do, not just what should they do to be forgiven. Peter told them how to receive forgiveness and the Holy Spirit, but he also stressed the need to be baptized as the way of professing their faith and joining other believers.

Forgiveness of sins and the gift of the Holy Spirit take place at conversion. The coming of the Spirit into a person's life is what marks the person as born anew into God's family (John 3:1–8; Rom. 8:9). The reason that believers can be filled with the Spirit many times in life is because the Spirit abides in our lives (Acts 4:8, 31; Eph. 4:30; 5:18).

> **39 For the promise is unto you, and to your children, and to all that are afar off, even as many as the Lord our God shall call.**

God's promise of forgiveness and the gift of the Spirit was for many more than heard Peter on that day. It was to fellow Jews and to Gentiles as well ("all that are afar off"). Earlier, Peter had said that "whosoever shall call on the name of the Lord shall be saved" (v. 21). In verse 39, he stressed that our calling on the Lord is in response to His calling of us. Peter was not implying that God restricts His call, but that God always takes the initiative in calling us.

Peter continued to exhort the people to save themselves from their evil generation (v. 40). About three thousand received his word and were baptized (v. 41).

III. The Common Life of the Believers (Acts 2:42–47)

Each baptized believer became part of a fellowship of faith and love. They committed themselves to teaching, fellowship, breaking of bread, and prayers (v. 42). Everyone was in awe of miracles done by the apostles (v. 43).

> **44 And all that believed were together and had all things common;**
>
> **45 And sold their possessions and goods, and parted them to all men, as every man had need.**

Verse 44 by itself might imply that everyone put everything into a common pool. Verse 45 and later references in Acts 4:32–5:2 show that the giving was voluntary and designed to meet specific needs that arose. These verses show the spirit of oneness that marked the early believers, and their generosity in meeting the needs of poor members.

The believers worshiped with one accord in the temple and had fellowship from house to house (v. 46). As they continued to praise the Lord, He continued to add more saved people to the church (v. 47).

The traditional site of the upper room, or Hall of the Coenaculum, in Jerusalem. Credit: *Biblical Illustrator*, Ken Touchton

APPLYING THE BIBLE

1. Filled with the Holy Spirit. John Hyde (1865–1912) was on a ship from England to India to serve as a missionary when he received a distressing telegram: "John Hyde, are you filled with the Spirit of God?" Angry, Hyde crumpled the telegram and put it in his pocket. "The audacity of somebody to ask me that question," Hyde said to himself. "Here I am a missionary, sincere, dedicated, leaving my home, going to another country. And someone has the nerve to ask me, 'Are you filled with the Holy Spirit?'"

But Hyde's anger soon turned to conviction and, down on his knees, he cried out to God: "Oh God, the audacity of me to think that I could pray or preach or witness or live or serve or do anything in my own strength and in my own power. Lord, fill me with your Spirit so I might have power to serve."[1]

John Hyde became one of the greatest missionary statesmen of all time because he realized that his greatest need was Holy Spirit empowerment (vv. 1–4). And so it was with the Jerusalem church.

2. The first biblical mention of the Holy Spirit coming upon a person. According to Herschel Hobbs in his book *The Origin of All Things*, the first mention in the Bible of the Holy Spirit coming upon a person is found in Genesis 41:38. Referring to Joseph, whom Pharaoh put in charge of storing up grain for the drought to come across the land, Pharaoh asked his advisers: "Can we find such a one as this is, a man in whom the Spirit of God is?" Hobbs adds that this is the first biblical mention of the Holy

Spirit coming upon a person, and it was spoken by a pagan.[2]

Old Testament studies show that the Holy Spirit came upon people whom God had chosen in order to empower them for a particular work. But at Pentecost, the Holy Spirit came upon all the believers and empowered them for Christian service (v. 3). His coming upon believers was not temporary and only for a given task, but a permanent gift.

3. Symbols for the Holy Spirit. Wind, fire, and tongue are three basic symbols used in the New Testament to describe the Holy Spirit and His ministry. Our lesson today uses two of those symbols: "wind" (v. 2) and "fire" (v. 3).

About "wind" as a symbol for the Holy Spirit, Benjamin P. Browne writes:
- Wind sings! Does the Holy Spirit work through our hymns singing of joy?
- Wind cleanses the air of pollution. How fresh the air we breathe when the wind blows away the foul air!
- Wind powerfully drives. The Holy Spirit is driving power—power to witness.
- The Holy Spirit creates patterns of beauty—as the wind paints portraits of beauty in the sand and on the sea, so the Holy Spirit beautifies our life.
- The Holy Spirit invigorates. As the sea is stirred to vast emotion by the wind, so the Holy Spirit within us stirs and invigorates us to live Christlike lives.

4. Peter's sermon. Charles Haddon Spurgeon once preached what he thought was one of his worst sermons. From beginning to end he had trouble.

Going home, Spurgeon fell on his knees and prayed: "Lord, God, Thou canst do something with nothing. Bless that poor sermon." He continued to pray the same prayer through the week, even at night when he would awaken. He then determined that the next Sunday morning he would redeem himself by preaching a great sermon.

The next Sunday morning Spurgeon was at his best. The service went beautifully and the message was delivered without any problem. At the close of the service the people crowded around Spurgeon and bragged on how well he had preached, and Spurgeon went home pleased with himself.

But the results? What came from the two sermons? From the sermon Spurgeon had struggled to preach and over which he felt such a failure, he was able to count forty-one conversions. But from his magnificent sermon preached the following Sunday, not a single soul was saved.

Spurgeon concluded that the difference was the Holy Spirit of God, who had used the one because of the humility with which it was preached, but could not use the other because of Spurgeon's pride.[3]

Peter's sermon on the Day of Pentecost was neither flashy nor fancy. His message was "Repent, and be baptized every one of you in the name of Jesus Christ for the remission of sins, and ye shall receive the gift of the Holy Ghost" (v. 38). And the results of the message are recorded in verse 41: "And the same day there were added unto them about three thousand souls."

The Holy Spirit's power in the service made the difference.

TEACHING THE BIBLE

▶ *Main Idea:* The Spirit's coming at Pentecost caused significant changes in the disciples' lives.
▶ *Suggested Teaching Aim:* To lead adults to explain the significance of the Spirit's coming at Pentecost.

A TEACHING OUTLINE

1. Use an illustration to introduce the lesson.
2. Prepare a teaching outline poster to guide you through the study.
3. Apply the lesson by identifying ways the Holy Spirit can make members' lives attractive today.

Introduce the Bible Study
Use "Filled with the Holy Spirit" in "Applying the Bible" to introduce the lesson.

Search for Biblical Truth
Prepare the following teaching outline. Write each point on a strip of paper and place it on the focal wall as you teach that point.
The Holy Spirit's Coming in Power
1. Signs of the Spirit's Coming (Acts 2:1–4)
2. Peter's Sermon (Acts 2:14, 29–33)
3. The People's Response (Acts 2:37–39)
4. The Believers' Common Life (Acts 2:44–45)

Point out the lesson on the quarter poster and place the lesson title on the focal wall. To overview the lesson, summarize the first paragraph under "Studying the Bible."

Place the first strip poster on the wall: *Signs of the Spirit's Coming.* On a chalkboard or large sheet of paper write the words below in bold. The italicized answers are suggested responses.

Who? (*All 120 of the disciples in the upper room.*)
What? (*Sound of rushing wind and tongues of fire.*)
When? (*Day of Pentecost, fifty days after Passover.*)
Where? (*In Jerusalem, possibly in the upper room.*)
How? (*Holy Spirit filled them with power.*)
Why? (*To tell people of all languages about Jesus.*)

Ask members to search Acts verses 1–4 for the answers to these questions. Use "Symbols for the Holy Spirit" in "Applying the Bible" to explain these symbols.

Place the second strip poster on the wall: *Peter's Sermon.* Present a brief lecture in which you cover the following: (1) David foresaw that God would keep his lineage alive by sending Christ. (2) Even though David's grave was known to them, Christ was alive. (3) The Holy Spirit could not come until Jesus had died, risen, and ascended to His Father.

Place the third strip poster on the wall: *The People's Response.* Write the following on a chalkboard or large sheet of paper: *The People's Conviction, Peter's Invitation.* Ask members to read silently verses 37–39 and to describe each of these elements. Ask: Did Peter mean that baptism is essential for forgiveness? (See comments on v. 38 in "Studying the Bible.")

Place the fourth poster strip on the focal wall: The Believers' Common Life. Ask members to characterize how the early believers responded. What characterized this sharing? (*It was voluntary.*)

Give the Truth a Personal Focus

Ask: Does the gospel still require a radical change in our lives today? What made this kind of activity possible in the early church? (*Holy Spirit.*) What will make it possible in our church? (*Holy Spirit.*) What will make it possible in your life?

Point out that the result of this sharing was that people were attracted to the gospel (v. 47). Let members suggest what they need to do to let the Holy Spirit make their lives attractive enough so that others will believe in Jesus.

---

1. James E. Hightower Jr., Compiler, *Illustrating Paul's Letter to the Romans* (Nashville: Broadman Press, 1984), 56–57.

2. Herschel H. Hobbs, *The Origin of All Things* (Waco, Tex.: Word Books, 1946), 152.

3. Adapted from Walter B. Knight, *Knight's Master Book of New Illustrations* (Grand Rapids, Mich.: Wm. B. Eerdmans Publishing Co., 1956), 288.

Healing and Preaching

Basic Passage: Acts 3:1–4:31
Focal Passages: Acts 3:1–8; 4:5–12

The spiritual impetus of Pentecost is apparent in subsequent events. Peter and John took the lead in a ministry of healing and preaching. They did not act in their own authority, but in the name of Jesus Christ. The healing of the lame beggar bore witness to the unique power of Jesus to save people and make them whole.

▶ ▶ ▶ ▶ ▶ ▶ ▶ ▶ **Study Aim:** *To explain how the healing and preaching of Peter and John bore testimony to Jesus Christ*

STUDYING THE BIBLE

LESSON OUTLINE
I. A Lame Beggar Healed (3:1–11)
  1. The beggar at the temple gate (vv. 1–2)
  2. Meeting Peter and John (vv. 3–5)
  3. Healed (vv. 6–8)
  4. Recognized by others (vv. 9–11)
II. Peter's Sermon (3:12–26)
III. Peter and John Before the Council (4:1–22)
  1. Arrested (vv. 1–4)
  2. Questioned (vv. 5–7)
  3. Peter's response (vv. 8–12)
  4. Warned and released (vv. 13–22)
IV. The Church's Prayer and Witness (4:23–31)

Peter and John healed a lame beggar at the temple gate, and the people were astonished (3:1–11). Peter used the occasion to preach a sermon that focused on the death and resurrection of Jesus, and called people to repent (vv. 12–26). The Sadducean leaders seized Peter and John and demanded that the apostles tell them by whose authority they were acting (vv. 1–7). Peter used the healed man as a testimony to the unique healing and saving power of Jesus (vv. 8–12). When the Sanhedrin warned Peter and John, the apostles said that they had to tell what they had seen and heard; and the council threatened them and let them go (vv. 13–22). The church prayed for strength to speak boldly; after being filled with the Spirit, they spoke God's word boldly (vv. 23–31).

I. A Lame Beggar Healed (Acts 3:1–11)
1. The beggar at the temple gate (vv. 1–2)

1 Now Peter and John went up together into the temple at the hour of prayer, being the ninth hour.

2 And a certain man lame from his mother's womb was carried, whom they laid daily at the gate of the temple which is called Beautiful, to ask alms of them that entered into the temple.

The first believers were Jews, who continued to worship in the temple (Acts 2:46). Peter and John, who often appeared together in the early chapters of Acts, went up into the temple at three in the afternoon, one of the prayer times. At one of the temple gates was a beggar, who had been lame from birth. Others brought him each day so he could ask for alms of the people who were entering the temple. Jewish teachings stressed giving alms to the poor and needy. Since showing devotion to God is expressed by showing kindness to others, people going to worship were a likely group to heed the beggar's requests for help.

2. Meeting Peter and John (vv. 3–5)

3 Who seeing Peter and John about to go into the temple asked an alms.

4 And Peter, fastening his eyes upon him with John, said, Look on us.

5 And he gave heed unto them, expecting to receive something of them.

As Peter and John approached the temple gate, the beggar saw them and asked them for money. The two apostles stopped and fixed their attention on the man. They told the beggar to look at them. The man looked at them because he expected to receive something from them. He did receive something; but what he received was not what he had expected—but something far better!

3. Healed (vv. 6–8)

6 Then Peter said, Silver and gold have I none; but such as I have give I thee: In the name of Jesus Christ of Nazareth rise up and walk.

7 And he took him by the right hand, and lifted him up: and immediately his feet and ankle bones received strength.

8 And he leaping up stood, and walked, and entered with them into the temple, walking, and leaping, and praising God.

Peter told the beggar that he had no silver or gold to give him, but would give him what he had. Then Peter invoked the name of Jesus to call the man to rise up and walk. Names have significance in the Bible. Invoking the name of Jesus was invoking the power of Jesus Himself. Peter and John had no authority within themselves to heal the man, but they represented One who did. Just as Jesus during His ministry healed people, so He continued to heal through the apostles.

Grabbing the beggar's right hand, Peter lifted him up. Even as he did, the man's bones were strengthened. The man sprang to his feet and began to walk about. Then he went into the temple with the two apostles. Entering the temple he walked and leaped about, praising God. Lame people were among those whom the Jewish law excluded from the inner courts of the temple (see Lev. 21:17–20; 2 Sam. 5:8). Now that the man was whole, he for the first time was able to enter the temple. Thus he received not only healing but also acceptance before God.

4. Recognized by others (vv. 9–11). The people recognized the man leaping about as the lame beggar. Word spread throughout the temple, and a crowd gathered.

II. Peter's Sermon (Acts 3:12–26)

Peter preached to the crowd in the temple. Disclaiming any personal power, Peter pointed to Jesus, whom they had crucified and God had raised from the dead (vv. 12–15). The man had been healed through faith in the name of Jesus (v. 16). They had acted in ignorance in crucifying Jesus, but His death fulfilled Scripture (vv. 17–18). Peter appealed to them to repent so the times of refreshing might come (vv. 19–21). Appealing to the Jews as the heirs of the prophets and the covenant, Peter called them to follow the One of whom the prophets foretold (vv. 22–26).

III. Peter and John Before the Council (Acts 4:1–22)

1. Arrested (vv. 1–4). Hearing of these events, the temple authorities came to where Peter and John were speaking to the people. The Sadducees (SAD joo sees) were the priestly party that administered the temple (v. 1). The apostles were preaching not only the resurrection of Jesus, but also the future resurrection of people. This greatly disturbed the Sadducees not only because they didn't believe in future resurrection, but also because any religious excitement threatened the status quo (v. 2). They seized Peter and John and put them in jail (v. 3). Meanwhile, many who heard the message believed, and the number of believers reached about five thousand men (v. 4).

2. Questioned (vv. 5–7)

5 And it came to pass on the morrow, that their rulers, and elders, and scribes,

6 And Annas the high priest, and Caiaphas, and John, and Alexander, and as many as were of the kindred of the high priest, were gathered together in Jerusalem.

7 And when they had set them in the midst, they asked, By what power, or by what name, have ye done this?

Since the council is mentioned in verse 15, this was probably a meeting of the council or Sanhedrin (SAN he drihn or san HE drihn). This supreme Jewish court was the council that condemned Jesus to death and sent Him to Pilate for the official sentence (Luke 22:66–71; John 18:28–31). It was made up of ruling priests, elders (lay members from the upper classes), and scribes (teachers of the law, most of whom were Pharisees). The high priest presided over the Sanhedrin.

Annas had been high priest from A.D. 6–15, but he was the power behind the scenes because five sons, a grandson, and a son-in-law attained the title. Strictly speaking, his son-in-law Caiaphas (KIGH uh fuhs or KAY yuh fuhs) was high priest from A.D. 18–36, but Annas continued to exert great influence. For example, when Jesus was arrested He was taken to Annas before being taken to Caiaphas (John

18:12–13, 24). Annas and his powerful family questioned Peter and John. They demanded to know who gave them authority for what they had done.

3. Peter's response (vv. 8–12)

8 Then Peter, filled with the Holy Ghost, said unto them, Ye rulers of the people, and elders of Israel,

9 If we this day be examined of the good deed to the impotent man, by what means he is made whole:

10 Be it known unto you all, and to all the people of Israel, that by the name of Jesus Christ of Nazareth, whom ye crucified, whom God raised from the dead, even by him doth this man stand here before you whole.

11 This is the stone which was set at nought of you builders, which is become the head of the corner.

12 Neither is there salvation in any other: for there is none other name under heaven given among men, whereby we must be saved.

Peter had denied the Lord when confronted by a girl in the courtyard of the high priest (Luke 22:54–57; John 18:15–17). Now Peter stood before the powerful men who had crucified Jesus. What made the difference? For one thing, Jesus had appeared alive; for another, He had sent His Spirit. Peter filled with the Spirit was a different man than Peter in his own strength.

Peter asked if they were being accused of doing a good deed for a helpless man. He said to his accusers that if that were the meaning of their question in verse 7, he wanted to make clear the authority for their actions. The man had been made whole in the name of Jesus. In describing Jesus, Peter used the title "Christ," which means "Messiah." Peter emphasized that they had crucified the Messiah, but God had raised Him from the dead. With Psalm 118:22 in mind, Peter said that Jesus was the stone whom they had rejected, but whom God made the cornerstone.

Peter declared that the healing of the man was a sign of the salvation offered only through Jesus. The Greek word translated "saved" in verse 12 is translated "made whole" in verse 9. This word can refer to physical healing, to deliverance from danger, or to salvation from sin and death. The healing of the man in the name of Jesus testifies to the salvation from sins offered in the name of Jesus.

4. Warned and released (vv. 13–22). The authorities were amazed at Peter and John, since they were ordinary people with no formal training (v. 13). Because the healed man was standing there, the authorities realized they could not deny his healing (v. 14). They decided that all they could do was to order the apostles to speak no more in the name of Jesus (vv. 15–18). Peter and John asked them whether it was right to obey God or men (v. 19). The apostles said that they had to speak what they had seen and heard (v. 20). The council realized that the people were praising God for the miracle of healing; therefore, they dared do no more than threaten the apostles and let them go (vv. 21–22).

IV. The Church's Prayer and Witness (Acts 4:23–31)

When Peter and John reported to the church, the church prayed (vv. 23–24). They recognized that the Scriptures foretold the hostility against God's anointed One by people like Herod and Pilate (vv. 25–28). They asked God to grant them boldness to speak in the face of the threats against them (v. 29). They asked Him to continue to heal through the name of Jesus (v. 30). After they prayed, the place was shaken; and after they were filled with the Holy Spirit, they spoke the word of God boldly (v. 31).

APPLYING THE BIBLE

1. How God heals. E. Stanley Jones (1884–1973) began his ministry as a Methodist missionary in India in 1907. Twice he was nominated for the Nobel Peace Prize. The author of twenty-nine books, his first and best-known novel was *The Great Christ of the Indian Road.*

Jones said God heals in one of several ways: (1) by medicine; (2) by surgery; (3) by proper nutrition; (4) by climate; (5) by mental suggestion; (6) by delivering the sick person from fears, self-centeredness, and guilt; (7) by the direct intervention of the Holy Spirit; and (8) by the resurrection.

Jones added that in this life our body will break down and healing may have to wait until the resurrection.[1]

Our lesson today clearly shows that the lame man was healed by the direct, immediate intervention of God (vv. 1–8).

2. Ministering to people's needs. In a "Fulfillment in Ministry Conference," Robert Dale told about a young seminarian who was called one night at midnight by an obnoxious parishioner. "George has gone to work without his teeth, and unless someone takes his teeth to him he won't be able to eat his lunch. I don't know who else to call. Will you please take his teeth to him?" she pleaded.

The young preacher asked the class how he should have responded to the call. "I know I am supposed to feed the flock, but this is ridiculous," he said.

Preachers have to do a good many strange things, but our main task is sharing the power and hope of the good news in Jesus Christ with people. This is what Peter and John did for the man in our lesson today.[2]

3. He didn't know what he was missing until he met Jesus. John Ericsson (1803–1889) was a Swedish-American engineer who invented screw propellers for ships. He had a Norwegian friend named Ole Bull who became a world-renowned violinist. But for many years, the two didn't see each other.

Once Bull contacted the wealthy, famous Ericsson and invited him to attend a concert and to listen to Bull play, but Ericsson declined, saying he had no ear for music.

Time and time again Bull invited Ericsson to a concert, but each time he declined. Finally, Bull said, "I'll bring my violin down to your shop and play," to which Ericsson replied, "If you do, I'll smash the thing to pieces."

Bull did it anyway, but he slipped up on Ericsson's blind side. Removing the strings and screws and apron on the violin, Bull pointed out to Ericsson the obvious defects and asked the scientist about sound waves and the right kind of wood from which to get the best resonance. To illustrate what he was talking about, Bull replaced the parts and brought the bow softly down upon the strings as Ericsson listened with rapt attention. Bull played on and on and when he finally paused, Ericsson said with a broken voice, "Play on! Don't stop. Play on. I never knew before what it was that was lacking in my life."[3]

The lame man never knew what he was missing until he met Peter and John, who told him about Jesus. Then he got a double treasure: healing and salvation.

4. The joy Jesus brings. American sculptor Lorado Taft (1860–1936) was well-known. On a summer vacation in the lake country of the northern United States, he and his family would hurry through their evening meal in order to watch the sunset. One evening, their maid asked if she could bring her parents to watch the sunset with the Tafts. Taft agreed, of course, but told the maid that her father and mother had seen hundreds of sunsets. "No, sir," she replied, "we never saw a sunset until you came."[4]

The poor lame man of our Scripture passage today, who was gloriously healed, had never known life or joy until Peter and John introduced him to Jesus. After that, all was new and different.

5. "Jehovah Ropheca." This is one of the names for God and it means, "I am the Lord that healeth thee" (Exod. 15:26). The Bible is full of instances of divine healing: God healed Abimelech (uh BIM eh lek) when Abraham prayed for him (Gen. 20:17); Moses prayed for Miriam and God healed her (Num. 12:13–14); weeping, Hezekiah turned to God in prayer and God healed Hezekiah (Isa. 38:4–5); Jesus healed the leper (Matt. 8:2–3); and many other instances of divine healing could be cited. Our lesson today is one of those instances of glorious, divine healing.[5]

TEACHING THE BIBLE

▶ *Main Idea:* The preaching and healing of Peter and John bore testimony to Jesus Christ.

▶ *Suggested Teaching Aim:* To lead adults to describe ways the preaching and healing of Peter and John bore testimony to Jesus Christ, and to identify ways they need to respond to Jesus.

A TEACHING OUTLINE

1. *Use an illustration to introduce the study.*
2. *Organize two study groups to study the biblical passages.*
3. *Apply the study by offering a simplified invitation.*

Introduce the Bible Study

Use "The Joy Jesus Brings" ("Applying the Bible") to introduce the Bible study.

Search for Biblical Truth

IN ADVANCE, enlist a member to summarize the first paragraph under "Studying the Bible" to set the context. Point out the lesson on the quarter poster.

Organize the class in two groups. Give each group one of the following assignments without the answers. (If you choose not to organize in groups, you can ask the questions to the class and let them respond as a group.)

Group 1—

Please read Acts 3:1–8 and answer the following questions.

(1) What time did Peter and John go to the temple? (3:00 P.M.)

(2) Why did they go? (To pray.)

(3) Whom did they encounter at the gate? (A beggar.)

(4) What did the man want from Peter and John? (Alms.)

(5) What did Peter tell the man? (He had no money, but he would give him what he had.)

(6) What did Peter do? (Took the man by the hand and lifted him up.)

(7) What was significant about the name Peter used to heal the man? (Invoking Jesus' name invoked Jesus power.)

(8) What happened to the man? (He was healed.)

(9) Where did the man go after he was healed? (Into the temple.)

Group 2—

Please read Acts 4:5–12 and answer the follow questions.

(1) What was the reaction of the Jewish leaders to the beggar's healing? (They arrested Peter and John.)

(2) Who were some of the religious leaders who opposed Peter and John? (Annas the high priest, Caiaphas, John, and Alexander.)

(3) What question did the religious leaders ask Peter and John? (By whose power had they performed the miracle?)

(4) What was the name of the group of religious leaders? (Sanhedrin.)

(5) What enabled Peter to speak before such a threatening group? (He was filled with the Holy Spirit.)

(6) To whom did Peter give the credit for the man's healing? (Jesus of Nazareth.)

(7) How did Peter identify Jesus to the Sanhedrin? (He was the one they had crucified.)

(8) What did this man's healing prove about Jesus? (That God had raised Him from the dead.)

(9) To what did Peter compare Jesus? (To a cornerstone that had been rejected.)

(10) What power did Peter say lay in Jesus' name? (He is the only source of salvation.)

Allow about ten minutes for study and then let the groups respond.

Give the Truth a Personal Focus

Ask members to look at verse 12 in their Bibles. If you have unsaved members present, be sensitive to the leadership of the Holy Spirit to use this time to present the gospel to them. Use the "How to

Become a Christian" feature on page 2 to share how a person can receive Christ.

If all of your members are Christians, use this time to encourage them to identify ways they can bear their testimony to Jesus this week. Close in a prayer of commitment.

---

1. E. Stanley Jones, *Abundant Living* (Nashville: New York: Abingdon Press, 1952), viii.

2. *Proclaim* Magazine (Nashville: Baptist Sunday School Board, July, August, September, 1976), 32.

3. R. L. Middleton, *Don't Disappoint God* (Nashville: Broadman Press, 1951), 59–61.

4. Robert J. Hastings, *A Word Fitly Spoken* (Nashville: Broadman Press, 1962), 54.

5. W. A. Criswell, *The Holy Spirit in Today's World* (Grand Rapids, Mich.: Zondervan Publishing House, 1966), 153.

Obedient to the Spirit

Basic Passage: Acts 4:32–5:42
Focal Passage: Acts 5:17–32

T he early church faced many challenges. Meeting the needs of the poor was one challenge. Another challenge was facing growing opposition. Yet another challenge was the appearance of hypocrisy within their own ranks. In facing each of these challenges, the believers found direction and strength from the Holy Spirit. Being obedient to Him, therefore, was a priority for them.

▶ ▶ ▶ ▶ ▶ ▶ ▶ ▶ **Study Aim**: *To testify how to be obedient to the Spirit*

STUDYING THE BIBLE

LESSON OUTLINE
I. Generosity and Hypocrisy (4:32–5:11)
    1. Giving to help the needy (4:32–37)
    2. Lying to God (5:1–11)
II. Awe and Church Growth (5:12–16)
III. The Apostles Before the Council (5:17–42)
    1. Arrest (5:17–18)
    2. Delivered (5:19–21)
    3. The missing prisoners (5:22–26)
    4. Accused (5:27–28)
    5. Peter's response (5:29–32)
    6. Gamaliel's advice (5:33–40)
    7. Release and renewed witness (5:41–42)

The church continued its ministry to the needy through the generous giving of people like Barnabas (4:32–37). By contrast, Ananias (an uh NIGH uhs) and Sapphira (suh FIGH ruh) lied to God and died as a result (5:1–11). As the apostles continued a ministry that included miracles, awe fell on the people, keeping some from joining, but encouraging true believers to be added to the church (vv. 12–16). The Sanhedrin arrested the apostles (vv.17–18). After an angel delivered them, the apostles returned to teach in the temple (vv. 19–21). The Sanhedrin, hearing the jail was empty, sent officers to arrest the apostles (vv. 22–26). The high priest accused them of filling Jerusalem with their teaching and making the rulers accountable for Jesus' death (vv. 27–28). Peter replied that they had to obey God, not man, and proceeded to bear witness to Jesus (vv. 29–32). When the Sadducees wanted to kill the apostles, Gamaliel advised restraint (vv. 33–40). When the apostles were released, they continued to teach and preach Jesus Christ (vv. 41–42).

I. Generosity and Hypocrisy (Acts 4:32–5:11)

1. Giving to help the needy (4:32–37). The spirit of oneness in the church was seen in how they shared with the needy among them. Those with property sold it and laid the proceeds at the apostles' feet, and money was given to all those who had needs (4:32–35). Barnabas exemplified this spirit by selling land and giving the money to the church (vv. 36–37).

2. Lying to God (5:1–11). Ananias and Sapphira sold something, but gave only part of the money (vv. 1–2). Peter accused Ananias of lying to the Spirit (v. 3). Ananias was under no obligation to sell the possession or to bring all the money to the apostles; but his sin was in claiming to have brought all (v. 4). Ananias fell down, died, and was buried (vv. 5–6). When his wife came in three hours later, Peter asked her if they had sold the land for a certain price, and she said yes (v. 7). After Peter accused her of testing the Spirit and told her of her husband's fate, she fell down, died, and was buried (vv. 8–10). As a result, great fear fell on the church and on all who heard about Ananias and Sapphira (v. 11).

II. Awe and Church Growth (Acts 5:12–16)

The apostles continued to do signs and wonders among the people (v. 12). A sense of awe caused people to be careful about joining the church (v. 13). In spite of this, true believers continued to be added to their number (v. 14). The apostles continued their ministry of healing the sick (vv. 15–16).

III. The Apostles Before the Council (Acts 5:17–42)

1. Arrest (vv. 17–18)

> 17 Then the high priest rose up, and all they that were with him, (which is the sect of the Sadducees,) and were filled with indignation,

> 18 And laid their hands on the apostles, and put them in the common prison.

Acts 5:17–42 hs much in common with Acts 4:5–22. These passages describe the first and second time the apostles were brought before the Sanhedrin. However, there are some differences. For one thing, only Peter and John were arrested the first time; the second time, all the apostles were imprisoned. The intensity of the two situations differed. In chapter 4, the authorities brought the apostles in for questioning and warned them to cease preaching in the name of Jesus. When the apostles continued their ministry, the Sadducees were angry at the apostles for defying their orders and jealous of their success with the people.

2. Delivered (vv. 19–21)

> 19 But the angel of the Lord by night opened the prison doors, and brought them forth, and said,

> 20 Go, stand and speak in the temple to the people all the words of this life.

21 And when they heard that, they entered into the temple early in the morning, and taught. But the high priest came, and they that were with him, and called the council together, and all the senate of the children of Israel, and sent to the prison to have them brought.

Because the Lord had work for the apostles, His angel delivered them at night in such a way that no one knew they had escaped. The angel ordered the apostles to return to where they had been arrested and do what they had been arrested for doing. They were told to continue to speak the words of life to the people. The apostles were obedient to the Word of God through the angel.

The Sanhedrin thought they were running things. By delivering the apostles, the Lord showed that He was in control. The last part of verse 21 shows the high priest, who still thought he was running things, calling together the Sanhedrin. Then he sent to the prison to have the helpless prisoners brought before them.

3. The missing prisoners (vv. 22–26)

22 But when the officers came, and found them not in the prison, they returned and told,

23 Saying, The prison truly found we shut with all safety, and the keepers standing without before the doors: but when we had opened, we found no man within.

24 Now when the high priest and the captain of the temple and the chief priests heard these things, they doubted of them whereunto this would grow.

25 Then came one and told them, saying, Behold, the men whom ye put in prison are standing in the temple, and teaching the people.

26 Then went the captain with the officers, and brought them without violence: for they feared the people, lest they should have been stoned.

These verses show the confusion and shock of the authorities. The officers went to the prison and found it empty, although the doors were shut and the guards were on duty. When this news was reported to the Sanhedrin, "they doubted of them whereunto this would grow." In other words, they wondered what would be the final outcome of all this. While the Sanhedrin was trying to absorb the news that the apostles were out of jail, someone reported that they were back in the temple teaching the people.

The captain shared the fear and confusion caused by the deliverance of the apostles from prison (v. 24). Now he personally led the officers back to the temple and quietly brought the apostles back to face the Sanhedrin. The captain used no violence for fear of the people, who held the apostles in awe.

4. Accused (vv. 27–28)

27 And when they had brought them, they set them before the council: and the high priest asked them,

28 Saying, Did not we straitly command you that ye should not teach in this name? and behold, ye have filled Jerusalem

with your doctrine, and intend to bring this man's blood upon us.

The apostles were brought back before the Sanhedrin. The high priest made two accusations against the apostles. First, they had disobeyed the order of the Sanhedrin not to teach in Jesus' name. In fact, the apostles had filled the city with their message. Second, the high priest charged that the apostles intended to hold them accountable for the death of Jesus. To lay blame for someone's blood was an Old Testament way of accusing the perpetrator of murder.

5. Peter's response (vv. 29–32)

29 Then Peter and the other apostles answered and said, We ought to obey God rather than men.

30 The God of our fathers raised up Jesus, whom ye slew and hanged on a tree.

31 Him hath God exalted with his right hand to be a Prince and a Saviour, for to give repentance to Israel, and forgiveness of sins.

32 And we are his witnesses of these things; and so is also the Holy Ghost, whom God hath given to them that obey him.

Peter's words in verse 29 are a restatement of what he said in his first defense before the Sanhedrin (Acts 4:19). As 1 Peter 2:13–14 shows, Peter believed in the God-ordained power of government. The Sanhedrin represented both political and religious authority; yet Peter refused to obey their clear order. Peter explained why. Although human authorities deserve respect and obedience, only God deserves ultimate obedience.

How did Peter know that he and the other apostles were obeying God? They had the clear command of the risen Lord to be His witnesses (Acts 1:8). When the angel delivered them from prison, he had told them to return to the temple and teach (Acts 5:20). The Spirit impressed them that these clear words were the Lord's will for them. Peter said as much in verse 32. The apostles were witnesses of the crucified and risen Lord. The Holy Spirit was the ultimate witness to Christ, as the Spirit worked in and through those who were obedient to Him.

Verses 30–31 show that Peter turned the trial into an opportunity for witnessing (see 1 Pet. 3:15). Verse 30 repeats the charge that the rulers had killed the Lord, adding that they killed Him by hanging Him on a tree, which Deuteronomy 21:23 says is a cursed death (see Gal. 3:13). In speaking of Christ's exaltation, Peter used two titles for Christ. Earlier Peter had spoken of "the Prince of life" (Acts 3:15). He used the words "salvation" and "saved" in pointing to Christ as the only One in whom salvation is found (Acts 4:12). Verse 31 introduces the title "Saviour" and emphasizes that salvation involves the possibility of repentance and the promise of forgiveness of sins.

6. Gamaliel's advice (vv. 33–40).

The Sanhedrin was in no mood to repent. Instead they began to talk of executing the apostles (v. 33). At this point, a leading Pharisee named Gamaliel (guh MAY lih ehl or guh MAYL yuhl) reminded them that two earlier self-proclaimed messiahs came to ruin (vv. 34–37). Gamaliel concluded that if such movements were not of God, they would fail (v. 38). However, if God was in a movement, no one could stop it; and those who opposed the movement would be opposing God (v. 39). The Sanhedrin did not kill the apostles, but had them beaten. Before they released the apostles, the Sanhedrin commanded them not to speak in the name of Jesus (v. 40).

7. Release and renewed witness (vv. 41–42). The apostles rejoiced that they were allowed to suffer for Jesus (v. 41). Each day found them in the temple and going from house to house as they continued teaching and preaching (v. 42).

APPLYING THE BIBLE

1. An offering for world relief. In one of the services at the 1950 Baptist World Alliance meeting in Cleveland, Ohio, an offering was taken for world relief and $2,700 was received. In one of the offering baskets, the ushers found two Cleveland transit tickets with the following notes: "I walked many miles to come here today, rather than using these tickets to ride a city bus. Will someone who lives in Cleveland please buy them and put the money in the relief offering? I paid twenty-five cents for them." When the note was read publicly, another offering was taken and $1,300 more was given.[1]

2. Oliver Wendell Holmes on lying. Oliver Wendell Holmes once said, "Sin has many tools and the lie is the handle that fits them all."[2]

The names of Ananias and Sapphira are synonymous with the word *liar* (vv. 1–11). It is a sad day when God calls the liar to face the consequences of his/her evil conduct.

The liar is a flatterer—Psalm 12:2: "With flattering lips and with a double heart do they speak."

The liar is deceitful—Psalm 55:21: "The words of his mouth were smoother than butter . . . his words were softer than oil, yet were they drawn swords."

The liar is a slanderer—Psalm 101:5,7: "Whoso privily slandereth his neighbor, him will I cut off . . . He that worketh deceit shall not dwell within my house: he that telleth lies shall not tarry in my sight."

It is a terrible thing to lie, but one cannot imagine the magnitude of the sin of lying to God as did Ananias and Sapphira.[3]

3. The cost and joy of obedience. Charles Haddon Spurgeon was a great English preacher. George Muller, also an Englishman, was a pioneer in caring for orphan children.

Spurgeon once preached in the three largest Baptist churches in Bristol, hoping to collect 300 pounds for his orphanage. He got the money and retired on the last night of his visit, satisfied he had been successful. But before he could fall to sleep, Spurgeon seemed to hear the Lord speaking to his heart: "Give that 300 pounds to George Muller."

Arguing with the Lord, Spurgeon responded, "But, Lord, I need that for my children in London." Again the Lord spoke to Spurgeon and he promised that the next day the money would be given to Muller.

Spurgeon went on to Muller's orphanage and found Muller on his knees before an open Bible.

"George," Spurgeon said, "God told me to give you this 300 pounds." And Muller replied, "Dear Mr. Spurgeon, I have been asking the Lord for that very sum."[4]

Being obedient cost Spurgeon, but it also paid great dividends. Being obedient cost Peter and John, as our lesson points out, but it also brought to them and the church great joy and increased effectiveness.

4. A contrast: light and dark. The first part of our lesson today gives us the sad experience of Ananias and Sapphira, who lied to God. That's the dark side of the lesson. The bright side of the lesson is seen in the obedience of Peter and the apostles even in the face of persecution.

Clarence E. Macartney, former Presbyterian leader and pastor of First Presbyterian Church, Pittsburgh, tells about a magnificent cathedral in Milan, Italy, and the inscriptions over the three great front doors.

"All that which pleases is but for a moment," is inscribed over the first door. Over the third door, a cross is carved with the inscription, "All that which troubles is but for a moment." But on the great center door, these words are inscribed: "That only is important which is eternal."[5]

TEACHING THE BIBLE

▶ *Main Idea:* The disciples' obedience to the Holy Spirit demonstrates how we should obey Him in our daily lives.

▶ *Suggested Teaching Aim:* To lead adults to examine the disciples' response to the Sanhedrin, and to identify ways they can obey the Holy Spirit in their lives.

A TEACHING OUTLINE

1. *Use an illustration to introduce the Bible study*
2. *Use a biblical simulation to summarize the Scripture study.*
3. *Let members write a modern-day case study or role play to describe a similar situation they could face today.*

Introduce the Bible Study

Use "A contrast: light and dark" in "Applying the Bible" to introduce the Bible study.

Search for Biblical Truth

IN ADVANCE, write the "Main Idea" of the lesson on a chalkboard or a large sheet of paper and place it on the focal wall.

Use the following biblical simulation to summarize the lesson. IN ADVANCE, enlist people to play the following roles. Give those enlisted a copy of their assignment and ask them to study the Scripture passage thoroughly before Sunday. You may want to serve as the announcer.

Television Announcer

Please read Acts 5:17–32 and think through the whole event to determine what questions people would want answered about this event. Use the questions listed in the other assignments. You will then interview the others to learn about events happening in Jerusalem. You may want to use a small microphone to simulate a television interview. Be careful to ask questions the interviewees will be able to answer.

First Member of the Sanhedrin

Please read Acts 5:17–32 and be prepared to be interviewed about the following: (1) Are you concerned about the teaching of the disciples? (2) How do you plan to arrest the disciples to stop such teaching?

Peter

Please read Acts 5:17–32 and be prepared to be interviewed about the following: (1) Since you were arrested and placed in jail, how did you get out? (2) Why would you come back to the temple and start preaching? (3) Why don't you get out of Jerusalem while you have time? (4) What did you tell the Sanhedrin about your escape? (5) Will you stop preaching?

Jailer

Please read Acts 5:17–32 and be prepared to be interviewed about the following: (1) How did the apostles escape? Did you get careless? Did someone slip in and let them out? (2) What did the Sanhedrin ask you about the escape? (3) What do you think will happen to you and your men? (4) What do you think about this new movement?

Gamaliel

Please read Acts 5:17–32 and be prepared to be interviewed about the following: (1) What do you think is the explanation of this escape from prison? (2) What did you tell these followers of Jesus? (3) What is your attitude toward this?

After the biblical simulation, allow members to ask questions to be sure they understand the biblical event. Point out the Main Idea of the lesson.

Give the Truth a Personal Focus

Organize members in groups of two or three. Ask them to write a modern-day case study or role play that would describe the same tension the apostles faced. Call on the groups to share their presentations.

Ask members to list ways they can be obedient to the Holy Spirit in their lives. List these ways on a chalkboard or a large sheet of paper. Ask members to choose one of these to emphasize this week in their lives.

---

1. Robert Hastings, *Proclaim* Magazine, Jan./Feb./Mar., 1993, 28–29.

2. Virginia Ely, *Devotion for Personal and Group Worship* (Westwood, N.J.: Fleming H. Revell Co., 1960), 97.

3. Ibid., 97.

4. Walter B. Knight, *Knight's Master Book of New Illustrations* (Grand Rapids, Mich.: Wm. B. Eerdmans Publishing Co., 1956), 445–46.

5. J. B. Fowler, Jr., *Illustrating Great Words of the New Testament* (Nashville: Broadman Press, 1991), 175.

Chosen to Serve

Focal Passage: Acts 6:1–8:3
Basic Passage: Acts 6:1–14

A new challenge faced the early church in Acts 6:1. For the first time, they were confronted by dissension within their own ranks. This led to the selection of seven men to meet a specific need. One of these was Stephen, whose witness for Christ stirred up such hatred that it led to Stephen's death and a wave of persecution that scattered the believers from Jerusalem.

▶ ▶ ▶ ▶ ▶**Study Aim:** *To serve faithfully in ways chosen by the Lord and the church*

STUDYING THE BIBLE

LESSON OUTLINE
I. Dissension and the Seven (6:1–7)
  1. Problem (6:1)
  2. Recommendation (6:2–4)
  3. Solution (6:5–6)
  4. Results (6:7)
II. Stephen's Ministry, Arrest, and Trial (6:8–7:1)
  1. Opposition (6:8–10)
  2. Accusations (6:11–12)
  3. Trial (6:13–7:1)
III. Stephen's Speech and Its Results (7:2–8:3)
  1. Survey of Abraham, Joseph, and Moses (7:2–34)
  2. Israel's persistent rejection (7:35–50)
  3. Rejection of the Messiah (7:51–53)
  4. Death of Stephen (7:54–60)
  5. Persecution (8:1–3)

The Greek-speaking members complained that their widows were being neglected (6:1). The apostles proposed a solution (vv. 2–4), which the church implemented by selecting seven men to meet this need (vv. 5–6). As a result, the church grew even more (v. 7). Stephen, one of the seven, aroused opposition by his bold witness (vv. 8–10). False accusations (6:11–12) led to a trial before the Sanhedrin (6:13–7:1). Stephen's defense involved a survey of familiar Old Testament figures (7:2–34). Stephen showed that Israel had a history of persistent rejection of God's word (vv. 35–50), which included that generation's rejection of the Messiah (7:51–53). Angry people stoned Stephen to death as he prayed for them (vv. 54–60). Among the bystanders was Saul, who spearheaded a persecution that scattered believers from Jerusalem (8:1–3).

I. Dissension and the Seven (Acts 6:1–7)
1. Problem (v. 1)

1 And in those days, when the number of disciples was multiplied, there arose a murmuring of the Grecians against the Hebrews, because their widows were neglected in the daily ministration.

In ancient society, widows were among the helpless members of society. The Old Testament commanded care for widows (Exod. 22:22; Deut. 10:18). The early church continued the practice (James 1:27). Widows were one of the groups whose needs were met by the church's sharing of goods (Acts 2:44–45; 4:32–35). Acts 6:1 shows that the Jerusalem church distributed food or money to buy food.

The word translated "Grecians" refers not to Greeks, but to Greek-speaking Jews. At this point, all the believers were either Jews or Gentile converts to Judaism. These Grecian Jews had lived outside the holy land and adopted Greek as their primary language. "Hebrews" refers to Aramaic-speaking Jews, who had lived within the holy land. The Jerusalem church consisted of both Grecian and Hebraic Jews. Each group had widows who needed the church's care. The Grecian Jews complained that their widows were being neglected in the daily distribution.

2. Recommendation (vv. 2–4)

2 Then the twelve called the multitude of the disciples unto them, and said, It is not reason that we should leave the word of God, and serve tables.

3 Wherefore, brethren, look ye out among you seven men of honest report, full of the Holy Ghost and wisdom, whom we may appoint over this business.

4 But we will give ourselves continually to prayer, and to the ministry of the word.

The twelve apostles realized the danger of dissension; therefore, they recommended that the church select seven men of good reputation, filled with the Spirit, and having true wisdom. These men were to be assigned to "serve tables." Serving tables is usually interpreted as distributing food, but the words can also refer to distributing money to buy food.

The apostles had a unique mission, since they were the only eyewitnesses of Jesus Christ. By handling the distribution to the widows, the seven would free up the apostles to concentrate on their main calling.

3. Solution (vv. 5–6)

5 And the saying pleased the whole multitude: and they chose Stephen, a man full of faith and of the Holy Ghost, and Philip, and Prochorus, and Nicanor, and Timon, and Parmenas, and Nicolas a proselyte of Antioch:

6 Whom they set before the apostles: and when they had prayed, they laid their hands on them.

The church was pleased by the apostles' recommendation; therefore, they chose the seven men named in verse 5. They brought them to the apostles. The apostles commissioned the seven by laying their hands on them.

The acts of Stephen and Philip are described in later passages. All we know of the others is their names and the fact that Nicolas was a Gentile who had accepted Judaism and then had become a believer. Since all seven had Greek names, they seem to have been chosen from among the Grecian Jews in the Jerusalem church. The later actions of Stephen and Philip show that at least two of the seven did much more than handle the distribution to widows. These two men were the first wave of Jewish believers to launch a mission to people other than Jews.

4. Results (v. 7)

> 7 And the word of God increased; and the number of the disciples multiplied in Jerusalem greatly; and a great company of the priests were obedient to the faith.

As a result of dealing with the problem, the church moved beyond dissension to a new burst of growth. The word bore a rich harvest, which included many priests.

II. Stephen's Ministry, Arrest, and Trial (Acts 6:8–7:1)

1. Opposition (6:8–10)

> 8 And Stephen, full of faith and power, did great wonders and miracles among the people.
>
> 9 Then there arose certain of the synagogue, which is called the synagogue of the Libertines, and Cyrenians, and Alexandrians, and of them of Cilicia and of Asia, disputing with Stephen.
>
> 10 And they were not able to resist the wisdom and the spirit by which he spake.

The miracles done through Stephen marked the power and favor of God on this remarkable man. Stephen also was a bold witness for Jesus Christ. Among those who heard his testimony were members of a synagogue made up of Grecian Jews. They had come to Jerusalem from places like Cyrene, Alexandria, Cilicia (sih LISH ih uh), and Asia (the Roman province by that name). Since Stephen's name marked him as a Grecian Jew, this may have been the synagogue to which he belonged. Unbelieving members of the synagogue argued with Stephen, but they were unable to withstand the wisdom and spiritual power of Stephen.

2. Accusations (6:11–12)

> 11 Then they suborned men, which said, We have heard him speak blasphemous words against Moses, and against God.
>
> 12 And they stirred up the people, and the elders, and the scribes, and came upon him, and caught him, and brought him to the council,

The opponents of Stephen got false witnesses to accuse Stephen of speaking blasphemous words against Moses and God. As a result, for the first time the people of Jerusalem and the Pharisees were stirred up against the believers. The previous opposition had been confined to the Sadducean (SAD joo see uhn) leaders (4:5–6; 5:17–18). The people had looked with favor on the believers (5:26), and the Pharisees had been neutral (vv.34-39). These groups were stirred up by charges that

Stephen was attacking the foundations of their faith in the God who gave them the law through Moses. They seized Stephen and took him to the Sanhedrin.

3. Trial (6:13–7:1)

13 And set up false witnesses, which said, This man ceaseth not to speak blasphemous words against this holy place, and the law:

14 For we have heard him say, that this Jesus of Nazareth shall destroy this place, and shall change the customs which Moses delivered us.

The false witnesses repeated their accusations before the Sanhedrin. They made two serious charges. For one thing, they accused Stephen of speaking against the temple. They quoted Stephen as saying that Jesus of Nazareth was going to destroy the temple. At the trial of Jesus, He had been accused of the same thing (Mark 14:57–58). Second, they accused Stephen of speaking against the law. They said that he advocated changing the customs that Moses had given the Jews.

Those who were there noted that Stephen's face looked like the face of an angel (6:15). Then the high priest asked him, "Are these things so?" (7:1).

III. Stephen's Speech and Its Results (Acts 7:2–8:3)

1. Survey of Abraham, Joseph, and Moses (7:2–34). At first glance, verses 2–34 appear to be only a survey of the lives of Abraham (vv. 2–8), Joseph (vv. 9–16), and Moses (vv. 17–34), which had little to do with the charges against Stephen. However, some key themes emerge even in verses 2–34. Stephen emphasized that key events in Israel's history took place outside the Holy Land (vv. 2–3,16,30). He also stressed that Joseph and Moses faced opposition from their own people (vv. 9, 26–28).

2. Israel's persistent rejection (7:35–50). Verses 35–43 add further examples of Israel's rejection of God's leadership through Moses. Stephen also mentioned Moses' promise of a prophet (v. 37). Although Stephen did not say so at the time, he believed that Jesus fulfilled the prophecy. Thus Stephen was implying that it was they, not he, who rejected God's Word through Moses.

Verses 44–50 provide Stephen's defense against the charge that he was opposed to the temple. Stephen emphasized God's presence in the movable tabernacle. In mentioning the temple, Stephen said that God does not live in man-made houses. Like the Old Testament prophets and Jesus, Stephen was critical of a religion that confined worship to a place (Jer. 7:1–16; John 4:19–24).

3. Rejection of the Messiah (7:51–53). Stephen accused his opponents of doing what their forefathers had done, resisting the Holy Spirit (v. 51). As their forefathers had persecuted the prophets, that generation had betrayed and murdered the Messiah (v. 52). Stephen also accused them of not keeping the very law they claimed to reverence (v. 53).

4. Death of Stephen (7:54–60). Stephen's words cut their hearts and infuriated them (v. 54). Stephen looked toward heaven and said that he saw "the Son of man standing on the right hand of God" (vv. 55–56). The mob stopped their ears, dragged Stephen outside the city, and stoned him (vv. 57–58). As Stephen died, he prayed for God to receive his spirit and to forgive the sin of the mob (vv. 59–60). The similarity to two of Jesus' prayers is striking (see Luke 23:34, 46).

5. Persecution (8:1–3). Among the witnesses to Stephen's death was Saul (7:58). He agreed with the action (8:1). So great was his opposition that he soon became the leader in a new wave of persecution that followed the death of Stephen (v. 3). The new persecution scattered the believers from Jerusalem into Judea, Samaria, and even beyond (8:1, 4; 11:19–21).

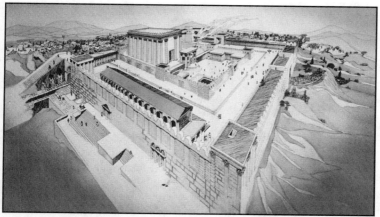

Reconstruction of Herod's Temple (20 B.C.–A.D. 70) at Jerusalem as viewed from the southeast. Credit: Bill Latta, Art Section Manager, Baptist Sunday School Board, Nashville, Tennessee

APPLYING THE BIBLE

1. A divided church. Churches have divided over a great many things, most of them foolish. For example, a beautiful colonial church in New England received a modern kitchen as a gift from a family. After the kitchen was dedicated, some of the women wanted to buy a newly invented electric automatic potato peeler. Other women wanted to do it the old-fashioned way: peel potatoes with knives. To buy the new electric potato peeler would make the work go too fast and the good ladies wouldn't have time to talk (gossip) about things happening in the community and church.

The controversy became so heated that the women lined up their husbands in support, and it became a full-blown church quarrel. Things became so bitter that when the pastor got up to preach on Sunday mornings the pro-potato parer party and the anti-potato parer party sat before him bristling at one another. As absurd as it seems, the church was so divided that the pastor resigned.[1]

The church at Jerusalem was divided because some of the people were being neglected (vv. 1–2). The concern of the people for the neglected widows was a valid one, but as the late Southwestern Seminary professor Ralph Baker used to tell us in class: "Whatever splits a Baptist church is wrong, I don't care how right it is!"

2. Working together. There's an old story about an ox and a colt which went to a spring to drink, but they began quarreling as to which should drink first. There was plenty of room for each of them to drink at the same time, but each was selfish and wanted to be first.

As they backed off and eyed each other for the battle that would decide the issue, they looked up and saw the buzzards circling above them, waiting to have the last word. According to the fable, the ox and the colt decided to drink together. Then, refreshed, they went on their way rejoicing.[2]

When the Jerusalem church quit quarreling, solved their problems, and began to work together, God's work prospered.

3. The solution to the church's problems. With the church divided, the apostles turned to finding a solution. That solution is pointed out in verse 3 where "seven men of honest report, full of the Holy Ghost and wisdom" were appointed to take care of the business of ministering to the needy.

Were these men deacons? They are not called deacons, but the root word from which *deacon* comes appears in verse 2: "serve" tables. This has led many to conjecture that these were the first deacons in the church.

Whether that is the case is immaterial. The solution to the problems in the church were some good men, and, no doubt, some good women as well. They were to be the buffers, the shock absorbers that stood between the offended parties. And every church needs people who will serve as these seven noble men in order to help the church run smoothly.

4. The devil attacks the growing church. The devil isn't concerned about dead churches. It's the growing church that concerns him.

The church was born at Jerusalem during the ministry of Jesus. At Pentecost, fifty days after the crucifixion, the church grew by three thousand souls (2:40–42). Shortly thereafter, about five thousand men believed, not counting women and children (4:4). And Acts 5:14 says: "And believers were the more added to the Lord, multitudes both of men and women." Then the church began to quarrel (6:1–2). Some godly men were called upon to help the church solve its problems and then the growth began again: "And the word of God increased; and the number of disciples multiplied in Jerusalem greatly; and a great company of the priests were obedient to the faith" (v. 7).

Henry Clarence Thiessen, a recognized New Testament scholar, suggests that in Jerusalem there may have been as many as twenty thousand Jews who had accepted Jesus as the Messiah.[3]

5. The Holy Spirit blessed the church greatly. Tertullian, the African Latin theologian (c. 160–225) wrote about the rapid spread of the church: "We are but of yesterday, yet we have filled your cities, islands, towns, and boroughs; we are in the camp, the senate and the

Forum. Our foes lament that every sex, age and condition, and the persons of every rank, are converts to the name of Christ." And within three centuries the Roman Empire itself capitulated unconditionally to the church of Jesus Christ. That's what happens when believers are united and filled with the Holy Spirit.

TEACHING THE BIBLE

▶ *Main Idea:* The way the early church handled controversy demonstrates how we can use differences to serve God faithfully.

▶ *Suggested Teaching Aim:* To lead adults to describe how the early church handled the controversy over distributing food to widows, and to identify ways they can serve the Lord and their church faithfully.

A TEACHING OUTLINE

1. Introduce the lesson with an illustration.
2. Use a brief lecture to teach Acts 6:1–7.
3. Use listening teams to teach Acts 6:8–14.
4. Identify elements that made Stephen faithful and apply these elements to members' lives.

Introduce the Bible Study

Use "A divided church" from "Applying the Bible" to introduce the lesson.

Search for Biblical Truth

IN ADVANCE, enlist a member to read the article in *Holman Bible Dictionary* (or other Bible dictionary) on "Stephen" and summarize the article for the class as a way to introduce the Bible study.

On a chalkboard or a large sheet of paper, write: "1. The Problem (6:1)." Present a brief lecture using the information in "Studying the Bible" that relates to this verse. Be prepared to explain the difference between Hebrews and Grecians.

Write: "2. The Recommendation (6:2–4)" and lecture briefly on these verses. Explain (1) why the apostles did not do the task, and (2) what the term "serving tables" can mean.

Write "3. The Solution (6:5–6)" and ask members to read these verses silently. Ask: (1) How many were chosen to serve the Grecian widows? (Seven.) (2) What do we know about these seven from later activities? (We know only about Stephen's and Philip's ministries; we know nothing about the other five.) (3) What do their names indicate about the seven men? (Their names were Greek which seems to indicate that they were chosen from the Grecian Jews.)

Write "4. The Results (6:7)" and briefly summarize these verses.

Enlist someone to read aloud Acts 6:8–14. Organize the class into three listening groups and make the following assignments:

Group 1—*Acts 6:8–10*

Why did Stephen stir up opposition? (He did wonders and

miracles.) Who opposed Stephen? (Grecian Jews from Cyrene and Alexandria who were members of the Synagogue of the Freedmen.)

Group 2—*Acts 6:11–12*

What did Stephen's enemies do to cause problems? (Enlisted false witnesses.) Why were the members of the Synagogue of the Freedmen so upset? (They felt Stephen was attacking the foundations of their faith in the God who gave the law.)

Group 3—*Acts 6:13–14*

What two serious charges did the Freedmen bring against Stephen? (Accused Stephen of speaking against the temple and accused him of speaking against the law.)

To complete the session, use the five points under "III. Stephen's Speech and Its Results" ("Studying the Bible") to summarize Stephen's defense before the Sanhedrin.

Give the Truth a Personal Focus

Ask members to take a moment and think of one or two reasons Stephen was so faithful to Christ. Then ask someone to write these on a chalkboard or a large sheet of paper.

Ask: What do you need to do to serve as faithfully as Stephen? Encourage members to find some place of service and to perform that service faithfully.

---

1. Benjamin P. Browne, *Illustrations for Preaching* (Nashville: Broadman Press, 1977), 73–74.

2. J. Ralph Grant, *Letters to Seven Churches and Other Sermons* (Grand Rapids, Mich.: Baker Book House, 1962), 53.

3. Henry Clarence Thiessen, *Introduction to the New Testament* (Grand Rapids, Mich.: Wm. B. Eerdmans Publishing Co., 1951), 136.

Philip: Witness to Outcasts

Basic Passage: Acts 8:4–40
Focal Passages: Acts 8:5–6, 26–38

P hilip, one of the seven, was among those scattered after the death of Stephen. Philip led the way in a breakthrough of the gospel to places outside Jerusalem and to people other than Jews. Philip preached the good news to the Samaritans, and he witnessed to an Ethiopian eunuch.

▶ ▶ ▶ ▶ **Study Aim:** *To share the good news with all kinds of people*

STUDYING THE BIBLE

LESSON OUTLINE
I. Philip in Samaria (8:4–25)
   1. Preaching Christ (8:4–8)
   2. Simon the magician (8:9–13)
   3. Peter and John in Samaria (8:14–17)
   4. Peter rebukes Simon (8:18–24)
   5. Preaching in the villages of Samaria (8:25)
II. Philip and the Ethiopian Eunuch (8:26–40)
   1. Led together by God (8:26–29)
   2. Scriptural witness to Jesus (8:30–35)
   3. Baptism and new joy (8:36–40)

Philip brought great joy to Samaria by preaching Christ there (vv. 4–8). Simon the magician was among those who believed and was baptized (vv. 9–13). When Peter and John came, they prayed that the Samaritan believers might receive the Holy Spirit (vv. 14–17). Peter rebuked Simon for trying to buy the Holy Spirit (vv. 18–24). Before returning to Jerusalem, they preached in many villages of the Samaritans (v. 25). An angel led Philip to an Ethiopian eunuch, and the Spirit led him to go to the eunuch's chariot (vv. 26–29). Finding the man reading Isaiah 53, Philip preached Jesus to him (vv. 30–35). The eunuch was baptized and went on his way rejoicing (vv. 36–40).

I. Philip in Samaria (Acts 8:4–25)
1. Preaching Christ (vv. 4–8). Philip was among those scattered from Jerusalem after the death of Stephen. The believers who were driven from Jerusalem went everywhere preaching the word (v. 4).

   5 Then Philip went down to the city of Samaria, and preached Christ unto them.

   6 And the people with one accord gave heed unto those things which Philip spake, hearing and seeing the miracles

which he did.

After the Northern Kingdom fell, most of the Israelites were either killed or taken into captivity. Other people were settled in the area. Over the years the people intermarried, and they became the Samaritans. The Samaritans believed in God and looked for a messiah. They were despised as half-breeds by the Jews. Several incidents in the ministry of Jesus show this strong animosity and also show that Jesus' love included the Samaritans (see Luke 9:51–56; 10:25–37; John 4:3–42).

Although Jesus had clearly told the apostles to witness in Samaria (Acts 1:8), several years had passed in which we have no record of any believer witnessing in Samaria until Philip went there. Philip carried out the kind of ministry for which Stephen died—a ministry not confined to Jews but including all people. Philip preached in Samaria, and they with one accord responded to his message. Philip also performed miracles there. Many were healed, and there was great joy in the city (vv. 7–8).

2. Simon the magician (vv. 9–13). A man named Simon had used magic to impress the people that he had the power of God (vv. 9–11). Many Samaritans believed the gospel of the kingdom and were baptized (v. 12). Simon also believed and was baptized (v. 13).

3. Peter and John in Samaria (vv. 14–17). When the Jerusalem apostles heard reports from Samaria, they sent Peter and John (v. 14). When the two apostles prayed and laid their hands on the Samaritans, they received the Holy Spirit (vv. 15–17). This special manifestation of the Spirit may have been God's way of blessing a significant breakthrough of the gospel to a new group.

4. Peter rebukes Simon (vv. 18–24). Simon asked to buy the ability to bestow the gift of the Holy Spirit (vv. 18–19). Peter rebuked Simon and said that the Samaritan's heart was not right toward God (vv. 20–21). The apostle called Simon to repent that he might be forgiven and delivered from his captivity to sin (vv. 22–23). Simon asked Peter to pray for him so that none of the judgments might fall on him (v. 24)

5. Preaching in the villages of Samaria (v. 25). As the apostles headed back to Jerusalem, they preached in the villages of Samaria.

II. Philip and the Ethiopian Eunuch
(Acts 8:26–40)

1. Led together by God (vv. 26–29)

26 And the angel of the Lord spake unto Philip, saying, Arise, and go toward the south unto the way that goeth down from Jerusalem unto Gaza, which is desert.

27 And he arose and went: and, behold, a man of Ethiopia, an eunuch of great authority under Candace (KAN duh see) queen of the Ethiopians, who had the charge of all her treasure, and had come to Jerusalem for to worship,

28 Was returning, and sitting in his chariot read Esaias the prophet.

29 Then the Spirit said unto Philip, Go near, and join thyself to this chariot.

The angel of the Lord offered no explanation for the instructions in verse 26. Philip was engaged in a fruitful ministry in Samaria; therefore, he may have wondered at the wisdom of leaving Samaria to go to a desert road. Philip, however, arose and went where the angel directed him. When Philip arrived at the desert road, he saw a chariot in which an important-looking foreigner was sitting and reading. The Spirit told Philip to go to this chariot.

Only later did Philip learn what verses 27–28 reveal about the man and what he was reading. He was from Ethiopia, a country south of Egypt, inhabited by people with black skin. He was a high government official, being in charge of the queen's treasury. He was a eunuch. He had been to Jerusalem to worship. He was reading from the prophet Isaiah.

This means that he was a Gentile who worshiped the God of Israel. Since he was a eunuch, he could not actually enter the temple as a worshiper (Deut. 23:1) or become an actual convert to Judaism. Although Judaism excluded him as a member, he got as close as possible to the holy temple as he worshiped God; and he was reading the sacred Scriptures. Such Gentiles were called God-fearers.

2. Scriptural witness to Jesus (vv. 30–35)

30 Then Philip ran thither to him, and heard him read the prophet Esaias, and said, Understandest thou what thou readest?

31 And he said, How can I, except some man should guide me? And he desired Philip that he would come up and sit with him.

Philip, sensitive to the Spirit's prompting, ran alongside the chariot and heard the man reading from the Scriptures. Letters on ancient scrolls were not easy to decipher; therefore, reading aloud was a way to pick one's way through a difficult passage. When Philip heard what the man was reading, he must have begun to realize why the Lord had sent him to this desert road at this particular time.

The apostles had needed the risen Lord to open to them the meaning of the Scriptures (Luke 24:45). This God-fearing Gentile was earnestly seeking truth in the Scriptures, and the Spirit led Philip to him. Although the Ethiopian was a high government official, he was open to the implied offer for help from the dusty Jewish traveler.

32 And the place of the scripture which he read was this, He was led as a sheep to the slaughter; and like a lamb dumb before his shearer, so opened he not his mouth:

33 In his humiliation his judgment was taken away: and who shall declare his generation? for his life is taken from the earth.

34 And the eunuch answered Philip, and said, I pray thee, of whom speaketh the prophet this? of himself, or of some other man?

35 Then Philip opened his mouth, and began at the same scripture, and preached unto him Jesus.

Philip must have been thrilled when he heard the eunuch reading Isaiah 53. He was reading verses 7–8, which told of someone being led as a sheep to the slaughter and going silently to an unjust death. The Ethiopian wanted to know who the silent sufferer was. Was the prophet writing of himself or someone else?

If the Ethiopian had asked this question to most first-century Jews, they would not have been able to give him much help. Jewish scholars debated the question. Some felt that Isaiah was speaking of himself. Others argued that Isaiah was speaking of the sufferings of the nation as a whole. Few thought the passage pointed to the Messiah, because most Jews didn't expect a suffering Messiah.

Philip quickly jumped on the man's question. The words "opened his mouth" signal that something significant was about to be said (see Matt. 5:2; Acts 10:34). Philip began with Isaiah 53:7–8, and preached Jesus to the Ethiopian. Philip knew that Jesus was the Suffering Servant foretold in Isaiah. During His ministry, Jesus had repeatedly predicted His suffering, death, and resurrection (Luke 9:22). Then He had done what Isaiah had prophesied and Jesus had foretold (Luke 22–24). After His resurrection, when Jesus opened the Scriptures to His followers, He doubtlessly dealt with Isaiah 53 (Luke 24:44–48). Philip's sermon is strong proof of that (see also 1 Pet. 2:24). The Suffering Servant was innocent of any wrong, but endured suffering and death according to God's will for the sins of others. Philip showed the eunuch how Jesus fulfilled this.

3. Baptism and new joy (vv. 36–40)

36 And as they went on their way, they came unto a certain water: and the eunuch said, See, here is water; what doth hinder me to be baptized?

37 And Philip said, If thou believest with all thine heart, thou mayest. And he answered and said, I believe that Jesus Christ is the Son of God.

38 And he commanded the chariot to stand still: and they went down both into the water, both Philip and the eunuch; and he baptized him.

Philip's sermon to the eunuch must have included instructions about baptism, for the Ethiopian asked what hindered him from being baptized. He had been excluded from Judaism. He wanted to know if any reason existed for him to be excluded from following Jesus. Fortunately, he asked Philip the question. Many of the early believers would have said that being a Gentile excluded him—unless he first became a Jew (something he couldn't do). Remember how Peter later resisted the Spirit's leadership in taking the gospel to another God-fearing Gentile. Only when the leadership of God was strong and persistent did Peter finally preach Christ to Cornelius (Acts 10:1–11:18).

Philip quickly received this man on the basis of his profession of faith in Christ. Since they were near water, Philip and the eunuch went down into the water together, and Philip baptized him. This is one of the passages that form the basis for the practice of believer's baptism by immersion.

The eunuch continued on his way rejoicing (v. 39). Philip went on his way and ended up at Caesarea, where Paul found him years later (v. 40; see Acts 21:8).

1. Winning one more soul. Rudyard Kipling, the renowned British poet who won the Nobel prize for literature, tells about being on a ship with William Booth, the founder of the Salvation Army.

The ship was docked in a south seaport and Kipling was drawn to the rail by the unusual noises he heard. There he saw William Booth walking back and forth, beating a tambourine as the crowd, which had come to see him off, wept and prayed.

Kipling didn't like all the noise and religious fervor and didn't hesitate to tell Booth. But Kipling said he never forgot Booth's reply: "Young feller, if I thought I could win one more soul to the Lord by walking on my head and playing a tambourine with my toes, I'd learn how."[1]

Stunned by Booth's sincerity, Kipling said he apologized. When Philip left Jerusalem and went to Samaria to preach, his message was the same as that of General William Booth. "[He] preached Christ unto them" (v. 5).

2. A joyous Christian, if possible. An elderly London lady once advertised in the newspaper for someone to live in her home and take care of her. Among the characteristics the lady wanted in a helper was, as she put it, "a joyous Christian, if possible."

Joy marked the life of Jesus and ought to mark the lives of His followers as well. Galatians 5:22 informs us that the Holy Spirit produces joy in the life of a yielded believer. If the joy is absent from a believer's heart and life, it is a grief to the Holy Spirit. Joylessness is not normal to the Christian life.

George Muller, the great English Christian who developed Britain's orphanage system, would not preach until his heart was full of joy and the grace of God. And the Moravians, whose daily life was marked by joy, convinced John and Charles Wesley that something was lacking in their lives. It wasn't too long after their association with the Moravians that they both came to know Christ as their Savior. They were trying to serve Christ, but they did not know Him. Joy was the magnet that pulled them to the Lord.

Our lesson today tells that after Philip preached in Samaria and led many of the people to Christ, "There was great joy in that city" (v. 8) Why not? That's the natural Christian life!

3. The condition of the unsaved. Although it is not in our lesson passage today, Ephesians 2 describes the condition of those who are unsaved, the Samaritans, the eunuch, and the people in our day, dead in sin (v. 1); living according the world (v. 2); servants to the flesh (v. 3); children of wrath (v. 3); and without Christ (v. 12). Also, they are aliens to God (v. 12); strangers to God (v. 12); without hope (v. 12); without God (v. 12); afar off from God (v. 13); and at enmity with God (v. 16).

But all can be changed when Jesus comes, as the Samaritans, the eunuch, and even Saul of Tarsus discovered.[2]

4. "The world is my parish." One of the greatest Christian leaders of history was John Wesley. An Anglican clergyman, Wesley and his brother Charles founded the Methodist Church. Born in 1703 in

Epworth, England, John Wesley died in 1791. At the age of eighty-six, Wesley preached a hundred sermons in sixty towns in nine weeks. His last sermon was preached on February 23, 1791, on the text, Isaiah 55:6. His last word was, "Farewell." The day before he died, with his last remaining strength he said, "The best of all is, God is with us!"

Wesley was well known for his statement, "I look upon all the world as my parish."

In our lesson today, the Great Commission of Jesus was being fulfilled by the church (Matt. 28:19–20). And His last commandment to the church was being carried out by the church: "Ye shall receive power, after that the Holy Ghost is come upon you: and ye shall be witnesses unto me both in Jerusalem, and in all Judaea, and in Samaria, and unto the uttermost part of the earth" (Acts 1:8). The good news had broken out of Jerusalem and Philip (8:4–8), as well as Peter and John (8:25), carried the gospel into despised Samaria.

There was no stopping it now! And, eventually, the gospel was carried to the whole world as Jesus commanded.

TEACHING THE BIBLE

▶ *Main Idea:* Philip's witness to the Samaritans and the Ethiopian shows how we should witness to all kinds of people.
▶ *Suggested Teaching Aim:* To lead adults to examine elements of Philip's witness to the Samaritans and the Ethiopian, and to identify some people with whom they will share the good news.

A TEACHING OUTLINE

1. Use an illustration to introduce the lesson.
2. Use a monologue to summarize Philip's actions in Samaria.
3. Use a "chain of events" poster to explain Philip's experience with the Ethiopian eunuch.
4. Identify some people with whom members can share the gospel.

Introduce the Bible Study

Use "The world is my parish" from "Applying the Bible" to introduce the lesson.

Search for Biblical Truth

IN ADVANCE, place a map of the first-century world on the wall. Be sure the map shows Jerusalem, Samaria, and Gaza. Begin the study by locating these places to show how the gospel began to spread.

IN ADVANCE, enlist a member to prepare a two- to three-minute report from *Holman Bible Dictionary* or another Bible dictionary on "Samaritans." Call for the report.

IN ADVANCE, enlist a member to prepare a two-minute monologue on Philip that explains how he left Jerusalem after Stephen's death and felt led to go to Samaria and preach the gospel there. Include some of the information in Acts 8:7–25 in the monologue.

On a chalkboard or a large sheet of paper, draw a large chain with four links. Above each link write one of the following Scripture references: Acts 8:26–29; Acts 8:30–31; Acts 8:32–35; Acts 8:36–38. Draw the links large enough so you can write a summary of each Scripture inside the link to form a chain of events.

Ask members to open their Bibles to Acts 8:26–29 and read these verses silently. Assign each verse to a different person (or ask for volunteers), and suggest they put the verse in their own words. Call for reports.

Use the comments on these verses from "Studying the Bible" to add any additional information. Locate Samaria and Gaza on the map.

Ask members to give a title to this section. (It might be something like "Led Together by God," but let them choose.)

Ask members to read Acts 8:30–31 silently. Use the comments in "Studying the Bible" to explain why the Ethiopian was reading aloud. Ask members to give a title to this section. (It might be something like "Philip Meets the Ethiopian.")

Ask members to read Acts 8:32–35 silently. Ask: What passage of Scripture was the Ethiopian reading? (Isa. 53.) What did the Ethiopian want to know about the passage? (Of whom the prophet spoke.) What was Philip's response? (Used the passage to preach Jesus.)

Ask members to give a title to this section. (It might be something like "Scriptural Witness to Jesus.")

Ask members to read Acts 8:36–38 silently. Write the following questions on slips of paper and distribute to members. Let them read the questions and see if members can answer. If not, be prepared to answer the questions. (1) What hindered the eunuch from becoming a Jew? (His physical mutilation.) (2) What barriers did Philip say would keep the Ethiopian from believing in Jesus? (Nothing!) (3) What did Philip say was required for the Ethiopian to be baptized? (Believing on Jesus with all his heart.) (4) What would seem to indicate that Philip immersed the Ethiopian? (They both went down into the water.)

Ask members to give a title to this section. (It might be something like "Baptism and New Joy.")

Give the Truth a Personal Focus

Ask: What would we have to do today to imitate Philip's actions? (Among other answers, follow the Spirit's direction and share the gospel with people of all races.)

Ask members to suggest some people or groups of people with whom they can share the gospel and suggest what they can do to reach them. Close with prayer that they will allow the Spirit to lead them to these people this week.

1. Scott Moody, *Proclaim* Magazine—Oct., Nov., Dec. 1992, 27–28—from Charles Ludwig, *Mother of an Army* (Minneapolis: Bethany House, 1987).

2. Hugh R. Horne, *Light on Great Bible Themes* (Grand Rapids, Mich.: Wm. B. Eerdmans Publishing Co., 1964), 61.

Saul Becomes a Disciple

Focal Passage: Acts 9:1–31
Basic Passages: Acts 9:1–6, 10–20

N ext to Jesus Himself, Paul exerted more influence on the shape of Christianity than any other leader. He was converted from being a fierce persecutor to being the apostle and missionary to the Gentiles. So important was Saul's conversion that the Book of Acts records it three times (9:1–31; 22:3–21; 26:2–23).

▶ ▶ ▶ ▶ ▶ ▶ ▶ ▶ ▶ **Study Aim:** *To distinguish the distinctive aspects of Saul's conversion from the aspects that constitute all true conversions*

STUDYING THE BIBLE

LESSON OUTLINE
I. Saul on the Damascus Road (9:1–9)
    1. Saul the persecutor (9:1–2)
    2. The Lord's appearance to Saul (9:3–6)
    3. Blind and helpless (9:7–9)
II. Ananias and Saul (9:10–19)
    1. Lord's instructions to Ananias (9:10–12)
    2. Lord's purpose for Saul (9:13–16)
    3. The ministry of Ananias to Saul (9:17–19)
III. The New Saul (9:20–31)
    1. Bold witness in Damascus (9:20–22)
    2. Plot against Saul in Damascus (9:23–25)
    3. Reception in the Jerusalem church (9:26–28)
    4. Witness and dangers in Jerusalem (9:29–30)
    5. The church at peace and growing (9:31)

Saul headed to Damascus to continue his persecution of believers (vv. 1–2). On the way, the Lord Jesus appeared to him and spoke to him (vv. 3–6). Saul was led into Damascus blind and helpless (vv. 7–9). Meanwhile, the Lord told a disciple named Ananias to go and help Saul (vv. 10–12). When Ananias replied that Saul was a persecutor, the Lord told him of His purpose for Saul (vv. 13–16). Ananias opened Saul's eyes and baptized him (vv. 17–19). Saul's bold witness in Damascus amazed everyone (vv. 20–22). When his enemies plotted to kill Saul, his followers enabled him to escape (vv. 23–25). With the help of Barnabas, Saul was accepted by the Jerusalem church (vv. 26–28). Saul's bold witness caused the brothers to send Saul to Tarsus (vv. 29–30). The church experienced a period of peace and further growth (v. 31).

I. Saul on the Damascus Road (Acts 9:1–9)
1. Saul the persecutor (vv. 1–2)

1 And Saul, yet breathing out threatenings and slaughter against the disciples of the Lord, went unto the high priest,

2 And desired of him letters to Damascus to the synagogues, that if he found any of this way, whether they were men or women, he might bring them bound unto Jerusalem.

Verse 1 picks up where Acts 8:1–3 left off. Saul had been wrecking the Jerusalem church by entering homes and sending believers to jail (8:1). Acts 26:10 shows that he voted for the death of believers who came to trial. Acts 9:1 reveals he was continuing to threaten the church in Jerusalem. Meanwhile, Saul had become concerned about the spread of "this way" to other places. He asked for and received letters from the high priest to the synagogues in Damascus. The letters introduced Saul and armed him with authority to apprehend any believers and to bring them as prisoners to Jerusalem.

2. The Lord's appearance to Saul (vv. 3–6)

3 And as he journeyed, he came near Damascus: and suddenly there shined round about him a light from heaven:

4 And he fell to the earth, and heard a voice saying unto him, Saul, Saul, why persecutest thou me?

5 And he said, Who art thou, Lord? And the Lord said, I am Jesus whom thou persecutest: it is hard for thee to kick against the pricks.

6 And he trembling and astonished said, Lord, what wilt thou have me to do? And the Lord said unto him, Arise, and go into the city, and it shall be told thee what thou must do.

Acts 22:6 says it was about noon, and Acts 26:13 says a light brighter than the sun shone around Saul. A voice called Saul by name and asked him, "Why persecutest thou me?" When Saul asked the identity of the speaker, he was told that the One being persecuted by Saul was none other than Jesus. This was Saul's ultimate moment of truth. He had been persecuting believers, claiming that their faith in Jesus was blasphemous. Suddenly, Saul realized that he had been totally wrong. He had been persecuting the Son of God by persecuting His people. He, not they, was the blasphemer.

The last part of verse 5 implies that Saul had already been feeling some pangs of conscience about his persecution. However, Saul had repressed whatever conviction he had been feeling as he continued his zealous persecution. But now, confronted by the Lord Himself, Saul was stopped in his tracks. The Lord told him to go into Damascus where he would be told what to do.

3. Blind and helpless (vv. 7–9).

Those with Saul saw the light and heard but didn't understand the voice (v. 7; see Acts 22:9). When Saul staggered to his feet, he couldn't see. His companions led him as a blind man into Damascus (v. 8). During the three days of blindness, Saul neither ate nor drank (v. 9). The aggressive persecutor had become a broken and helpless person.

We are not told what went through Saul's mind, but his experience must have helped him later to form his doctrine of salvation by grace. He had discovered that he was a guilty sinner who deserved only destruction, yet no thunderbolts of wrath fell. Instead the Lord reduced him to an awareness of his own helplessness as he awaited what the Lord would do.

II. Ananias and Saul (Acts 9:10–19)

1. Lord's instructions to Ananias (vv. 10–12)

10 And there was a certain disciple at Damascus, named Ananias; and to him said the Lord in a vision, Ananias. And he said, Behold, I am here, Lord.

11 And the Lord said unto him, Arise, and go into the street which is called Straight, and inquire in the house of Judas for one called Saul, of Tarsus: for, behold, he prayeth,

12 And hath seen in a vision a man named Ananias coming in, and putting his hand on him, that he might receive his sight.

Saul had been right about believers being in Damascus. The Lord spoke in a vision to one of them named Ananias. Ananias, like Samuel of old, responded quickly to the Lord's call (1 Sam. 3:4–14). The Lord instructed Ananias to go to where Saul of Tarsus was praying. Saul too had seen a vision. In his vision he saw a man named Ananias restoring his sight.

Verses 11–12 give further insight into what Saul was doing during his three-day fast. He was praying; and although he was blind, he saw a vision.

2. Lord's purpose for Saul (vv. 13–16)

13 Then Ananias answered, Lord, I have heard by many of this man, how much evil he hath done to thy saints at Jerusalem:

14 And here he hath authority from the chief priests to bind all that call on thy name.

15 But the Lord said unto him, Go thy way: for he is a chosen vessel unto me, to bear my name before the Gentiles, and kings, and the children of Israel.

16 For I will shew him how great things he must suffer for my name's sake.

Ananias was aware of Saul's persecution of the saints in Jerusalem and of his evil mission to Damascus. Ananias was not refusing to do what the Lord said, but he was displaying the kind of honesty that characterizes so many Bible prayers.

The Lord replied by telling Ananias of His purpose for Saul. The Damascus road revelation was no accident, for Saul was a chosen instrument of the Lord. Saul was to bear the Lord's name before Gentiles, kings, and Jews. The blindness was a lesson for Saul in suffering for the Lord's sake.

3. The ministry of Ananias to Saul (vv. 17–19)

17 And Ananias went his way, and entered into the house; and putting his hands on him said, Brother Saul, the Lord, even Jesus, that appeared unto thee in the way as thou camest, hath

sent me, that thou mightest receive thy sight, and be filled with the Holy Ghost.

18 And immediately there fell from his eyes as it had been scales: and he received sight forthwith, and arose, and was baptized.

19 And when he had received meat, he was strengthened. Then was Saul certain days with the disciples which were at Damascus.

Ananias obeyed the Lord. When he met Saul, he made clear that he had been sent by the Lord Jesus. Ananias called him "Brother Saul," not as a fellow Jew but as a fellow believer. He told Saul that he had come so that Saul might regain his sight and receive the Holy Spirit. When Ananias laid his hands on Saul, his sight returned as he had seen in the vision (v. 12). Then Saul was baptized. After he ate, he was strengthened. He stayed for a while with the disciples at Damascus.

III. The New Saul (Acts 9:20-31)

1. Bold witness in Damascus (vv. 20–22)

20 And straightway he preached Christ in the synagogues, that he is the Son of God.

Saul, who had come to Damascus to destroy the church, now declared boldly that Jesus Christ is the Son of God. The knowledge of his original mission was well known in Damascus; therefore, when Saul preached Christ, everyone was amazed. At first, people couldn't believe their eyes and ears. They asked if this was not the one who had persecuted Jerusalem believers and had come to arrest disciples in Damascus (v. 21). When they realized this was Saul the persecutor, the testimony of Saul grew in strength and confounded his opponents (v. 22).

2. Plot against Saul in Damascus (vv. 23–25). Being unable to withstand his testimony, Saul's enemies plotted to kill him (v. 23). Saul learned of the plot and of his enemies' daily watch at the gates (v. 24). Saul's friends saved him by lowering him through an opening in the city wall under cover of night (v. 25).

3. Reception in the Jerusalem church (vv. 26–28). At some point Saul spent some time in Arabia; but after three years the former persecutor returned to Jerusalem (Gal. 1:15–18). When Saul tried to join the Jerusalem church, they were afraid of him and didn't believe he had really become a disciple (v. 26). Barnabas, however, lived up to his reputation as an encourager (Acts 4:36–37) by standing up for Saul. Barnabas took him to the apostles, and vouched for what happened on the Damascus road, and told how Saul had preached boldly in Damascus (v. 27). Barnabas' testimony for Saul must have convinced the apostles, because Saul moved about freely in Jerusalem (v. 28).

4. Witness and dangers in Jerusalem (vv. 29–30). Saul became a bold witness for Christ in Jerusalem. Like Stephen, Saul became involved in debates with the Grecian Jews, who plotted to kill him (v. 29; see Acts 6:9–14). Before this could happen, the believers hustled

Saul to Caesarea and from there to Tarsus (v. 30).

5. The church at peace and growing (v. 31). With the conversion of its chief persecutor, the church experienced a period of peace and further growth.

The city wall of biblical Damascus. Credit: William B. Tolar, Vice President for Academic Affairs and Provost, Southwestern Baptist Theological Seminary, Fort Worth, Texas

APPLYING THE BIBLE

1. Saul the persecutor. F. J. Huegel, in his book *The Cross of Christ*, tells about the persecution of Christians during the Boxer Rebellion in China in 1900. It was a persecution directed mainly against foreigners and Chinese Christians.

The Boxers captured a Christian mission school, erected a cross, and sent word to the faculty and students that anyone who would trample on the cross would go free. Those who did not do so, they were warned, would be killed. The first seven students who came out of the school trampled on the cross and their lives were spared, but the next student, who was a girl, knelt before the cross and was shot on the spot. The remaining students, about one hundred of them, followed her example and were killed.

Saul was a persecutor of the Christians before he was saved (Acts 9:1-2). He even consented to the death of Stephen, the first known Christian martyr (7:54–8:1). This courage in the face of certain death, such as was demonstrated by Stephen and the Chinese Christian students, has been multiplied millions of times through the ages. And many times, as in the case of Saul, the martyrdom of the saints has led to the conversion of the persecutors.

2. Noted conversions. Every salvation experience is unique and miraculous, but let me share with you the conversion experiences of a few noted people:

William Cowper, born in England in 1731, was a poet and hymn writer who was plagued throughout his life with long periods of depression and despondency. On more than one occasion, Cowper attempted suicide. In "The Task, Book III," Cowper refers to his emotional problems and describes himself as "a stricken deer that left the herd." But during one of his stays in a private hospital he was converted as he read his Bible. His greatest contribution to Christianity, although he wrote more than sixty-eight hymns, is the familiar hymn, "There Is a Fountain Filled with Blood."

Martin Luther, born in Germany in 1483, was a "good" Catholic who entered the priesthood after having been frightened by a terrible thunderstorm. Although he fasted more than was required, did excessive penitences, starved himself, mortified his body, and confessed at great length both real and imagined sins, still he found no peace.

Luther was saved while studying Paul's Epistle to the Romans, when he discovered that "the just shall live by faith." He said he "felt myself to be reborn." As we all know, he became a catalyst for the Protestant Reformation that sent the world reeling in a new direction.

John Wesley was born in England in 1703. Reared an Anglican, and the son of an Anglican clergyman, Wesley had no intention of leaving the Anglican Church but, eventually, he and his brother Charles founded the Methodist Church. Wesley served as a chaplain in colonial Georgia but later testified, "I went to America to convert the Indians; but oh! who shall convert me?"

Through the influence of Peter Bohler, a Moravian preacher, and other Moravians who were so joyous in their relationship to Christ, Wesley said he discovered he lacked "that faith whereby alone we are saved."

The rest is history. On May 24, 1738, while attending a Moravian devotional meeting at Aldersgate, Wesley was listening to Luther's *Preface to the Epistle to the Romans* when he had that spiritual experience with Christ that forever changed his life.[1]

Others certainly could be told and many of them describe the same kind of traumatic experience Saul had on the road to Damascus. But remember: all people are saved exactly the same way through repentance from sin and faith in Jesus Christ, but conversion affects sinners differently. The experience of most of us is far gentler, though just as real as the experience of Paul and these others cited.

3. Speak a good word for Jesus. In his book *Beside the Bonnie Brier Bush*, Ian Maclaren tells about a Scottish boy named John, whose mother was ambitious for him to become a minister. "During her final illness, she called John to her bedside and gave him her watch and chain. Then holding John's hand, and with a mother's word of counsel, she said: 'You follow Christ, and if He offers you a cross, you will not refuse it, for He always carries the heavy end Himself. . . . If God calls you to the ministry, you will not refuse, and the day you preach in yonder old church, speak a good word for Jesus Christ.'"[2]

After Paul's conversion on the Damascus road, he boldly "spoke a good word for Jesus" everywhere he went, and became the greatest preacher of the gospel since Jesus Christ.

TEACHING THE BIBLE

▶ *Main Idea:* Saul's experience on the Damascus road demonstrates that certain aspects of his conversion differ from the aspects that constitute all true conversions.

▶ *Suggested Teaching Aim:* To explore the significance of Saul's conversion, and to distinguish the distinctive aspects of Saul's conversion from the aspects that constitute all true conversions.

A TEACHING OUTLINE

1. Use an illustration to introduce the study.
2. Use a biblical outline to guide you through the lesson.
3. Challenge members to identify aspects of Saul's conversion that must be present in all true conversions.

Introduce the Bible Study

Use "Saul the persecutor" in "Applying the Bible" to introduce the session.

Search for Biblical Truth

IN ADVANCE, place a map showing Jerusalem and Damascus on the focal wall. Locate these two places and point out that somewhere between these two cities a conversion took place that changed the world. Share the information in the opening paragraphs of the introduction to this lesson.

IN ADVANCE, write the following outline on a chalkboard or a large sheet of paper. Cover each point until you are ready to use it.

Saul Becomes a Disciple

1. Saul on the Damascus Road (Acts 9:1–6)
2. Ananias and Saul (Acts 9:10–19)
3. The New Saul (Acts 9:20)

Call attention to the outline and uncover the first point: 1. Saul on the Damascus Road (Acts 9:1–6). Ask for a volunteer to read Acts 9:1–6. Ask: What is the background of this passage? (Stephen's stoning.) Why do you think Saul was so violent in his opposition to this new way of belief? (Your response, but consider: Saul may have felt guilt over not following Jesus after he saw how Stephen died.) What word from Jesus indicated that Saul may have been feeling some pangs of conscience about his activities? ("It is hard for thee to kick against the pricks.") What response from Saul indicated that he was sincere in seeking God's will? ("What wilt thou have me to do?")

Uncover the second point on the outline: 2. Ananias and Saul (Acts 9:10–19). Ask for a volunteer to read Acts 9:10–19. Briefly summarize verses 7–9. Ask: How would you have felt if you had been Ananias? What indicated that God was working on both fronts? (God had told Saul a man by the name of Ananias would come to him.) What had God chosen Saul to do that made Saul's conversion so special? (God had chosen Saul to appear before kings, Gentiles, and Jews.) Why do you think God chose Saul? (Your response, but consider: God in His wisdom chose Saul just as he had chosen Abraham, Jacob, David, and a host of others.) What term of address showed Ananias had accepted Saul's conversion as genuine? ("Brother.") What, according to verse 18, was the first thing that Paul did after his vision was restored? (He was baptized.) What do you think Paul did during those "certain days" he spent with the disciples at Damascus? (Your response, but consider: possibly Saul learned all he could from them about Jesus.)

Uncover the third outline point: 3. The New Saul (Acts 9:20). Ask a volunteer to read Acts 9:20. Ask: What did Saul do now that he was a believer? (Preached.) What do you think would have been Paul's outline for his first sermon?

Give the Truth a Personal Focus

Use "Noted conversions" from "Applying the Bible." Ask: How do these conversions and Saul's differ from yours? What aspects of Saul's conversion were unique to his experience? What aspects must be present in all true conversions? (Meeting Jesus and giving one's life to Him is the only aspect that we must duplicate in Saul's conversion.)

If you have unsaved members present, use this opportunity to encourage them to meet Jesus.

---

1. For a fuller discussion of these conversions, see J. B. Fowler, Jr., *Illustrating Great Words of the New Testament* (Nashville: Broadman Press, 1991), 153–56.
2. R. L. Middleton, *Don't Disappoint God* (Nashville: Broadman Press, 1951), 128.

Gentiles Receive the Spirit

Basic Passage: Acts 10:1–11:18
Focal Passages: Acts 10:30–39, 44–48

Acts 10:1–11:18 describes an important breakthrough of the gospel. God led Peter to realize that His plan included receiving Gentile believers for salvation and fellowship. Philip had led a Gentile God-fearer to faith in Christ, but that apparently was considered an isolated case. Peter preached to a number of Gentiles, and he and his companions saw the Holy Spirit come on these Gentile believers. The Jerusalem church was forced to recognize that God offered salvation to Gentile believers.

▶ ▶ ▶ ▶ ▶ ▶ ▶ ▶ **Study Aim:** *To recognize the significance of the coming of the Spirit on Cornelius and his household*

STUDYING THE BIBLE

LESSON OUTLINE
I. Peter Sent by God to the House of Cornelius (10:1–22)
  1. Vision of Cornelius (10:1–8)
  2. Vision of Peter (10:9–16)
  3. Spirit's command to Peter (10:17–23)
II. Peter at the House of Cornelius (10:24–48)
  1. Getting acquainted (10:24–33)
  2. Peter's sermon (10:34–43)
  3. Spirit falls on Gentiles (10:44–48)
III. Peter's Report to the Jerusalem Church (11:1–18)
  1. Criticism of Peter (11:1–3)
  2. Peter's explanation (11:4–17)
  3. Praise by the church (11:18)

Cornelius (Kawr NEE lih uhs) had a vision about sending for Peter (10:1–8). Peter had a vision about eating unclean food (vv. 9–16). When the messengers from Cornelius arrived, the Spirit led Peter to go with them (vv. 17–23). When Peter heard what Cornelius said, he realized that God doesn't consider any person common or unclean (vv. 24–33). Peter preached the gospel to Cornelius, his family, and friends (vv. 34–43). After the Spirit fell on the Gentiles, Peter saw no reason not to have them baptized (vv. 44–48). Peter was criticized by some in Jerusalem for eating with uncircumcised men (11:1–3). Peter told the events recorded in chapter 10 (vv. 4–17). The church recognized that God had offered life to repentant Gentiles (v. 18).

The ancient seaport of Joppa. Credit: William B. Tolar, Vice President for Academic Affairs and Provost, Southwestern Baptist Theological Seminary, Fort Worth, Texas

I. Peter Sent by God to the House of Cornelius (Acts 10:1–22)

1. Vision of Cornelius (vv. 1–8). While he was praying, a God-fearing Roman centurion named Cornelius saw a vision of an angel (vv. 1–3). The angel told Cornelius that his prayers and gifts had been heard by God (v. 4). The angel told Cornelius to send from Caesarea to Joppa and to make contact with a man named Peter (vv. 5–6). Cornelius sent two servants and a devout soldier to Joppa (vv. 7–8).

2. Vision of Peter (vv. 9–16). On the next day while Peter was praying, he saw a vision (vv. 9–10). He saw a great sheet filled with all kinds of animals, and he heard a voice telling him to kill and eat (vv. 11–13). When Peter objected that he had never eaten anything common or unclean, the voice said, "What God hath cleansed, that call not thou common" (vv. 14–15). This happened three times (v. 16).

3. Spirit's command to Peter (vv. 17–23). While Peter was wondering about the meaning of the vision, the three messengers from Cornelius arrived (vv. 17–18). The Spirit told Peter that He had sent them and to go with them (vv. 19–20). The messengers told Peter about Cornelius and his vision (vv. 21–22). The next day, Peter took some Jewish brothers and went with the messengers (v. 23).

II. Peter at the House of Cornelius (Acts 10:24–48)

1. Getting acquainted (vv. 24–33). When they arrived on the following day, they found that Cornelius had invited relatives and close friends (v. 24). When Cornelius bowed before Peter, the apostle told the Roman that he was just a man (vv. 25–26). Peter told the group that Jews were forbidden to have fellowship with Gentiles, but that God had taught him not to call any man common or unclean (vv. 27–28). Then Peter asked Cornelius why he had sent for him (v. 29).

30 And Cornelius said, Four days ago I was fasting until this hour; and at the ninth hour I prayed in my house, and, behold,

a man stood before me in bright clothing,

31 And said, Cornelius, thy prayer is heard, and thine alms are had in remembrance in the sight of God.

32 Send therefore to Joppa, and call hither Simon, whose surname is Peter; he is lodged in the house of one Simon a tanner by the sea side: who, when he cometh, shall speak unto thee.

33 Immediately therefore I sent to thee; and thou hast well done that thou art come. Now therefore are we all here present before God, to hear all things that are commanded thee of God.

Verses 30–33 summarize the events of verses 1–8. Cornelius was a God-fearing Gentile. That is, he believed in and sought to worship the God of the Jews; but he had not actually been circumcised in order to become a proselyte (convert) to Judaism. He prayed and gave alms—marks of Jewish piety.

Thus, in many ways, Cornelius was like the Ethiopian eunuch. Both were God-fearing Gentiles. They were seekers who believed and practiced the Jewish religion without actually becoming members. These two men were alike in another way: God recognized their earnest sincerity and sent believers to witness to them of Jesus Christ. Thus Peter, like Philip, found eager seekers whose hearts the Lord had prepared for the seed of the gospel.

2. Peter's sermon (vv. 34–43)

34 Then Peter opened his mouth, and said, Of a truth I perceive that God is no respecter of persons:

35 But in every nation he that feareth him, and worketh righteousness, is accepted with him.

The words "opened his mouth" show that something significant was about to be said (see Matt. 5:2; Acts 8:35). Verses 34–35 are a restatement in different words of the basic idea in verse 28. When Peter had the vision telling him to eat unclean animals, he didn't understand. However, when God led him to the house of a Gentile, whom Jews considered unclean, Peter saw what God was trying to teach him. He was not to call any man common or unclean (v. 28). Or to put it another way: God has no favorites, but accepts people of every nation who love and serve Him.

This is the meaning of the words "no respecter of persons." On the surface, the English words might be misunderstood to mean that God doesn't respect persons. The wording goes back to the Old Testament commands to judges not to show respect of persons (Deut. 1:17; 16:19). The judges were not to pass judgment based on a person's face or appearance. In other words, justice is supposed to be blind and not be partial toward the rich, powerful, or attractive. God is like that, and His people are also to avoid prejudice (James 2:1).

36 The word which God sent unto the children of Israel, preaching peace by Jesus Christ: (he is Lord of all:)

37 That word, I say, ye know, which was published throughout all Judaea, and began from Galilee, after the baptism which John preached;

38 How God anointed Jesus of Nazareth with the Holy

Ghost and with power: who went about doing good, and healing all that were oppressed of the devil; for God was with him.

39 And we are witnesses of all things which he did both in the land of the Jews and in Jerusalem.

Peter's sermon focused on Jesus Christ. Peter stated his assumption that these Gentiles living in Caesarea had already heard much about Jesus of Nazareth. Although Peter said that God sent Jesus to the Jews, Peter showed his new insight by adding "he is Lord of all." Peter spent more time on the life of Jesus than he had in earlier sermons to Jews. He began with the baptism of John. The reference to being anointed with the Holy Spirit probably points to the Spirit's descent on Jesus at His baptism (see Luke 3:22). Peter emphasized that the miracles of Jesus were part of His ministry of doing good to people.

Although Cornelius and the other Gentiles had heard some things about Jesus, this was the first time they had heard one of the eyewitnesses. Peter bore witness to the death and resurrection of Jesus (vv. 39–41). Peter also said that Jesus was ordained to be Judge of all (v. 42). The apostle stressed the invitation that applied to all, including his Gentile audience: "To him give all the prophets witness, that through his name whosoever believeth in him shall receive remission of sins" (v. 43). Peter had used "whosoever" in preaching to Jews at Pentecost (Acts 2:21); now he realized that "whosoever" included all people, not just Jews.

3. Spirit falls on Gentiles (vv. 44–48)

44 While Peter yet spake these words, the Holy Ghost fell on all them which heard the word.

45 And they of the circumcision which believed were astonished, as many as came with Peter, because that on the Gentiles also was poured out the gift of the Holy Ghost.

46 For they heard them speak with tongues, and magnify God. Then answered Peter,

47 Can any man forbid water, that these should not be baptized, which have received the Holy Ghost as well as we?

48 And he commanded them to be baptized in the name of the Lord. Then prayed they him to tarry certain days.

What happened here is often called "the Gentile Pentecost." As Peter was preaching to them, the Spirit came on them; and they began to speak with tongues. A similar thing had happened when Peter and John came to Samaria to meet those who had believed at Philip's preaching (Acts 8:17). These two comings of the Spirit were signs of breakthroughs of the gospel to new groups—to Samaritans and to Gentiles. Something observable was needed to convince Jewish believers that God welcomed Gentiles on the basis of their faith. Peter had been careful to take six witnesses with him to Caesarea (10:23; 11:12). These men were astonished that the Spirit fell on Cornelius, his relatives, and friends.

Peter's question in verse 47 is like the Ethiopian's question in Acts

8:36. Many Jewish believers excluded Gentiles unless the Gentiles had first been circumcised and come under the Jewish law. Peter and the other Jews at Caesarea had seen the same Spirit come on uncircumcised Gentiles. None of them dared forbid that these new believers be baptized.

III. Peter's Report to the Jerusalem Church (Acts 11:1-18)

1. Criticism of Peter (vv. 1–3). When news of these events reached Jerusalem, Peter was criticized by those "of the circumcision" (vv. 1–2). These Jewish believers insisted that Jews should not eat with anyone who had not been circumcised (v. 3). The basis for this was that uncircumcised people ate unclean food. Strict Jews believed that eating with such a person made the Jews themselves unclean.

2. Peter's explanation (vv. 4–17). Peter summarized the events that had led him to go to the house of Cornelius. He went because the Spirit led him, and he took with him six Jews to witness what happened (vv. 4–12). Peter then told what had happened in the house of Cornelius, stressing the coming of the Spirit on the Gentiles (vv. 13–16). He summed up his case by saying: "Forasmuch then as God gave them the like gift as he did unto us, who believed on the Lord Jesus Christ; what was I, that I could withstand God?" (v. 17).

3. Praise by the church (v. 18). Faced with such facts, the church at Jerusalem praised God for opening the door to Gentiles who believed. But later events showed that the issue was far from settled (see Acts 15:1–5).

APPLYING THE BIBLE

1. Mankind's search for God. The distinguished missionary E. Stanley Jones tells about watching a Hindu woman in India one day prostrating herself on the ground, arising to prostrate herself again and again, moving toward a flame burning in the ground hundreds of miles away. In their superstition, the Hindus thought it was a place where they could find God, although it was nothing more than natural gas escaping from the ground. When Jones asked the woman what she was doing, in broken English she replied: "Vision of Him! Vision of Him!"

Mankind's search for God is universal and timeless. Near Thebes, in Egypt, one can see the ruins of the Temple of Karnak. It is a marvelous ruin, unique in its architectural features. One gazes with amazement at the vista of gigantic columns decorated with religious symbols sculptured in curious designs. The wealth and splendor of Thebes, now in ruins, gives evidence of the quest for God of the ancient Egyptians.

At Baalbek, in Syria, there are nine acres covered with the ruins of once magnificent and ornate temples, built two thousand years ago. These ruins, like those at Thebes, are an ancient testimony to mankind's search for God.

In Ephesus, the ruins of the Temple of Diana, and in Athens, the ruins of the Parthenon, all testify to the same thing. They give proof to the statement of Russian novelist Leo Tolstoy: "God is He without Whom one cannot live."

Cornelius, like all those who came before him and all who have come after him, was seeking God when he sent for Simon Peter (10:1–8).

2. "I want God." What is the thing you most want in life? What is the one thing you most need? What is the one thing on which your heart is set above all other things? English poet and novelist Rudyard Kipling gives us his answer. During a serious illness the nurse asked Kipling, "Do you want anything?" and Kipling replied, "I want God."[1]

3. God is love. A farmer once painted on his weathervane the words, "God is love." When someone asked him if he meant to imply that the love of God is as fickle as the wind, the farmer answered: "No, the love of God is certainly not fickle. I mean that whichever way the wind blows, God is love. "In life," he said, "if the cold wind blows out of the north, God is love. If the wet wind blows from the east, God is love. If life's wind blows gently from the south or the west, God is always love."[2]

God's love for the Jews was an accepted fact, but could God love a Gentile? As the winds of grace blew across Jerusalem and out to the Gentile world, they revived and refreshed a Gentile centurion named Cornelius. What an epochal development this was as the Gentiles entered the kingdom of God by grace. As Peter told Cornelius, "God is no respecter of persons" (v. 34).

4. It is at the cross that we find God. Only the cross reveals the depth of the love of God (Rom. 5:8). Neither the beauty of creation nor the magnificence of the universe reveal God's love for sinners. That love is only expressed at the cross.

An artist once created an unusual picture of Jesus on the cross. The sky is darkened and Christ hangs in sharp relief against the black background. Gazing at the painting, one observes a second figure seeming to emerge from the shadows. It is God the Father standing behind Jesus. The nails through the hands of Jesus also go through the hands of the Father. The nails through the feet of Jesus also penetrate the feet of God. And the crown of thorns on the brow of Jesus is also on the Father's head. It is the artist's way of saying that the death of Jesus on the cross reveals the love and the suffering of God for sinners.[3]

5. The people God uses. In one of my early pastorates, there was a farmer who went to church regularly with his wife, but he was not a Christian. He told me on one occasion how he was brought to Jesus.

There was a young man in the church who stood about six feet three inches tall, weighed two hundred pounds and was a fine specimen of young manhood—about twenty-two years of age. He was a devout Christian, although he had the mind of a child.

"He is the one," the farmer friend said, "who led me to Jesus.

"He never said a word to me," my friend said, "but during each invitation time in the service he would turn completely around in his pew toward the front and stare at me in my pew toward the back.

Finally, I could no longer stand his penetrating gaze, and in a morning worship service, I walked down the aisle and told the pastor I was giving my heart to Jesus."

God is full of surprises! I am surprised at the people God uses to get His work done. Our lesson today is a classic example of that very thing. Peter was a prejudiced Jew, and Cornelius was a hated Gentile. But, directed by the Holy Spirit, God responded to the call of Cornelius, shared the gospel with him, and led him to Christ. The gospel was breaking out of its Jewish boundaries and penetrating the Gentile world.

TEACHING THE BIBLE

▶ *Main Idea:* The coming of the Spirit on Cornelius and his household shows that the gospel is for all people.
▶ *Suggested Teaching Aim:* To lead adults to describe the significance of the Spirit's coming on Cornelius and his household, and to list implications of that experience.

A TEACHING OUTLINE

1. Use an illustration to introduce the study.
2. Let members write an outline of the passage.
3. Let members develop four principles to guide their understanding of the implications of the passage for sharing the gospel with all people.

Introduce the Bible Study
Use "God is love" in "Applying the Bible" to introduce the lesson.
Search for Biblical Truth
IN ADVANCE, enlist a member to present a monologue of Cornelius' vision (Acts 10:1–8) and a member to present a monologue of Peter's vision (Acts 10:9–16). Use the material in "3. Spirit's command to Peter" to summarize Acts 10:17–23. (See "Studying the Bible" for each of these.)

IN ADVANCE, place a map on the wall and locate Joppa and Caesarea.

IN ADVANCE, write the following Scripture references on a large sheet of paper (without the heading and place them on the focal wall):
Gentiles Receive the Spirit
Acts 10:30–33—Cornelius Explains His Actions
Acts 10 34–35—Peter Expresses a Great Truth
Acts 10:36–39—Peter Preaches Jesus
Acts 10:44–48—The Spirit Falls on Gentiles

Leave space opposite each reference to write a title for that reference. (The titles above are suggestions only; let members come up with their ideas.)

Ask a volunteer to read Acts 10:30–33. Give a brief lecture in which you cover the following points: (1) Cornelius was a God-fearing Gentile; (2) Cornelius was similar in some ways to the Ethiopian eunuch; and (3) God approved of his praying and almsgiving. Let members suggest a title for the passage.

Ask a third of the class to take Acts 10:34–35 and write a title for it and be prepared to summarize the passage for the rest of the class. Ask a third of the class to take Acts 10:36–39, write a title for it, and be prepared to summarize the passage for the rest of the class.

Ask a third of the class to take Acts 10:44–48, write a title for it, and be prepared to summarize the passage for the rest of the class.

Allow about five minutes for study, and then call on the three groups to report. Write the titles on the chalkboard or a large sheet of paper.

Give the Truth a Personal Focus

Read the "Main Idea" of the lesson and ask members to think what principles they can draw from this lesson that would state that the gospel is for all people.

Look at the first outline point and let members suggest a principle. (Many possibilities but consider: God works with the unsaved and the saved at the same time to bring the unsaved to salvation.)

Look at the second outline point and let members suggest a principle. (Because God does not show partiality to any nation, we should share the gospel with them all.)

Look at the third outline point and let members suggest a principle. (God chose Jesus to bring freedom and salvation to all people.)

Look at the fourth outline point and let members suggest a principle. (God gives His Spirit to all who truly believe on Him.)

Ask members to take these four statements (or the ones they wrote) and put them together in a paragraph that would express what this passage teaches about God's good news being for all people.

---

1. Joey Faucette, Jr., *Proclaim*, July–September 1992, 27.

2. A. Dudley Dennison, Jr., *Windows, Ladders, and Bridges: An Anthology of Illustrations for Public Speakers and Ministers* (Grand Rapids, Mich.: Zondervan Publishing House, 1976), 129.

3. Ibid., 92.

The Church
at Antioch

Basic Passage: Acts 11:19–30; 12:24–25
Focal Passage: Acts 11:19–30; 12:24–25

T he church at Antioch represents one of the breakthroughs of the gospel in the Book of Acts. This church, which was in one of the large cities of the Roman Empire, was the first to include large numbers of Jewish and Gentile believers. Here believers were first called Christians. It was a church with a big heart, sending financial help to Jewish brothers and sending missionaries to the world of the day.

▶ ▶ ▶ ▶ ▶ ▶ ▶ ▶ ▶ **Study Aim:** *To describe the characteristics of the first people to be called Christians*

STUDYING THE BIBLE

LESSON OUTLINE
I. Establishing the Church at Antioch (11:19–26)
    1. Witnessing to Jews and Greeks (11:19–21)
    2. Barnabas at Antioch (11:22–24)
    3. The first "Christians" (11:25–26)
II. Sending Help to Judean Believers (11:27–30; 12:24–25)
    1. Deciding to send help (11:27–29)
    2. Sent by Barnabas and Saul (11:30)
    3. Mission accomplished (12:24–25)

When Greek-speaking believers preached in Antioch to Gentiles as well as Jews, many believed and turned to the Lord (11:19–21). Barnabas came from the Jerusalem church and rejoiced when he saw evidences of God's grace in Antioch (vv. 22–24). Barnabas brought Saul to Antioch to help teach these people, who were called Christians (vv. 25–26). The church at Antioch decided to send financial help to help the Judean believers during a famine (vv. 27–29). The mission was carried out by Barnabas and Saul (v. 30). These two completed the mission and returned to Antioch with John Mark (12:24–25).

I. Establishing the Church at Antioch
(Acts 11:19–26)

1. Witnessing to Jews and Greeks (vv. 19–21)

19 Now they which were scattered abroad upon the persecution that arose about Stephen travelled as far as Phenice, and Cyprus, and Antioch, preaching the word to none but unto the Jews only.

20 And some of them were men of Cyprus and Cyrene, which, when they were come to Antioch, spake unto the

Grecians, preaching the Lord Jesus.

21 And the hand of the Lord was with them: and a great number believed, and turned unto the Lord.

Earlier we read how Philip went to Samaria when believers were scattered from Jerusalem after the death of Stephen (Acts 8:4–5). Verse 4 says that the scattered believers went everywhere preaching the word. Philip went to Samaria. Other unnamed believers went to Phoenicia (fuh NISH ih uh or fuh NISH uh) along the coastal plain north of Judea, to the island of Cyprus, and as far north as to Antioch. Many important events in the early church were carried out by people whose names are mentioned in Scripture, but the Bible doesn't tell us the names of these people who were used by God for a great breakthrough of the gospel. They were the vanguard of hosts of believers who have been used over the centuries, but whose names are unknown to Christian historians.

Antioch was a thriving seaport near the mouth of the Orontes River in Syria. It was the third largest city of the Roman Empire, with only Rome and Alexandria being larger. It was thoroughly Greek in culture and language, although all kinds of people lived there, including a large group of Jews. Various religions and pagan life-styles flourished in Antioch.

As we noted in comments on the lesson about Stephen, most of the believers who were scattered from Jerusalem were Grecian Jews, who like Stephen and Philip wanted to take the gospel to all people. In their earliest preaching, they spoke only to fellow Jews. Probably like Stephen and like Saul's later practice, they went first to the Jewish synagogues.

However, some of the believers from Cyprus and Cyrene began to preach the Lord Jesus to Greeks in Antioch. The title "Lord" was a common Gentile title for gods and special rulers; therefore, the title "Lord" was more easily understood by Gentiles than the Jewish title "Christ." The evidence of the Lord's hand was seen in the great number of Gentiles who believed and turned to the Lord.

These were not the first Gentiles to hear the gospel, for we have already seen how the Ethiopian eunuch and Cornelius believed. However, the Ethiopian was considered an isolated case; and although the Jerusalem church praised God for the conversion of Cornelius, the church made no attempt to follow up by evangelizing Gentiles. The new thing in Antioch was the large numbers of Jewish believers who preached to Gentiles, the large number of Gentile converts, and the fact that the Gentile believers became a part of the same church with Jewish believers.

2. Barnabas at Antioch (vv. 22–24)

22 Then tidings of these things came unto the ears of the church which was in Jerusalem: and they sent forth Barnabas, that he should go as far as Antioch.

23 Who, when he came, and had seen the grace of God, was glad, and exhorted them all, that with purpose of heart they would cleave unto the Lord.

24 For he was a good man, and full of the Holy Ghost and of

faith: and much people was added unto the Lord.

As the Jerusalem church had sent Peter and John to Samaria when they heard of the work of Philip (8:14), so the Jerusalem church sent Barnabas to Antioch. Barnabas was an excellent choice for such a mission. He was a kind and good man of faith who was full of the Spirit of God. He had shown himself to be an encourager by his generosity to the needy (4:36–37) and by befriending Saul the former persecutor (9:26–27).

When Barnabas arrived in Antioch, he saw many evidences of God's grace at work in and among this church of believing Jews and Gentiles. He encouraged and exhorted them to remain true to their Lord.

3. The first "Christians" (vv. 25–26)

25 Then departed Barnabas to Tarsus, for to seek Saul:

26 And when he had found him, he brought him unto Antioch. And it came to pass, that a whole year they assembled themselves with the church, and taught much people. And the disciples were called Christians first in Antioch.

Barnabas recognized that these new converts needed instruction in the Scriptures and the apostles' doctrine. Many of them were Gentiles who lacked any knowledge of the Scriptures. They also had heard nothing of Jesus until the believers preached to them. Many of them came out of pagan religions and immoral ways of living.

Barnabas saw an opportunity to "kill two birds with one stone." The new converts in Antioch needed to be taught. Saul of Tarsus needed an opportunity to exercise his considerable gifts in a broader arena. So Barnabas went to Tarsus to ask Saul to come to Antioch and help him. This makes twice that Barnabas was God's instrument in encouraging Saul to become the great servant of God that he became.

Saul had been in Tarsus for several years. This was his native city (Acts 9:11). He had gone back to Tarsus when his zealous testimony in Jerusalem resulted in a plot to kill him (vv. 28–30). When Barnabas found Saul, he brought him to Antioch. Then these two choice servants of the Lord spent an entire year teaching a large number of people in the Antioch church. This says something about the importance of the teaching ministry of the church.

This passage contains the first use of the word *Christians*. Prior to this time, the followers of Christ were called believers, disciples, brothers, and "those of the way." At Antioch, they were first called Christians. The title occurs only two other times in the New Testament. Herod Agrippa II used it when refusing Paul's impassioned appeal for the king to receive Christ (Acts 26:28). Peter used it once in a persecution setting: "If any man suffer as a Christian, let him not be ashamed" (1 Pet. 4:16).

The title means those belonging to or identified with Christ. The title seems to have been used first by unbelievers in describing the followers of Christ. They heard the believers speaking and singing about Christ. They heard them talking about living like Christ. They named them Christians. Originally, the title may have been intended as a term of derision; but eventually believers in Christ accepted it as a good description of those who build their lives around their commitment to Christ.

II. Sending Help to Judean Believers (Acts 11:27-30; 12:24-25)

1. Deciding to send help (11:27-29)

27 And in these days came prophets from Jerusalem unto Antioch.

28 And there stood up one of them named Agabus, and signified by the spirit that there should be great dearth throughout all the world: which came to pass in the days of Claudius Caesar.

29 Then the disciples, every man according to his ability, determined to send relief unto the brethren which dwelt in Judaea.

Agabus (Ag uh buhs) was a prophet who seems to have been based in Judea, but who traveled about. Paul encountered him later at Caesarea (sess uh REE uh)(Acts 21:10–11). Agabus predicted an extensive famine. The reign of Claudius (KLAW dih uhs) Caesar (A.D. 41–54) was marked by crop failures in a number of areas, including Judea.

The believers in Antioch were determined to do what they could to help fellow believers in Judea. They followed the usual biblical practice of each giving as he was able (see 1 Cor. 16:2; 2 Cor. 8:12). Keep in mind that the church at Antioch was made up of many Gentiles, and the church in Judea was Jewish. Also remember that there was no love lost between Jews and Gentiles. Before their conversion, the Gentile Christians in Antioch would not have lost any sleep over a famine in Judea. However, now that they shared a common faith in the Lord Jesus, they saw the Jewish believers as brothers in the same family of faith.

2. Sent by Barnabas and Saul (11:30)

30 Which also they did, and sent it to the elders by the hands of Barnabas and Saul.

The church at Antioch made an offering and entrusted this money to the two who had encouraged and taught them in the way of Christ. Thus Barnabas and Saul traveled together to Judea on this special mission. The church trusted them not only to deliver the offering but also to express the love for Jewish believers of their Gentile brothers and sisters.

3. Mission accomplished (12:24-25)

24 But the word of God grew and multiplied.

25 And Barnabas and Saul returned from Jerusalem, when they had fulfilled their ministry, and took with them John, whose surname was Mark.

Between Acts 11:30 and 12:24 is the record of the persecution by Herod Agrippa I. He had launched a vicious attack on the church, which resulted in the death of James the brother of John and in the imprisonment of Peter. The Lord delivered Peter and struck down the persecutor. These events enabled the word of God to grow and multiply.

Another event in Acts 12:1–23 was the first mention of John Mark, who went back to Antioch with Barnabas and Saul. Mark was mentioned in verse 12 because the church held a prayer meeting in the house of Mary, Mark's mother.

Barnabas and Saul completed their mission. This prepared them for another kind of mission, which is described in the following chapters.

APPLYING THE BIBLE

1. God's word for His people. The word we most commonly use to describe those who have received Christ is *Christians.* We also frequently use the word *believers.* But God's word for His people is *saints.*

The word *Christian* appears only three times in the Bible: Acts 11:26; Acts 26:28; and 1 Peter 4:16. The word *believer* appears two times: Acts 5:14 and 1 Timothy 4:12. The word *disciple* appears numerous times, mostly in the Gospels, referring to those immediate disciples who walked with Jesus. Acts uses the word about thirty-one times, and most of those references describe those who became followers of Jesus through the preaching of the gospel.

But God's word for His people is *saints.* Look in a good concordance, and you will discover that *saint* appears something like ninety-nine times in the Bible. If my count is correct, it appears thirty-seven times in the Old Testament and sixty-two times in the New Testament.

2. What it means to believe. Luke states in 11:21: "And the hand of the Lord was with them: and a great number believed, and turned unto the Lord." But what does it mean to believe?

Harold T. Bryson recounts the well-known story of Blondin, a famous tightrope walker who lived in the latter part of the nineteenth century. The story appears in James E. Hightower's book, *Illustrating Paul's Letter to the Romans.*

Once Blondin strung a tightrope across Niagara Falls. Thousands of curious onlookers had gathered to watch Blondin walk the tightrope from the Canadian to the American side of the falls. Thousands cheered his name as he stepped on the high rope.

Silencing the crowd, Blondin said to them, "I am going to walk across the Niagara Falls on the tightrope, but this time I will carry someone on my shoulders. Do you believe in me?"

"We believe! We believe!" shouted the excited crowd.

"Then which of you will be the lucky person to have Blondin carry him across the falls?" Blondin asked.

Heavy silence fell over the crowd. But in a few minutes one of the onlookers moved slowly toward Blondin, climbed up on his shoulders, and had the thrill of his life as Blondin carried him safely across to the American side of the falls.

All the people agreed that they believed Blondin could do it, but only one man believed in Blondin enough to trust him.[1]

3. "Mr. Encourager." Barnabas was a great encourager. According to Acts 4:36, his name was Joses and the apostles gave him the name "Barnabas." The King James Version says, "Which is, being interpreted, The son of consolation." The New International

Version translates it as "Joseph . . . which means Son of Encouragement."

In one of his books, the late Huber Drumwright has a chapter titled, "Mr. Encourager." It is a magnificent study of Barnabas, who was a great encourager to the Gentile believers (11:22–24). Unlike so many Christians who major on orthodoxy and minor on attitude, Barnabas had a good word for everyone he met. And the disciples recognized that gift.

4. Vince Lombardi, another encourager. The fabled coach of the Green Bay Packers, Vince Lombardi, was one of the greatest football coaches who ever coached. When he died of cancer in 1969, tributes poured in from all over the country. All who knew him, especially those who had played under him, held him in awe.

Although Lombardi was praised for his coaching skill, perhaps Frank Gifford, the ABC sports commentator who played under Lombardi when he was offensive coach of the New York Giants, paid him the greatest compliment: "When we played a game, I couldn't have cared less about the headlines on Monday. All I wanted was to be able to walk into the meeting on Tuesday morning and have Vinny give me that big grin." And Sam Huff, who was a linebacker for the Washington Redskins, said that "receiving a compliment from Coach Lombardi was like receiving the crown from the king."[2]

To what better pursuit could we give ourselves than magnifying the Christian grace of being an encourager to the people with whom we come into contact? That was the kind of man Barnabas was.

TEACHING THE BIBLE

▶ *Main Idea:* The church at Antioch displayed characteristics that we can practice today.
▶ *Suggested Teaching Aim:* To lead adults to describe the characteristics of the first people to be called Christians, and to identify characteristics they will practice today.

A TEACHING OUTLINE

1. Use a graffiti wall to create interest.
2. Use questions and answers to teach the truths of the lesson.
3. Help members identify characteristics of the early church that they can apply to their lives.

Introduce the Bible Study
IN ADVANCE, place a large sheet of paper on the wall and provide markers for members to use. As they enter, ask them to go to the graffiti wall and write characteristics of Christians.

To begin the session, read the characteristics and point out that the lesson today describes the characteristics of the first people to be called Christians.

Search for Biblical Truth

IN ADVANCE, enlist a member to prepare a two- to three-minute report on Antioch (of Syria) using *Holman Bible Dictionary* or another Bible dictionary. Call for the report and locate Antioch on a map to show how the gospel is spreading.

Ask members to open their Bibles to Acts 11:19–21 and read the passage silently. Ask: What impact did Stephen's death have on the spread of the gospel? What impact does persecution have on the spread of the gospel today? To whom did the first preachers who left Jerusalem preach the gospel? (Locate Phenice, Cyprus, and Antioch on the map.) With whom do we most often share our faith today? Who first shared the gospel with Grecians in Antioch? Who often makes the best witnesses today? What was the result then and now when the gospel is shared?

Ask members to read silently Acts 11:22–24. Ask: How did Barnabas get involved in the ministry at Antioch? What made Barnabas such a good representative from the Jerusalem church? What other roles has Barnabas played up to this point in the spread of the gospel? (Sold property [Acts 4:36] and befriended Saul [Acts 9:27].) What was Barnabas' response when he saw what was going on in Antioch?

Ask members to read silently Acts 11:25–26. DISCUSS: Why do you think the term *Christian* was (was not) a term given by their opponents?

Ask members to read silently Acts 11:27–30. Ask: Who was Agabus? What was the situation that caused his prophecy? What did the church in Antioch do that proved they had had a life-changing experience when they believed in Jesus? (Gentiles gave money to feed Jews.) What good principle of stewardship did the church demonstrate by sending both Barnabas and Saul to Jerusalem with the money? (Two trusted people handled the money to reduce suspicion.)

Ask members to read silently Acts 12:24–25. Use the comments in "Studying the Bible" to explain the events between Acts 11:30 and 12:24. Point out that Acts 12:25 introduces a significant character, John Mark, and that the gospel continued to grow.

Give the Truth a Personal Focus

Ask: What characteristics of the early church can you identify? As members mention these, write them on the graffiti wall along with the characteristics the members listed as they came in. Be sure the following are included: sharing the gospel with people who are different, encouraging others (Barnabas), and growing in grace.

Ask: Who do you know who needs to hear the gospel message? How can you share it? How can you be an encourager? What evidence do you see that you are growing in God's grace? Are you willing to share your physical resources with those in need?

1. J. B. Fowler, Jr., *Illustrating Great Words of the New Testament* (Nashville: Broadman Press, 1991), 26. (From James E. Hightower, *Illustrating Paul's Letter to the Romans* [Nashville: Broadman Press, 1984], 31-32.)

2. Jack Gulledge, *Proclaim*, July, Aug., Sept. 1992, 25. (Adapted from *Reader's Digest*, Dec. 1970, "We Remember Lombardi," Jerry Krammer, 159–62.)

Mission to Gentiles

Basic Passage: Acts 13–14
Focal Passages: Acts 13:1–5; 14:1–7, 24–27

T he church at Antioch sent out Barnabas and Saul as
missionaries. Although they began in each locale by going first
to the Jews, they met increasing resistance from fellow Jews and
increasing acceptance from Gentiles. Early in chapter 13, Paul became
the leader in this mission to Gentiles.

▶ ▶ ▶ ▶ **Study Aim:** *To describe and explain the missionary strategy of
Paul and Barnabas*

STUDYING THE BIBLE

LESSON OUTLINE
  I. Commissioned as Missionaries (13:1–3)
  II. Mission to Cyprus (13:4–12)
  III. Mission to Antioch of Pisidia (13:13–52)
    1. The journey (13:13–15)
    2. Paul's sermon (13:16–41)
    3. Paul's response to Jewish rejection (13:42–52)
  IV. Mission to Iconium (14:1–7)
  V. Mission to Lystra and Derbe (14:8–21a)
    1. Mistaken for gods (14:8–13)
    2. Paul's sermon (14:14–18)
    3. Paul almost killed (14:19–20a)
    4. Derbe (14:20b–21a)
  VI. Return to and Report to Antioch (14:21b–28)
    1. Retracing their steps (14:21b–25)
    2. Report to the Antioch church (14:26–28)

The Spirit led the Antioch church to send out Barnabas and Saul
(13:1–3). They went first to Cyprus, where a Roman proconsul was
converted and Paul emerged as team leader (vv. 4–12). They went
through Perga (PUR guh) to travel to Antioch of Pisidia (pih SID ih
uh) (vv. 13–15). Paul preached in the synagogue and invited people to
be justified through faith in Christ (vv. 16–41). Although many
believed, violent Jewish rejection caused Paul to announce that he was
going to the Gentiles (vv. 42–52). Paul and Barnabas encountered a
similar mixture of faith and rejection in Iconium (14:1–7). After they
healed a cripple in Lystra (LISS truh), the pagan people wanted to
worship Paul and Barnabas as gods (vv. 8–13). When the apostles
realized what was happening, Paul preached to them of the one true
God (vv. 14–18). Opponents from other cities arrived and led the
crowd to stone Paul, who was almost killed (vv. 19–20a). The apostles
then went to Derbe (DUR bih), where they preached to many (vv.
20b–21a). Rather than taking the shortest route back, Paul and

Barnabas went back through the places where new believers needed encouragement and leadership (vv. 21b–25). Finally, they arrived in Antioch, where they reported on what God had done (vv. 26–28).

I. Commissioned as Missionaries (Acts 13:1–3)

1 Now there were in the church that was at Antioch certain prophets and teachers; as Barnabas, and Simeon that was called Niger, and Lucius of Cyrene, and Manaen, which had been brought up with Herod the tetrarch, and Saul.

2 As they ministered to the Lord, and fasted, the Holy Ghost said, Separate me Barnabas and Saul for the work whereunto I have called them.

3 And when they had fasted and prayed, and laid their hands on them, they sent them away.

Five leaders of the Antioch church are mentioned in verse 1. We know nothing about three of them except what is said in this verse. During a time of fasting, the church heard the Spirit telling them to set aside Barnabas and Saul for the work to which God had called them. After a time of fasting and prayer to prepare for this work, the church commissioned the two and sent them out. Someone might have objected: "These are our two best leaders." Or they could have said, "We have just begun to evangelize our own city; why send missionaries to other places?" No such objections are recorded. Instead the church at Antioch showed themselves to be Great Commission Christians.

II. Mission to Cyprus (Acts 13:4–12)

4 So they, being sent forth by the Holy Ghost, departed unto Seleucia; and from thence they sailed to Cyprus.

5 And when they were at Salamis, they preached the word of God in the synagogues of the Jews: and they had also John to their minister.

The two missionaries were accompanied by John Mark, whom we met in Acts 12:12, 25. Mark was kin to Barnabas (Col. 4:10). The team went to Seleucia (sih LYOO shih uh), the main port for Antioch. From there they sailed the sixty miles to the large island of Cyprus. Barnabas was from Cyprus (Acts 4:36), and believers from Cyprus were among those who first preached to Gentiles in Antioch (11:20).

Arriving in Salamis (SAL uh miss), the port on the eastern side of Cyprus, the missionaries went to the Jewish synagogues. This practice became an ongoing strategy of Barnabas and Saul. Jews were found throughout the Roman Empire. There were enough Jews in Salamis that the city had more than one synagogue. A synagogue was a place of worship and instruction as well as a center for fellowship among Jews.

The synagogues provided a beginning point for Christian missionaries. Jews believed in God, the promise of a Messiah, and the Scriptures. Thus, Jewish Christians were able to begin from their common beliefs and preach Jesus as the promised Messiah.

The missionaries journeyed across the island to Paphos (PAY fahs), where Paul preached to a Roman official named Sergius Paulus (SURH jih uhs-PAW luhs). When Paul was opposed by a Jewish sorcerer named Bar-Jesus, the Spirit led Paul to pronounce blindness on the villain. Impressed by this, the Roman believed (13:6–12).

III. Mission to Antioch of Pisidia (Acts 13:13–52)

1. The journey (vv. 13–15). The missionaries traveled north to Perga in Pamphylia (pam FIL ih uh), where John Mark left them (v. 13). Then they journeyed to Antioch of Pisidia, where they went to the synagogue on the Sabbath (v. 14). After the Scripture reading, the visitors were asked to share any word of exhortation (v. 15).

2. Paul's sermon (vv. 16–41). Paul reviewed highlights of Israel's history up to David, stressing God's faithfulness to His promises (vv. 16–22). Paul preached Jesus' coming, death, and resurrection as the fulfillment of God's scriptural promises (vv. 23–37). Paul appealed for his hearers to receive forgiveness and justification through faith in Jesus (vv. 38–41).

3. Paul's response to Jewish rejection (vv. 42–52). After Paul preached, many Jews and Gentile proselytes believed (vv. 42–43). When the whole city turned out on the next Sabbath, the synagogue leaders began to speak against what Paul was saying (vv. 44–45). Paul and Barnabas said that since the Scriptures offered salvation to all people, they would go to the Gentiles (vv. 46–49). When city leaders expelled the missionaries, they went to Iconium (vv. 50–52).

converts

IV. Mission to Iconium (Acts 14:1–7)

1 And it came to pass in Iconium, that they went both together into the synagogue of the Jews, and so spake, that a great multitude both of the Jews and also of the Greeks believed.

2 But the unbelieving Jews stirred up the Gentiles, and made their minds evil affected against the brethren.

3 Long time therefore abode they speaking boldly in the Lord, which gave testimony unto the word of his grace, and granted signs and wonders to be done by their hands.

4 But the multitude of the city was divided: and part held with the Jews, and part with the apostles.

5 And when there was an assault made both of the Gentiles, and also of the Jews with their rulers, to use them despitefully, and to stone them,

6 They were ware of it, and fled unto Lystra and Derbe, cities of Lycaonia, and unto the region that lieth round about:

7 And there they preached the gospel.

Iconium (igh KOH nih uhm) lay about ninety miles southeast of Antioch of Pisidia. The apostles followed their usual pattern of going to the Jewish synagogue when they arrived. This shows that Paul's words about turning to the Gentiles in Acts 13:46 did not mean that he would neglect Jews. The synagogue was the best place to gain an initial hearing because of the common faith in God, the Scriptures, and the Messiah. The synagogue was also a good place to make contact with those Gentiles who believed in God and the Scriptures.

As at Antioch, many Jews and Gentiles believed; but then unbelieving Jews stirred up opposition. Paul and Barnabas continued speaking boldly and doing miracles in the city. Eventually the entire community was divided by either supporting or opposing the missionaries. When Paul and Barnabas learned of a plot to kill them, they fled to Lystra and Derbe. As they went through the countryside, they preached the gospel.

V. Mission to Lystra and Derbe
(Acts 14:8-21a)

1. Mistaken for gods (vv. 8-13). In Lystra, Paul healed a cripple (vv. 8-10). The pagan people mistook Paul and Barnabas for Mercury and Zeus (Jupiter), and were preparing to offer sacrifices (vv. 11-13).

2. Paul's sermon (vv. 14-18). When the missionaries realized what was happening, they protested that they were only human beings; but they said that they had come to preach the living God who created all things (vv. 14-15). As they told of God's forbearance and goodness, they were able to restrain the pagans from worshiping them (vv. 16-18).

3. Paul almost killed (vv. 19-20a). Opponents from Antioch and Iconium stirred up the crowd, who stoned Paul and left him for dead (v. 19). When the disciples gathered around him, Paul got up (v. 20a).

4. Derbe (vv. 20b-21a). Paul and Barnabas went on to Derbe, where they preached and taught many.

VI. Return to and Report to Antioch
(Acts 14:21b-28)

1. Retracing their steps (vv. 21b-25). The shortest, easiest, and safest route back to Antioch of Syria was to continue southeast; however, the missionaries retraced their steps through all the places they had been (v. 21b). They encouraged believers and selected leaders in each city (vv. 22-23).

> **24 And after they had passed throughout Pisidia, they came to Pamphylia.**
>
> **25 And when they had preached the word in Perga, they went down into Attalia.**

They made their way back through Pisidia to Pamphylia. When they came to Perga, they preached—something they had not done when they passed through it earlier (13:13-14). Then they went to the seaport of Attalia (at uh LIGH uh), as they prepared to sail back to Antioch of Syria, their home base.

2. Report to the Antioch church (vv. 26-28)

> **26 And thence sailed to Antioch, from whence they had been recommended to the grace of God for the work which they fulfilled.**
>
> **27 And when they were come, and had gathered the church together, they rehearsed all that God had done with them, and how he had opened the door of faith unto the Gentiles.**

Since Paul and Barnabas had been sent out from the Antioch

church, they returned to it and reported on what had happened. They emphasized two things: (1) Everything that had happened for good had been the work of God, who had worked through them; (2) the missionary work of Paul and Barnabas clearly showed that God had opened a door of faith for Gentiles to be saved.

APPLYING THE BIBLE

1. Gentile church becomes a missionary church. Isn't it unique that the Antioch church, which was established through the missionary ministries of the Jerusalem church, now sends out its own missionaries (Acts 13:1–3)? That's the way it ought to be. We read regularly about churches in the mission field that are now sending missionaries to other parts of the world. And, embarrassingly, some of them are even sending missionaries to America! But do you know of any nation in the world that more needs the gospel—yet has more of the gospel—than America?

2. The importance of missions. The Book of Acts is the missionary book of the New Testament. Read Acts closely and see how the early churches majored on getting the gospel out to the world. And the missionaries—such as Barnabas and Saul (v. 2)—were highly regarded and revered by their contemporaries.

We have lost much of that awe for those who leave home and loved ones to carry the gospel to the uttermost parts of the earth. For example, in the eleventh edition of the *Encyclopedia Britannica*, fewer than five hundred words are written about Adoniram Judson, America's great pioneer missionary to India and Burma. But when Judson's son wrote the biography of his father, the life story of this great missionary required more than five hundred pages![1]

3. William Carey's challenge. Missions had its beginning in the heart of God and was communicated to the church through Jesus. The Great Commission (Matt. 28:19–20) is the greatest missions mandate ever spoken.

In response to that mandate from Jesus, there grew in the heart of a shoe cobbler named William Carey the conviction that he ought to become a foreign missionary. It was a time in church history when such thinking was frowned upon. The attitude seemed to be, "If God wants to save the heathen, He will save him without your help."

Carey was reared in the Church of England, and the church's cold attitude toward getting the gospel out to the whole world chilled Carey. Commissioned as a Baptist preacher, he walked sixteen miles to his chapel at Barton, England, to preach to the poor people. But all the while, there was growing in his heart the conviction that his work lay beyond the sea.

In 1776, at a meeting of Baptist ministers in Northampton, Carey proposed that Christ intended for the gospel to be carried to the ends of the earth. But the aged chairman of the ministers rebuked Carey with the words, "You are a miserable enthusiast."

In 1792, at the annual ministers' meeting at Northampton, Carey preached from Isaiah 54:1–2, encouraging his brethren to "attempt

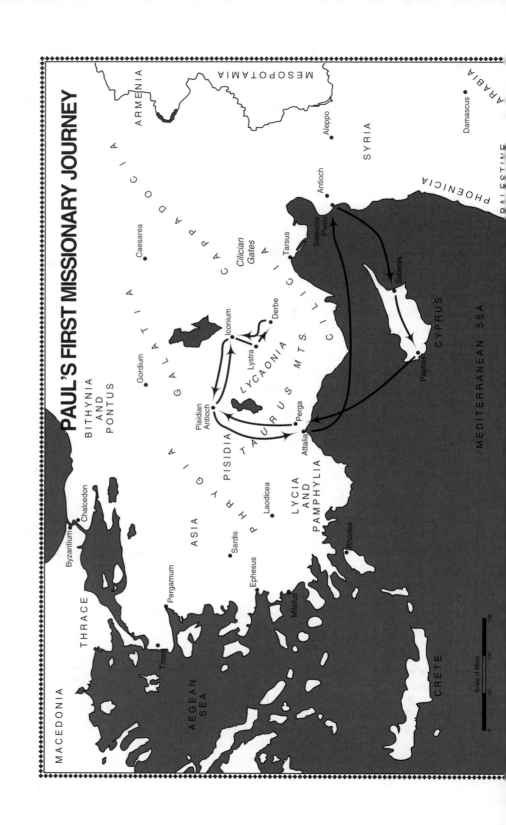

PAUL'S FIRST MISSIONARY JOURNEY

MACEDONIA

THRACE

BITHYNIA
AND
PONTUS

ARMENIA

MESOPOTAMIA

GALATIA

CAPPADOCIA

Byzantium
Chalcedon

Gordium

Caesarea

ASIA

PHRYGIA

PISIDIA

Pisidian
Antioch

Iconium

Derbe

Lystra

Cilician
Gates

Tarsus

LYCAONIA

CILICIA

TAURUS MTS.

Pergamum

Sardis

Laodicea

Ephesus

LYCIA
AND
PAMPHYLIA

Perga

Attalia

SYRIA

Aleppo

Antioch

Seleucia
Pieria

PHOENICIA

PALESTINE

Damascus

ARABIA

Miletus

Troas

AEGEAN
SEA

Rhodes

CYPRUS

Salamis

Paphos

MEDITERRANEAN SEA

CRETE

Scale of Miles

0   50   100   150

great things for God! And expect great things from God." Carey persisted in his vision of reaching out to heathendom and in January 1793, he and Dr. John Thomas, a surgeon, were commissioned, as were Paul and Barnabas, to carry the gospel to India, where it had never gone before.[2]

It was the start of something bigger than Carey or Thomas could ever have imagined. Today, we recognize William Carey as the father of modern missions. Christian missionaries serve, following Carey's example, all over the world.

4. The important contributions of missionaries.

(1) The whole of the New Testament was written by foreign missionaries.

(2) The Epistles, called letters, in the New Testament were written to individuals and are all addressed to converts of foreign missionaries.

(3) Every Epistle in the New Testament that was addressed to a church was written by a foreign missionary.

(4) In the first missionary community (Antioch), the disciples were first called Christians.

(5) All of the apostles were missionaries except one, and he was a traitor.

(6) Most of the problems in the Jerusalem church, the mother church, were related to missionary procedure.

(7) The New Testament emphasizes that missionary service of whatever sort is the highest expression of the Christian life.[3]

TEACHING THE BIBLE

▶ *Main Idea:* The church at Antioch's mission to Gentiles models for us what true missionary strategies should be.
▶ *Suggested Teaching Aim:* To lead adults to describe and explain the missionary strategy of Paul and Barnabas, and to outline their own missionary strategy.

A TEACHING OUTLINE

1. Use an illustration to introduce the lesson.
2. Let the class arrange the events of the text in proper order.
3. Let the class identify strategies the early missionaries used.
4. Let the class identify strategies that will help them in their mission work.

Introduce the Bible Study

Use "William Carey's challenge" from "Applying the Bible" to begin the lesson.

Search for Biblical Truth

IN ADVANCE, place a map of the journeys of Paul on the focal wall and use it to locate the places mentioned in the text.

IN ADVANCE, write the following main events of the lesson on strips of paper and place at random on the focal wall. Do not include the numbers. (1) The Holy Spirit spoke to them while they worshiped. (2) The group commissioned Barnabas and Saul. (3) Barnabas, Mark, and Saul sailed to Cyprus. (4) The missionaries went first to the Jewish synagogue. (5) Many Jews in Iconium believed. (6) Unbelieving Jews stirred up trouble. (7) Unbelieving Jews and Gentiles planned to stone the missionaries. (8) The missionaries escaped when they became aware of the plot and went to Lycaonia. (9) The missionaries revisited the cities in which they had started new work. (10) The missionaries returned to Antioch and told the church all that had happened.

IN ADVANCE, ask a volunteer to read Acts 13:1–5; 14:1–7, 24–27 aloud so the reader can look up the pronunciation of the names in the text. Call for the Scripture to be read at one time and ask members to arrange the strips in the proper order.

After members have arranged the strips in proper order, ask them to look specifically at 13:1–3. (If you wish, you could organize the class in four groups.) Ask: What missionary strategies do you see in these verses that would be good for mission groups to follow today? Write these on a chalkboard or a large sheet of paper. (Let members make suggestions; these are intended only as a guide: they worshiped and fasted; they were in a position to hear God's voice; the larger group affirmed and supported the missionaries by commissioning them.)

Ask members to look at verses 4–5. Ask: What missionary strategies do you see in these verses that would be good for mission groups to follow today? (Led by Holy Spirit; first went to the synagogue where people had some knowledge of what they were talking about.)

Ask members to look at 14:1–7. Ask: What missionary strategies do you see in these verses that would be good for mission groups to follow today? (Continued even in the face of opposition; went elsewhere when they saw they could no longer minister effectively.)

Ask members to look at verses 21b–27. Ask: What missionary strategies do you see in these verses that would be good for mission groups to follow today? (They returned to the new converts and sought to ground them in the faith; they reported to and were responsible to the church; they did not go off on their own.)

Give the Truth a Personal Focus

Ask members to look at the strategies used by Paul and Barnabas and to identify a strategy that will help them in their mission work. (For example, they may need to place themselves in a position of worship so God can speak to them; they may need to be sure new converts are grounded in the faith.)

1. Walter Russell Bowie, *Men of Fire* (New York: Evanston, London: Harper & Row, 1961), 180.

2. Ibid., 177–78.

3. Walter B. Knight, *Knight's Master Book of New Illustrations* (Grand Rapids, Mich.: Wm. B. Eerdmans Publishing Co., 1956), 415.

The Jerusalem Conference

Basic Passage: Acts 15:1–35
Focal Passages: Acts 15:1–2, 6–18

One of the crucial issues facing the early church was the basis for admitting Gentiles. One group insisted that the only way for a Gentile to become a Christian was first to become a Jew. The other group received Gentile believers on the basis of their faith in Jesus Christ. A conference at Jerusalem was convened to seek to resolve this issue.

▶ ▶ ▶ ▶ ▶ **Study Aim:** *To explain the issues discussed and the decisions made by the Jerusalem Conference*

STUDYING THE BIBLE

LESSON OUTLINE
I. A Divisive Issue (15:1–5)
    1. Disruption in Antioch (15:1–2)
    2. Trip to Jerusalem (15:3)
    3. Debate in Jerusalem (15:4–5)
II. Discussion and Speeches (15:6–21)
    1. The meeting (15:6)
    2. Discussion and Peter's speech (15:7–11)
    3. Report of Barnabas and Paul (15:12)
    4. James's speech (15:13–21)
III. Decision and Implementation (15:22–35)
    1. Selecting representatives (15:22)
    2. Writing a letter (15:23–29)
    3. Reporting to the church at Antioch (15:30–35)

When people from Judea debated Paul and Barnabas about their reception of Gentiles, a decision was made to take the issue to Jerusalem (vv. 1–2). When Paul and Barnabas told churches on the way about the conversion of Gentiles, the churches rejoiced (v. 3). When they reported in Jerusalem, converted Pharisees insisted that believing Gentiles must be circumcised and keep the Mosaic law (vv. 4–5). A meeting was called (v. 6). Following discussion, Peter reminded them of what God had taught them in the conversion of Cornelius (vv. 7–11). Barnabas and Paul then made their report (v. 12). James quoted Scripture to support the reception of Gentiles, and asked only that Gentile believers respect certain Jewish scruples (vv. 13–21). The church selected Barsabas and Silas to tell Gentile churches about the decision (v. 22). A letter to the Gentile churches was written (vv. 23–29). The Antioch church rejoiced when they heard the report of Paul and Barnabas, the letter, and

Barsabas (BAHR suh buhs) and Silas (vv. 30–35).

I. A Divisive Issue (Acts 15:1-5)

1. Disruption in Antioch (vv. 1–2)

1 And certain men which came down from Judaea taught the brethren, and said, Except ye be circumcised after the manner of Moses, ye cannot be saved.

2 When therefore Paul and Barnabas had no small dissension and disputation with them, they determined that Paul and Barnabas, and certain other of them, should go up to Jerusalem unto the apostles and elders about this question.

Some Jewish believers from Judea disrupted the Antioch church by telling Gentile believers that they weren't saved. These visitors insisted that Gentiles could be saved only if they were circumcised. In other words, before a Gentile could follow the Messiah of Israel, the Gentile had to become a Jew. Paul and Barnabas had been assuring Gentile believers that faith was the only requirement for salvation. Therefore, when Paul and Barnabas heard what these Judeans were saying, they strongly disagreed.

The Antioch church recognized that this crucial issue must be resolved. They, therefore, sent Paul, Barnabas, and some other members (Titus, for example, according to Gal. 2:1) to confer with the apostles and elders in Jerusalem.

2. Trip to Jerusalem (v. 3). As the Antioch delegation made the long journey to Jerusalem, they visited churches along the way. Wherever they went, they told of the conversion of Gentiles, and the churches rejoiced.

3. Debate in Jerusalem (vv. 4–5). Arriving in Jerusalem, Paul and Barnabas reported on the success of their work among Gentiles (v. 4). Pharisaic believers were quick to challenge them by insisting that Gentile believers must be circumcised and keep the Mosaic law (v. 5).

II. Discussion and Speeches (Acts 15:6-21)

1. The meeting (v. 6)

6 And the apostles and elders came together for to consider of this matter.

Some Bible students think this was a private meeting with only the church leaders. More likely, the entire congregation was present. They certainly were by verse 12.

2. Discussion and Peter's speech (vv. 7–11)

7 And when there had been much disputing, Peter rose up, and said unto them, Men and brethren, ye know how that a good while ago God made choice among us, that the Gentiles by my mouth should hear the word of the gospel, and believe.

8 And God, which knoweth the hearts, bare them witness, giving them the Holy Ghost, even as he did unto us;

9 And put no difference between us and them, purifying their hearts by faith.

At the beginning of the meeting was much discussion. Then Peter arose to speak. He reminded them that the Lord had chosen him as an early witness to Gentiles. He was obviously referring to Cornelius, his relatives, and friends. Peter had made a full report of this to the Jerusalem church, and they had praised God for offering repentance to Gentiles (see Acts 10:1–11:18).

Peter had made no requirement that Cornelius and the other Gentiles be circumcised before God would accept them. His previous training would have led him to take such a position, but God sent His Spirit on the Gentile believers as a token of His acceptance. God considers people pure or impure on grounds other than the food they eat or the group to which they belong (see Acts 10:28). He purifies hearts through faith (see v. 43). God made no difference between Gentile believers and Jewish believers (see v. 34).

> 10 Now therefore why tempt ye God, to put a yoke upon the neck of the disciples, which neither our fathers nor we were able to bear?

> 11 But we believe that through the grace of the Lord Jesus Christ we shall be saved, even as they.

Peter pleaded with his fellow Jewish believers not to place the yoke of circumcision and the law on Gentiles. Peter was not renouncing his Jewish heritage. He was still a circumcised Jew who kept the law to the best of his ability. However, he had come to see—as Paul so often taught (see Acts 13:39)—that people are not saved by being Jews and keeping the law. The only way of salvation for Jews as well as Gentiles is by faith in Christ.

3. Report of Barnabas and Paul (v. 12)

> 12 Then all the multitude kept silence, and gave audience to Barnabas and Paul, declaring what miracles and wonders God had wrought among the Gentiles by them.

Peter's speech quieted the congregation so that Barnabas and Paul could give their report. They had given this report in Antioch (14:27) and in churches on the way to Jerusalem (15:3). This is the second time they had reported in Jerusalem (see v. 4). The earlier report had led to a vigorous debate. Therefore, now that Peter had prepared the way, people listened quietly as Barnabas and Paul told of the wonders wrought among the Gentiles.

Paul was a controversial figure in Jerusalem. Peter and James were respected leaders. Paul restricted his speaking to a report of what had happened. He wisely allowed Peter and James to present the arguments for accepting Gentiles by faith alone.

4. James's speech (vv. 13–21)

> 13 And after they had held their peace, James answered, saying, Men and brethren, hearken unto me.

When the congregation remained quiet, James spoke. This was not James the apostle, who had been killed in the persecution of Herod Agrippa I (see Acts 12:1). This was James, the half brother of Jesus, to whom Jesus had appeared after His resurrection (1 Cor. 15:7). After Peter was forced to flee Jerusalem during Agrippa's persecution, James became the leader (Acts 12:17). When Paul returned years later, James was leader in the church (21:18–25). No one questioned his commitment to his Jewish heritage. His word would carry strong weight on this issue.

14 Simeon hath declared how God at the first did visit the Gentiles, to take out of them a people for his name.

15 And to this agree the words of the prophets; as it is written,

16 After this I will return, and will build again the tabernacle of David, which is fallen down; and I will build again the ruins thereof, and I will set it up:

17 That the residue of men might seek after the Lord, and all the Gentiles, upon whom my name is called, saith the Lord, who doeth all these things.

18 Known unto God are all his works from the beginning of the world.

James built on the foundation of what Peter had said. Peter's speech had emphasized his personal experience with Cornelius. James emphasized biblical support for a mission to Gentiles. James believed that God's plan was to call out from the Gentiles "a people for his name." In other words, God's chosen people included believers from both Jews and Gentiles.

James said that this was the teaching of the prophets. Then he quoted one of the prophets to prove his case. He quoted Amos 9:11–12. This is one of many passages from the Old Testament prophets that predicted the restoration of Israel and the inclusion of Gentiles. Acts 15:14–18 shows that the New Testament presents the people of God as including Gentile and Jewish believers. James quoted Amos as evidence that the Scriptures supported the direction taken by Barnabas and Paul in receiving Gentile believers without requiring them to become Jews.

James stated his conclusion in verses 19–21. His opinion was that they should not trouble Gentile converts with questions about circumcision and the Jewish law (v. 19). He did request that Gentiles respect Jewish scruples about food offered to idols, immorality, and eating meat from which the blood had not been drained (v. 20). These Jewish scruples were based on the Mosaic law, which continued to be taught and read in all the synagogues (v. 21).

III. Decision and Implementation (Acts 15:22–35)

1. Selecting representatives (v. 22). The Jerusalem church and its leaders were pleased with what James proposed. They selected two of their number—Barsabas and Silas—to go with Paul and Barnabas.

2. Writing a letter (vv. 23–29). A letter was sent to the Gentile believers in Antioch, Syria, and Cilicia (v. 23). The letter acknowledged that the Gentiles had been disturbed by those who preached circumcision (v. 24). The letter praised Barnabas and Paul for their courageous work (vv. 25–26). The letter introduced Barsabas and Silas, who would confirm the message of the letter (v. 27). The

Jerusalem Conference followed the Holy Spirit in not laying any additional burden on Gentile believers (v. 28). They did ask Gentiles to observe the Jewish scruples mentioned by James (v. 29).

3. Reporting to the church at Antioch (vv. 30–35). The letter was read to the Antioch church, who rejoiced at its contents (vv. 30–31). Barsabas and Silas added their personal encouragement (vv. 32–34). Paul and Barnabas continued to teach and preach in Antioch (v. 35).

APPLYING THE BIBLE

1. Confusion over conversion of the Gentiles. Sometimes we are so confused that we want to spell the word with a *k*. And sometimes confusion is funny.

Take for example this humorous confession:

(1) A bulletin from a church in La Puente, California, carried the announcement, "The fifth grade choir will sing, 'No One Knows the Trouble I've Been.'"

(2) In Cherry Hill, New Jersey, the church bulletin announced that in the morning worship service they would sing together, "I Heard the Bills on Christmas Day."

(3) There was a church in Connecticut that announced one of the hymns for the morning would be, "Gold Will Take Care of You."

(4) A church in Alexandria, Virginia, announced in its bulletin: "Next Sunday Mrs. S. will be the soloist at the morning service. Pastor G. will preach on the subject, 'It's a Terrible Experience.'"

After the Gentiles began to respond to the gospel, Satan went to work and confusion reigned. Some of the Jerusalem brethren came to Antioch and announced that the Gentiles could be saved only by conforming first to the Mosaic law of circumcision (15:1–2). The Antioch church went to work to correct the confusion by sending Paul and Barnabas to Jerusalem to speak to the apostles abut the matter.

2. Too often the church is out of touch with reality. Benjamin P. Browne tells about the little boy who sat quietly and solemnly by the side of a fishing pool watching his cork.

"What are you fishing for?" a passerby asked.

"Sharks," the little boy replied.

"But there are no sharks in that pool, my little friend," said the stranger.

"There ain't no fish in the pool neither," the boy answered, "so I might as well fish for sharks as anything else."[1]

3. Not by works of righteousness. Years ago a barbers' union in Chicago advertised that a certain brand of soap would change one's life. They went down to Madison Street and picked up the filthiest derelict they could find and used their soap on him: bath, shave, shampoo, the works. They bought the poor man a fine suit, put him up in an exquisite hotel suite and advertised in the newspapers the next day: "See what we have done, we have made a new man with soap." But, of course, it didn't really work, for he was no new man at all. About a week later there was a small item on page 13 of the paper written by some nosy, irreverent reporter, stating: "The man made over by the barbers' union was found last night on Madison Street drunk, dirty and disillusioned."² The Jerusalem Council was a great victory for the Gentile converts. They were freed forever from the requirements of conforming to the Jewish law before they could be saved. As a result, what a legacy has been handed to us who are Gentiles!

4. The influence of the early missionaries. Charles Dickens (1812–1870), the noted English novelist well known for his *David Copperfield, Oliver Twist, A Tale of Two Cities,* and *A Christmas Carol,* was visiting the English city of York on one occasion. A woman unknown to Dickens stopped him on the street and pleaded with him, "Mr. Dickens, will you let me touch the hand that has filled my house with many friends?"³

Think of the people, multiplied millions of them, who have been touched by the influence of the early Christian missionaries. Peter, Paul, and Barnabas were three of this group of selfless servants of Christ who brought many friends into God's kingdom, but thousands of other missionaries have followed and are following in their wake.

TEACHING THE BIBLE

▶ *Main Idea:* The Jerusalem Conference shows how believers can handle their differences.

▶ *Suggested Teaching Aim:* To lead adults to explain the issues discussed and the decisions made by the Jerusalem Conference, and to identify how they can settle differences in a Christlike way.

A TEACHING OUTLINE

1. Use a case study to create interest in the lesson.
2. Use strip posters of the outline to involve members.
3. Use a variety of teaching methods to guide the study.
4. Lead members to identify a process for settling differences they face in a Christlike way.

Introduce the Bible Study

Share the following case study: Downtown Suburban Church had a crisis on their hands. A small but vocal group of members felt called to begin a mission work with an ethnic group in their city. Other members of the church declared that they would not allow "those people" in the church building. It looked like the church was headed for a split. A friend came to you and asked what you thought should be done. You said . . .

Let several respond and then read the "Suggested Teaching Aim." Point out the church has always had conflict, but Acts gives guidelines for dealing with conflict.

Search for Biblical Truth

IN ADVANCE, write the following on strips of paper and tape these to the backs of six chairs: (1) The Problem: Circumcision (Acts

15:1); (2) The Solution: A Conference (Acts 15:2,6); (3) The Discussion: Peter (Acts 15:7–9); (4) The Warning: No Burden (Acts 15:10–11); (5) The Discussion: Barnabas and Paul (Acts 15:12); (6) The Agreement: God-honoring (Acts 15:13–18).

Ask members to find the six strips and ask the person with the first strip to read the title and place it on the focal wall. Share these points: (1) Jews came to Antioch from Jerusalem. (2) They preached that one had to become a Jew by being circumcised as Moses taught in order to become a Christian. These men are often called Judaizers.

Ask the person with the second strip to read the title and place it beneath the first strip. Ask members to open their Bibles to Acts 15:2, 6 and scan the verses. Ask: What was Paul and Barnabas's reaction to this false teaching? What was their first response? What did the church do after the Judaizers refused to back down on their teaching?

Ask the person with the third strip to read the title and place it beneath the second strip. Ask members to read verses 7–9 and to paraphrase it. Write their paraphrase on a chalkboard as members suggest how the verse should be phrased. After they have done this, use "Studying the Bible" to make any comments needed to understand the verses.

Ask the person with the fourth strip to read the title and place it on the wall. Share the following points: (1) Peter was not renouncing his Jewish heritage; (2) he had discovered that people are not saved by keeping the law, but by believing in Jesus.

Ask the person with the fifth strip to read the title and place it on the wall. Ask a volunteer to read aloud verse 12. Ask: Why do you think Barnabas and Paul had so much influence in the meeting? What miracles and wonders do you think they might have shared with the group?

Ask the person with the last strip to read the title and place it on the wall. Read aloud verse 13 and identify James as the halfbrother of Jesus. Use "Studying the Bible" to explain James' argument. Briefly summarize verses 19–21 to give the agreement they arrived at and how they communicated this message to the Gentile churches.

Give the Truth a Personal Focus

Read the "Teaching Aim" again and ask members to identify how they can settle differences in a Christlike way based on the information in this lesson. The following is a suggested approach; your members may suggest something different: (1) Identify the problem; (2) agree to work toward a solution; (3) allow free and open discussion of all viewpoints; (4) be certain the solution is not contrary to the basic teachings of the Bible; (5) be certain the agreement is God-honoring. Ask members to identify one area in which they will apply these principles.

---

1. Benjamin P. Browne, *Illustrations for Preaching* (Nashville: Broadman Press, 1977), 19.

2. Source unknown.

3. Clarence Macartney, *Macartney's Illustrations* (New York, Nashville: Abingdon-Cokesbury Press, 1945), 120.

A Gospel Unhindered by Geography

Basic Passage: Acts 15:36–16:40
Focal Passages: Acts 16:9–10, 13–15, 25–34

A missionary is someone who crosses barriers to take the gospel to those who have not heard. The barriers may be geographic, language, racial, or anything that keeps people from hearing the gospel. Judged by this definition, Paul was a true missionary.

▸▸▸▸▸▸ ▸ ▸ **Study Aim:** *To explain why Paul went to Philippi and to describe what happened there*

STUDYING THE BIBLE

LESSON OUTLINE
 I. **Paul and Barnabas Disagree (15:36–41)**
 II. **Following the Lord's Direction (16:1–12)**
   1. Revisiting churches (16:1–5)
   2. Seeking the Spirit's leading (16:6–8)
   3. Answering the Macedonian call (16:9–12)
 III. **Mission Work in Philippi (16:13–40)**
   1. Lydia's conversion and baptism (16:13–15)
   2. Healing a slave girl (16:16–18)
   3. Accused, beaten, and imprisoned (16:19–24)
   4. Loosed from their chains (16:25–28)
   5. Jailer's salvation and baptism (16:29–34)
   6. Gaining recognition from local officials (16:35–40)

After a disagreement about taking John Mark, Paul and Barnabas formed separate missionary teams (15:36–41). Paul took Silas and visited places he had been before (16:1–5). Paul was led by the Spirit to Troas (vv. 6–8). When he saw the vision of the man of Macedonia (mass uh DOH nih uh), Paul and his team went there (vv. 9–12). Lydia and her household believed, were baptized, and extended hospitality to Paul and his team (vv. 13–15). Paul cast a spirit of divination out of a slave girl (vv. 16–18). The girl's owners brought charges against Paul and Silas, which resulted in their being beaten and imprisoned (vv. 19–24). At midnight, an earthquake freed Paul and the other prisoners; but Paul assured the jailer that all the prisoners were still there (vv. 25–28). The jailer and his household believed and were baptized (vv. 29–34). Paul refused to leave town until the city officials publicly escorted them (vv. 35–40).

I. Paul and Barnabas Disagree (Acts 15:36–41)

After some days in Antioch, Paul asked Barnabas to go with him to

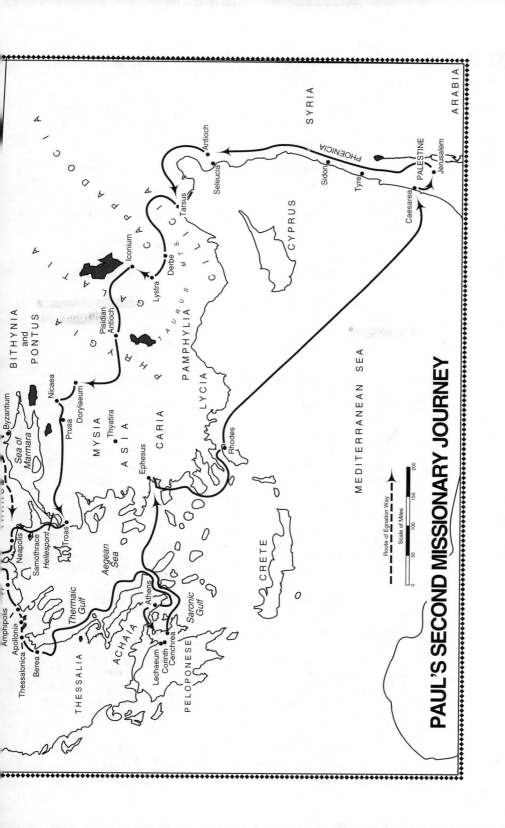

PAUL'S SECOND MISSIONARY JOURNEY

visit the churches they had started earlier (v. 36). Barnabas wanted to take Mark with them (v. 37). Because of Mark's earlier desertion, Paul didn't think that taking him again was a good idea (v. 38). The disagreement was so sharp that Barnabas took Mark and went to Cyprus, while Paul took Silas and went through Syria and Cilicia encouraging the churches (vv. 39–41).

II. Following the Lord's Direction (Acts 16:1–12)

1. Revisiting churches (vv. 1–5). While revisiting Derbe and Lystra, Paul selected Timothy to join him and Silas (vv. 1–3). As they visited churches, Paul and Silas shared the letter from the Jerusalem Conference (v. 4). The churches experienced growth in faith and converts (v. 5).

2. Seeking the Spirit's leading (vv. 6–8). After visiting the churches of Phyrgia (FRIG ih uh) and Galatia, Paul was forbidden by the Spirit from preaching in Asia (v. 6). They passed through Mysia (MISS ih uh or MISH ih uh), but the Spirit would not let them go to Bithynia (bih THIN ih uh) (v. 7). As a result, they ended up at Troas (v. 8).

3. Answering the Macedonian call (vv. 9–12)

9 And a vision appeared to Paul in the night; There stood a man of Macedonia, and prayed him, saying, Come over into Macedonia, and help us.

10 And after he had seen the vision, immediately we endeavoured to go into Macedonia, assuredly gathering that the Lord had called us for to preach the gospel unto them.

As he waited in Troas, Paul saw a vision of a man of Macedonia; and he and the others concluded that this was God's way of calling them to go to Macedonia. Troas was on the Aegean Sea only a few miles from the Dardanelles. Macedonia was a Roman province in northern Greece on the other side of the Aegean Sea. Luke apparently joined the team of Paul, Silas, and Timothy as they headed for Macedonia. Beginning with verse 10, the description of the team went from "they" to "we." They sailed to Neapolis (nih AP uh lihs) and then went to the city of Philippi (FILL ih pigh), a Roman colony (vv. 11–12).

III. Mission Work in Philippi (Acts 16:13–40)

1. Lydia's conversion and baptism (vv. 13–15)

13 And on the sabbath we went out of the city by a river side, where prayer was wont to be made; and we sat down, and spake unto the women which resorted thither.

As we have seen, Paul's strategy was to go first to a Jewish synagogue. Apparently, Philippi did not have enough Jewish men to form a synagogue. However, on the Sabbath a group of women met on the riverbank to pray. Paul spoke to them.

14 And a certain woman named Lydia, a seller of purple, of the city of Thyatira, which worshipped God, heard us: whose heart the Lord opened, that she attended unto the things which

were spoken of Paul.

Lydia, who had come to Philippi from Thyatira (thigh uh TIGH ruh), ran a business selling purple goods. Lydia was a Gentile god-fearer, who worshiped the God of Israel. Thus she was in the same category as the Ethiopian eunuch and Cornelius, not an actual convert to Judaism but a worshiper of the one true God. As Lydia listened that day, her heart was open to all that Paul said.

15 And when she was baptized, and her household, she besought us, saying, If ye have judged me to be faithful to the Lord, come into my house, and abide there. And she constrained us.

Some have tried to build a case for infant baptism from household baptisms like the one in Acts 16:15. Two other examples show that this was not an automatic baptizing of all the family and servants of Lydia. Instead, the family and servants heard the gospel and believed before they were baptized. This was clearly the case with the households of Cornelius and the jailer (Acts 10:33–48; 16:32–33).

Lydia insisted that Paul and his friends accept the hospitality of her home. This verse plus Acts 16:40 shows that the Philippian church probably met in Lydia's house.

2. Healing a slave girl (vv. 16–18). As the believers went to prayer, a slave girl with a spirit of divination followed and declared, "These men are the servants of the most high God, which shew unto us the way of salvation" (vv. 16–17). After the girl continued to do this for many days, Paul cast the spirit out of her (v. 18).

3. Accused, beaten, and imprisoned (vv. 19–24). Having lost their source of profit, the owners of the girl dragged Paul and Silas before the magistrates (v. 19). They called them Jewish troublemakers who undermined the Roman way of life (vv. 20–21). When the mob became inflamed, the magistrates ordered Paul and Silas beaten and imprisoned (vv. 22–23). The jailer put them in the inner prison and fastened their feet in stocks (v. 24).

4. Loosed from their chains (vv. 25–28)

25 And at midnight Paul and Silas prayed, and sang praises unto God: and the prisoners heard them.

The Bible often tells us to rejoice in times of trouble (Matt. 5:10–12; Rom. 5:3; James 1:2; 1 Pet. 1:6–7). Paul and Silas sang praises to God while their backs were raw and bloody, their feet were in stocks, and they were in prison on false charges. The source of their joy was obviously not in outward circumstances. They could rejoice because they were doing the will of God.

26 And suddenly there was a great earthquake, so that the foundations of the prison were shaken: and immediately all the doors were opened, and every one's bands were loosed.

27 And the keeper of the prison awaking out of his sleep, and seeing the prison doors open, he drew out his sword, and would have killed himself, supposing that the prisoners had been fled.

28 But Paul cried with a loud voice, saying, Do thyself no harm: for we are all here.

November
19
1995

An earthquake shook the prison with such force that the doors were opened and the chains fell from the prisoners. Since the jailer was responsible for the prisoners, he would have been disgraced and punished for allowing them to escape. Paul stopped him from killing himself by calling out from the inner prison that all the prisoners were still there.

5. Jailer's salvation and baptism (vv. 29–34)

29 Then he called for a light, and sprang in, and came trembling, and fell down before Paul and Silas,

30 And brought them out, and said, Sirs, what must I do to be saved?

The trembling was not just the result of the earthquake and the fear that the prisoners had escaped. The pagan jailer had become aware of his need for salvation from something worse than could be caused by earthquake or sword. The word *saved* was often used of being saved from danger or death. However, the man had become aware of the need to be saved in a deeper sense. Perhaps he had heard what the slave girl had said about Paul and Silas (v. 17). Perhaps he had heard the hymns that Paul and Silas sang (v. 25). Something had made him aware of his need for salvation.

31 And they said, Believe on the Lord Jesus Christ, and thou shalt be saved, and thy house.

32 And they spake unto him the word of the Lord, and to all that were in his house.

Paul answered the question in a straightforward way. Then Paul spoke the word of the Lord to the jailer and to his household. Since the jailer had no background in Judaism, Paul may also have said some of the things he elsewhere used in sermons to Gentiles who knew nothing about the Scriptures or the God of Israel (see Acts 14:15–17; 17:22–31). However, his sermon focused on explaining the meaning of the promise in verse 31. Like Philip, "he preached unto him Jesus" (Acts 8:35).

In earlier sermons, Paul (13:38–39) and Peter (10:43) had preached faith in Christ as the way of salvation. But nowhere else is the question asked so simply as in verse 30, and nowhere else is the answer so clear as in verse 31. Saving faith is more than intellectual assent to truths about Jesus Christ. A person can believe the facts about God and His Son, and still not exercise saving faith. For faith to be real, it must involve personal trust in and commitment to the Lord Jesus Christ.

33 And he took them the same hour of the night, and washed their stripes; and was baptized, he and all his, straightway.

34 And when he had brought them into his house, he set meat before them, and rejoiced, believing in God with all his house.

After the jailer and his household heard the word and believed, they were baptized. Evidence of the jailer's sincerity is also seen in his washing the wounds of the prisoners and feeding them. With their faith in God came a new sense of joy.

6. Gaining recognition from local officials (vv. 35–40). Early the next day, the magistrates sent word to set Paul and Silas free and tell them to leave Philippi (vv. 35–36). Paul pointed out that he and Silas were Roman citizens who had been punished without a trial. He refused to leave town quietly; instead, he demanded that the magistrates escort them out of town (v. 37). The magistrates were terrified when they discovered Paul and Silas were Roman citizens; therefore, they came to the jail and asked Paul and Silas to leave town (vv. 38–39). First, however, Paul and Silas went to Lydia's house and encouraged the band of brothers and sisters in Christ (v. 40).

The traditional site of the prison of Paul and Silas at Philippi. Credit: Scofield Collection, Dargan Research Library, Nashville, Tennessee.

APPLYING THE BIBLE

1. The conversion of Pocahontas. We don't know much about the influence of the clergymen who settled in Jamestown. We know a good deal about the Pilgrims and the Puritans, but what about their preachers?

One of these who deserves honorable mention was Alexander Whitaker, who came to Virginia in 1611. He was a graduate of St. John's College, Cambridge, and had what seemed to be a promising career ahead of him at home. But Whitaker sacrificed his ministry in England, dedicated himself to the new world, and had a notable ministry in the Jamestown area. The most noted of his converts was Pocahontas, the daughter of Powhatan. Pocahontas married Captain John Smith, the leader of the Jamestown settlers, who claimed she had saved his life.

2. David Livingstone and missions. No name is more revered and sacred in mission history than that of David Livingstone. Influenced by pioneer African missionary Dr. Robert Moffatt, whose daughter Livingstone later married, Livingstone said: "All I am and all I possess means nothing except in connection with the kingdom of God."

After having spent the night with his parents, praying and reading the Bible, he got up before daylight, read Psalm 121, then accompanied by his father, walked to Glasgow to catch a boat for Africa.

For three decades Livingstone served Christ faithfully in Africa as a missionary physician. He died on his knees in prayer; his heart was cut from his body as he had requested and buried under a tree in Africa, and his body was carried overland nine hundred miles by the natives who loved him. Placed on board a ship sailing for England, Livingstone's body was carried back home, where it lies buried today in Westminster Abbey.

TEACHING THE BIBLE

▶ *Main Idea:* Paul's experience in Philippi portrays a gospel unhindered by geography.

▶ *Suggested Teaching Aim:* To lead adults to describe the events surrounding Paul's visit to Philippi, and to identify some with whom they will share the gospel.

A TEACHING OUTLINE

1. Use a graffiti wall to identify barriers.
2. Organize the class into three groups and make assignments.
3. Ask the group to complete statements that apply the text to life.

Introduce the Bible Study

IN ADVANCE, draw a rock wall on a large sheet of paper (or write the word *Barriers* on a large sheet of paper) and ask members as they enter to name barriers of any sort they encounter in life. Read these and suggest that the spread of the gospel encountered many barriers, but it overcame them. Point out that today's lesson shows the spread of the gospel into Macedonia and acceptance by one who had no previous connection with the Jewish religion.

Search for Biblical Truth

Organize the class into three groups and make the following assignments:

Group 1—

Read Acts 16:9–10 and be prepared to share the following information with the rest of the class. (1) Locate Macedonia and Philippi on a map. (2) Explain why Paul felt he should go to Macedonia. (3) Why do you think the description of the team went from "they" to "we" in 16:10?

Group 2—

Read Acts 16:13–15 and be prepared to share the following information with the rest of the class. (1) Why did Paul go to the river side on a Sabbath? (2) Who was Lydia and what did she do to earn a living? (3) What was Lydia's response to the gospel?

Group 3—

Read Acts 16:25–34 and be prepared to share the following

information with the rest of the class. (1) Why were Paul and Silas in jail? (2) What was Paul and Silas' response to their imprisonment? (3) How were they released? (4) What did the jailer do? (5) What was significant about Paul's words to the jailer? (6) What was the jailer's response?

Allow three to five minutes for study. Briefly set the stage by summarizing verses 1–8 and then call for reports. Briefly summarize verses 35–40 after Group 3 has reported.

Give the Truth a Personal Focus

Read the following and let members complete them to make an application to life. (The italicized statements are suggestions only.) After members have suggested answers, discuss the implications of each statement.

1. Studying Paul's vision in Troas and the missionary party's immediate response can motivate adults to be ready to meet people's spiritual needs as God makes known the needs (vv. 9–10).

2. Studying the missionary party's going to a place of prayer and speaking to the women can inspire adults to seek out opportunities to share the good news (v. 13).

3. Studying Lydia's being converted and offering her house for the missionaries' use can teach adults that believers are to make their resources available for Christ's work (vv. 14–15).

4. Studying Paul and Silas' singing in prison can encourage adults to look for ways to share their faith in difficult circumstances (v. 25).

5. Studying Paul's stopping the jailer from killing himself can remind adults that believers are to do good to people who mistreat them (vv. 26–28).

6. Studying the jailer's question and the missionaries' witness can make adults aware that they must be prepared to share the gospel at any time and in any place (vv. 29–32).

Power of the Gospel

Basic Passage: Acts 18:18–19:41
Focal Passages: Acts 19:1–6, 11–20

P art of Paul's missionary strategy was to target cities. One of his most effective missionary ventures was in the city of Ephesus. This was the largest city of Asia Minor and the site of the temple of the goddess Artemis (AHR tih mihs) or Diana. The power of the gospel was demonstrated in a variety of ways in Ephesus.

▶ ▶ ▶ ▶ ▶ ▶ ▶ ▶ ▶ **Study Aim:** *To describe the ways in which the power of the gospel was shown in Paul's Ephesian ministry*

STUDYING THE BIBLE

LESSON OUTLINE
  I. Contacts with Ephesus (18:18–28)
    1. Paul passing through Ephesus (18:18–23)
    2. Apollos in Ephesus (18:24–28)
  II. God's Power at Ephesus (19:1–20)
    1. Disciples of John the Baptist (19:1–7)
    2. Word spread throughout Asia (19:8–10)
    3. Extraordinary miracles (19:11–12)
    4. Jewish exorcists (19:13–16)
    5. Confessing sins (19:17–20)
  III. Paul's Future Plans (19:21–22)
  IV. Near Riot at Ephesus (19:23–41)
    1. Demetrius stirs up the image–makers (19:23–27)
    2. A wild mob (19:28–34)
    3. Order restored (19:35–41)

On Paul's way from Antioch to Jerusalem, he stopped briefly at the synagogue in Ephesus (18:18–23). When Apollos came to Ephesus, Priscilla and Aquila (uh KWIL uh) instructed him more fully (vv. 24–28). When Paul returned to Ephesus, he led twelve of John the Baptist's disciples to believe, be baptized, and receive the Spirit (19: 1–7). While Paul was at Ephesus, everyone in the province of Asia heard the gospel (vv. 8–10). God performed extraordinary miracles through Paul (vv. 11–12). When some Jewish exorcists used the name of Jesus, the demoniac attacked them (vv. 13–16). Believers who had practiced occult arts confessed their sins and burned their books (vv. 17–20). Paul planned to go to Jerusalem and then to Rome (vv. 21–22). Demetrius (dih MEE trih uhs), a maker of images of the goddess, accused Paul to the other imagemakers (vv. 23–27). He and the others stirred up a mob (vv. 28–34). Words of warning from a city official restored order (vv. 35–41).

I. Contacts with Ephesus (18:18–28)

1. Paul passing through Ephesus (vv. 18–23). When Paul left Corinth, he took with him Priscilla and Aquila (v. 18). When they came to Ephesus, Paul visited briefly in the synagogue, and Priscilla and Aquila stayed (v. 19). Although the Ephesians asked Paul to stay, he said he had to go to Jerusalem; but he promised to return (vv. 20–21). After going to Jerusalem and Antioch, Paul traveled through Galatia and Phrygia, strengthening the disciples (vv. 22–23).

2. Apollos in Ephesus (vv. 24–28). Apollos, a Jewish believer and eloquent speaker, came to Ephesus (v. 24). He was diligent in teaching the things of the Lord, but he knew only the baptism of John (v. 25). When Priscilla and Aquila heard him speak, they privately explained to him the way of God more perfectly (v. 26). Apollos went to Corinth in Achaia (uh Kay yuh or uh KIGH uh), where he preached Christ with great power (vv. 27–28).

II. God's Power at Ephesus (19:1–20)

1. Disciples of John the Baptist (vv. 1–7)

1 And it came to pass, that, while Apollos was at Corinth, Paul having passed through the upper coasts came to Ephesus: and finding certain disciples,

2 He said unto them, Have ye received the Holy Ghost since ye believed? And they said to him, We have not so much as heard whether there be any Holy Ghost.

3 And he said unto them, Unto what then were ye baptized? And they said, Unto John's baptism.

4 Then said Paul, John verily baptized with the baptism of repentance, saying unto the people, that they should believe on him which should come after him, that is, on Christ Jesus.

5 When they heard this, they were baptized in the name of the Lord Jesus.

6 And when Paul had laid his hands upon them, the Holy Ghost came on them; and they spake with tongues, and prophesied.

When Paul arrived at Ephesus, he met twelve (v. 7) disciples of John the Baptist. They had been baptized with the baptism of John, but they had no knowledge of Pentecost and probably not of the cross and resurrection. Paul explained that John's baptism was designed to point to Christ Jesus. John's baptism was preparatory to faith in Jesus Christ. When these men heard the gospel, they believed and were baptized. Paul laid his hands on them, and they received the Spirit and spoke with tongues.

2. Word spread throughout Asia (vv. 8–10). Following his usual pattern in a new city, Paul went first to the synagogue. He spent three months there before opposition led him to move with the believers to another building (vv. 8–9). During a two-year period, everyone in the province of Asia heard the word of the Lord Jesus (v. 10).

3. Extraordinary miracles (vv. 11–12)

11 And God wrought special miracles by the hands of Paul.

12 So that from his body were brought unto the sick handkerchiefs or aprons, and the diseases departed from them, and the evil spirits went out of them.

During Paul's ministry in Ephesus, God worked special miracles through him. The sick were healed. Evil spirits were cast out. So great was God's power that God even used things that Paul had touched. Visible demonstrations of God's power were used to combat great evil and point people to what God was doing. The miracles of Acts 19:11–12 were demonstrations of divine power that challenged the stranglehold of pagan idolatry in Ephesus.

4. Jewish exorcists (vv. 13–16)

13 Then certain of the vagabond Jews, exorcists, took upon them to call over them which had evil spirits the name of the Lord Jesus, saying, We adjure you by Jesus whom Paul preacheth.

14 And there were seven sons of one Sceva, a Jew, and chief of the priests, which did so.

15 And the evil spirit answered and said, Jesus I know, and Paul I know; but who are ye?

16 And the man in whom the evil spirit was leaped on them, and overcame them, and prevailed against them, so that they fled out of that house naked and wounded.

The practice of various occult arts was common in the ancient world, and seems to have been especially prevalent in Ephesus. Earlier in Acts, Simon the magician tried to buy the Holy Spirit from Peter and John (8:18–19). In Ephesus, some traveling Jewish exorcists had seen Paul cast out demons in the name of Jesus. Therefore, these exorcists added the name of Jesus to the other impressive-sounding names they used in performing exorcisms.

Luke records what happened to seven such exorcists, the sons of a Jew named Sceva (See vuh), who claimed high priestly lineage. They commanded the evil spirits to come out in the name of "Jesus whom Paul preacheth." When they tried this on one particular demoniac, the evil spirit said that he knew Jesus and Paul, but not the exorcists. Then the demoniac attacked the would-be exorcists, beat them, and sent them fleeing naked from the house.

5. Confessing sins (vv. 17–20)

17 And this was known to all the Jews and Greeks also dwelling at Ephesus; and fear fell on them all, and the name of the Lord Jesus was magnified.

The news about the sons of Sceva spread throughout Ephesus. Everyone—Jews and Greeks—heard about it. The effect of this incident was similar to the effect of the judgment on Ananias and Sapphira (see Acts 5:11). Verse 17 records two effects of the news about the exorcists who had been judged for their use of the name of Jesus. Judgment on the selfish use of the name of Jesus struck fear into the hearts of all. The positive result was a new sense of reverence and praise for the Lord Jesus.

18 And many that believed came, and confessed, and shewed their deeds.

19 Many of them also which used curious arts brought their books together, and burned them before all men: and they counted the price of them, and found it fifty thousand pieces of silver.

Many believers in Ephesus had continued to practice the same occult arts that they had done before believing in Jesus. When they heard what happened to Sceva's sons, they were convicted of their own sins. They had not necessarily been doing exactly the same thing as the exorcists—using the name of Jesus in their black magic; however, they had continued their old practices after believing in the Lord Jesus.

Their conviction led these believers to confess their sins not only to God but also openly to others. Essential to their occult practices were books containing such things as incantations, magic spells, astrological charts, fortunetelling secrets, and so forth. When the believers confessed such things, they showed their sincerity by destroying the books they had used in their dark practices. They publicly burned scrolls, whose total monetary value was great.

20 So mightily grew the word of God and prevailed.

Acts 19:1–19 describes various displays of the power of the gospel at Ephesus: conversions, bold witnessing, extraordinary miracles, judgment on misuse of the Lord's name, and believers confessing their sins and destroying their books of black magic. As a result of these evidences of the power of the gospel, the Word of the Lord spread even further, and His power became even more evident.

III. Paul's Future Plans (Acts 19:21–22)

Paul was planning a trip through Macedonia to Achaia (Corinth). He then was going on to Jerusalem. Although he did not mention it here, he was going to Jerusalem with an offering from Gentile churches for Jewish believers. Then he hoped to travel to Rome (v. 21; see Rom. 15:24–26). Meanwhile, Paul sent Timothy and Erastus (ih RASS tuhs) to Macedonia, but he stayed for a while longer in Ephesus (v. 22).

IV. Near Riot at Ephesus (Acts 19:23–41)

1. Demetrius stirs up the imagemakers (vv. 23–27). Demetrius was one of many who made a good living from silver images of the goddess Diana (v. 23). He stirred up other imagemakers by saying that Paul's work threatened not only their jobs but also their religion (vv. 24–27).

2. A wild mob (vv. 28–34). The angry cries of the imagemakers caused a mob to seize two believers (vv. 28–29). Paul wanted to appear before the crowd, but his disciples and friendly political leaders warned him against doing this (vv. 30–31). Most of the confused mob didn't even know what was going on (v. 32). A man named Alexander tried to speak, but the mob drowned out his voice when they realized he was a Jew (vv. 33–34).

3. Order restored (vv. 35–41). A city official got the mob's attention by affirming the greatness of their religion (v. 35). He advised them not to do anything rash (v. 36). He denied that Paul was guilty of any crime; and if Demetrius thought he was guilty, he should make his accusations through legal channels (vv. 37–39). The official warned that this kind of crowd action could attract the attention of high government officials (v. 40). Then he dismissed them (v. 41).

APPLYING THE BIBLE

1. The gospel bears fruit. During World War II when General Stilwell retreated from Burma, he and his retreating troops were concerned for their lives as they passed through the Nauga Hills, which reputedly was where the headhunters lived. But much to their surprise, as they quietly slipped through the jungle they heard music. The tunes were familiar but they could not understand the words. Listening closely, they were amazed to discover that the natives were singing hymns that the soldiers had learned as boys in their churches.

Paul Geren was one of those American soldiers in the retreating company and he tells how he and the others moved cautiously in the direction of the music. They found the people who were singing, and they also found a Baptist church! The gospel seeds planted by Ann and Adoniram Judson 125 years before were still bearing fruit.

Paul's ministry in Ephesus was strategic. It was a great city, where paganism flourished in the worship of Artemis or Diana, the goddess of fertility. But Paul's ministry there, though controversial and extremely difficult, yielded precious fruit. Long after Paul had passed from the scene, the Ephesian church, the mother church of Asia Minor, was still holding aloft the gospel torch.

2. The power of influence. Nothing in this world is as permanent or as powerful as one's influence. Dwight L. Moody, the great American evangelist, was led to Christ as a boy while working in Holton's shoe store in Boston, by Edward Kimball, his Sunday School teacher. Moody has been called the most powerful influence for righteousness in the nineteenth century.

Moody's influence spread to other men: John R. Mott, the great Methodist missionary statesman who raised more than $300 million for Christ's work in America; Sir Wilfred Grenfell, the pioneer British medical missionary to Labrador; Robert E. Speer, the American Presbyterian missionary statesman; Henry Drummond, the British scientist and theologian who wrote the finest little book ever penned on 1 Corinthians 13, titled, *The Greatest Thing in the World*; and Sherwood Eddy, the Kansas boy educated at Yale and Princeton whose worldwide work with the Young Men's Christian Association had a major impact.[1]

And who can adequately describe the influence of Priscilla and Aquila who were ministering in Ephesus (v. 26)? Apollos, an Alexandrian, mighty in preaching skills, came to Ephesus and was preaching only the baptism of John (v. 25). He did not yet know about the death, burial, and resurrection of Jesus; and Aquila and Priscilla instructed him and, no doubt, Apollos developed into a powerful Christian preacher (v. 26).

3. Satan's opposition. Anywhere the work of God begins to prosper, that's where Satan really goes to work.

Daniel Defoe, the author of *Robinson Crusoe*, wrote about the devil and his work:

> Wherever God erects a house of prayer,
> The devil always builds a chapel there;
> And 'twill be found upon examination,
> The latter has the largest congregation.[2]

Ephesus was no exception. God blessed Paul's ministry there and Satan opposed it (vv. 13–16). And although at times Satan may seem to have the upper hand, God always has the final word.

4. The power of the gospel. Many years ago a small, weak-looking black boy was sold as a slave in Nigeria. He looked so miserable that slave buyers laughed at the suggestion of paying for him, but one finally bought him for a roll of tobacco. Then the boy was put on board a British slave ship. Liberated sometime later, the boy, grown to young manhood, was put in the charge of some Christian missionaries.

Many years later, the boy, now a man, addressed church dignitaries, statesmen, and nobles in St. Paul's Cathedral, London, when he was appointed the first bishop of Nigeria. His name was Bishop Samuel Crowther, who spent the rest of his life preaching the gospel and building up the Anglican Church in Nigeria.[3]

TEACHING THE BIBLE

▶ *Main Idea:* The gospel's power as revealed at Ephesus shows that God was blessing Paul's ministry.

▶ *Suggested Teaching Aim:* To lead adults to describe the ways in which the power of the gospel was shown in Paul's Ephesian ministry, and to identify what they need to change in their lives for God's Word to move freely through them.

A TEACHING OUTLINE

1. Use an illustration to introduce the study.

2. Use lecture and questions and answer to guide the Bible study.

3. Lead members to identify what they need to do in their lives to allow God's message to move to the world.

Introduce the Bible Study

Use "The gospel bears fruit" in "Applying the Bible" to introduce the lesson.

Search for Biblical Truth

IN ADVANCE, copy the following on a large sheet of paper and place on the focal wall. Cover the outline points until you are ready to use them.

    I. Contacts with Ephesus (Acts 18:18–23)
    II. God's Power at Ephesus (Acts 19:1–20)
        1. Disciples of John the Baptist (19:1–7)
        2. Word spread throughout Asia (19:8–10)
        3. Extraordinary miracles (19:11–12)
        4. Jewish exorcists (19:13–16)
        5. Confessing sins (19:17–20)
    III. Paul's Future Plans (19:21–22)
    IV. Near Riot at Ephesus (19:23–41)

Uncover the first point. To set the context, summarize I. "Contacts with Ephesus" by using the material in "Studying the Bible." Be sure you identify Apollos and describe Priscilla and Aquila's role in instructing him.

Uncover II. "God's Power at Ephesus" and 1."Disciples of John the Baptist (19:1–7)." Ask members to read 18:1–7 silently. On a map, locate Corinth (where Apollos was) and Ephesus (where Paul was). Ask: How did these people hear the teaching they had received? (We do not know; someone may have been in Judah and heard John preach and brought the message of repentance back.) What essential parts of the gospel message did they lack? (Probably the cross, resurrection, and Pentecost.) What was the significance of the speaking in tongues in 19:6? (The coming of the Holy Spirit further affirmed the ministry to disciples of John.)

Uncover 2. "Word spread throughout Asia" and briefly summarize these verses.

Uncover 3. "Extraordinary miracles" and ask members to search 19:11–12 to find what made the miracles so unusual. (Pieces of cloth that Paul had touched used in miracles.)

Uncover 4. "Jewish exorcists" and ask members to skim 19:13–16. Ask: Why was this experience so significant? (Served as a warning to others who would try to misuse the power of the Holy Spirit.) What other experience in Acts is similar to this? (Simon the magician—8:18–19). DISCUSS: What practices today could be compared to the attempt to misuse the power of the Holy Spirit?

Uncover 5. "Confessing sins" and ask members to look at 19:17–20 to find the outcome of this experience. (Fear fell and the name of the Lord was magnified.)

DISCUSS: Compare this experience at this stage of the church's development to the earlier experience of Ananias and Sapphira (see 5:11).

Ask: What evidence did the Ephesians give that their conversion was real? (Burned books on the occult.) What was the result of this

visible experience? (Word of God grew.)
Uncover points III. and IV. and briefly summarize them.

Give the Truth a Personal Focus

Ask members to examine their lives to see what they need to remove for God's Word to move through them to the world. Close in prayer for courage and conviction to make the changes necessary.

1. J. D. Douglas, *Who's Who in Christian History* (Wheaton, Ill.: Tyndale House, 1992); also see Lewis L. Dunnington, *Power to Become* (New York: The Macmillan Co., 1956), 60.

2. See J. B. Fowler, Jr., *Illustrating Great Words of the New Testament* (Nashville: Broadman Press, 1991), 151–60.

3. Walter B. Knight, *Knight's Master Book of New Illustrations* (Grand Rapids, Mich.: Wm. B. Eerdmans Publishing Co., 1956), 255.

God's Promise of Deliverance

INTRODUCTION

These nine studies from the Book of Isaiah deal with God's promises to deliver Israel and to bring a better day to all God's people. These studies run through January 1996. The studies for February 1996 are "On God's Love for All People (Jonah, Ruth)" and will be introduced before the first lesson in February.

Unit I, "The Coming of a New Day," consists of five lessons that deal with various aspects of the coming of the new day and the good news that God promised through the prophet Isaiah. Although there is considerable repetition of themes in the Book of Isaiah, the five lessons focus on the following aspects of the new day: comfort, encouragement, joy, righteousness and peace, and sharing good news. Passages in Unit I are from the following chapters in Isaiah: 40; 51; 9; 11; 60; and 61. The Christmas lesson also includes verses from Luke 2:1–20.

Unit II, "The Ministry of the Suffering Servant," is a study of some of the passages in Isaiah that refer to the Servant of the Lord. The four lessons deal with the Servant's call, mission, steadfast endurance, and victory. Passages in Unit II are from the following chapters of Isaiah: 42; 49; 50; 52; 53.

A Time of Comfort

Basic Passage: Isaiah 40:1–11
Focal Passage: Isaiah 40:1–11a

Like most of the last half of the Book of Isaiah, Isaiah 40 was written in poetic language. Doing full justice to the power and beauty of such a passage requires that it be sung. Whenever I read this great passage, I think of these same words being sung in a presentation of Messiah by Handel.

▶ ▶ ▶ ▶ ▶ ▶ ▶ ▶ ▶ **Study Aim:** *To state the basis for the message of comfort in Isaiah 40:1–11*

STUDYING THE BIBLE

LESSON OUTLINE
  I. Words of Comfort (Isa. 40:1–2)
    1. A message of comfort from God to His people (Isa. 40:1)
    2. Loving words of pardon for sin (Isa. 40:2)
  II. Prepare the Way of the Lord (Isa. 40:3–5)
    1. Preparing for the King's coming (Isa. 40:3–4)
    2. The revelation of God's Glory to all people (Isa. 40:5)
  III. Mortal Man and the Eternal Word of God (Isa 40:6–8)
    1. Mortal human beings (Isa. 40:6–7)
    2. The eternal word of God (Isa. 40:8)
  IV. Good News of God's Strength and Tenderness (Isa. 40:9–11)
    1. Proclaim good news (Isa. 40:9)
    2. God's strength and tenderness (Isa. 40:10–11)

The Lord called the prophets and others to proclaim His message of comfort to His people (v. 1). In words of love, they were to announce the end of captivity, pardon for sin, and the end of punishment (v. 2). A voice cried out to prepare a way for the Lord's coming (vv. 3–4). All flesh would see the Lord's glory (v. 5). The certainty of God's promise is seen by contrasting the frailty and mortality of human beings (vv. 6–7) with the eternally abiding word of God (v. 8). Jerusalem was called to declare the good news to the cities of Judah (v. 9). The Lord has the strength of a king but the tender care of a shepherd (vv. 10–11).

I. Words of Comfort (Isa. 40:1–2)
1. A message of comfort from God to His people (v. 1)
1 Comfort ye, comfort ye my people, saith your God.

Although the ultimate fulfillment of Isaiah's words was in the coming of the incarnate Word in Jesus Christ, a prior application of the message was to the Jewish exiles in Babylon. People in every generation need the message of comfort and encouragement in this passage. This was certainly true of the Jewish exiles. Isaiah 40:27 reflects their sense of despair. They thought God had forgotten them and their plight (see also Ps. 137:1–4).

Notice the words "my people" and "your God." What comfort those simple words contained! The people thought God had forgotten them. The message of comfort begins with the assurance that they were His people and He was their God.

Notice also the word *ye*, an old English word for the plural of *you*. God was calling many to spread His message of comfort. This surely included the prophets, but it also included anyone who experienced God. Paul wrote that when believers have experienced God's comfort in their own lives, they are to share that comfort with others (2 Cor. 1:4).

Isaiah's earlier call was to declare judgment (Isa. 6). By contrast, Isaiah 40 is a call to bring comfort. Someone has said that a preacher's job is to comfort the afflicted and afflict the comfortable. Most of the prophets contain a mixture of messages of judgment and hope. Words of judgment are needed when hearts are sinful and cold. Words of hope are needed when hearts are broken and discouraged.

2. Loving words of pardon for sin (v. 2)

> **2 Speak ye comfortably to Jerusalem, and cry unto her, that her warfare is accomplished, that her iniquity is pardoned: for she hath received of the Lord's hand double for all her sins.**

The first part of verse 2 literally means "speak to the heart." Elsewhere in the Old Testament, this is used to speak words of encouragement, affection, and love. God here spoke words of love to His people. The words contain three assurances: (1) The allotted time of their captivity was over. "Warfare" refers to a soldier's time of service. (2) Their iniquity was pardoned. This was the basis for the other assurances. (3) They had been punished more than enough for their past sins.

II. Prepare the Way of the Lord (Isa. 40:3–5)

1. Preparing for the King's coming (vv. 3–4)

> **3 The voice of him that crieth in the wilderness, Prepare ye the way of the LORD, make straight in the desert a highway for our God.**
>
> **4 Every valley shall be exalted, and every mountain and hill shall be made low: and the crooked shall be made straight, and the rough places plain.**

In ancient times, as a king approached, a herald went before him announcing his coming. Also builders went ahead of him to ensure that the road was worthy of a king's travel. If a king was traveling through an area where there was no road, a new road was built. These are the practices reflected in verses 3–4. The voice is that of the herald. The rest of the passage describes the work of the road builders. The king needed a road that was level and smooth. Therefore, some valleys had to be filled; and some mountains had to be cut down.

The voice in verse 3 followed up on verses 1–2 by announcing the coming of the Lord. We Christians recognize this passage as one quoted by John the Baptist to describe himself and his task (Matt. 3:3; Mark 1:2–3; Luke 3:3–6; John 1:23). John repeatedly denied that he himself was the Messiah. He described his own role as that of the herald who prepared the way for the Lord.

The more immediate application of the prophet's words was preparation for the Lord's coming to lead His people out of Babylonian captivity. Thus as the exiles awaited deliverance, the voice called for preparations to be made for His coming.

2. The revelation of God's glory to all people (v. 5)

5 And the glory of the Lord shall be revealed, and all flesh shall see it together: for the mouth of the Lord hath spoken it.

The word *glory* is used to describe the indescribable the revelation of the full majesty and power of God's presence. When Moses prayed to see God's glory, he was told that no man could see God's face and live; but God hid Moses in a cleft of the rock and caused His glory to pass by (Exod. 33:18–23). The ark of the covenant signified God's glory with His people (1 Sam. 4:22). Ezekiel described how the glory of God left the temple because of the persistent rebellion of Judah (Ezek. 11:33), but God promised that the glory would return (Ezek. 43:4). Isaiah 40:5 predicted that when the Lord came to His people, they would see His glory. The ultimate fulfillment of this is Jesus Christ (John 1:14).

Verse 5 predicted that the revelation of God's glory would be to all people, not just to Israel. This is one of many passages in Isaiah that predicts the universal scope of God's plan. Luke is the Gospel that gives special emphasis to the intention of God to reveal Himself to all people. When Luke described how John the Baptist quoted Isaiah 40, he was careful to include verse 5 (see Luke 3:6). From the beginning, God's plan has included all people. He chose Israel as a special people through whom to send the Savior of all people.

III. Mortal Man and the Eternal Word of God (Isa. 40:6–8)

1. Mortal human beings (vv. 6–7)

6 The voice said, Cry. And he said, What shall I cry? All flesh is grass, and all the goodliness thereof is as the flower of the field:

7 The grass withereth, the flower fadeth: because the spirit of the Lord bloweth upon it: surely the people is grass.

Notice that each of the four parts of Isaiah 40:1–11 begins with a voice. The source of the voice at the beginning of verse 6 is not identified. Neither is the one who heard the voice identified. The voice could have been God or an angel. The one who heard could have been the prophet or someone else. The voice said to cry out. The one who heard asked, "What shall I cry?"

A twofold answer to the question is given. The message of verses

6b–7 is clear. Just as grass withers and flowers fade, so do human beings grow old and die.

2. The eternal word of God (v. 8)

8 The grass withereth, the flower fadeth: but the word of our God shall stand for ever.

Verse 8 sums up the two parts of the message. Humans, like grass and flowers, grow old and die. By contrast, however, the word of God stands forever. The Old Testament views words as extensions of the speaker's personality. Thus the word of God is the extended reach and power of God Himself. No wonder Isaiah 55:11 says that God's word never comes back empty but always accomplishes the purpose for which it was sent forth.

What choices did the exiles have when they heard the message of Isaiah 40? They could have trusted in some device of their own to try to secure deliverance and new life. They could have continued to wallow in their doubts and despair. Or, they could have believed the promise of God's word that He was coming to redeem them and to lead them home. God may not act when we want Him to act or in the way we expect Him to act, but God's word is true and His promises will come to pass in His own time and way.

IV. Good News of God's Strength and Tenderness (Isa. 40:9–11)

1. Proclaim good news (v. 9)

9 O Zion, that bringest good tidings, get thee up into the high mountain; O Jerusalem, that bringest good tidings, lift up thy voice with strength; lift it up, be not afraid; say unto the cities of Judah, Behold your God!

Hebrew poetry often repeats the same basic thought in slightly different words. We see this in the first half of verse 9. Zion or Jerusalem was summoned to bring good news. The New Testament often uses a word translated "gospel" or more literally "good news." Isaiah 40:9 was one of the Old Testament proclamations of good news. Jerusalem was called to tell good news to the cities of Judah. The good news was "Behold your God!" Jerusalem represented all the people of God. They as well as the prophets were to join in telling good news. This principle applied to the good news of deliverance from exile; it applies even more to telling the good news of deliverance from sin and death through Jesus Christ.

2. God's strength and tenderness (vv. 10–11)

10 Behold, the Lord God will come with strong hand, and his arm shall rule for him: behold, his reward is with him, and his work before him.

11 He shall feed his flock like a shepherd.

The good news is that the God who reveals Himself to us is both strong and tender. He is the eternal God, Creator of heaven and earth. No power is so great as His strength. On the other hand, He is as gentle as the shepherd who tenderly cares for his flock. Verse 10 is one of many Bible descriptions of God's strength; verse 11 is

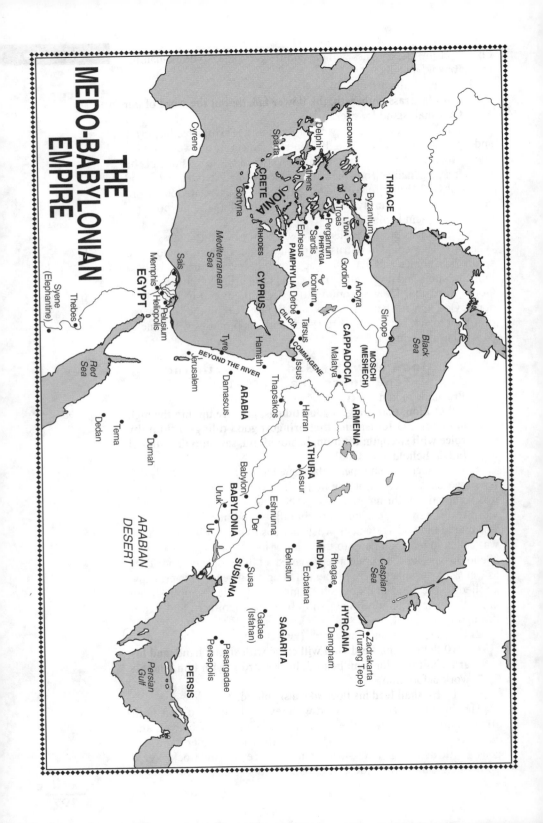

one of many words of God's tender love. The simple prayer expresses the most profound biblical theology: "God is great, and God is good."

Only the first part of verse 11 is in the focal passage, but be sure and read the rest of the verse to see the full description of God's tender care of His own: "He shall gather the lambs with his arm, and carry them in his bosom, and shall gently lead those that are with young." This reminds us of Psalm 23.

APPLYING THE BIBLE

1. **Light in the darkness**. Surely, the most-beloved piece of music in Christendom is the one often heard at this season of the year. It is Handel's Messiah, but like so many great human accomplishments, it was inspired in Handel's heart in a time of personal crisis and darkness.

The year was 1741. Handel walked the dark streets of London thinking of his past triumphs, yet despairing of his future. Misfortune, ill health, and bankruptcy dogged him. His audiences had dwindled, and a cerebral hemorrhage had partially paralyzed him. At sixty, he felt life had passed him by.

Then the miracle happened! Returning to his shabby apartment, he found a bulky package on his desk from Charles Jennens, who asked Handel to write the music for *A Sacred Oratorio*. The *Oratorio,* filled with passages about the promised Messiah from Isaiah, challenged Handel's discouraged heart. With lightening speed and divine inspiration he wrote: "He was despised and rejected of men. . . . Comfort ye, comfort ye my people, saith your God."

For hours on end he wrote, jumping up often from his chair to play a passage on his harpsichord. "Hallelujah!" he would shout aloud, as the tears rolled down his cheeks.

When the *Messiah* was done, after days of almost nonstop labor, Handel fell on his bed and slept for seventeen hours from complete exhaustion.

But the music Handel composed in his darkest hours has brought light, hope and comfort to millions since that day in 1741. God still comforts His people (v. 1).

2. **The words we most need to hear.** Nansen, the great Arctic explorer, took a carrier pigeon with him on one of his expeditions to the North Pole. For two years he was stranded in those frigid waters and frozen wastelands, and the world thought Nansen was lost forever.
One day he wrote a message to his wife and put it in a tiny vial under the frail bird's wings. Nansen then turned the bird loose, and it flew two thousand miles over the frozen northland, always south, home to Norway. At last it landed on Mrs. Nansen's windowsill, and she gathered the exhausted, trembling little messenger up into her warm hands. She read the message that all was well with her husband and that soon he would be home.

They were the words she most needed to hear, as God's words

through Isaiah to the lonely, disconsolate exiles were the words they most needed to hear. "All is well," he told them, "and soon you will be home! Hold on to your faith!"

3. Set free by the Savior. No American president stirs the emotions of the peoples of the world as does the hallowed memory of Abraham Lincoln.

In Boston's Park Square there is a touching statue of Abraham Lincoln with two slaves kneeling before him. The president is striking the chains off the wrists of the slaves. There is a look of compassion and kindness on Lincoln's face, and the slaves are gazing up at the president in grateful wonderment. The remarkable bronze work is a powerful testimony to the joy of being set free.

God was about to set His people free. Isaiah was to give them the good news. Isaiah's message to the Jews had been one of divine judgment. Now it was a message of divine grace to captives set free from their bondage (v. 2). They had suffered enough for their sins. Pardon, freedom, and restoration were immediately before them. What glorious news!

But behind this immediate scene of exiles being pardoned and set free from captivity is a greater and grander message: Jesus, our Savior and Lord, has died and been raised from the dead to set sinners free from their sins. Hallelujah, what a Savior (John 8:36)!

TEACHING THE BIBLE

▶ *Main Idea:* God comforts His people when they hurt.
▶ *Suggested Teaching Aim:* To lead adults to describe the way God would comfort His people in Babylon, and to identify ways He comforts us today.

A TEACHING OUTLINE

1. Introduce the lesson with an illustration.
2. Have members fill in a chart to study the lesson.
3. Identify ways God comforts us and ways we can share God's comfort with others.

Introduce the Bible Study

Use "Light in the darkness" from "Applying the Bible" to introduce the study.

IN ADVANCE make a unit poster, listing on it the title of each lesson this quarter, the Scriptures being studied, and the "Main Idea." Make an arrow from colored paper and use it to highlight each week's session. Read the title, Scripture references, and the main idea for December 3.

Search for Biblical Truth

On a chalkboard or a large sheet of paper, write:

A Time of Comfort
Isaiah 40:1–11

	Speaker	To Whom Spoken	Message: Immediate/Ultimate
First Voice (40:1–2):			
Second Voice (40:3–5):			
Third Voice (40:6–8):			
Fourth Voice (40:9–11):			

Ask members to open their Bibles to Isaiah 40:1–2. Explain the setting of this passage as a message to the Babylonian captives. The people had been taken to Babylon in 586 B.C. when Babylon had captured Jerusalem. Now God was describing what was going to happen when it was time for His people to come home.
Speaker: God.
To Whom Spoken: Babylonian captives
Message: Comfort then and now.
Ask them next to look at 40:3–5 and fill in the chart:
Speaker: A human voice, possibly a prophet.
To Whom Spoken: God's people in seventh century B.C. and first century A.D.
Message: Prepare the way for God to come to His people.
Ask them to look at 40:6–8 and fill in the chart:
Speaker: God/angel.
To Whom Spoken: Prophet.
Message: Humans do not last; God's word does.
Ask members to look at 40:9–11a and fill in the chart:
Speaker: Possibly Zion or Jerusalem.
To Whom Spoken: Cities of Judah.
Message: God will care for His people.
Be sure to point out that this chapter has an immediate fulfillment in God's coming to the Babylonian captives, but the ultimate fulfillment is given in the New Testament in John the Baptist's proclamation of Jesus' coming.
Ask a volunteer to read Luke 3:1–6. Ask: What similarities do you see in the two accounts? what differences?

Give the Truth a Personal Focus
On a chalkboard or a large sheet of paper write "Comfort ye my people." Ask members to list ways that God comforts us today.
Point out that the "ye" is plural and that this command is still valid for us today. Ask members to list ways they can comfort people today. Point out that helping others get ready for God's coming is the greatest comfort they can offer.

A Time of Encouragement

Basic Passage: Isaiah 51:1–8
Focal Passages: Isaiah 51:1–6

T he Bible deals honestly with negative as well as positive feelings of people of faith. Throughout the last part of Isaiah are several passages in which people expressed their doubts and despair. For example, Isaiah 49:14 reads: "But Zion said, The Lord hath forsaken me, and my Lord hath forgotten me." Such feelings as these were addressed in many of Isaiah's prophecies. In the lesson for December 3, we saw a message of comfort in Isaiah 40:1–11. The passage for December 10 sounds a similar note by speaking a message of encouragement.

▶ ▶ ▶ ▶ ▶ ▶ ▶ ▶ **Study Aim:** *To identify the elements of encouragement in Isaiah 51:1–6*

STUDYING THE BIBLE

LESSON OUTLINE
  I. Heritage and Hope (Isa. 51:1–3)
    1. Pursuing righteousness and seeking God (Isa. 51:1)
    2. Remember your heritage of faith (Isa. 51:2)
    3. Be encouraged by God's bright promises (Isa. 51:3)
  II. Bright Hope (Isa. 51:4–6)
    1. Hope for all people (Isa. 51:4–5)
    2. Eternal hope (Isa. 51:6)
  III. Fear Not (Isa. 51:7–8)
    1. Human reproaches (Isa. 51:7)
    2. The end of the ungodly (Isa. 51:8)

Isaiah 51:1–8 is divided into three stanzas, each beginning with a call for God's people to hearken to words of encouragement (vv. 1,4,7). God's people are described as pursuing righteousness and seeking God (v. 1). They were told to remember the faith of Abraham and Sarah (v. 2). They also were called to look to a future in which the wilderness would blossom like the garden of Eden (v. 3). The people of Israel were part of God's plan toward which the nations looked for light and hope (vv. 4–5). The heavens and earth will vanish away, but God's righteousness and salvation will abide forever (v. 6). Those who fear the reproach of others should realize that humans are mortal, but God's righteousness and salvation are forever (vv. 7–8).

I. Heritage and Hope (Isa. 51:1–2)
1. Pursuing righteousness and seeking God (v. 1)

1 Hearken to me, ye that follow after righteousness, ye that seek the Lord: look unto the rock whence ye are hewn, and to the hole of the pit whence ye are digged.

The word *hearken* in verses 1, 4, and 7 reminds us that people must be willing to listen to the word of God. Often our doubts and despair arise because we are listening more to other voices than we are to the voice of God. In the midst of our strivings, God says, "Be still, and know that I am God" (Ps. 46:10).

The word *follow* means more than follow halfheartedly; it means to "pursue." It is a strong word like the word *seek* to describe those who "seek the Lord." A number of passages from the New Testament illustrate what was meant. I think especially of two from the Sermon on the Mount: "Blessed are they which do hunger and thirst after righteousness" (Matt. 5:6). "Seek ye first the kingdom of God and his righteousness" (Matt. 6:33).

Those who pursue righteousness and seek God with all their heart are in the minority in every generation. Most people are not pursuing righteousness or seeking God with all their heart. People of faith must swim upstream against the current of a world that lives by different standards and values. Thus people of faith often need to renew their faith by hearing God's Word remind us of what is right, true, and lasting.

We need to remember the rock from which we were hewn. This is a figurative way of calling us to remember who we are and whose we are. We need to remember that we belong to God and thus we also belong to God's people. We are like a rock from God's quarry. Each of us is one of many rocks from God's quarry.

2. Remember your heritage of faith (v. 2)

2 Look unto Abraham your father, and unto Sarah that bare you: for I called him alone, and blessed him, and increased him.

Remember is a big word in the Bible (see Exod. 32:13; Deut. 5:15). The children of Israel were called to remember their heritage of faith by remembering how God led earlier people of faith. Verse 2 called the discouraged Jewish exiles to remember Abraham and Sarah.

God reminded them that He called Abraham when he was alone. When God called Abraham, he had few prospects of becoming a father, much less the father of a great nation. When God promised to make of him a great nation, Abraham and Sarah were well past the age of bearing children. From a human point of view, the promise of God had no chance of becoming true; but from God's point of view, the promise was sure (compare Rom. 4:18; Heb. 11:8–12).

People of faith in every generation are children of Abraham (Gal. 3:9); therefore, his faith should inspire us to trust and obey God no matter how bleak our prospects seem. The discouraged exiles had been battered by defeat, exile, and humiliation. They were few in number and weak by comparison to their conquerors. God's word to the exiles was to remember Abraham and Sarah's faith, and put it into practice in their own day. If God could make a great nation from one old couple, He certainly could restore that nation no matter how few or weak they were.

3. Be encouraged by God's bright promises (v. 3)

> 3 For the Lord shall comfort Zion: he will comfort all her waste places; and he will make her wilderness like Eden, and her desert like the garden of the Lord; joy and gladness shall be found therein, thanksgiving, and the voice of melody.

Verse 2 called the people to look back and draw strength from their heritage of faith. Verse 3 called them to look to the future and to find comfort and encouragement for the present.

God used a striking figure to contrast their future life to their present plight. When the exiles looked at their situation, they felt as if they were in a desert or a wilderness. Israel had a period of wilderness-wandering in their history; it preceded their entry into the promised land. However, the prophet went back further in human history to find an image that would describe the blessed future God has for His people. He said that God was going to turn their wilderness into a new garden of Eden.

Such a future would be a time of joy and gladness—two words often found together in the Old Testament. Often these words describe the future bliss of God's people (see Isa. 35:10; 51:11). At other times, the same words describe the present experience of those who walk with the Lord (see Ps. 51:8).

Verse 3 also describes the experience of God's people in terms of thanksgiving that is expressed in songs of praise. The Book of Psalms and many other Bible passages show that thanksgiving and praise are part of the experience of God's people. Our songs of praise now point to the songs of thanksgiving and praise that will reverberate through heaven.

II. Bright Hope (Isa. 51:4–6)

1. Hope for all people (vv. 4–5)

> 4 Hearken unto me, my people; and give ear unto me, O my nation: for a law shall proceed from me, and I will make my judgment to rest for a light of the people.
>
> 5 My righteousness is near; my salvation is gone forth, and mine arms shall judge the people; the isles shall wait upon me, and on mine arm shall they trust.

Verses 4–5 maintain the future look of verse 3. Although the words are addressed to the Old Testament people of God, the promises include people of other nations who would come to believe. God promised that His law and justice would light all people. That seems to be the meaning of the words "light of the people." The idea is spelled out more clearly in God's words through Isaiah about the Servant of God: "I will also give thee for a light to the Gentiles, that thou mayest be my salvation unto the end of the earth" (Isa. 49: 6; see 42:6).

The basic word of assurance and encouragement in Isaiah 51:1–8 is summed up at the beginning of verse 5. The time of God's righteousness was near; already His salvation had gone forth. Among those who waited for the fulfillment of this promise were both the people of Israel and also people of other nations. The last part of verse 5 presents a vivid picture of this. God said that the people of the distant islands were waiting for His salvation. Many of them would someday come to trust in the Lord.

In our recent study of the Book of Acts, we saw the beginning of the fulfillment of this promise. Christian history tells the thrilling story of how missionaries crossed barriers of distance, language, and culture to tell the good news. Even in our day, many who have not heard are still waiting for the message of divine salvation.

2. Eternal hope (v. 6)

6 Lift up your eyes to the heavens, and look upon the earth beneath: for the heavens shall vanish away like smoke, and the earth shall wax old like a garment, and they that dwell therein shall die in like manner: but my salvation shall be for ever, and my righteousness shall not be abolished.

In last week's lesson, we saw how Isaiah 40:8 contrasted the mortality of human life with the eternal God and His word (Isa. 40:6–8). Isaiah 51:6 also mentions the reality of death for human beings and contrasts it with the eternal nature of divine righteousness and salvation. This passage takes the contrast a step farther by contrasting God's righteousness and salvation with the temporary nature of even the heavens and earth. It is one thing to say that our lives are as sure to end as the grass and flowers are to fade. We have all seen enough of passing seasons and human deaths to know the temporary nature of grass, flowers, and humans. But we have never seen the heavens and earth pass away. They appear to be eternal.

The Bible, however, reminds us that this is not true. We sometimes ask, "What's this world coming to?" One answer is that it's coming to an end. God created the heavens and the earth; and someday, in God's own time, He will bring to an end the present heavens and earth, although He promises to create a new heavens and new earth. Nothing is said about the new heavens and earth in Isaiah 51:6— only the end of the present heavens and earth. However, later in Isaiah is the promise of new heavens and a new earth (65:17; 66:22). God's Word in 2 Peter 3:10–14 describes the destruction of the present creation and then says that "we, according to his promise, look for new heavens and a new earth, wherein dwelleth righteousness" (2 Pet. 3:13).

Believers throughout the centuries have been challenged and inspired by this vision of hope. We are better able to live righteous lives when we live our lives in light of eternity, rather than compromise with the world's transient ways. We are better able to endure troubles and trials, knowing that God's eternal kingdom will come and His will shall be done.

III. Fear Not (Isa. 51:7–8)

1. Human reproaches (v. 7). Some of God's people in every age have been ridiculed for their faith. At such times, people of faith are tempted to fear their tormentors so much that they forget who they are and whose they are. The ringing message of Scripture at such times is not to fear human reproaches and persecution.

2. The end of the ungodly (v. 8). Verse 6 focused on the end of the heavens, earth, and human life.

Verse 8 focuses on the end of those who set themselves against God by persecuting God's people. They flourish only for a short time, but soon they perish. By contrast, the righteousness and salvation of God are eternal.

APPLYING THE BIBLE

1. The emptiness in man's heart. Sir William Osler (1849–1919) was a Canadian physician and one of Canada's greatest medicinal teachers. It was he who discovered the presence in the blood stream of blood platelets. Also, he helped to found the National Tuberculosis Association in 1904. Highly respected in his day, Osler once declared: "The human heart has a hidden want science cannot supply."

Long ago Isaiah identified that emptiness of the human heart and urged the people of Israel to "seek the Lord" with all their hearts (v. 1).

As Augustine put it in the forth century A.D., there is a "God blank" in each of us which only God can fill.

2. God of the past? Thomas Carlyle, the noted Scottish writer who authored several books including *The French Revolution*, said he believed in a God up to the time of Oliver Cromwell, who ruled England from 1649 to 1658.

Is God a God of the past or of the present? He is both. He was the God of the past who led Abraham and Sarah and the patriarchs, but He was also the God of the Israelites who were struggling with the crises of their day. Here Isaiah calls on the Jews to remember the God of their fathers and to seek Him with all their hearts (v. 2) and to take courage from how He dealt with Abraham.

3. The encouragement faith produces. Verse 2 reminded the exiles of their heritage and the faithfulness of God. Verse 3 encourages them to look to the future in faith, knowing that God is dependable.

Nicholas Poussin, one of the leading French painters of the sixteenth century, and a poet friend were examining Poussin's painting of Jesus healing the two blind men of Jericho.

"What to you is the most remarkable thing about the painting?" the poet asked Poussin.

Answering his own question, he said that it must surely be the presence of Christ or the happy expression on the faces of the men whose sight had been restored.

"No," Poussin replied, "it is the cane resting on the steps of the house." Continuing, he said that one of the blind men had been sitting on the steps leaning on his cane. But when he heard Jesus was coming, he discarded his cane and stumbled out to Jesus in faith, believing his sight would be restored.

Faith in God produces encouragement to act. The Israelites were encouraged to trust God, who had led their fathers, to lead and bless them as well. Their faith would encourage them to believe in a better tomorrow (v. 3), they were told.

Do we not need that same encouragement that faith produces as we face our problems today?

4. The power of hope. In his book *The Christ of the Centuries*, R. C. Campbell tells about a woman who was saved by hope.

The poor London woman was in such despair that she was determined to take her life by throwing herself into the Thames River. On her way down the street to end it all, she was distracted by a group of people who were looking in a store window. Curious, she stopped to see what they were looking at and discovered it was a painting by George Frederick Watts, titled, "Hope." In the painting, a woman is sitting limply atop a globe of the world clutching a lyre whose strings all but one are broken, but she will play her music as best she can on the only string there is.

The poor, despairing woman got the message as God spoke to her through the painting. She left the crowd and went to her home determined to do the best she could with what she had.

God's message of hope for tomorrow was given to Israel by Isaiah. Their salvation was at hand. A better day was dawning. That promise was particularly fulfilled for them when they returned from exile, but it was finally and fully fulfilled when the Messiah was born in Bethlehem.

5. Only God is eternal. From beginning to end, the Bible warns us that all living things die: plants, animals, people, you and I as well. Nothing escapes the Grim Reaper.

This is brought home forcefully to those who visit the study of General Robert E. Lee at Washington and Lee University. There everything is in place just as Lee left it when he left his study for the last time. His memory is one of the sweetest in the southland. He was a genius in battle, honored and loved by all who knew him, but he died as all men and women must, leaving his work unfinished.

When his funeral service was held, the great hymn "How Firm a Foundation" was sung, reminding all that we are mortal and only God is eternal.

The Israelites were reminded in our Scripture lesson that all things perish, "shall vanish away like smoke" but God and His salvation and righteousness shall abide forever (v. 6).

TEACHING THE BIBLE

▶ *Main Idea:* God's encouragement of His people shows that He cares when we are discouraged.

▶ *Suggested Teaching Aim:* To describe how God encouraged Israel, and to identify ways we can share God's encouragement with others.

A TEACHING OUTLINE

1. Introduce the Bible study by sharing an illustration.
2. Prepare a teaching outline poster.
3. Present a series of brief lectures on each outline point, followed by a discussion question.
4. Identify ways members were encouraged and choose a person they will seek to encourage this week.

Introduce the Bible Study

Share the illustration, "The power of hope" from "Applying the Bible" to introduce the lesson. Point to the title of the lesson on the unit poster you used last week and read the "Main Idea."

Search for Biblical Truth

Write the following teaching outline on a large sheet of paper and place it on the wall. Cover the points until you are ready to discuss them.

A Time of Encouragement

1. Look Back at the Past (Isa. 51:1–2)
2. Look Forward to the Future (51:3)
3. Look Inward at God's Permanence (51:4–6)

Uncover the first point. Ask a volunteer to read Isaiah 51:1–2. Give a brief lecture in which you cover the following:

(1) Isaiah 51:1 contains two commands: "hearken" and "look."

(2) Those who hearken must be willing to listen ("follow. . . seek") to God's Word.

(3) Remembering the "rock" from which we are "hewn" is a figurative way of calling us to remember who we are and whose we are.

(4) Remembering is important to the biblical faith.

DISCUSS: Why was Abraham such a good example of biblical faith?

Uncover the second point on the teaching outline. Present a brief lecture covering these points:

(1) Verses 1–2 called the people to look back and draw strength from their heritage; verse 3 calls them to look to the future to find encouragement for the present.

(2) God will turn a wilderness of wandering into a garden of Eden.

(3) Joy and gladness are results of God's comfort.

DISCUSS: What wilderness are you in that you would like God to turn into a garden?

Uncover the third point on the teaching outline. Present a brief lecture covering these points:

(1) Although addressed to Old Testament Israel, the promise applies to other nations who believe in God.

(2) God's law and justice would light all people.

(3) God's righteousness is near; His salvation has gone forth. This

has been fulfilled in Jesus.

(4) People in distant lands are waiting to hear the good news.
DISCUSS: What can you do to take the gospel to those who do not
know God?

Give the Truth a Personal Focus

Write *Encouraged* and *Discouraged* on a chalkboard or a large sheet
of paper. Ask members to think of a time when they were discouraged.
What helped them the most? the least? List these on the chalkboard or
sheet of paper. Let members suggest other steps they can take to encourage people. Ask: Who do you know who is discouraged? Based on
the "Encouraged" list, what can you do to help encourage this person?

Urge members to seek to encourage one person this week.

A Time of Joy

Basic Passage: Isaiah 9:1–7
Focal Passages: Isaiah 9:1–7

everal great times of divine intervention in the Bible began with the birth of a child. We think especially of the birth and deliverance of Moses (Exod. 2:1–10) and of the birth of Samuel (1 Sam. 1–2). Isaiah the prophet spoke of the birth of a child in passages like 7:14 and 9:6. However these prophecies may have been understood by Isaiah and the people of his day, Christians see the ultimate fulfillment in the birth of Jesus Christ. Matthew 1:21–23 quotes Isaiah 7:14 as fulfilled in the birth of Jesus. Isaiah 9:1–2 is quoted in Matthew 4:12–16 of the ministry of Jesus; and Christians consider Jesus to be the One whose name is "called Wonderful, Counsellor, The mighty God, The everlasting Father, The Prince of Peace" (Isa. 9:6).

▶ ▶ ▶ ▶ ▶ ▶ ▶ ▶ ▶ **Study Aim:** *To identify New Testament fulfillments of Isaiah 9:1–7*

STUDYING THE BIBLE

LESSON OUTLINE
  I. Light in the Darkness (Isa. 9:1–2)
    1. Galilee (Isa. 9:1)
    2. A great light (Isa. 9:2)
  II. The Joy of Victory and Peace (Isa. 9:3–5)
    1. Joy (Isa. 9:3)
    2. Victory (Isa. 9:4)
    3. Peace (Isa. 9:5)
  III. The Birth of a Child (Isa. 9:6–7)
    1. The child and His names (Isa. 9:6)
    2. His reign (Isa. 9:7)

The region of Galilee had often been the first to feel the enemy's fury, but God would reverse its fortunes (v. 1). Those who walked in darkness in the land of the shadow of death would see a great light from God (v. 2). They would experience a joy like a farmer's at harvest, and a solder's in victory (v. 3). God would grant His people a victory comparable to the victory over Midian in Gideon's time (v. 4). The bloody garments of warfare would be burned (v. 5). A child would be born whose reign and special names marked him as the divine Prince of Peace (v. 6). The fulfillment of God's promise to David would be accomplished by the zeal of the Lord of hosts (v. 7).

I. Light in the Darkness (Isa. 9:1–2)
1. Galilee (v. 1)
    1 Nevertheless the dimness shall not be such as was in her vexation, when at the first he lightly afflicted the land of Zebulun and

the land of Naphtali, and afterward did more grievously afflict her by the way of the sea, beyond Jordan, in Galilee of the nations.

The last few verses of chapter 8 refer to darkness coming as a result of the people's sins. Isaiah 8:19–20 refers to the fate of those who turn to spiritualists and fortunetellers and reject God's Word: "There is no light in them" (Isa. 8:20). When they face hunger and despair, they curse God; "and they shall be driven to darkness" (Isa. 8:22). The word "nevertheless" in Isaiah 9:1 shows that Isaiah was about to present a contrast to that spiritual darkness caused by sin.

Verse 1 refers to the northernmost part of the land of Israel. After the conquest, the tribes of Zebulun and Naphtali were settled in the northern part of the land of Canaan (Josh. 19:10–16, 32–39). At various times in history including the first century that area was called Galilee. Because of its exposed position, this northern region suffered from the raids and invasions of enemy nations. In Isaiah's day, the Assyrian Empire attacked Israel. The first area to be subjugated by the fierce and brutal Assyrians was the northern region.

By its proximity to Gentile nations, the region of Galilee was subject to more Gentile influence than the southern regions around Jerusalem. In fact, in the time of Jesus, the Jews of Jerusalem and Judea looked down on Galilean Jews (see John 7:41, 52; Acts 2:7).

Isaiah 9:1 predicted a reversal of fortunes for the region of Galilee. The following translation brings out this meaning: "Nevertheless, there will be no more gloom for those who were in distress. In the past he humbled the land of Zebulun and the land of Naphtali, but in the future he will honor Galilee of the Gentiles, by the way of the sea, along the Jordan" (NIV). This interpretation is consistent with the prediction of verse 2 that light would shine out of darkness; and it is consistent with the quotation of Isaiah 9:1–2 in Matthew 4:15–16.

When Jesus launched His Galilean ministry with Capernaum as His headquarters, Matthew saw this as a fulfillment of Isaiah 9:1–2.

The region that had so often suffered from the attacks of enemies and the ridicule of other Jews became the region favored by so much of Jesus' ministry.

2. A great light (v. 2)

2 The people that walked in darkness have seen a great light: they that dwell in the land of the shadow of death, upon them hath the light shined.

Darkness and light are familiar symbols in the Bible for evil and good, for sin and salvation. In a couple of weeks, we will look at another of Isaiah's familiar promises that uses these symbols: "Arise, shine; for thy light is come, and the glory of the Lord is risen upon thee" (Isa. 60:1). Isaiah 9:2 pictures people who walked in darkness in a land of the shadow of death. The joyous prophecy is that a great light would shine on them.

Although the emphasis in verse 1 is on the rays of light first shining in Galilee, verse 2 and the New Testament show that the rays of this light will extend to the ends of the earth. Jesus is the light of the world (John 8:12).

II. The Joy of Victory and Peace (Isa. 9:3–5)

1. Joy (v. 3)

3 Thou hast multiplied the nation, and not increased the joy: they joy before thee according to the joy in harvest, and as men rejoice when they divide the spoil.

The coming of light in the darkness of sin and death would result in joy. The prophet looked beyond the time when Israel was a small remnant to a time when God would increase the nation. Isaiah used two human analogies to illustrate the joy that God would give His people. It would be like the joy of the farmer in a bountiful harvest. It would also be like the joy of victory when the victors divide the spoils of the enemy.

Throughout much of this prophecy, Isaiah used tenses that usually refer to past actions. However, the prophets often used such tenses to communicate the certainty of the fulfillment of divine promises. The events were described as if they had already happened because they were sure to happen.

2. Victory (v. 4)

4 For thou hast broken the yoke of his burden, and the staff of his shoulder, the rod of his oppressor, as in the day of Midian.

Continuing the analogy of victory in warfare, Isaiah described God's deliverance of Israel from powerful enemies. The words "yoke," "staff," and "rod" all refer to subjection by an enemy. In actual history, both Israel and Judah fell before powerful enemies; however, the prophet knew that ultimate victory belongs to the Lord. Isaiah compared this future deliverance to the victory that God gave over Midian in the time of Gideon (see Judg. 6–7). The victory of Gideon was actually the victory of the Lord. Gideon was a reluctant leader. Only a handful of men were selected to attack the vast hosts of the Midianites. Just as God gave victory over Midian, so will He win the final battle over vast and powerful evil forces.

3. Peace (v. 5)

5 For every battle of the warrior is with confused noise, and garments rolled in blood; but this shall be with burning and fuel of fire.

Verse 5 continues the picture of victory from verses 3–4. The emphasis in verse 5 is on the peace that follows the victory. The verse describes the bloody garments of battle being burned in the fire. Compare this description with Isaiah 2:4, which predicts the coming age of peace by describing implements of war like swords and spears being remade into implements of peace like plowshares and pruning hooks.

III. The Birth of a Child (Isa. 9:6–7)

1. The child and His names (v. 6)

6 For unto us a child is born, unto us a son is given: and the government shall be upon his shoulder: and his name shall be called Wonderful, Counsellor, The mighty God, The everlasting Father, The Prince of Peace.

The background to Isaiah 9:6–7 and to the messianic hope in general was God's promise to David recorded in 2 Samuel 7:4–17. God promised that David's dynasty would continue forever. The word *messiah* means an anointed one. Since kings were anointed with oil in ancient Israel, *messiah* became synonymous with *king*. It was natural for the people of Israel to view this promise in earthly terms. Even in Jesus' day, this was the kind of messiah expected by most Jews. Some Bible students think that the prophet Isaiah had hoped that Hezekiah would be the fulfillment of Israel's hope for a messiah. Although Hezekiah proved to be one of Judah's best kings, his imperfections became all too apparent to the prophet especially toward the end of his life (see Isa. 39). Although some Bible scholars disagree, Isaiah 9:6 refers to something far more than another merely human king of David's line. The ultimate fulfillment surely fits only the kind of Messiah whom God sent into the world in the birth of Jesus. The names of the Child in verse 6 go beyond what mere humans might be, no matter how great. (Next month we will study Isaiah's prophecies of the Suffering Servant, which describe how the Messiah would fulfill His mission of salvation.)

2. His reign (v. 7)

7 Of the increase of his government and peace there shall be no end, upon the throne of David, and upon his kingdom, to order it, and to establish it with judgment and with justice from henceforth even for ever. The zeal of the Lord of hosts will perform this.

The Davidic descent of the coming King is made clear in verse 7. The scope of His realm will be great. The peace of His reign will be everlasting. The fruits of His reign other than peace will be justice and righteousness. When they heard this prophecy of Isaiah, the people of his day may well have asked, "How will this ever be possible?" The final sentence of verse 7 gives the answer: "The zeal of the Lord of hosts will perform this."

This truth is similar to the conversation of Mary with the angel Gabriel in Luke 1:26–38. After the angel announced to her that she was to bear a son to be called Jesus, Gabriel added: "He shall be great, and shall be called the Son of the Highest: and the Lord God shall give unto him the throne of his father David: And he shall reign over the house of Jacob for ever; and of his kingdom there shall be no end" (Luke 1:32–33). Mary asked, "How shall this be, seeing I know not a man?" (Luke 1:34). Gabriel answered, "The Holy Ghost shall come upon thee, and the power of the Highest shall overshadow thee: therefore also that holy thing which shall be born of thee shall be called the Son of God" (Luke 1:35).

God can do what is impossible from a human point of view. Isaiah did not understand how God would bring this great promise to fulfillment, but the prophet was sure that the Lord would be able to do it in His own way and in His own time. Isaiah trusted God to do what only God can do.

APPLYING THE BIBLE

1. Man's sin ruins everything. American historian Will Durant said that sin destroys everything it touches: We learned how to build airplanes and turned them into "Hellcat" fighter planes; discovered atomic energy and made bombs that will kill millions; invented machinery to lighten burdens in our factories and turned our cities into slums and our rivers into sewers; learned to make motion pictures and use them to demoralize womanhood and destroy moral values; and invented television that dumps filth into every American home. Is it any wonder then that the two monkeys who left the jungle to see how man lived could stand it only two hours and then rushed back to their jungle where they could find a bit of tranquility?[1]

2. Light. According to the *World Book Encyclopedia*, every living thing needs light to live, and the changing patterns of sunlight on the earth determine our seasons.

The light of the sun rules our daily lives. We work when it is light and rest when it is dark (or we used to!). Sunlight provides energy for all life, and without sunlight all living things would die because there would be nothing to eat. Also, sunlight deposited on the earth thousands of years ago has stored its energy in coal far below the earth's surface. When coal or oil are burned to produce light for our homes and factories, the light shines in our darkness because it was stored in the earth long ago. Now factories run day and night, even in the darkness, thanks to the sunlight. Light from the outer limits of the heavens takes millions of years to reach us, although it travels toward us at the speed of nearly six trillion miles a year. To better understand this, suppose a clock had been set ticking 32,000 years ago. From that time to this it would have ticked only about a million million times, but that is only one–sixth of the number of miles that light travels in one year.[2]

Physical light is both amazing and important. But how much more amazing and important is the spiritual light of God promised in verse 2 of today's lesson. The final fulfillment of this promise came to pass with the birth of our Lord Jesus, who is the Light of the world. Through His ministry and the Gospels which record it, "The people that walked in darkness have seen a great light!"

3. The promise of light fulfilled. Although we know verses 6–7 are a clear prophecy of the birth of the Messiah hundreds of years after Isaiah, the immediate application to the Jews of Isaiah's day was one of hope and encouragement. To them, "messiah" became synonymous with *king,* as our writer points out. Even in Jesus' day, the people expected a messiah who would deliver them from their problems and supply their immediate needs. But the final fulfillment of all the hopes bound up in the expected "Messiah" was in Jesus Christ, born in a manger in Bethlehem.

4. If Christ had not come. A group of historians once amused themselves by writing a book, titled, *If, or History Rewritten.* Some of the "ifs" they discussed were these: *if* Robert E. Lee had not lost the Battle of Gettysburg; *if* the Moors in Spain had not been defeated; *if* Booth's bullet had missed Lincoln; and *if* Napoleon had escaped to America.

But the greatest and most important *if* of history is this: What if Christ had not been born (John 15:22). It would be like imagining a day without sunrise, a sky with no sun, a world without water, or an earth with no abundant supply of food.³

But thanks be to God, He has come and, as Isaiah says in verse 6: "His name shall (be) called Wonderful, Counsellor, The mighty God, The everlasting Father, The Prince of Peace."

5. Only one gate. The ancient city of Troy (Troas) had only one gate: one way in and one way out. But that one gate was not adequate to keep out the invaders, and she fell and was destroyed.

There is only one way to the Father and heaven and that way is Jesus Christ (John 14:6). Through that one gate, multiplied millions of repentant sinners have passed to find forgiveness and life eternal.

As a result, His kingdom has spread from heart to heart, nation to nation, and today millions serve Him and call Him Lord. Truly, as verse 7 states: "Of the increase of his government and peace there shall be no end."

TEACHING THE BIBLE

▶ *Main Idea:* Isaiah's prophecies demonstrate that God does give hope and joy in the midst of conflict.
▶ *Suggested Teaching Aim:* To examine Isaiah's prophecies in 9:1–7, and to identify ways that Jesus' coming provides hope and joy to us.

A TEACHING OUTLINE

1. Use an illustration from "Applying the Bible" to introduce the lesson.
2. Use a map, lecture, a poster, and questions and answers to teach the lesson.
3. Use small groups to determine how Jesus' coming provides hope and joy to us today.

Introduce the Bible Study

Use "The promise of light fulfilled" in "Applying the Bible" to introduce the lesson. Locate the lesson title on the unit poster and read the "Main Idea." Ask members to describe the darkest situation physically or emotionally they ever experienced. Ask: What did you want when you were lost in the darkness? Point out that in our spiritual life, God provides us light through Jesus.

Search for Biblical Truth

On a map showing the tribal claims, locate Zebulun [ZEB yoo luhn] and Naphtali [NAF tuh ligh]. Point out that Nazareth, where Jesus grew up, lay in what had been the territory of Zebulun.

Use "Studying the Bible" to summarize briefly the background of chapter 8 and how it prepares the way for the "Nevertheless" in 9:1.

Ask members why they think Naphtali and Zebulun would have been attacked often by foreign armies. Explain that in Isaiah's day the

Assyrian army had attacked the Northern Kingdom and that the first area to be conquered was the northern region. Briefly summarize the commentary on 9:1 in "Studying the Bible."

Ask a volunteer to read 9:2–5. Point out that God was going to bring joy to the people who had been afflicted. Ask: To what did Isaiah compare the joy the people would experience (9:3)? (Joy of harvest and dividing spoils.) To what historical event did Isaiah refer in 9:4? (Gideon.) Why was this a good comparison?

On a chalkboard or a large sheet of paper write:

(1) The Child and His Names (9:6)

(2) His Reign (9:7)

Use "Studying the Bible" to give a brief overview of who Isaiah may have understood the child to be. Ask members to look at 9:6 and to list all the names for the Child. List these on the poster. Point out that the names of the Child describe someone far beyond human strength; only Jesus can ultimately fulfill this prophecy.

Ask: What is the scope of the coming King's reign? (Unlimited.) How long will peace last? (Everlasting.) What are the fruits of His reign? (Peace, justice, righteousness.) What is the certainty of His reign? (Zeal of the Lord.)

Give the Truth a Personal Focus

Organize the class into three groups and make the following assignments:

Group 1: Isaiah 9:1–2
Group 2: Isaiah 9:3–5
Group 3: Isaiah 9:6–7

Ask the groups to search their assigned Scripture to see how many New Testament references they can find. After four to five minutes call for reports.

Then ask the same groups to identify ways Jesus' coming provides hope and joy to us. Close in a prayer of thanksgiving for God's wonderful Son.

---

1. J. Wallace Hamilton. *Ride the Wild Horses* (Old Tappan, N.J.: Fleming H. Revell, 1962) 70.

2. *World Book Encyclopedia*, vol. 12 (Chicago: Field Enterprises, 1950), 248–55.

3. Clarence F. Macartney. *Macartney's Illustrations* (New York, Nashville: Abingdon–Cokesbury Press, 1955), 52.

A Time of Righteousness and Peace

Basic Passage: Isaiah 11:1–9; Luke 2:1–20
Focal Passages: Isaiah 11:1–6; Luke 2:10–14

In this study of Isaiah, the passages for December 17 and 24 have been selected because of their relation to our celebration of the birth of Jesus Christ. Isaiah 9:1–7 and 11:1–9 are strong passages about the Messiah. The emphasis in Isaiah 11:1–9 is on the personal characteristics of the coming King. Along with this passage, we will study the story of the birth of Jesus in Luke 2:1–20.

▶ ▶ ▶ ▶ **Study Aim:** *To celebrate the birth of Jesus in light of biblical teachings*

STUDYING THE BIBLE

LESSON OUTLINE
I. A Prophecy of the Messiah (Isa. 11:1–9)
  1. Branch of Jesse (Isa. 11:1)
  2. The Spirit of the Lord (Isa. 11:2)
  3. Righteous Judge (Isa. 11:3–5)
  4. Reign of peace (Isa. 11:6–9)
II. The Birth of the Savior (Luke 2:1–20)
  1. The birth of Jesus (Luke 2:1–7)
  2. The announcement to the shepherds (Luke 2:8–14)
  3. The shepherds' response (Luke 2:15–20)

God promised that a green sprout would come forth from the roots of the stump of Jesse, David's father (Isa. 11:1). He would be endowed with the Spirit of the Lord and with all the qualities of that Spirit (Isa. 11:2). He would become a righteous Judge, who provides justice and deliverance for the poor and who condemns the wicked by His righteous word (vv. 3–5). His reign of peace will mean that nature will be remade and the whole earth will be filled with the knowledge of God (Isa. 11:6–9).

Mary and Joseph went to Bethlehem to be taxed, and there Jesus was born and laid in a manger (Luke 2:1–7). The angels announced to shepherds the good news of the Savior's birth, which means glory to God and joy and peace to those who are the objects of God's grace (Luke 2:8–14). The shepherds saw the newborn King and told the good news, while Mary treasured in her heart all that had happened (Luke 2:15–20).

I. A Prophecy of the Messiah (Isa. 11:1–9)

1. Branch of Jesse (v. 1)

1 And there shall come forth a rod out of the stem of Jesse, and a Branch shall grow out of his roots.

Isaiah 10:12–34 contrasts the arrogant strength of the Assyrians with the weakness of the remnant of Israel. The prophet predicted that the mighty cedar forest of Assyrian might would be cut down. Isaiah 11:1 is set against that background. Verse 1 compared the ruling house of Judah to the stump of a tree, from the roots of which would come a green sprout. The green sprout is a sign that the roots have life that will be renewed.

God had promised David an everlasting kingdom; however, after the exile, Judah had no ruling king of David's line. The birth of Jesus of David's line fulfilled that promise. The name of Jesse, David's father, was used in verse 1 to show that only God's power could reconstitute the line of David and fulfill the promise.

2. The Spirit of the Lord (v. 2)

2 And the spirit of the Lord shall rest upon him, the spirit of wisdom and understanding, the spirit of counsel and might, the spirit of knowledge and of the fear of the Lord.

Isaiah predicted that the Spirit of the Lord would rest on the Messiah in a special way. The results of the Spirit's presence were described in three pairs of characteristics. He would have special wisdom and understanding. He would provide good counsel and provide the power to accomplish the counsel. He would magnify the knowledge and fear of the Lord.

Jesus was conceived by the Holy Spirit (Luke 1:35). The Spirit descended on Him in a special way at His baptism (Luke 3:22). When Jesus began His ministry, He quoted Isaiah 61:1, "The Spirit of the Lord is upon me" (Luke 4:18).

3. Righteous Judge (vv. 3–5)

3 And shall make him of quick understanding in the fear of the Lord: and he shall not judge after the sight of his eyes, neither reprove after the hearing of his ears:

4 But with righteousness shall he judge the poor, and reprove with equity for the meek of the earth: and he shall smite the earth with the rod of his mouth, and with the breath of his lips shall he slay the wicked.

5 And righteousness shall be the girdle of his loins, and faithfulness the girdle of his reins.

The Old Testament instructed judges to be impartial and to base their judgments on righteousness and truth. Unfortunately, the prophets had to condemn judges for taking bribes to favor the wealthy and powerful. The poor and meek often were falsely condemned. Therefore, Isaiah 11:3–5 was good news to poor and oppressed people. The Messiah would base His judgments not on outward appearances (v. 3). Instead He would provide justice for the poor and meek; and He would condemn the wicked with His word (v. 4). He would be girded with righteousness and truth (v. 5).

4. Reign of peace (vv. 6–9)

> 6 The wolf also shall dwell with the lamb, and the leopard shall lie down with the kid; and the calf and the young lion and the fatling together; and a little child shall lead them.

The righteous reign of the Messiah will result in an age of peace. Isaiah describes this time of peace in various ways in his prophecies. People will turn their implements of war into implements of peace (2:4). They will burn the bloody garments of warfare (9:5). Nature itself will be remade so that predatory beasts like wolves, leopards, and lions will abide in peace with their former prey; and a little child will lead them all (11:6).

Verses 7–9 elaborate on this picture of peace. The reason for the new earth is stated in verse 9: "The earth shall be full of the knowledge of the Lord, as the waters cover the sea."

II. The Birth of the Savior (Luke 2:1–20)

1. The birth of Jesus (vv. 1–7). Luke's account of the birth of Jesus is the most familiar biblical account. Many Christians have memorized these beautiful and powerful words. Prior to chapter 2 is the account of the announcement to Mary of the miracle to be wrought in her by the Holy Spirit (1:26–38). Matthew 1:18–25 supplements Luke's account by telling how God revealed to Joseph the miracle of the conception and birth. His name would be Jesus, for He would save His people from their sins (v. 21). He would be the virgin-born Emmanuel of Isaiah 7:14 (v. 23).

Luke 2:1–5 explains how it was that Joseph and Mary happened to be in Bethlehem when Jesus was born. Verses 6–7 explain how it was that Jesus came to be born in a manger.

2. The announcement to the shepherds (vv. 8–14). In the time of Jesus, shepherds were of the lower social and economic strata of society. God chose to announce the birth of His Son to shepherds on a hillside, not in the homes of the rich and famous (v. 8). The shepherds were understandably afraid when suddenly "the glory of the Lord shone round about them" (v. 9).

> 10 And the angel said unto them, Fear not: for, behold, I bring you good tidings of great joy, which shall be to all people.

The word translated "bring good tidings" in verse 10 is often translated "preach the gospel" (see Luke 4:18). The word was used in the first century of someone telling good news. Likewise the noun usually translated "gospel" means "good news" (see Mark 1:1,14; 1 Cor. 15:1). These words were used in the first century of all kinds of good news that people told to one another. The Lord chose this ordinary word to announce the best of all the good news this tired old world has ever heard.

The angel announced good news of "great joy." The Old Testament pointed to a coming age of joy (Isa. 9:3). The angel announced to the shepherds that the promised time of joy had dawned.

From a small group of shepherds on a hillside near Bethlehem, the good news was designed by God "for all people." In our study of Isaiah, we have noted the predictions of a worldwide scope of the Messiah's work (see Isa. 11:9; 40:5; 51:4–5). The rest of the Gospel of Luke and the Book of Acts show how the angel's words were fulfilled. The mission of Paul and others to Gentiles was based on God's eternal plan.

11 For unto you is born this day in the city of David a Saviour, which is Christ the Lord.

12 And this shall be a sign unto you; ye shall find the babe wrapped in swaddling clothes, lying in a manger.

The good news of great joy for all people was the coming of the One who was born that day. Jesus was born in the city of David as a sign that He was the Messiah who fulfilled God's promise to David of an everlasting kingdom. Each of the three titles in verse 11 is significant. "Saviour" means that He came to save people from sin and death. "Christ" is the Greek version of the Hebrew "Messiah." "Lord" was a common title used by Gentiles of their gods or their rulers, and by the Jews of their God. Jesus Christ the Savior is Lord in the sense of being God's Son with sovereignty over all things.

The shepherds were told that the circumstances in which they would find the newborn King would be a sign to them of the truth of the angel's announcement. He would be found wrapped in strips of cloths and lying in an animal's feeding trough.

13 And suddenly there was with the angel a multitude of the heavenly host praising God, and saying,

14 Glory to God in the highest, and on earth peace, good will toward men.

The first heavenly messenger was alone; but after the announcement of verses 10–12, the angel was joined by a huge heavenly choir. They were praising God for what He was doing in sending His Son to be the Savior.

Their words of praise focused on two fruits of this great event: glory and peace. To give glory to God is to praise and magnify God for who He is and what He has done. Another way to put it is this: to glorify God is to make His reputation equal to His character. In the eyes of many people, God's reputation is unworthy of who God really is. When people come to see and know God as He truly is, He is glorified. The sending of His Son shows who God is and what He is like (John 3:16).

God is to be glorified for His gift of peace. The word translated "good will" is used in the Bible of God's good will to people, not of humanity's good will. Thus the idea is not that God has sent His peace for a select group of people of good will. The good news is that God has given His peace as a gift of His grace or good will toward people of all kinds. Peace, like joy, is a fruit of God's grace in sending His Son.

3. The shepherds' response (vv. 15–20). The shepherds showed themselves to be worthy of the honor of being the first to hear the good news of the Savior's birth. They decided to obey the directions of the angel and went and found Mary, Joseph, and the newborn

King (vv. 15–16). Not only were they the first humans to hear the good news; but they also became the first humans to tell the good news to others. They spread the good news of what they had seen and heard that night (v. 17). Those who heard the shepherds' story wondered at what they had been told (v. 18). As for Mary, she treasured in her heart all that had happened (v. 19). Meanwhile, the shepherds glorified and praised God for what they had seen and heard (v. 20).

APPLYING THE BIBLE

1. A root out of dry ground (53:2). One of the memorable works of Michelangelo stands in a park in the ancient city of Florence, Italy. Known as *David Slaying Goliath*, it is a work of beauty, grace, and strength. David, the young shepherd, stands poised to hurl the stone from his sling that would kill Goliath and deliver Saul's army.

But Michelangelo carved this most striking marble work from stone that had been discarded. He took unlikely material and from it created a masterpiece.

Isaiah 11:1, at which we are looking today, "contrasts the strength of the Assyrians with the weakness of the remnant of Israel," as our writer points out. But from that "stump of a tree," a most unlikely source, God would bring forth the Messiah who would save His people from their sins. At that time in Israel's history it seemed "the stem of David" was lifeless and utterly impotent, but in time God would bring forth from David's seed the divine "Branch" Jesus Christ.

2. Christ is all things to us. In his book *The Must of the Second Birth,* the late R. G. Lee shows us that Christ is all things to those who trust and love him: "To keep Christ out of your life is like taking heat out of fire, melody out of music, color out of rainbows, numbers out of mathematics, water out of the ocean, mind out of metaphysics, sap out of trees, [and] all light out of day."

Continuing, Lee wrote: "Christ is the power of God to guide you; the might of God to uphold you; the wisdom of God to teach you; the eye of God to watch over you; the ear of God to hear you; the Word of God to give you speech; the hand of God to protect you; the shield of God to shelter you; and the host of God to defend you."[1]

Writing long before the birth of Jesus, Isaiah said the same thing: He is our Wisdom, our Counsellor, our Strength, and our Teacher (v. 2).

3. Hope for a nobody. Missionary Howard Thurman, Elizabeth Yates tells us in her book about the dedicated missionary-preacher, once visited India and met a poor, little boy from one of the villages. That night after the Thurmans had gone to bed, there was a timid knock at their door.

It was the little boy, one of India's "untouchables." Politely, he said, "I listened to your words tonight and have come to ask you if you can give hope to a nobody?"

Falling on his knees before Thurman, the boy listened quietly as the missionary told him about the sweet Savior who specializes in giving hope to the world's nobodies.

4. A king without a crown. Scottish evangelist-author Henry Drummond, perhaps best remembered for his masterful little book, *The Greatest Thing in the Word* (a study of 1 Cor. 13), once said: "There are so many more mysteries on the outside of the Bible than there are in it, that I have ceased to worry over those in it." And the greatest of all these mysteries is told in the Christmas story: how God became man in Jesus Christ.

Author Guy King relates that on one occasion it was announced that King George V of England (1865–1936) would visit a certain hospital in London. There was special excitement in the children's ward, as one might expect.

At about four o'clock in the afternoon the matron brought in a small group of visitors, one of whom was ever so kind, who patted the children on the head and spoke gently to them.

One little boy was sorely disappointed because he felt he had missed seeing the king. Expressing his disappointment to one of the aides, the little fellow said, "But the king didn't come."

"Why, sonny," she replied, "don't you remember the gentleman who patted you on the head and spoke kindly to you? That was the king."

"But he didn't have his crown on," the little boy exclaimed.[2]

When the promised Messiah was born in Bethlehem, He didn't have on His crown. But, nonetheless, He was and is the King of Kings and Lord of Lords whose birthday we will celebrate tomorrow (Luke 2:1–20).

5. The humble birth of Jesus. When other notables have been born, their advent has been marked by the roar of guns, or by great strains of music, or by the waving of flags. But when Jesus was born there was no demonstration of earthly honor. He was born to a poor, unknown peasant couple, in a borrowed barn, and welcomed by humble shepherds from the fields. But, remember, that great hearts often beat beneath the garb of poverty!

TEACHING THE BIBLE

▶ *Main Idea:* The Old Testament predicts the birth of Jesus as described in the New Testament.

▶ *Suggested Teaching Aim:* To lead adults to examine Isaiah's prophecies of Jesus' birth, and to identify ways we experience His peace.

A TEACHING OUTLINE

1. Introduce the lesson with an illustration.

2. Organize members into three groups to examine the Old Testament passage.

3. Use the same three groups to examine the New Testament passage.

4. Use a creative drawing exercise and music to close the session.

Introduce the Bible Study

Introduce the lesson by sharing "Hope for a nobody" from "Applying the Bible." Point out that hope is the reason for Christmas.

Search for Biblical Truth

Point out the lesson on the unit poster and read the "Main Idea."

Present a three-minute lecture in which you cover the background of Isaiah 11:1 based on "Studying the Bible." Organize the class into three groups and make the following assignments (or do this activity as a group):

Group 1: Branch (Isa. 11:1)
Group 2: Spirit (Isa. 11:2)
Group 3: Judge (Isa. 11:3–5)

Ask groups to explain their word in the setting of their verse.

Ask a volunteer to read Isaiah 11:6 and another to read Luke 2:14. Ask members to listen for the idea that runs through these two passages of Scripture that ties them together. (*Peace.*)

Ask members to keep their same groups and make the following assignments:

Group 1: Sign (Luke 2:11–12)
Group 2: Joy (Luke 2:10)
Group 3: Peace (Luke 2:13–14)

Ask members to compare and contrast their assignment from Luke with their previous verse from Isaiah. Point out that while the verses are not intended as a direct parallel, the Old Testament passages can give a fuller meaning to the New Testament passages; the reverse is also true.

Allow about five minutes for study and then call for reports.

DISCUSS: How does Isaiah's precise prophecy add meaning to the birth of Jesus for us today?

Give the Truth a Personal Focus

Remind members of the stump image Isaiah used. Point out that the setting of this passage is so important because it came at a time when everything appeared to be hopeless. At that moment, God reminded His people that He had not forgotten them.

Ask the three groups to discuss ways they have experienced God's peace. Give each group a large sheet of paper and colored markers. Ask them to draw their concept of peace and share it with the class, along with ways they have experienced God's peace.

As an alternate activity, ask members to write a carol about peace. Suggest that they select a familiar tune and sing it for the class.

Close by singing "I Heard the Bells on Christmas Day" (No. 98, *The Baptist Hymnal*, 1991). Assure members that there is hope for them and for all people in Jesus Christ.

---

1. R. G. Lee, *The Must of the Second Birth*, (Westwood, N.J.: Fleming H. Revell 1959), 50.

2. Guy King, *Salvation Symphony* (London: Marshall, Morgan and Scott LTD, 1946), 20–21.

A Time for Sharing Good News

Focal Passage: Isaiah 60–61
Focal Passages: Isaiah 60:1–4; 61:1–4

A number of themes are intertwined throughout the Book of Isaiah. We have been looking at some of these: comfort, encouragement, joy, righteousness, peace, good news. Although each lesson title during December has focused on one or two of these, most of the passages contain all or most of these themes. This is surely true of Isaiah 60–61. The emphasis is on telling good news, but the passages contain most of the other themes.

▶ ▶ ▶ ▶ ▶ ▶ ▶ ▶ **Study Aim:** *To discover what we can learn from Isaiah 60–61 about our opportunities to share good news*

STUDYING THE BIBLE

LESSON OUTLINE
 I. Let Your Light Shine (Isa. 60:1–22)
  1. Reflecting the light of God's glory (Isa. 60:1–2)
  2. Results of the coming of light (Isa. 60:3–14)
  3. The everlasting light (Isa. 60:15–22)
 II. Messenger and Message of Good News (Isa. 61:1–11)
  1. Messenger and message (Isa. 61:1–3)
  2. Everlasting covenant (Isa. 61:4–11)

Zion was told to arise and shine with the reflected light of God's glory (60:1–2). As a result, Gentiles would be attracted to the light and Jews would return (60:3–14). The light of God's glory would become an everlasting light (60:15–22). The One anointed with God's Spirit would tell the good news and minister to the deepest needs of hurting people (61:1–3). God would make an everlasting covenant with His priestly people (61:4–11).

I. Let Your Light Shine (Isa. 60:1–22)

1. Reflecting the light of God's glory (vv. 1–2)
 1 Arise, shine; for thy light is come, and the glory of the Lord is risen upon thee.
 2 For, behold, the darkness shall cover the earth, and gross darkness the people: but the Lord shall arise upon thee, and his glory shall be seen upon thee.
These verses paint a picture of darkness over all the earth. The prophet was looking into the future and foreseeing a time when God's light would pierce through the darkness. The light is described as rising like the sun, but this light is not the sun. This light is the glory of the

Lord. Isaiah 60:19 gives further insight into this light: "The sun shall be no more thy light by day; neither for brightness shall the moon give light unto thee: but the Lord shall be unto thee an everlasting light, and thy God thy glory." The final chapters of Isaiah have much in common with the closing chapters of the Book of Revelation. For example, Revelation 21:23 uses language like that in Isaiah 60 to describe the new Jerusalem in the new heaven and new earth.

The word *glory* in the Old Testament referred to the majesty of the presence and power of God. The glory of God is often described in connection with the tabernacle and the temple (Exod. 40:34–35; 1 Kings 8:11). Although no building could contain the God of all the earth, God chose to reveal Himself in a special way in the midst of His people. Ezekiel described how the people continued to sin against the Lord, even turning the temple into a place of pagan worship. Ezekiel described how the glory of God left the temple (Ezek. 10:4,18; 11:2–23), but the prophet also promised that the glory of God would return (Ezek. 43:1–5).

The New Testament uses both words: "light" and "glory" of Jesus Christ (John 1:14; 8:12). Thus in the new Jerusalem, "the Lamb is the light thereof" (Rev. 21:23).

Isaiah 60 is addressed to the future Zion or Jerusalem. Verse 1 begins with two imperatives. First, Zion was told to arise. The word shows that Zion had fallen on hard times and was crushed to the earth. God called her to arise, much as Jesus called those whom He healed to arise (see Mark 5:41; Luke 7:14). The word called for faith and obedience, but the command also showed that God would give the strength to arise.

Shine is used in a way similar to Matthew 5:16: "Let your light so shine before men, that they may see your good works, and glorify your Father which is in heaven." Believers are the "light of the world" (Matt. 5:14) only in the sense of reflecting the light of Him who is the ultimate Light of the world. In the same way, Zion is to shine by reflecting the light of the glory of the Lord which arises upon her.

2. Results of the coming of light (vv. 3–14)

3 And the Gentiles shall come to thy light, and kings to the brightness of thy rising.

4 Lift up thine eyes round about, and see: all they gather themselves together, they come to thee: thy sons shall come from far, and thy daughters shall be nursed at thy side.

The arising of the light of God's glory on Zion would result in Gentiles coming to the light. They would be attracted by it. In our recent study of the Book of Acts, we saw how the good news was shared with and accepted by Gentiles.

Verse 4 describes Zion as a mother unto whom her sons and daughters return from afar. This is one of many Old Testament descriptions of the restoration of Israel. Some of these promises were fulfilled in the return from Babylonian exile, but many refer to a restoration in the Messianic Age.

Verses 5–9 elaborate on the joy of Zion at the return of her sons and daughters and the coming of Gentiles. Zion would watch the Gentiles stream to her (v. 5). They bring flocks and herds, gold and incense and offer them to the Lord (v. 6–7). Many come in ships, bringing themselves and wealth from afar (vv. 8–9).

Verses 10–14 show how Gentiles would serve in Zion. Strangers would build her walls (v. 10). The gates of Zion would remain open day and night (v. 11; this is another picture of the new Jerusalem in Rev. 21:25.) Those who continue to resist the Lord would face judgment (v. 12). The sanctuary would be beautified (v. 13). Even those that afflicted Zion would join others in calling her: "The city of the Lord, The Zion of the Holy One of Israel" (v. 14).

3. The everlasting light (vv. 15–22). Although forsaken and hated, Zion would be made a joy forever (v. 15). Zion would know that the Lord is Redeemer and Savior (v. 16). Peace and righteousness would characterize Zion (v. 17). Her walls would be called salvation and her gates praise (v. 18). The Lord would be in her an everlasting light (vv. 19–20). The righteous people would inherit the land forever (v. 21). The Lord would being this to pass in His own time (v. 22).

Students of the Bible recognize the similarities between the future Zion of Isaiah 60 and the new Jerusalem of Revelation 21:23–26. The new Jerusalem will have no need for the sun or moon because the Lord will be the light (v. 23). The gates will remain open (v. 25). The Gentiles will be among the saved who bring their glory and honor to the new Jerusalem (vv. 24, 26).

II. Messenger and Message of Good News (Isa. 61:1–11)

1. Messenger and message (vv. 1–3)

1 The spirit of the Lord God is upon me; because the Lord hath anointed me to preach good tidings unto the meek; he hath sent me to bind up the brokenhearted, to proclaim liberty to the captives, and the opening of the prison to them that are bound;

2 To proclaim the acceptable year of the Lord, and the day of vengeance of our God; to comfort all that mourn.

Christians immediately recognize this as the passage that Jesus read in the synagogue at Nazareth. He identified Himself and the ministry He had come to perform as the ultimate fulfillment of Isaiah's prophecy (Luke 4:17–21).

We cannot know how clearly the prophet understood the ultimate fulfillment of his inspired prophecies. Sometimes prophecies had an immediate application as well as an ultimate fulfillment. Some students of the Old Testament think that the prophet spoke of himself as anointed with God's Spirit for the purpose of telling God's good news. Other Old Testament students think that the prophet had in mind the Servant mentioned in a number of other passages in the closing chapters of Isaiah. We will study several of these passages in January, ending with the most famous description of the Suffering Servant in Isaiah 52:13–53:12.

Although the word *servant* is not used in Isaiah 61, the description of the One anointed with the Spirit is similar to the description of the

Servant as One upon whom God placed His Spirit (Isa. 42:1). In last week's lesson, we saw how the Messiah was described in the same way (see comments on Isa. 11:2).

The first task of the One anointed with the Spirit was to proclaim the good news to the meek or poor. Many ancient prophets and all Christian witnesses have been called to tell the good news in the name of the Lord. The good news we tell is centered in Jesus Christ. He is more than a Spirit-filled prophet telling good news; He Himself is the good news. The rest of Isaiah 61:1–2 describes various aspects of the good news He makes possible.

First, He exemplified these things in His ministry and made them possible through His mission of salvation. He came to heal the broken-hearted, to liberate prisoners, to comfort those who mourn. His death and resurrection provided salvation from the sin and death that impris-ons and destroys.

3 To appoint unto them that mourn in Zion, to give unto them beauty for ashes, the oil of joy for mourning, the garment of praise for the spirit of heaviness; that they might be called trees of righteousness, the planting of the Lord, that he might be glori-fied.

The words of verse 3 are not in Luke's account of what Jesus read from Isaiah 61; however, Jews often quoted only a part of a familiar passage when they had the whole passage in mind. Whether this was true of Jesus in quoting Isaiah 61:1–2, verse 3 reinforces the message of the first two verses. The result of the Lord's ministry was and is on peo-ple who hurt. He came to replace mourning with joy and heaviness with praise. The work of the Lord in our lives results in righteousness that glorifies the Lord.

Because the New Testament makes Christlikeness the goal of every believer, we are called to tell the good news and to perform a caring ministry to people who hurt. Notice the words in verses 1–3 that de-scribe people of every age, including our own. Many mourn and are brokenhearted. Many are enslaved and imprisoned. Christ came to meet their needs. They all need to hear the good news. They all need His caring touch. He wants to work through us to do just that.

2. Everlasting covenant (vv. 4–11)

4 And they shall build the old wastes, they shall raise up the former desolations, and they shall repair the waste cities, the desolations of many generations.

Verse 4 returns to the language of exile and of restoration to the land. The wasted ruins of the past would be rebuilt. In the new order of things, people of other nations would tend flocks (v. 5). God's people would perform their God-ordained role as priests in His name (v. 6; see Exod. 19:6; 1 Pet. 2:9; Rev. 1:6). Their former shame would be replaced with everlasting joy (v. 7). God would recompense them for the former wrongs done to them, and He would make with them an everlasting covenant (v. 8). They would be known far and wide as the people whom the Lord has blessed (v. 9). The contemplation of such glory caused the prophet to break forth into joyful thanksgiving (v. 10). God's salvation is as certain as the earthly process of sowing and growing (v. 11).

APPLYING THE BIBLE

1. God is still alive and at work. When Evangelist John Wesley came down for breakfast one morning, his wife immediately sensed he was not in good spirits. Going upstairs, she dressed in black and came back down to join him. "Who is dead?" Wesley asked when he saw her somber dress. "God is dead," his wife announced sadly. "Oh, no! That is not so," Wesley exclaimed. "From your countenance and attitude, I assumed He was," she replied.

Isaiah assures his people, who have been severely tested by their trials, that God is still alive and active among them, and calls upon them to respond joyously and faithfully to His presence and promises.
Although our burdens may be heavy, our days trying and our nights full of despair, our blessed Lord calls us to respond joyfully to His presence among us. This is no time to give up! We are to "arise, shine; for thy light is come and the glory of the Lord is risen upon thee" (60:1). What optimism this gives to life!

2. Lights are made to shine. Jesus told us that we must not put our light under a bushel. We are His light, appointed to serve Him and shine in a dark world.

Bishop Gerald Kennedy of California related an experience of his friend Bishop Trice Taylor. Once when Taylor was in Liberia, he was visited by an old chief who said, "We believe in God, but sometimes He is so far away it seems. Today, you be God for us."

Augustine said that God became man that man might become like God. Certainly, we know we cannot be God to any person, but we understand the spirit in which the Liberian chief made his request. But we can be like God, through Christ, and let His light shine out to others through us. And that's what Isaiah calls God's people to be and do (vv. 1–2).

3. The good news is for everyone. The good news of God's grace was first proclaimed to the Jews, as the Book of Acts shows us. But the good news of God's grace is for everyone and is too great to be confined to one race or people.

When Adoniram Judson, the first American missionary to sail from America's shores, was offered the position as the associate pastor to Dr. Griffin, pastor of the largest church in New England, Judson refused.

His parents urged Judson to accept the position, pleading, "You will be so near home." But young Judson replied, "I shall never live near Boston. I have much farther to go."

The good news of the Savior's birth, death, and resurrection would first be declared to the nation of Israel. But it would only begin there, and had much farther to go, even extending to the hated Gentiles (vv. 3–4).

On the day of Pentecost this prophecy was fulfilled, at least in part. Acts 2 shows the gospel being preached both to Jews and Gentiles and then being carried into all the Mediterranean world as the travelers, who had come from afar to Jerusalem, returned to their homes bearing the good news.

4. The nail-scarred hand. B. B. McKinney was perhaps the most-beloved and best-known music director produced by Southern Baptists.

In the early 1920s, McKinney was on the music faculty of Southwestern Seminary, in Fort Worth, when he was invited to lead the music for a Sunday School conference to be held in the small town of Allen, Texas, about fifty miles northeast of Fort Worth.

During the invitation that followed the message, the preacher urged the unbelievers to place their hand in the nail-scarred hand of Jesus. Impressed by the plea, McKinney wrote the preacher's words on an envelope he had in his pocket. Going to his room, McKinney wrote both the words and music of the song by that title. Often we have sung his song:

> *Have you failed in your plan*
> *of your storm tossed life?*
> *Place your hand in the nail-scarred hand;*
> *Are you weary and worn from its*
> *toil and strife?*
> *Place your hand in the nail-scarred hand.*[1]

Isaiah no doubt did not fully understand all the future implications of what he was telling the people of Israel, but we know today for we have the full revelation in Jesus Christ. In verses 1–3, Isaiah writes about the future and the day when "good tidings" would be preached to the meek and broken hearted. It is an ancient promise with an eternal application: it is by placing our hand in the nail-scarred hand of Jesus that spiritual prisons are opened to sinners and broken hearts are healed. Jesus applied this prophecy of Isaiah to Himself (61:1–3), telling the people of Nazareth: "This day is this scripture fulfilled in your ears" (Luke 4:17–21).

5. "Life with Christ is an endless hope, without Him a hopeless end." Anonymous.

TEACHING THE BIBLE

▶ *Main Idea:* God's instructions to Zion demonstrate that His people are to take every opportunity to share the good news.
▶ *Suggested Teaching Aim:* To lead adults to examine God's charges to Zion, and to identify opportunities they have to share the good news.

A TEACHING OUTLINE

1. Use an illustration to introduce the lesson.
2. Examine how three words are used in the Old and New Testament.
3. Identify the actions and results in Isaiah 61:1–4.
4. Identify ways members can share good news.

Introduce the Bible Study
Introduce the lesson by sharing "The good news is for everyone" in

"Applying the Bible." Point to the unit poster and read the "Main Idea" of the lesson.

Search for Biblical Truth

Make the following poster:

Reflecting the Light of God's Glory
Isaiah 60:1–4

Old Testament   **New Testament**
Light
Glory
Shine

Organize the class into three groups. Assign each group one of the words. Ask them to search Isaiah 60:1–4 to find how their word or concept is used. After three to four minutes, call for reports.

Then ask the same groups to consider how these same three words apply to Jesus and/or His followers in the New Testament. (See "Studying the Bible" for this information.) Encourage members to use their cross-reference Bibles and to think of ways the New Testament used these words. After three to four minutes, call for reports.

Ask members to turn to Isaiah 61:1–4. Present a brief lecture using the information in "Studying the Bible" to identify the person referred to in these verses. Explain that many prophecies had an immediate and an ultimate fulfillment. In this passage, the ultimate fulfillment can only be fulfilled by Jesus. Ask members to find all the words that describe actions (verbs) of the Messenger.

Action	Result
Anointed	to preach
Preach	good tidings
Sent	bind up
Bind Up	brokenhearted
Proclaim	liberty to captives
Open	the prisons
Proclaim	acceptable year of the Lord
Comfort	all the mourners
Appoint	to them who mourn
Give	beauty for ashes, oil of joy, garment of praise, wastes

Read Luke 4:17–21 and point out that Jesus chose these verses from Isaiah to describe His ministry.

Give the Truth a Personal Focus

Ask members to read Isaiah 61:1–3 and interpret the *me* in (61:1) as themselves. Ask them to suggest ways they can fulfill these actions in the name of Christ. For example, how has God anointed them to preach? To whom can they preach good news?

As members suggest ideas, write them on the above poster under *Result.* Read the "Suggested Teaching Aim" and encourage members to accept that God has called all believers to be messengers of His good news. Point out the many different ways God's messengers can share the good news. Close in prayer that members will take this lesson seriously.

---

1. © Copyright 1924. Renewal 1952 Broadman Press (SESAC). All rights reserved.

The Servant's Call

Basic Passage: Isaiah 42:1–9
Focal Passage: Isaiah 42:1–9

I n the earlier chapters of Isaiah are several prophecies of the Messiah (9:1–7; 11:1–9). In the latter part of Isaiah are a number of prophecies of the Servant of the Lord. In several of these, Israel is identified as the servant of the Lord (Isa. 41:8–9). At other times, the Servant is presented as an individual. Christians see Jesus Christ as the perfect Servant of the Lord. Isaiah 42:1–4, for example, is quoted in Matthew 12:17–21 as being fulfilled in Jesus and His ministry.

▶ ▶ ▶ ▶ ▶ ▶ ▶ ▶ ▶ **Study Aim:** *To describe the Servant's call*

STUDYING THE BIBLE

LESSON OUTLINE
I. Introducing the Servant (Isa. 42:1–4)
　1. The Servant of the Lord (Isa. 42:1)
　2. The Servant's ministry (Isa. 42:2–4)
II. Commissioning the Servant (Isa. 42:5–9)
　1. Creator and sustainer of life (Isa. 42:5)
　2. Called for mission (Isa. 42:6–7)
　3. The true and living God (Isa. 42:8–9)

God introduced His Servant, who was chosen to bring saving judgment to Gentiles (v. 1). God described the Servant as using the power of love, not force (vv. 2–4). The Creator who spoke these words deserves all praise (v. 5). Addressing the Servant, the Lord reinforced His mission to bring light to Gentiles (vv. 6–7). The one true God keeps His promises and fulfills His purposes (vv. 8–9).

I. Introducing the Servant (Isa. 42:1–4)
1. The Servant of the Lord (v. 1)
　1 Behold my servant, whom I uphold; mine elect, in whom my soul delighteth; I have put my spirit upon him: he shall being forth judgment to the Gentiles.
The exclamation "behold" was used in Isaiah 40:9 to announce the Lord's self-revelation. It was used in Isaiah 41:24,29 to declare the nothingness of idols. Here the word begins God's presentation of His Servant. The emphasis is on the fact that the Servant is the Lord's Servant. Notice the repetition of the words "my" and "mine."

The word *elect* means "chosen." Israel was chosen by the Lord; so was the individual Servant chosen by God. Being chosen by God involves both a privilege and a responsibility. One of Israel's problems was that they thought being God's chosen people was a privilege, but they failed to recognize that being chosen by God was also a responsibility. The two are inseparable.

God promised to uphold His Servant. This means that the Lord laid hold of His Servant as an instrument of doing His will. The word uphold also implies that God would supply the strength to fulfill God's mission.

The words "in whom my soul delighteth" were echoed in the voice from heaven at the baptism of Jesus. The first part of the words, "This is my beloved Son" (Matt. 3:17; see also Mark 1:11; Luke 3:22), reflects Psalm 2:7, one of the messianic psalms. The second part, "in whom I am well pleased," reflects Isaiah 42:1, one of the Servant passages. Because the Servant fulfilled His mission through suffering and death, these words of divine favor also foreshadow the cross.

Privilege and responsibility are included also in the promise by God to put His Spirit on His Servant. We noted a similar promise in Isaiah 61:1. Both references point to the coming of the Spirit on Jesus at His baptism and the many references to the Spirit's blessings on His ministry. Being endowed with God's Spirit is a promise that His strength will provide power for completing the mission.

The Servant's mission is summed up in the last part of verse 1. The Old Testament use of the word "judgment" means more than our word *judgment.* It expresses the mercy and grace of God as well as His holiness and righteousness (see Isa. 30:18). Thus it includes the idea of providing salvation as well as exercising judgment. Thus the Servant was to provide salvation and exercise judgment for all people, Gentiles as well as Jews.

2. The Servant's ministry (vv. 2–4)

2 He shall not cry, nor lift up, nor cause his voice to be heard in the street.

3 A bruised reed shall he not break, and the smoking flax shall he not quench: he shall being forth judgment unto truth.

4 He shall not fail nor be discouraged, till he have set judgment in the earth: and the isles shall wait for his law.

The Servant's ministry is described both in terms of what He would and what He would not do. What He would not do is set forth in seven negatives (see the words "nor" or "not"). What He would do is set forth in terms of judgment.

The two references to "judgment" in verses 3 and 4 make three when placed with the reference in verse 1. This threefold emphasis shows that the Servant's ministry would be focused toward providing saving judgment for all people.

The word *cry* is often used in the Old Testament of the weak crying out to the strong for help, especially of those who cry out to God. As applied to Jesus, the words do not mean that Jesus did not call on God in prayer, for His entire life was lived in communion with the Father. He prayed before the cross and while on the cross; however, the Servant was a silent sufferer. He did not summon legions of angels to rescue Him, as He could have done (Matt. 26:53–54). As Isaiah 53:7 describes Him, he was silent in the face of those who tormented and killed Him.

The descriptions of the Servant's ministry in verses 2–3 point to a ministry of gentle persuasion, rather than one that uses force. This does not mean that the Servant would not cry out against entrenched forces of evil; but it does mean that He would rely on the power of love, not on other kinds of power to achieve His mission.

This seems to be the point of the quotation of Isaiah 42:1–4 in Matthew 12:17–21. Matthew had just described Jesus' response to fierce opposition against Him. The controversies with the Pharisees had become such that they were plotting His death (Matt. 12:1–14). The response of Jesus was to withdraw quietly, to continue to heal the sick, and to instruct His disciples not to tell who He was (Matt. 12:15–16). This was necessary to keep people from ascribing to Jesus their false expectations of a powerful earthly messiah.

The first part of verse 4 implies the difficulties faced by the Servant. Verse 4 thus supplements verse 3. Verse 3 stresses that His ministry would be gentle, but verse 4 shows that the gentleness would not be weakness. No one would face such difficulties as the Servant of the Lord; yet He would not fail or be discouraged.

II. Commissioning the Servant (Isa. 42:5–9)

1. Creator and sustainer of life (v. 5)

5 Thus saith God the Lord, he that created the heavens, and stretched them out; he that spread forth the earth, and that which cometh out of it; he that giveth breath unto the people upon it, and spirit to them that walk therein.

Verse 5 makes clear that the One speaking of His Servant was none other than the Lord God, Creator and sustainer of all things. All other truths about God are built on the foundational revelation of Him as Creator. Thus references to Him as Creator are not confined to Genesis 1–2, but are found throughout the Bible. The Book of Isaiah contains many references to God as Creator (see 40:12–13, 26, 28).

What is the purpose of verse 5 in this passage? It clearly identified the One who called the Servant. It also linked the Servant's ministry to the eternal purpose of the Creator. This ensured the success of the Servant's mission and ministry.

2. Called for mission (vv. 6–7)

6 I the Lord have called thee in righteousness, and will hold thine hand, and will keep thee, and give thee for a covenant of the people, for a light of the Gentiles;

7 To open the blind eyes, to bring out the prisoners from the prison, and them that sit in darkness out of the prison house.

Verses 1–4 were the words of the Lord introducing the Servant. Verses 6–7 were addressed to the Servant. (Notice the words "thee" and "thine" in v. 6.) Verses 6–7 constitute the Servant's call. These verses addressed to the Servant supplement the words about the Servant's call in verses 1–4.

The middle of verse 6 expresses the reassurance implied in verse 5. That is, the Servant was assured that the Lord who created all things was the One who called Him; and the One who called Him would hold His hand and keep Him.

Verses 6–7 also reinforce other words about the Servant's mission. The word "righteousness," like the word *judgment,* points not only to the Servant's righteousness but also to His mission of making people right with God. The scope of the Servant's saving work is a familiar theme in the Book of Isaiah. The Servant would be a light for the Gentiles. We have already noted this in studies of other passages (see 9:1; 11:9; 40:5; 51:4–5; 60:3), and we will see it in later studies.

The words "a covenant of the people" are parallel to the words "a light of the Gentiles." The Servant would provide saving light for the nations through a new covenant offered to all who commit themselves to Him (Jer. 33:31–34).

Verse 7 provides further commentary on the meaning of the Servant being a "light of the Gentiles." Three vivid pictures are used to illustrate the reality of divine salvation. One is the picture of blind people being made to see through the Servant's ministry. The second is of prisoners being liberated from their prisons by the Servant. The third contrasts the darkness of the prison to the light into which the prisoners are delivered by the Servant. All of these images bring to mind many incidents in the ministry of Jesus the Servant of God. They also depict vivid symbols of the inward experiences of those who have come to know the Servant's saving power.

3. The true and living God (vv. 8–9)

8 I am the Lord: that is my name: and my glory will I not give to another, neither my praise to graven images.

9 Behold, the former things are come to pass, and new things do I declare: before they spring forth I tell you of them.

Verse 8 is another reminder like verse 5 of the One who spoke these words. The Lord God is the only true and living God. Other gods are only the creations of human beings. All praise and glory is due only to the true God.

Because the Lord God is true and living, His word is true and living. His word accomplishes the purpose for which the Lord sends it forth (Isa. 55:8–11). Verse 9 was a reminder that God's past promises had come to fruition. By the same token, the promises He made about the future would surely come to pass. In this context, the reference is to God's promises to and about the Servant. We have seen the fulfillment of much of what the Lord promised in the coming of Christ. We have confidence that all His promises will come to pass in God's own time and in His own way.

APPLYING THE BIBLE

1. **Rights and responsibilities.** Rights and responsibilities go together. They are inseparable.

The late Dr. Clarence Cranford, who served as pastor of the Calvary Baptist Church of Washington, D. C., relates that once he was invited to speak in a college chapel service. When Cranford asked the school's president what he would emphasize if he were giving the address, the president replied: "Emphasize responsibility. Young people today are quick to demand their rights," he said, "but they are slow to accept their responsibilities."

Israel rightly saw themselves as the chosen people. They eagerly accepted their God-given rights, but they were slow to accept their responsibility of sharing that blessing of God's grace with others outside their culture.

God's perfect Servant, Jesus Christ, accepted this divine right of sonship, but He also accepted the responsibility that went with it: "I have put my spirit upon him [right]; he shall bring forth judgment to the Gentiles [responsibility]" (v. 1).

Keswick Week preacher George Duncan said that mature Christians accept not only their grace-rights, but also accept the responsibility that goes with grace. The Holy Spirit in us reveals Himself not in ecstatic emotion, but in character that is changed to produce the fruit of the Spirit (Gal. 5:22–26).

2. What Jesus refuses to do. Gladly and willingly Jesus did many things: "He went about doing good." But there were also some things Jesus refused to do that are noted in verses 2–4.

Notice the negative prophecies pointing to what God promised Messiah would not: "He shall not cry, nor lift up, nor cause his voice to be heard in the street" (v. 2). His ministry would be marked by quiet love, not boisterous noise and ostentation; "A bruised reed shall he not break, and the smoking flax shall he not quench" (v. 3). This surely points to the tenderness and patience He would show to those all but defeated by life. The bruised reed could easily be extinguished, and the flax, which lighted the room and smoked only when the oil was about gone, could be extinguished with only a breath. But the gentle Savior will not deal harshly and impatiently with poor sinners with heavy burdens and broken hearts.

3. Every weed a potential flower. Gardeners and lovers of flowers know the name Luther Burbank (1849–1926). A well-known American horticulturist, Burbank said he saw every weed as a potential flower. What divine insight this noted botanist possessed! He worked patiently with the cactus, a prickly foe full of sharp thorns, until the most delicate woman could rub her cheeks against the soft velvet of its petals without any discomfort.

God's promised Servant would share His love with the Gentiles, Israel's most despised foes, change their lives and bring them into the kingdom, turning a hostile and hated people into trophies of marvelous grace (v. 6).

Thank God for the "Light of the Gentiles." Because God's Servant is this, we all of us Gentiles are participants in and sharers of God's grace by faith.

4. The bells of grace toll above the world's noise. Clarence McCartney, the late, well-known Pittsburgh Presbyterian minister, told a legend about the church that had no bells.

According to the legend, a ship bearing bells for the church at Bottreaux, on England's stormy, southwest coast, was floundering in the stormy coastal waters near Bottreaux. A sailor on board, hearing the distant church bells at Tintagel sounding above the roar of the sea, audibly thanked God that they would soon be safely in port. But the wicked, godless captain rebuked the lad and told him to give thanks for a good steersman, a sturdy ship, and a ready sail.

As though the sea were responding to the blasphemous captain, the waves and wind suddenly increased, the ship was crushed against the rocks, and the bells went down with the ship and were lost to the churning sea.

The legend says that now when one walks along the rough coast at Bottreaux the bells can be heard tolling beneath the churning waters.[1]

Today, the noise, clamor, and sin of the world do all they can to stifle the bells of grace, but in thousands of churches across the land the peals of grace's bells are still heard: "Come! Come!" They call to all people and races!"

TEACHING THE BIBLE

▶ *Main Idea:* God's call to His Servant shows that He calls people to serve in specific tasks.

▶ *Suggested Teaching Aim:* To lead adults to examine God's call to His Servant, and to identify some tasks to which God has called them.

A TEACHING OUTLINE

1. Share an illustration to begin the lesson.

2. Enlist a member to prepare a report on the Servant of the Lord.

3. Examine the introduction and commissioning of the Servant.

4. Have members sign a commitment card, indicating their decision to be servants this year.

Introduce the Bible Study

Share the following illustration. As a woman came out of a Michigan grocery store with a bag of groceries, the sack ripped and apples began rolling all over the sidewalk. She was at a loss to know what to do. She started to pick them up, but she had nothing to put them in. Many people walked by, either pretending not to see her plight or smiling in amusement. Then a man came out of the store with an empty sack in his hand and began helping her. The man was none other than Governor G. Mennen Williams.[2]

Point out that we are all called to serve in small areas of life as well as the larger areas.

Search for Biblical Truth

IN ADVANCE, enlist a member to prepare a two- to three-minute report on "Servant of the Lord" in the *Holman Bible Dictionary* or another Bible dictionary. Call for the report at this time.

On a chalkboard or a large sheet of paper write:

The Servant's Call

I. Introducing the Servant (Isa. 42:1–4)

II. Commissioning the Servant (Isa. 42:5–9)

Cover the second point until you are ready to introduce it.

Ask members to open their Bibles to Isaiah 42:1. Point out that privilege and responsibility are two sides of the same coin. Ask, what part of verse 1 indicates privilege? responsibility? (See "Studying the Bible.")

Ask members to look at 42:2–4. Ask: What will the Servant of the Lord not do? (Seven negatives.) List these on a chalkboard or a large sheet of paper. What word expresses the positive side of His ministry? (Judgment.) How does this passage describe Jesus?

Uncover the second point on the teaching outline. Point out that 42:5 identifies the One who called and commissioned His Servant. Point out that 42:6–7 were addressed to the Servant and could be referred to as His call. Ask: What two tasks did God give His Servant in 42:6? (Covenant and light.) Point out that the Servant would provide saving light for the nations through a new covenant offered to all who commit themselves to Him.

Give the Truth a Personal Focus

IN ADVANCE, prepare the following service commitment card for each member:

In the Lord's Service . . .

Because I accept the responsibility as well as the privilege of following Christ, I commit myself to the following:

_____

_____

Date:_____ Signed: _____

Ask members to look at the seven negatives the Servant will not do and see if they can agree on one word to describe all of these. (Their response, but consider: gentle or comforting.) Ask: How can you be gentle in your ministry? How can you help bring judgment?

Distribute the commitment cards. Ask members to decide on one specific act they will make a part of their life this new year. Suggest they sign the commitment card and keep it in their Bibles as a way of reminding them of this decision. Close in a prayer of commitment.

---

1. Clarence E. McCartney, *McCartney's Illustrations* (New York, Nashville: Abingdon-Cokesbury, 1945) 302.

2. *Our Daily Bread*, February 20, 1978.

The Servant's Mission

Focal Passage: Isaiah 49:1–6
Focal Passage: Isaiah 49:1–6

T he Hebrew word for "servant" means a person at the disposal of another to do his work, represent his interests, and carry out his will. The word is found many times throughout the Old Testament. It was often used of the servants of a king or of a god. People of faith referred to themselves as servants of the Lord. As we saw in the previous lesson, sections of the Book of Isaiah use the word *servant* in distinctive ways. The New Testament often quotes these passages to present Jesus Christ as the ultimate fulfillment of Isaiah's prophecies of the Servant of the Lord. Certain themes are repeated in Isaiah's references to the Servant of the Lord: call, mission, ministry, suffering, victory, and so forth. The title for January 14, "The Servant's Mission," is taken from one of the themes in Isaiah 49:1–6.

▶ ▶ ▶ ▶ **Study Aim:** *To identify the Servant of Isaiah 49:1–6 and to describe His mission*

STUDYING THE BIBLE

LESSON OUTLINE
I. The Testimony of the Servant (Isa. 49:1–4)
  1. Called of God (Isa. 49:1)
  2. Equipped to speak (Isa. 49:2)
  3. Commissioned to glorify God (Isa. 49:3)
  4. Encouraged to persevere (Isa. 49:4)
II. Scope of the Mission (Isa. 49:5–6)
  1. To Israel (Isa. 49:5)
  2. To all the world (Isa. 49:6)

The Servant of the Lord testified to the world that He was called from His mother's womb (v. 1). He was preserved by God to speak God's word (v. 2). God's servant Israel was to glorify God (v. 3). When the Servant was tempted to give up, He remembered He was in God's hand to do God's will (v. 4). The scope of His mission included the restoration of Israel (v. 5) and salvation to the ends of the earth (v. 6).

I. The Testimony of the Servant (Isa. 49:1–4)
1. Called of God (v. 1)
1 Listen, O isles, unto me; and hearken, ye people, from far; The Lord hath called me from the womb; from the bowels of my mother hath he made mention of my name.

Although Isaiah 49:1–6 repeats some of the themes of Isaiah 42:1–9, God was the One speaking in Isaiah 42, while the Servant was the speaker in Isaiah 49. Isaiah 49:1–6 is a testimony of the Servant. Another distinctive of Isaiah 49:1–6 is that the testimony was addressed to the whole world. The picture in verse 1 is of the Servant speaking to the nations as a representative of the Lord God. Isaiah 49:1–6 begins and ends by stressing the universal scope of the Servant's mission. We have already seen this theme of the universal scope of the Messiah-Servant's mission in Isaiah 9:1; 11:9; 40:5; 42:1, 4; 51:4–5; 60:3.

The lesson for January 7 focused on "The Servant's Call," as presented by God in Isaiah 42:1–9. Isaiah 49:1 is the Servant's testimony about a distinctive aspect of that call. The Servant described His call in words similar to language Jeremiah used to describe his call: "Before I formed thee in the belly I knew thee; and before thou camest forth out of the womb I sanctified thee, and I ordained thee a prophet unto the nations" (Jer. 1:5).

If these words are applied to Jesus Christ, the New Testament presents Him as the eternal Word of God who became flesh (John 1:1–3,14). His conception was not only planned by God but miraculously achieved by God's Spirit in the womb of a virgin (Luke 1:26–38).

2. Equipped to speak (v. 2)

2 And he hath made my mouth like a sharp sword; in the shadow of his hand hath he hid me, and made me a polished shaft; in his quiver hath he hid me.

This passage, like most of the other Servant passages in Isaiah, was written in Hebrew poetic language and form. Notice the first half of verse 2. The Servant compared his words to a sharp sword and testified that He was hid with the shadow of God's hand. In the second half of the verse, the Servant compared himself to a polished shaft (arrow or spear) and testified that God had hid Him in His quiver. Two ideas thus are presented. For one thing, the Servant testified that God equipped Him to speak words that are like a sharp sword or a polished spear. Second, God protected the Servant.

The power of God's word is a theme not only in Isaiah, but throughout the Scripture. Since the Servant would be the representative of God, His words would have the power of God's word. Isaiah elsewhere described God's word as the extension of God Himself, with a power that accomplishes the purpose for which God sent forth His Word (Isa. 55:8–11). Isaiah 49:2 also brings to mind the words of Hebrews 4:12: "The word of God is quick, and powerful, and sharper than any two-edged sword."

The Old Testament often uses the picture of someone being hidden by the Lord. The person is being preserved or protected by God. For example, David testified, "For in the time of trouble he shall hide me in his pavilion: in the secret of his tabernacle shall he hide me" (Ps. 27:5).

3. Commissioned to glorify God (v. 3)

3 And said unto me, Thou art my servant, O Israel, in whom I will be glorified.

This is one of many verses in the Book of Isaiah that identifies Israel as the servant of the Lord. Some of these passages refer to Israel as God's chosen servant (see Isa. 41:8–9). Some even refer to Israel as God's servant formed from the womb (see Isa. 44:2, 21–24). If we had only these verses, we might conclude that Isaiah identified the servant as the nation of Israel, God's chosen people. However, before making this identification, two factors need to be considered.

One factor is that the Servant in Isaiah is described as ministering to Israel in Isaiah 49:5–6. How can Israel minister to itself? The other factor is that the New Testament presents Jesus Christ as the ultimate fulfillment of the servant passages in Isaiah. We have already noted how Isaiah 42:1–4 was quoted in Matthew 12:17–21. Isaiah 49:6 is echoed in Luke 2:32 and quoted in Acts 13:47. Later (on Jan. 28) we will look at the most famous servant passage—Isaiah 52:13 53:12—in which the Servant's sufferings are described. This was the passage the Ethiopian eunuch was reading when Philip presented Jesus as the fulfillment (see Acts 8:26–40).

The best way to interpret passages like Isaiah 49:1–6 is to recognize that the chosen people of God were called to be God's servant people. They were specially chosen to be a blessing and to be priests to all nations. This is clear in the calls of Abraham and the covenant with the Israelites at Mount Sinai (Gen. 12:1–3; Exod. 19:5–6). However, as the history of Israel unfolded, the prophets recognized that most Israelites were too sinful to fulfill God's purpose. Finally, prophets like Isaiah came to see that the call to Israel was to be ultimately fulfilled in one Servant, who was of Israel, but whose mission was to all people. Thus we have passages that refer to Israel as God's servant, for this was God's intent; but God's mission would be fulfilled not by the nation as a whole, but by one perfect Israelite.

In either case, the mission of both Israel and the Servant was to glorify God. When Jesus came, He reflected the glory of God (John 1:14; 17:1, 4)). Likewise, God's true people in every age have this as their ultimate mission in life. As Paul wrote in his magnificent passage about God the Father, Son, and Spirit, we are to be to the praise of the glory of His grace (Eph. 1:6, 12, 14).

4. Encouraged to persevere (v. 4)

4 Then I said, I have laboured in vain, I have spent my strength for nought, and in vain: yet surely my judgment is with the Lord, and my work with my God.

The Israelites as God's servants often expressed sentiments like those in the first part of verse 4. Isaiah, for example, quoted the exiled Israelites as saying, "My way is hid from the Lord, and my judgment is passed over from my God" (Isa. 40:27). Jesus, who was tempted as we are, must at times also have been tempted to grow discouraged as He faced difficulties and opposition. His prayers in Gethsemane and on the cross represent His struggles with such feelings (Matt. 26:38–46; 27:46). Notice that although the Servant was tempted to feel this way, He remembered that He and His fate were ultimately in the hands of God, not in human hands. He overcame these temptations, and lived and died in trust and obedience to the Heavenly Father.

II. Scope of the Mission (Isa. 49:5-6)

1. To Israel (v. 5)

5 And now, saith the Lord that formed me from the womb to be his servant, to bring Jacob again to him, Though Israel be not gathered, yet shall I be glorious in the eyes of the Lord, and my God shall be my strength.

The Servant was quoting the words of God to Him. Verse 5 makes three points, two of which have already been made earlier in Isaiah 49: (1) The Lord formed the Servant from the womb (see v. 1). (2) The Lord gave His Servant the mission of gathering Israel. (3) The Lord promised to provide honor and strength to His Servant (see vv. 2, 4).

The restoration of Israel is a familiar theme in the prophets. As we have already noted in comments on verse 3, verse 5 demands that we interpret verse 3 as meaning more than the nation of Israel. If Israel was the servant, how could Israel restore Israel? The Old Testament promise is the restoration of a remnant of Israel through the Servant whom God would send from Israel.

2. To all the world (v. 6)

6 And he said, It is a light thing that thou shouldest be my servant to raise up the tribes of Jacob, and to restore the preserved of Israel: I will also give thee for a light to the Gentiles, that thou mayest be my salvation unto the end of the earth.

What was the "light thing" of which God spoke? It was the Servant's mission to restore Israel. The point is not that this part of the Servant's mission was unimportant. The point is that the restoration of Israel is only a small part of the Servant's mission, which includes the whole world.

As we noted in comments on verses 1 and 3, verse 6 represents a familiar theme in the Book of Isaiah. Isaiah saw what had been inherent in God's call of Israel from the beginning. God chose Israel for a worldwide mission. God wanted to call all people to come to Him. He started with one nation, which was to model true faith and be a missionary nation to all nations. Most of the people of Israel, however, continued to see God's choice of them as a privilege, not as a responsibility.

Only the choicest of Israelites saw the truth in Old Testament times. Isaiah was one of them. No wonder the New Testament quotes so often from the Book of Isaiah. As we saw from our study of the Book of Acts, the biggest struggle in the first-century church was over this issue. One group of Jewish believers wanted to exclude Gentiles unless they first became Jews. Paul and others insisted that God's purpose had always been to make Christ a light for the whole world and to provide salvation for believers to the ends of the earth.

Thus when Paul and Barnabas went as missionaries, they went first to the Jewish synagogues; but they didn't confine themselves to Jews. For example, when they met fierce opposition in the synagogue at Antioch of Pisidia, they began to witness to Gentiles. They justified this action by quoting Isaiah 49:6 (see Acts 13:47). Paul saw the mission of the Servant of Isaiah 49:6 fulfilled in Christ and in followers of Christ who obey His Great Commission to take the good news to the ends of the earth.

APPLYING THE BIBLE

1. The true mark of greatness. According to Jesus, the great people are the servants. The disciples were eager to be served, but Jesus told them that the most important thing was serving. One can only serve God by serving others.

Several years ago, the school children of France were asked to name the greatest of all Frenchmen. They passed over Napoleon, who bathed Europe in its own blood, and chose Louis Pasteur, who did so much good for so many people. Napoleon strove for true greatness, but never found it. Pasteur did not seek it, but it found him as he humbly served others.

True greatness for the nation would be found not in keeping their divine blessings only to themselves, but in sharing them with others. In this unselfish act of service "I will be glorified" said the Lord (v. 3).

2. "I'd Rather Have Jesus." Recently, I heard George Beverly Shea sing "I'd Rather Have Jesus" on a Billy Graham broadcast. Well past eighty, Shea's voice is still remarkable. As a twenty-two-year-old clerk in a New York insurance firm, Shea was offered an attractive radio contract. Normally, he would have jumped at the opportunity, but Shea was struggling with God's call to the Christian music ministry.

One Sunday during the time he was struggling over his decision, he arose early to rehearse a hymn he was to sing in church that morning. Earlier, his mother had placed a poem on the piano, and as Shea prepared for the service his eyes fell on the poem. Almost without thinking, as he read the poem, he began to play a melody on the piano and the hymn for which this great Christian musician is best known was born. At the same time, Shea's life-commitment to the Christian ministry was made.[1]

Isaiah says of the Savior that from eternity God had chosen His only begotten Son for His saving ministry, "called from the womb" as the atoning sacrifice for our sins (v. 1).

Missionary E. Stanley Jones said about the uniqueness of Jesus: "If you call Him a man you will have to change your ideas of what man is, and if you call Him God you will have to change your ideas of what God is like."

3. The tool most often used by Satan. Discouragement is perhaps the tool Satan most frequently uses to hinder God's servants in their work.

The late C. Roy Angell once told a legend about the devil going out of business, so he decided to auction off his choicest tools: envy, jealousy, vengeance, hatred, resentment, and pride. But off to one side was a silver wedge which Satan claimed was his choicest tool.

"See how bright and shiny it is. I use it all the time," he told those gathered for the strange event. "I put it over there because it is worth more than all the other tools put together. It is the wedge of discouragement. If I can drive this wedge into the lives of the finest Christians, I can wreck their usefulness to God." [2]

4. God, our strength. The late Kansas Methodist Bishop William Quayle said that one night, as he wrestled with some problem, he couldn't get to sleep. Then, deep in the night, Quayle said that God walked into his room, stood at the foot of the bed, and said: "William, you go on to sleep for I am awake."

Among Scotland's finest preachers was a young man named Robert Murray McCheyne (1813–1843). He was pastor of St. Peter's Church in Dundee, and although he died at only thirty his impact on Scotland was very significant.

McCheyne wrote about discouragement and the strength God gave him to see it through: "At the very time when I was beginning to despair, God gave tokens of His presence." [3]

God's servants, both Israel and Jesus Christ, faced discouragement but found grace and strength in God (v. 5).

In our day, as we face discouragement, with Paul we can say: "I can do all things through Christ which strengtheneth me" (Phil. 4:13).

TEACHING THE BIBLE

▶ *Main Idea:* The Servant's mission is a reminder that all of God's people are to be on mission for Him.
▶ *Suggested Teaching Aim:* To lead adults to identify the Servant and describe His mission, and to identify ways they can be on mission for God.

A TEACHING OUTLINE

1. Use a graffiti wall to introduce the concept of "servant."
2. Use strip posters and a series of questions to identify the Servant and describe His mission.
3. Use an illustration to apply the lesson.

Introduce the Bible Study

Place a large sheet of paper on the wall. On it write: *What is a servant?* As members enter, ask them to go to the paper and, in graffiti fashion, write or draw their definition of a servant.

After all have had a chance to write, begin by reading the definitions or having members explain their drawings.

Search for Biblical Truth

IN ADVANCE on a sheet of posterboard, write the first sentence of the introduction to "Studying the Bible": "The Hebrew word for 'servant' means a person at the disposal of another to do his work, represent his interests, and carry out his will." Display this definition alongside the graffiti wall and see how many characteristics of this definition appear in the descriptions the members wrote. Do encourage members whose definitions may not have characteristics in their definitions.

IN ADVANCE, make the following two strip posters (or write them on a chalkboard or a large sheet of paper as you teach):

I. The Servant's Testimony (Isa. 49:1–4)
II. The Scope of the Mission (Isa. 49:5–6)

Place the first strip on the focal wall. Call on a volunteer to read Isaiah 49:1–4. Then use the following questions. Ask members to read the particular phrase that answers the question from their Bibles when possible.

(1) Who is speaking? (The Servant: "listen . . . unto me"; [v. 1].)

(2) Who called the Servant? ("The Lord hath called me" [v. 1].)

(3) To whom was the Servant called to minister? ("Isles . . . people from far" [v. 1].)

(4) What two images did the Servant use to describe God's equipping Him and God's care for Him? (*Equipping*: "sharp sword . . . polished shaft"; *Care*: "shadow of his hand . . . in his quiver" [v. 2].)

(5) Who is the Servant in the passage according to 49:3? ("Israel.") Use "Studying the Bible" to explain how Jesus became the perfect Israelite who fulfilled this passage.

(6) What thought encouraged the Servant? ("My judgment is with the Lord" [v. 4].)

Place the second strip poster on the focal wall and ask a volunteer to read Isaiah 49:5–6. Ask the following:

(1) What three points did the Servant make in verse 5? ("Formed me from the womb"; the Lord gave Him the mission "to bring Jacob again to him"; the Lord will make the Servant "glorious in the eyes of the Lord . . . and be my strength.")

(2) What was the "light thing" the Servant was to do? ("Raise up the tribes of Jacob, and to restore the preserved of Israel" [v. 6].) Use "Studying the Bible" to explain what this means.

(3) What was the complete task of the Servant? ("A light to the Gentiles, that thou mayest be my salvation unto the end of the earth" [v. 6].)

(4) How can only Jesus ultimately fulfill this prophecy? (See "Studying the Bible.")

Give the Truth a Personal Focus

Remind members that all believers are responsible for continuing the ministry of the Servant by sharing God with the world. Share "I'd rather have Jesus" from "Applying the Bible." Ask members to identify one area in which they will be on mission for God. Close with a prayer of commitment.

If you prefer a "Sanctity of Life" lesson, it can be found in the back of this book.

---

1. Robert Hastings, *A Word Fitly Spoken* (Nashville: Broadman Press, 1962), 42.

2. Ibid., 88.

3. Quoted in Keswick Week, 1958, by George B. Duncan: (Marshall, Morgan and Scott LTD, 1958), 16.

The Servant's Steadfast Endurance

Basic Passage: Isaiah 50:1–11
Focal Passage: Isaiah 50:4–11

The speaker in Isaiah 50:4–9 is not specifically identified by the word *servant,* but the word does appear in a reference about the Servant in verse 10. Thus this is another servant passage. As in Isaiah 49:1–11, the Servant Himself speaks in verses 4–9. As we move through the servant passages in Isaiah, the picture of the Servant comes into sharper focus. The climax is the picture of the Suffering Servant in Isaiah 52:13 53:12, but the picture in Isaiah 50 provides glimpses of the faithfulness of the Servant in service and suffering.

▶ ▶ ▶ ▶ ▶ ▶ ▶ ▶ **Study Aim:** *To identify the characteristics of the Servant in Isaiah 50:4–11 and list those that apply to Christians*

STUDYING THE BIBLE

LESSON OUTLINE
I. The Cause of Israel's Plight (Isa. 50:1–3)
    1. Israel's charge that God had forsaken her (Isa. 50:1)
    2. Israel's charge that God had not helped her (Isa. 50:2–3)
II. The Servant's Faithfulness (Isa. 50:4–9)
    1. Disciple and teacher (Isa. 50:4)
    2. Obedient Sufferer (Isa. 50:5–6)
    3. Divine help and vindication (Isa. 50:7–9)
III. Responses to the Servant (Isa. 50:10–11)
    1. Trust and obey (Isa. 50:10)
    2. Burned by their own fires (Isa. 50:11)

The cause of Israel's plight was the sins of the people (v. 1). The Lord is able to redeem His people and judge His enemies (v. 2). The Servant described Himself as a learner from God and an encourager of others (v. 4). He obediently endured abuse and insults (vv. 5–6). He trusted God for help and vindication against false charges (vv. 7–9). People should trust and obey God and His Servant (v. 10). Those who refuse God's light and live around their own fires will eventually be burned by them (v. 11).

I. The Cause of Israel's Plight (Isa. 50:1–3)
    1. Israel's charge that God had forsaken her (v. 1). Zion said, "The Lord hath forsaken me, and my Lord hath forgotten me" (Isa. 49:14). The covenant between God and Israel was like that of a husband and wife. God answered Israel's charge of desertion by asking Israel to show the divorce papers, which would prove that God had divorced Israel. No such papers existed because Israel had forsaken God. Her own

sins were the cause of her plight.

2. Israel's charge that God had not helped her (vv. 2–3). Back of verses 2–3 was the complaint that God had not come to Israel's aid in her time of trouble. God reminded Israel that He had the power to redeem His people just as He had done in the events of the Exodus.

II. The Servant's Faithfulness (Isa. 50:4–9)

1. Disciple and teacher (v. 4)

4 The Lord God hath given me the tongue of the learned, that I should know how to speak a word in season to him that is weary: he wakeneth morning by morning, he wakeneth mine ear to hear as the learned.

Verse 4 focuses on the Servant's tongue and ear. The Servant's tongue was the tongue of a disciple, ready to receive and to speak God's word. His ear was attuned to God's messages. The Servant listened for and heard God's word, which was fresh each morning. This was the inspiration and basis for His ministry of teaching and encouragement.

The word "learned" is similar to the New Testament word "disciple," which means a learner. Christian disciples are teachable followers of Christ, who become lifetime learners from Him. They learn through study of God's Word, and they learn through prayer. As Christians live as disciples, we are following One who was the perfect disciple of His Father.

True disciples may not always be teachers in the formal sense, but all who learn from God have words to share with others who need God's Word. Verse 4 says that the Servant spoke God's word at critical times to those who were weary and discouraged. All disciples have been called to a ministry of encouragement in the name of Christ.

2. Obedient sufferer (vv. 5–6)

5 The Lord God hath opened mine ear, and I was not rebellious, neither turned away back.

6 I gave my back to the smiters, and my cheeks to them that plucked off the hair: I hid not my face from shame and spitting.

Verse 5 is tied to verse 4 by the emphasis on the open ear. As in verse 4, the Servant was open and responsive to whatever the Lord God said. Verses 5–6 apply this to obedience in the face of opposition. The Servant did not turn away when God led Him in a ministry that brought such opposition as is described in verse 6.

Verses 5–6 reveal two important truths about the Servant. For one thing, the Servant would be abused by enemies. Second, He would endure this in obedience to the will of God. These verses, therefore, anticipate the more complete description of the Suffering Servant in Isaiah 52:13–53:12 (which we will study on January 28).

The Servant allowed enemies to beat His back, pluck out His hair and beard, and spit in His face. These were acts of abuse and insult. For example, plucking out or cutting the hair of one's head and beard was considered a deep insult in Old Testament times (see Isa. 7:20; 2 Sam. 10:4). Christians cannot read such verses as Isaiah 50:6 without thinking of the things endured by Jesus before and during His crucifixion.

During His trials, His accusers slapped Him and spit in His face (Matt. 26:67). Before He was crucified, His back was scourged (Matt. 27:26; Mark 15:15). Jesus was turned over to the soldiers, whose mockery included hitting Him in the head and spitting on Him (Matt. 27:30; Mark 15:19).

3. Divine help and vindication (vv. 7–9)

7 For the Lord God will help me; therefore shall I not be confounded: therefore have I set my face like a flint, and I know that I shall not be ashamed.

8 He is near that justifieth me; who will contend with me? let us stand together: who is mine adversary? let him come near to me.

9 Behold, the Lord God will help me; who is he that shall condemn me? lo, they all shall wax old as a garment; the moth shall eat them up.

Verses 7 and 9 begin with the same words, "The Lord God will help me." The Servant who heard and obeyed the Word of God endured suffering in accordance with the will of God (see vv. 5–6). The Servant trusted in the strength and help of God to be able to endure such abuse and insults.

The words "set my face like flint" mean that the Servant would make Himself like flint in the face of the accusations and abuse of His enemies. This brings to mind the description of Jesus in Luke 9:51: "And it came to pass, when the time was come that he should be received up, he steadfastly set his face to go to Jerusalem." The Servant's steadfast endurance and abiding commitment are clear in the similar description of Isaiah 50:7.

The language of Isaiah 50:8–9a is that of a courtroom and trial. The following translation brings out this meaning:

> He who vindicates me is near.
> Who then will bring charges against me?
> Let us face each other!
> Who is my accuser?
> Let him confront me!
> It is the Sovereign Lord who helps me.
> Who is he that will condemn me? (NIV).

The Servant's earlier abuse and insults were given a judicial setting in verses 8–9a. The Servant expressed not only the false charges of His accusers but also His trust that God would vindicate Him. In the Gospels, the vindication of Jesus came through His resurrection (see Acts 2:36). The world in its sin pronounced Jesus guilty, but God reversed the verdict. Through raising Jesus from the dead, God declared the world guilty and vindicated and exalted His Son.

Isaiah 50:8–9a reminds Christians of the language of Paul in Romans 8:33–34: "Who will bring any charge against those whom God has chosen? It is God who justifies. Who is he that condemns? Christ Jesus, who died more than that, who was raised to life is at the right hand of God and is also interceding for us" (NIV). Paul's words show that although Isaiah 50:8–9a applied directly to the Servant, the words also apply to each servant of the Lord who suffers false charges and insults.

The final part of verse 9 speaks of the fate of those who set themselves against God, His Servant, and their servants. They will grow old and wear out like old clothes, and finally will be destroyed as old clothes are destroyed by moths. This figure is used elsewhere in the Old Testament (see Isa. 51:8; Job 13:28; Hos. 5:12). The figure speaks not only of the inevitable ruin of the aging process but also of the corrupting power of sin.

III. Responses to the Servant (Isa. 50:10–11)
1. Trust and obey (v. 10)

10 Who is among you that feareth the Lord, that obeyeth the voice of his servant, that walketh in darkness, and hath no light? let him trust in the name of the Lord, and stay upon his God.

The interpretation of verse 10 depends on where one puts the question mark. Since the original manuscripts didn't have question marks, this is something that translators and interpreters must decide. Some place the question mark after the word "servant." Others place it after the word "light." Still others place it at the end of the verse.

If the question mark is placed at the end of the verse, all the descriptions of verse 10 apply to the Servant. He is the One who should be obeyed because He Himself lived a life of trust and obedience. If the question mark is placed after the word "servant" or the word "light," the meaning is that people should obey the Servant by living a life of trust and obedience. We cannot be sure of the exact meaning of this specific verse, but we do know that the Bible in many verses teaches two truths: (1) The divine Servant Jesus showed perfect trust and obedience to the Father. (2) Followers of the Lord should follow the example and obey the commandments of the divine Servant.

2. Burned by their own fires (v. 11)

11 Behold, all ye that kindle a fire, that compass yourselves with sparks: walk in the light of your fire, and in the sparks that ye have kindled. This shall ye have of mine hand; ye shall lie down in sorrow.

The people addressed in verse 11 are those who refuse to trust and obey the Lord. They do not walk in the light of the Lord. Instead, they light their own fires to provide light and warmth. Possibly, there is also the suggestion that they light their fires to shoot flaming arrows at the Servant of the Lord. In either case, the picture is of the judgment that comes on them. By walking in the light of their own fires, they eventually are consumed in fires of their own making. The words "lie down" refer to dying (see Isa. 14:8; Job 20:11; Ezek. 32:21). The words "in sorrow" show that it is a sorrowful end.

In one sense, their judgment was that they reaped what they sowed. The last part of verse 11 reminds us that such judgment is also from the hand of God. He has made a moral and spiritual universe in which He has ordained that people be judged by being burned in fires that they themselves have set.

1. Sin finds us out. Jack Gulledge tells about a four-year-old child who was abducted from a hospital in England, sexually assaulted, and beaten to death.

A large glass bottle was found under the bed of the dead child with a fresh set of twenty fingerprints on it. Police fingerprinted everyone having any connection with the hospital, but none matched the prints on the bottle.

The police then divided the city into fourteen districts, worked fourteen-hour shifts, checked each of the city's 35,000 houses, and collected more than 46,000 fingerprints.

After two months of arduous work, they still had not identified the killer. Six months later they found the guilty man, and Peter Griffiths was arrested, tried, and hanged for the brutal murder. He was the 46,253rd person fingerprinted. Ten of the prints on the bottle were his.[1]

It took a long time, and a lot of dedicated, hard work, but the police finally got their man.

Sin always catches up with us. There is no hiding from God. One may run from God, but none can hide from God.

When we feel forsaken by God we need to take a look into our hearts. God hasn't moved away and left no forwarding address. Rather, we are the ones who have moved!

2. The power of a word. English minister Robert William Dale (1829–1895) was a Congregational minister, one of the great preachers of his day. Terribly discouraged and depressed one day, he met a woman he did not know on the streets of Birmingham. She spoke to Dale, only saying, "God bless you, Dr. Dale." Dale later said that with her warm, sincere greeting the mists broke and the sunlight shone into his soul. "I breathed the free air of the mountains of God," he said. Her word of encouragement was what he needed. It was "a word in season" (v. 4) "a word fitly spoken" (Prov. 25:11).

Who can measure or weigh the worth of a word when encouragement is desperately needed? God's Servant, who is none other than Jesus Christ, always had the right word for the discouraged and, as one writer puts it, the people gathered around Him to hear His words as moths gather around a light.

As disciples of Jesus we need to remember that everyone we meet is hurting. Who knows what the right word from us can mean to one who is hurting?

3. The courage to go on. William Tyndale (1492?–1536) was one of England's leaders in the Protestant Reformation. For our English Bible we owe an everlasting debt to Tyndale. He is famous for his translation of the new Testament from Greek into English. When the work was completed, he could not get it published in England. But with the help of Martin Luther, it was published in Germany and smuggled back into England. In 1535, he was imprisoned for his "crime" and confined to a castle near Brussels. In 1536, he was taken from prison, strangled to death, and his body was burned.

In one of his last preserved written words, Tyndale wrote to the commissary of the prison: "I entreat you . . . to send me my Hebrew Bible, grammar, and dictionary that I may spend my time in that pursuit."

Like the Savior, the Servant of our lesson today, Tyndale suffered indescribable abuse, but he refused to give up. Courage, born of faith, sustained Tyndale and the Savior in their most trying hours (see Luke 9:51).

In our kind of world that scorns the Word of God and mocks the people of God, we must not quit and recant our faith in Christ. It takes courage to go on, but that courage is available in abundance from our God (vv. 9–10).

Take courage from English Baptist preacher John Bunyan, author of *The Pilgrim's Progress*, who was often so terrified that he was afraid to go out on the streets, afraid that the village green would open up and hell would swallow him.

But he pressed on, drawing upon that divine strength that never fails, and his life and works have blessed and strengthened millions. This has been the victorious spirit of God's servants through the ages. Courage is not the absence of fear; rather, it is going on in spite of fear.

TEACHING THE BIBLE

▶ *Main Idea:* The Servant's steadfast endurance demonstrates how we should respond to God.
▶ *Suggested Teaching Aim:* To lead adults to describe the Servant's steadfast endurance, and to list those characteristics that apply to Christians.

A TEACHING OUTLINE

1. Use questions to introduce the lesson.
2. Use a poster to identify the faithfulness of the Servant and how that faithfulness can encourage us.
3. Use group discussion to identify responses to the Servant.
4. Use small groups to apply the lesson.

Introduce the Bible Study

Ask: What was the most difficult task you ever had to complete? What made it so hard? What helped you get through the task?

Search for Biblical Truth

IN ADVANCE, write the following on a chalkboard or a large sheet of paper:

The Faithfulness of the Servant

Description of Servant	Description of Jesus	Application to Us

Ask members to open their Bibles to Isaiah 50:1. Explain that this passage, as the rest of the Servant poems, describes Jesus in many ways, but that it also describes how Christians are to live. Ask members to look for both of these applications as they study.

Use "Studying the Bible" to summarize 50:1–3. Then write the words *disciple* and *teacher* under Description of Servant. Ask: How does 50:4 portray the servant as a disciple and teacher? (Tongue of a disciple; ear tuned to God's message.)

DISCUSS: What was the most encouraging thing anyone has ever done for you? What can you do to encourage others? (Write answers on poster.)

Ask members to look at 50:5–6. Write Obedient Sufferer on the poster. Describe how these verses applied to the Servant. Ask: How do these verses describe Jesus?

DISCUSS: What helps you obey God when you face opposition? (Write answers on poster.)

Ask members to look at 50:7–9. Write Source of Strength on the poster. Describe how these verses applied to the Servant. Read the translation in "Studying the Bible." Ask: How do these verses describe Jesus?

DISCUSS: How has God provided for your needs when you faced great difficulty and hardship? (Write answers on poster.)

Ask members to look at 50:10–11. If members have various translations, ask several to read 50:10 and note the differences. Use "Studying the Bible" to explain the significance of where the question mark is placed. Be sure to remind members that question marks were not a part of the original manuscripts and that any translation is an interpretation of the text. Share the two conclusions in "Studying the Bible": (1) the divine Servant Jesus showed perfect trust and obedience to the Father; (2) followers of the Lord should follow the example and obey the commandments of the divine Servant.

DISCUSS: In what areas of your life do you need to obey the Lord more fully?

Ask members to look at 50:11 and to suggest what Isaiah was saying. If members have various translations, ask them to read the verse aloud. Point out that the verse describes the judgment of those who refuse to obey the Servant's message.

DISCUSS: Are the wicked punished by their own sins, or does God send specific punishments on them?

Give the Truth a Personal Focus

Organize the class into three groups. Assign each group one of the segments of the above poster. Ask them to discuss ways their passage applies to them and then share their ideas with the rest of the class.

---

1. Jack Gulledge, *Inspirational Talks* (Nashville: Broadman Press, 1986), 60.

The Servant's Victory

28
1996

Basic Passage: Isaiah 52:13–53:12
Focal Passages: Isaiah 53:1–6, 10–11

I saiah 52:13–53:12 is the most familiar servant passage in Isaiah. Most of the verses are quoted in the New Testament. For example, the Ethiopian eunuch was reading Isaiah 53:7–8 when Philip joined him and told him of Jesus (Acts 8:30–35). The theme of Isaiah 52:13–53:12 is this: the Suffering Servant was victorious through His suffering on behalf of others.

▶ ▶ ▶ ▶ **Study Aim:** *To identify aspects of Christ's sufferings and victory found in Isaiah's picture of the Suffering Servant*

STUDYING THE BIBLE

LESSON OUTLINE
  I. From Humiliation to Exaltation (Isa. 52:13–15
  II. Rejection of the Servant (Isa. 53:1–3)
   1. Who has believed? (Isa. 53:1)
   2. A root out of dry ground (Isa. 53:2)
   3. Despised and rejected (Isa. 53:3)
  III. The Suffering of the Servant for Us (Isa. 53:4–6)
   1. The cause of His suffering (Isa. 53:4)
   2. With His stripes we are healed (Isa. 53:5)
   3. Our spiritual plight (Isa. 53:6)
  IV. The Servant's Unjust Death (Isa. 53:7–9)
  V. God's Will and the Servant's Victory (Isa. 53:10–12)
   1. The fulfillment of God's will (Isa. 53:10)
   2. Justification (Isa. 53:11)
   3. Intercessor for sinners (Isa. 53:12)

God described the humiliation and exaltation of His Servant (52:13–15). Although the word went forth, people didn't believe (53:1). They saw nothing in His unlikely origin or in His appearance to attract them (53:2). The Servant was despised and rejected (53:3). Although people thought He was suffering for His own sins, He was actually suffering for others (53:4). He suffered and died for our sins, so that we could be made whole (53:5). All of us are sinners, but God provided salvation for us by laying on the Servant our sins (53:6). The innocent Servant suffered and died for the sins of others (53:7–9). The Servant's suffering and death were the will of God because this led to the Servant's exaltation and the salvation of many (53:10). The Servant was pleased because His death for others made possible the justification of sinners (53:11). Through His suffering and death, the Servant became the Intercessor for sinners (53:12).

I. From Humiliation to Exaltation
(Isa. 52:13–15)

God referred to His Servant in verse 13 the same way as in Isaiah 42:1: "Behold, my servant." Verse 13 presents the wisdom and exaltation of the Servant. Verse 14 presents the humiliation of the Servant. Verse 15 focuses on His redemptive mission to kings, who fell silent in awe of what they saw and heard.

II. Rejection of the Servant (Isa. 53:1–3)

1. Who has believed? (v. 1)

1 Who hath believed our report? and to whom is the arm of the Lord revealed?

Verses 1–6 were spoken by some group. Notice the word "our" in verse 1 and the words "we," "us," and "our" in the rest of the verses. Bible students have made several suggestions about the identity of the speakers in verses 1–6: (1) the kings of Isaiah 52:15; (2) Israel as a whole; (3) a faithful remnant within Israel; or (4) the prophets. Although we cannot tell for sure who asked the questions of verse 1, we do know the answer to their questions. God had revealed Himself, but the people as a whole had refused to believe His word or to accept His revelation (see John 12:37–38; Rom. 10:16).

2. A root out of dry ground (v. 2)

2 For he shall grow up before him as a tender plant, and as a root out of a dry ground: he hath no form nor comeliness; and when we shall see him, there is no beauty that we should desire him.

The first part of verse 2 uses similar language to Isaiah 11:1, which described the Messiah as a sprout out of the root of Jesse. A root out of dry ground has little hope of survival, much less growing into a flourishing plant. Thus, from an unlikely beginning and of humble origins, the Servant became the One through whom God would do great things.

The last part of verse 2 may be making the same point as the description of the Servant in Isaiah 52:14. That is, the appearance of the Servant would become so marred by His suffering that people would be repulsed by Him. Or the meaning may be that the outward appearance of the Servant was not attractive enough to draw people to Him. His strength was not in His outward appearance as a human being.

3. Despised and rejected (v. 3)

3 He is despised and rejected of men; a man of sorrows, and acquainted with grief: and we hid as it were our faces from him; he was despised, and we esteemed him not.

The words "sorrows" and "grief" literally mean "pains" and "sickness." This could mean that He was sick of body or spirit, or it could mean that He voluntarily bound Himself in the sickness and pain of humanity. This is the view stated in the first part of verse 4 (see below).

Matthew 8:17 quotes Isaiah 53:4 as fulfilled in the healing ministry of Jesus.

The last part of verse 3 reinforces the picture of rejection of the Servant. He was despised. People didn't care about Him. This shows how little they understood who He was and what He was doing.

III. The Suffering of the Servant for Us
(Isa. 53:4–6)

1. The cause of His suffering (v. 4)

4 Surely he hath borne our griefs, and carried our sorrows: yet we did esteem him stricken, smitten of God, and afflicted.

Many people assumed that suffering was the result of the sins of the sufferer. The Book of Job shows that some people who suffer are not being punished by God for their sins. Isaiah presents another kind of sufferer—one who suffers for others. The last part of verse 4 states the initial assumption about the cause of the Servant's suffering. They thought He was smitten by God for His sins. The first part of the verse, however, shows that He suffered not for Himself but for others.

2. With His stripes we are healed (v. 5)

5 But he was wounded for our transgressions, he was bruised for our iniquities: the chastisement of our peace was upon him; and with his stripes we are healed.

Verse 5 makes three points: (1) The suffering of the Servant resulted in His death. The language denotes a violent and painful death. (2) The suffering and death of the Servant were for our sins. Verse 4 says that He bore our griefs and sorrows. Verse 5 makes clear that this includes our "transgressions" and "iniquities." (3) The Servant's suffering and death for our sins make possible our salvation. "Chastisement of our peace" means "chastisement which leads to our peace."

Peter's use of parts of verses 5–6 shows how the early Christians interpreted these verses. Referring to Jesus, Peter wrote: "Who his own self bare our sins in his own body on the tree, that we, being dead to sins, should live unto righteousness: by whose stripes ye were healed. For ye were as sheep going astray; but are now returned unto the Shepherd and Bishop of your souls" (1 Pet. 2:24–25).

3. Our spiritual plight (v. 6)

6 All we like sheep have gone astray; we have turned every one to his own way; and the Lord hath laid on him the iniquity of us all.

Verse 6 reveals three biblical truths about human sin: (1) Everyone has sinned. (2) The basic and universal human sin is that each one has decided to go his own way, not to walk with God in His way. (3) The result of our turning from God is that we are separated from God and one another by our sins. (This is implied in the words "gone astray" and "into his own way.")

The last line in verse 6 makes clear that the suffering and death of the Servant for our sins was in accordance with the plan and will of God. This clarifies the meaning of the last part of verse 4. The Servant was "smitten of God, and afflicted" in the sense that "the Lord hath laid on him the iniquity of us all."

Although we cannot know who were the original speakers of verses 4–6, all of us are the "we," "us," and "our" of verses 4–6. We all of us have gone astray from God. The Servant suffered and died for our sins yours and mine. And with His stripes, we all who believe are saved and made whole!

IV. The Servant's Unjust Death (Isa. 53:7–9)

The Servant was the Lamb of God who went silently to His death (v. 7). He was unjustly accused and killed (v. 8a). Yet even in this description of the mistreatment of the Servant by wicked people, we are reminded that from God's point of view, the Servant died for the sins of the people (v. 8b). In His death and burial He was associated with the wicked and with the rich (v. 9a). The Servant suffered although He Himself was an innocent and good man (v. 9b).

V. God's Will and the Servant's Victory (Isa. 53:10–12)

1. The fulfillment of God's will (v. 10)

10 Yet it pleased the Lord to bruise him; he hath put him to grief: when thou shalt make his soul an offering for sin, he shall see his seed, he shall prolong his days, and the pleasure of the Lord shall prosper in his hand.

The word "pleased" means that the Servant's suffering and death for human sin were God's will, not that God found pleasure in seeing the Servant suffer and die. The pleasure resulted from achieving the end result of the sacrificial death of the Servant. This meaning is clear in the following translation:

> Yet it was the Lord's will to crush him and cause him to suffer,
> and though the Lord makes his life a guilt offering,
> he will see his offspring and prolong his days,
> and the will of the Lord will prosper in his hand (NIV).

The references to offspring and long life are Old Testament symbols of enduring life and success in the sight of God. Thus verse 10 points to God's will in the suffering and death of the Servant, and in His victory and enduring success. The New Testament sees the latter fulfilled in Jesus' resurrection, exaltation, the salvation of many through His Spirit, and His coming sovereignty over all things.

2. Justification (v. 11)

11 He shall see the travail of his soul, and shall be satisfied: by his knowledge shall my righteous servant justify many; for he shall bear their iniquities.

The first part of verse 11 points to the satisfaction of the Servant in fulfilling the Father's will through His suffering and death. Hebrews 12:2 refers to Jesus as "the author and finisher of our faith; who for the joy that was set before him endured the cross, despising the shame, and is set down at the right hand of the throne of God."

The rest of the verse refers to what the New Testament calls justification by faith. "His knowledge" means our knowledge of Him. Through our knowledge of Him, Christ God's righteous Servant justifies many. Although we are sinners (v. 6), He makes us right with God. This is possible because He died for our sins.

3. Intercessor for sinners (v. 12). Verse 12 sounds the note of victory with which the passage began in Isaiah 52:13. The Servant will be exalted among the great and divide the spoils of His victory over sin and death (v. 12a). Because He died a sinner's death for sinners, He became the great Intercessor for sinners (v. 12b). (See Heb. 7:25.)

APPLYING THE BIBLE

1. Opposition to the word of God. Opposition to and unbelief in the Bible are nothing new.

In A.D. 303, Roman Emperor Diocletian sought to destroy all the Bibles. In his attempt to stamp out Christianity, he persecuted and killed many humble believers. Christians found with Bibles were burned to death along with their Bibles. After two years of insane persecution and Bible burning, Diocletian erected a monument reading, "Extinct is the name of Christians." But just twenty-five years later Emperor Constantine, sympathetic to Christians, offered a reward for copies of the Bible. Within just twenty-four hours, fifty copies of the Bible were brought out of hiding and presented to the emperor.

American lawyer and agnostic Robert Ingersoll fought the Bible all his life. Once, in a lecture against the Bible, he declared: "In fifteen years I'll have this book in the morgue." But the Bible has outlived Ingersoll, and there are more copies of it in existence today—and more believers in it today—than there were when Ingersoll made his foolish remarks.

French philosopher Voltaire (1694–1778) said that in one hundred years the Bible would be extinct. But when the one hundred years were up, Voltaire was dead, and the house in which he had lived was owned and used by the Geneva Bible Society in its work of printing and distributing Bibles. Since his time millions of Bibles have been published, but some years ago ninety-two volumes of Voltaire's works were sold for a total of two dollars.

Long ago, God asked the question: "Who hath believed our report? and to whom is the arm of the Lord revealed?" (v. 1).

2. A root out of dry ground. Great men and women have been produced by unlikely soil. Consider, for example, Abraham Lincoln, our martyred and most-beloved president. Born in poverty and obscurity in Kentucky in 1809, Lincoln had almost no formal education but was self-taught. Studying by a log fire at night, Lincoln kept saying to himself, "I will study and get myself ready and someday my opportunity will come."

And come it did when he was elected president in 1860 to lead the nation through its greatest crisis—the Civil War. Unlikely soil produced one whom many believe to be our greatest president.

Verse 2 of today's lesson shows us that God's Servant the Savior came from an unlikely source. But as Renan, the French historian wrote, "He is the hinge upon whom the ages turn. Where we came from is unimportant. What we become is the thing that counts!"

3. No beauty to behold Him. In the 1880s, T. DeWitt Talmage was the sensational pastor of a Brooklyn, New York, church. Whether his information is correct, one can only surmise, but Talmage said that twenty centuries ago Publius Lentulus wrote a letter to the Roman Senate describing Jesus.

"A man of stature somewhat tall; His hair the color of a chestnut fully ripe, plain to the ears, whence downward it is more orient, curling and waving about the shoulders; in the midst of His forehead is a stream or partition of his hair; forehead plain and very delicate; His face without spot or wrinkle, a lovely red; His nose and mouth so forked that nothing can be represented; His beard thick, in color like His hair and not very long; His eyes, quick and clear.[1]

But Isaiah said, "There is no beauty that we should desire him" (v. 2). Jesus' attractiveness was not in His physical appearance, but in His spiritual power.

4. The Suffering Savior. The physical suffering of Jesus on the cross was immense, but His spiritual suffering was greater by far. Bearing the sins of all humankind, He died as a sinner rejected by the Father whose love and presence He had shared from eternity (Matt. 27:46).

He was tried six times: three trials in the ecclesiastical courts and three trials in the civil courts. His beard was plucked, and He was crowned with a crown of thorns and mockingly robed in a regal, purple robe. He was jeered, spat upon, laughed at, and made to carry His cross in public humiliation. Nailed naked and inhumanely to the cross, He died among thieves and the jeers of the Roman soldiers. But, on Easter God had the last word, as He always does.

About our suffering Savior, Isaiah said: "But he was wounded for our transgressions, he was bruised for our iniquities: the chastisement of our peace was upon him; and with his stripes we are healed" (v. 5). Our only response to this kind of love must be humble, obedient love and service.

TEACHING THE BIBLE

▶ *Main Idea:* The Servant's victory shows how God can bring victory out of suffering.

▶ *Suggested Teaching Aim:* To lead adults to identify aspects of Christ's suffering found in the description of the Servant, and to identify ways God can give them victory in suffering

A TEACHING OUTLINE

1. Use an illustration to introduce the lesson.
2. Use sentence strips to overview the lesson.
3. Use a lesson outline to guide the study.
4. Read a hymn to "Give the Truth a Personal Focus."

Introduce the Bible Study

Introduce the lesson by using "The Suffering Savior" in "Applying the Bible." Read the "Main Idea" of the lesson.

Search for Biblical Truth

IN ADVANCE on strips of paper, write the statements in the opening paragraph under "Studying the Bible." Distribute these to the people in your class. Ask them to read the statements to summarize the lesson.

Copy the following lesson outline on strips of paper and place on the focal wall as you teach:

I. From Humiliation to Exaltation (Isa. 52:13–15)
II. Rejection of the Servant (Isa. 53:1–3)
III. The Suffering of the Servant for Us (Isa. 53:4–6)
IV. The Servant's Unjust Death (Isa. 53:7–9)
V. God's Will and the Servant's Victory (Isa. 53:10–12)

Place the first poster strip on the wall and ask members to open their Bibles to Isaiah 52:13. Briefly summarize the material on these verses in "Studying the Bible."

Place the second strip on the wall. Ask: Who is speaking in 53:1? (See four suggestions in "Studying the Bible.")

Ask a volunteer to read Isaiah 11:1 and ask members to compare the ideas in 11:1 and 53:2. Ask members to suggest what the last half of 52:2 means. (See "Studying the Bible.")

Ask a volunteer to read 53:3. Write on a chalkboard or a large sheet of paper: *Sorrows = pains; Grief = sickness.*

Ask a volunteer to read Matthew 8:17. Point out how the New Testament saw Jesus' healing ministry fulfilling this verse.

Place the third strip on the focal wall. Ask: How did the Servant's suffering differ from most suffering? (It was for others.) Present a brief lecture in which you share the three points which "Studying the Bible" makes about 53:5 and the three biblical truths about human sin mentioned in 53:6. Point out that we are the ones for whom Jesus suffered.

Place the fourth poster on the wall. Briefly summarize the information in "Studying the Bible" on these three verses.

Place the fifth outline point on the wall. Ask a member to read another translation (preferably NIV) of 53:10. Ask: How is this verse fulfilled in Jesus' life? (Resurrection.)

Point out that Hebrews 12:2 is a commentary on the first half of 53:11. Point out that the Servant's justification is possible because He died for our sins.

Give the Truth a Personal Focus

Read the words to "When I Survey the Wondrous Cross."

> When I survey the wondrous cross,
> On which the Prince of glory died,
> My richest gain I count but loss,
> And pour contempt on all my pride.

Point out that because of Jesus' death on the cross for us, He is able to bring victory out of our suffering. The only appropriate response to His suffering is to say:

> Were the whole realm of nature mine,
> That were a present far too small;
> Love so amazing, so divine,
> Demands my soul, my life, my all.[2]

Read again the Main Idea and close in prayer.

---

1. Fowler's personal file, source unknown.
2. No. 144, *The Baptist Hymnal*, 1991.

God's Love for All People (Jonah, Ruth)

INTRODUCTION

This four-lesson study is taken from two short Old Testament books: Jonah and Ruth. Both of these short books have this in common: each emphasizes that God's love includes people other than the descendants of Israel.

The first two lessons are taken from the Book of Jonah. This prophetic book is a narrative about Jonah rather than prophetic messages by the prophet Jonah. The first lesson tells how Jonah tried in vain to flee from God's call. The second lesson reveals the heart of the book's message in Jonah's anger that God spared the repentant people of Nineveh.

The last two lessons are based on the Book of Ruth. The third lesson shows Ruth's loyalty to her mother-in-law and her acceptance of the God of Israel. The fourth lesson deals with the kindness of Boaz to Ruth and Naomi, the marriage of Boaz and Ruth, and the birth of their son.

Jonah Flees from God

Basic Passage: Jonah 1–2
Focal Passages: Jonah 1:1–4,10–15,17; 2:1,10

When most people think of Jonah, they think only of Jonah being swallowed by a great fish. This is part of what happened, but it isn't the real message of the Book of Jonah. The real message doesn't become clear until Jonah explained why he was angry about the repentance and deliverance of Nineveh. Jonah then explained that he had fled from the Lord's call precisely because he knew that God was a merciful God (Jonah 4:2). Jonah hated the foreign Ninevites so much that he wanted God to destroy them, not save them. The point of the book, therefore, is that God's people sometimes resist God's loving purpose for all people, especially people they dislike. The lesson of the first two chapters focuses on what happens when people of faith disobey God's call.

▶ ▶ ▶ ▶ ▶ ▶ ▶ ▶ **Study Aim:** *To understand the reason and results of Jonah's flight from obeying God's call*

STUDYING THE BIBLE

LESSON OUTLINE
I. God's Call and Jonah's Rebellion (Jonah 1:1–3)
  1. God's call to Jonah (Jonah 1:1–2)
  2. Jonah's rebellion (Jonah 1:3)
II. God's Response to Jonah's Rebellion (Jonah 1:4–16)
  1. Storm at sea (Jonah 1:4–6)
  2. Finding the guilty party (Jonah 1:7–10)
  3. Deciding what to do (Jonah 1:11–14)
  4. Jonah cast into the sea (Jonah 1:15–16)
III. Jonah's Prayer and Deliverance (Jonah 1:17; 2:10)
  1. The fish (Jonah 1:17)
  2. Jonah's prayer (Jonah 2:1–9)
  3. Jonah's deliverance (Jonah 2:10)

When God called Jonah to go to Nineveh (1:1–2), Jonah got on a ship headed for Tarshish (1:3). God responded by sending a storm (1:4–6). When the sailors discovered that Jonah was the cause of the trouble and a worshiper of the Creator of earth and seas, they were more frightened than ever (1:7–10). After they had tried in vain to row to land, the sailors prayed to God before casting Jonah overboard (1:11–14). When the sailors threw Jonah overboard, the sea calmed; and the sailors offered a sacrifice and vows to God (1:15–16). Jonah was swallowed by and survived for three days and nights in a great fish prepared by God (1:17). Jonah prayed (2:1) a prayer of gratitude for deliverance (2:2–9), and the fish vomited Jonah out on dry land (2:10).

I. God's Call and Jonah's Rebellion
(Jonah 1:1–3)

1. God's call to Jonah (vv. 1–2)

1 Now the word of the Lord came unto Jonah the son of Amittai, saying,

2 Arise, go to Nineveh, that great city, and cry against it; for their wickedness is come up before me.

Jonah, the son of Amittai, is mentioned in 2 Kings 14:23–25 as a prophet during the reign of Jeroboam II, king of Israel. The Book of Jonah begins like many of the prophetic books with a reference to the word of the Lord coming to the prophet (see Ezek. 1:3; Jer. 1:2; Hos. 1:1; Joel 1:1; Mic. 1:1). Jonah's call included three words of command: "Arise," "go," and "cry." Jonah was told to arise and go to Nineveh, the capital of the brutal Assyrians. Their evil reputation made them feared and hated throughout the ancient world. Jonah was told to cry out against the city because of their sins. In typical biblical language, the wickedness of the city is described as coming up before the Lord (compare Gen. 4:10; Jer. 2:22; Hos. 7:2).

2. Jonah's rebellion (v. 3)

3 But Jonah rose up to flee unto Tarshish from the presence of the Lord, and went down to Joppa; and he found a ship going to Tarshish: so he paid the fare thereof, and went down into it, to go with them unto Tarshish from the presence of the Lord.

God had told Jonah to arise and go to Nineveh. Instead, Jonah rose and went the opposite direction. He went down to Joppa, an ancient seaport on the Mediterranean. Joppa is the modern Jaffa, which is now part of the city of Tel Aviv. Jonah paid the fare for a trip to Tarshish, which most people think was at the other end of the Mediterranean in what is now Spain.

Jonah surely knew better than to think that he could find a place where he could escape the presence of the Lord. Later He confessed faith in "the God of heaven, which hath made the sea and the dry land" (v. 9). From the beginning he must have known, like the writer of Psalm 139, that God's presence is everywhere.

Why did Jonah try to run from God? At this point in the story, we might think he was afraid of confronting the fierce Assyrians with their sins. However, he later showed himself to be a man of courage (see 1:12; 3:3–4). Jonah later confessed that he ran from God because he feared that the people of Nineveh might repent and be spared by the mercy of God (4:2). He was angry because they were not destroyed by God (4:9–11).

II. God's Response to Jonah's Rebellion
(Jonah 1:4–16)

1. Storm at sea (vv. 4–6)

4 But the Lord sent out a great wind into the sea, and there

was a mighty tempest in the sea, so that the ship was like to be broken.

Notice the word "but" at the beginning of verses 3 and 4. God called Jonah, but he fled. Jonah tried to flee from God on an out-bound ship, but the Lord sent a destructive storm. The force of the storm is seen in the words "mighty tempest" and in the threat that the ship was likely to break up.

The sailors were brave men who likely had ridden out many a storm, but the fury of this storm terrified them. Each prayed to his own god for deliverance. They began to throw the cargo overboard in an attempt to lighten the ship. Meanwhile Jonah was in a deep sleep in the inner part of the ship (v. 5). The captain aroused Jonah from his sound sleep and told him to call on his God (v. 6).

2. Finding the guilty party (vv. 7–10)

Assuming that the storm was caused by a god for the offense of someone on board, the sailors cast lots to find the guilty party.

When they did, the lot fell on Jonah (v. 7). They gave Jonah an opportunity to explain by asking him a number of questions about himself (v. 8). Jonah replied that he was a Hebrew, who feared the Lord God, Creator of earth and seas (v. 9).

10 Then were the men exceedingly afraid, and said unto him, Why hast thou done this? For the men knew that he fled from the presence of the Lord, because he had told them.

Earlier the sailors had been frightened by the storm. Now that Jonah had spoken of His God as Creator, they were even more afraid. Earlier they had feared the storm; now they also feared the Lord God of Jonah. Apparently when Jonah first boarded the ship, he told them that he was running from his God. They had not thought much about it until the terrible storm came and Jonah described His God as Creator of earth and sea. They put two and two together and realized that Jonah's great God had caused the storm because of Jonah's rebellion.

3. Deciding what to do (vv. 11–14)

11 Then said they unto him, What shall we do unto thee, that the sea may be calm unto us? for the sea wrought, and was tempestuous.

12 And he said unto them, Take me up, and cast me forth into the sea; so shall the sea be calm unto you: for I know that for my sake this great tempest is upon you.

To the sailors' credit, they were still reluctant to harm Jonah. We might have expected these terrified, heathen sailors to throw Jonah overboard when they first suspected that he was the one who had offended his God. Instead they asked Jonah what they should do with him. Jonah was the one to recommend that he be cast into the sea. He promised that the sea would grow calm if the sailors threw the guilty Jonah into the sea. Why would he suggest that his own life be taken? One motivation may have been a desire to spare others from death on his account.

13 Nevertheless the men rowed hard to bring it to the land; but they could not: for the sea wrought, and was tempestuous

against them.

14 Wherefore they cried unto the Lord, and said, We beseech thee, O Lord, we beseech thee, let us not perish for this man's life, and lay not upon us innocent blood: for thou, O Lord, hast done as it pleased thee.

Even after Jonah told the sailors to throw him into the sea, they were reluctant to do so. They thought that throwing him into the sea would surely result in his death. When finally the sailors realized they could not reach land, no matter how hard they rowed, they concluded that God Himself had determined Jonah's fate.

Before throwing him overboard, however, the heathen sailors prayed to the Lord God. They fervently besought the Lord not to hold Jonah's death against them. Their reference to "innocent blood" does not mean that Jonah was innocent before God; it means that he was innocent of doing anything against them that led them to take his life. The last part of verse 14 means that they were acting on God's behalf to do what they thought He wanted them to do to throw Jonah overboard.

4. Jonah cast into the sea (vv. 15–16)

15 So they took up Jonah, and cast him forth into the sea: and the sea ceased from her raging.

Feeling that they had no other choice, the sailors finally picked up Jonah and threw him into the angry sea. As a result the mighty tempest stopped. The sailors were so impressed by this display of power and justice by the Lord God that they feared Him and offered a sacrifice and vows to Him (v. 16).

III. Jonah's Prayer and Deliverance
(Jonah 1:17; 2:10)

1. The fish (1:17)

17 Now the Lord had prepared a great fish to swallow up Jonah. And Jonah was in the belly of the fish three days and three nights.

If the Lord could create heaven and earth, He could prepare a great fish of some kind to swallow Jonah; and He could keep Jonah alive inside the fish. The miracle was not in the fish swallowing him but in Jonah staying alive for three days and nights. The sailors and probably Jonah himself thought that God's plan was for Jonah to perish in the sea. God didn't use the fish to destroy Jonah but to deliver him. The prophet was saved from drowning by the fish. Judging from the prayer that follows and by Jonah's later obedience to the Lord's call, God used the experience in the fish to discipline and correct the prophet.

2. Jonah's prayer (2:1–9)

1 Then Jonah prayed unto the Lord his God out of the fish's belly.

Troubles have a way of teaching people to pray. Jonah's prayer in verses 2–9 expressed gratitude to God for deliverance. God heard his prayer from the depths of distress and at the gate to death (v. 2). His physical danger (v. 3) was compounded by his sense of being alienated from God (v. 4). God answered his prayer from the very portals of death (vv. 5–7). The prophet declared the emptiness of idols (v. 8) even as he praised God for deliverance (v. 9).

3. Jonah's deliverance (2:10)

> 10 And the Lord spake unto the fish, and it vomited out Jonah upon the dry land.

Jonah must have realized that God was trying to tell him something. He had left from dry land trying to run from God. Now the fish vomited him up back on dry land. No wonder the next few verses describe how Jonah obeyed the Lord's call when it came again.

Restored gate at the site of the ancient city of Nineveh of Assyria. Credit: William B. Tolar, Southwestern Baptist Theological Seminary, Fort Worth, Texas.

APPLYING THE BIBLE

1. Who is on the Lord's side? Abraham Lincoln was a great storyteller. He used stories to make a point, defuse a volatile situation, or simply to entertain.

To his cabinet that opposed him on a matter, except for one member, Lincoln told about an Illinois revival preacher who asked all in the congregation who were on the Lord's side to stand. Quickly, the entire audience stood except for one inebriated man who had wandered into the service. The preacher then asked that all who were on the devil's side to stand, and the drunk struggled to his feet and said: "I don't know what you said, preacher, but whatever it was I want you to know I am with you and will stand by your side!"

Nineveh, the great and wicked capital city of the cruel Assyrians, was certainly not on the Lord's side. But loving all people, even the most depraved, God called His servant Jonah, a Jew, to go to the wicked city and call it to repentance.

2. Preachers and preaching. Since the beginning of time, God has been calling his servants to preach His word to the people. The Bible is filled with the names of God's faithful proclaimers.

Richard Baxter, the great seventeenth-century English preacher said: "I have preached as never such to preach again."

Robert Murray McCheyne, the magnificent Scottish preacher who died at only thirty, said, "A preacher should never preach on everlasting punishment without tears."

In an English cathedral there is a tomb in which reposes the body of a preacher of earlier times. His epitaph reads: "He was a painful preacher of the truth."

Jonah is numbered among those who accepted the divine call to proclamation. He ran from the call at first, but God dealt with Jonah and, reluctantly, he did what God had called him to do.

3. Sin is rebellion against God. We are all sinners, but the preacher's sin casts a dark and heavy cloud over the work of the kingdom.

Such was the case with Henry Ward Beecher (1813–1887), one of the greatest preachers of the last century. Beecher was accused of committing adultery with Elizabeth Tilton when he was pastor of Brooklyn's Congregationalist Plymouth Church. Beecher was brought to trial, which lasted for six months. It was scandalous, and according to one account received more newspaper coverage than any event, up to that time, except the Civil War.

Although Beecher was found innocent of the charge, many believed he was guilty. And the publicity generated did irreparable damage, not only to Beecher but also to God's work in the northeast.[1]

In our day we have seen the same thing. The newspapers and televisions of our land have been filled with charges of fraud and immorality leveled against a number of well-known American preachers and priests. What great harm has been done by their self-centered rebellion against God. Jonah is usually remembered for his rebellion against God's call.

4. The great fish. Was Jonah really swallowed by a great fish? Could one survive three days and nights in a fish? Skeptics say "no," but the word of God says "yes," and we believe it.

James Bartley served as a seaman on the whaler the "Star of the East." Bartley fell overboard in February, 1891, and could not be found. When the whale they were trying to land as Bartley fell overboard was pulled up on deck and cut open, they found Bartley in its stomach. Bartley was alive but unconscious. After three weeks he was well enough to describe being forced down the slippery throat of the great white whale, and the terrible heat of its stomach. Bartley recovered after being treated in a London hospital, but his skin was permanently tanned by the gastric juices in the whale's stomach.

Ask Bartley if Jonah's story is only legend—that to survive in a fish's stomach is impossible. Guess what his reply would be?[2]

5. Repentance. Repentance is that voluntary change in the mind of the sinner in which he turns from sin, writes theologian Augustus Strong. It is sorrow for sin as committed against goodness and justice and therefore hateful to God and hateful in itself, Strong said. In the belly of the great fish, Jonah experienced firsthand in his own heart the repentance he was to preach to the Assyrians.

▶ *Main Idea:* The reason and results of Jonah's flight from obeying God's call show God's persistence in dealing with His people.

▶ *Suggested Teaching Aim:* To lead adults to describe the reason and results of Jonah's flight from obeying God's call, and to decide to accept a task from which they have been running in an attempt to escape God.

A TEACHING OUTLINE

1. Use an illustration to introduce the Bible study.

2. Use a map to locate significant places.

3. Prepare a study guide for each member to use as you lecture.

4. Challenge members to commit themselves to a ministry which they have been reluctant to accept.

Introduce the Bible Study

Use "Preachers and preaching" from "Applying the Bible" to introduce the lesson. Point out that many of us are like Jonah in that we refuse to accept certain tasks to which God has called us.

Search for Biblical Truth

Set the background of the lesson by pointing out Joppa, Nineveh, and the possible location of Tarshish on a map. Prepare a lesson outline on a chalkboard or a large sheet of paper by copying the three bold phrases below. Cover the phrases until you are ready to discuss them.

Prepare the following study guide for each member:

Study Guide
I. God's Call and Jonah's Rebellion (Jonah 1:1–3)

1. Where outside the Book of Jonah is Jonah mentioned? (2 Kings 14:23–25.)

2. What three verbs or action words did Jonah's call include? ("Arise," "go," "cry.")

3. To what nation did God tell Jonah to preach and why did Jonah not want to preach to them? (Assyrians, whose capital was Nineveh; they were a brutal people.)

4. Where did Jonah start and in what direction was it in relationship to Nineveh? (Tarshish, and it was in the opposite direction.)

5. Why did Jonah try to flee? (He feared the people of Nineveh would repent, and God would be merciful to them.)

II. God's Response to Jonah's Rebellion (Jonah 1:4–16)

6. What did God do to keep Jonah from going to Tarshish? (Sent a great wind.)

7. What was Jonah's explanation of the storm? (God the Creator of heaven and earth sent it.)

8. What was Jonah's suggestion for calming the storm? (Throw him overboard.)

9. Why did Jonah suggest his own life be taken? (Possibly to save others.)

10. How could the sailors refer to Jonah as "innocent" (1:14)? (He was innocent in that he had not harmed the sailors.)

11. What happened when they threw Jonah in the sea? (Sea became calm, and the sailors offered sacrifice to God.)

III. Jonah's prayer and Deliverance (Jonah 1:17, 2:10)

12. In this section the second unusual creation by God appears. What was it? (First a great wind, now a great fish.)

13. What was the miracle in this case? (Not the fish swallowing Jonah, but Jonah staying alive three days.)

14. What did Jonah finally do? (Prayed.)

15. What was God's response to Jonah's prayer? (Told the fish to deposit Jonah on the shore.)

Present a lecture in which you cover each of these points on the study guide. Ask members to write their answers. When you have finished, go over the answers to be sure members have correct answers.

Give the Truth a Personal Focus

Read the last part of the "Suggested Teaching Aim." Ask members to turn their study guides over and list some tasks to which God has called them but to which they have not responded. Now ask them to write why they should expect any different treatment from God than Jonah got. Encourage them to commit themselves to accepting a ministry they have previously refused.

---

1. J. B. Fowler, Jr., *Illustrating Great Words of the New Testament* (Nashville: Broadman Press, 1991), 168.

2. Ibid., 126.

God Shows Mercy

Basic Passage: Jonah 3–4
Focal Passages: Jonah 3:1–5,10; 4:1–5,11

I n a sense, Jonah represented Israel's attitude toward its missionary calling. This calling to all nations was inherent in the call of Abraham (Gen. 12:1–3) and in the covenant with Israel (Exod. 19:5–6). As we saw in our study of the Book of Isaiah, this aspect of Israel's mission was spelled out repeatedly (see Isa. 9:1; 11:9; 40:5; 42:1,6; 49:6; 51:4–5; 60:3). Throughout most of the Old Testament, Israel compromised its distinctive faith and way of life, and was thus disqualified to be a missionary nation. At other times, they emphasized their distinctive calling to the exclusion of any concern for Gentiles. The twofold theme of God's love for all people and Israel's reluctance to fulfill its missionary calling is emphasized in the Book of Jonah.

▶ ▶ ▶ ▶ ▶ ▶ ▶ ▶ ▶ **Study Aim:** *To explain why Jonah was angry when God spared Nineveh and what God tried to teach the angry prophet*

STUDYING THE BIBLE

LESSON OUTLINE
  I. Jonah's Preaching and Nineveh's Repentance (Jonah 3:1–10)
   1. God's second call to Jonah (Jonah 3:1–2)
   2. Jonah's obedience (Jonah 3:3–4)
   3. Nineveh's repentance (Jonah 3:5–9)
   4. God's response (Jonah 3:10)
  II. Jonah's Anger and God's Response (Jonah 4:1–11)
   1. The reason for Jonah's anger (Jonah 4:1–3)
   2. God's response to Jonah's anger (Jonah 4:4)
   3. Jonah waiting outside the city (Jonah 4:5)
   4. God dealing with Jonah (Jonah 4:6–8)
   5. Jonah's continuing anger (Jonah 4:9)
   6. What God tried to teach Jonah (Jonah 4:10–11)

When God called Jonah the second time (3:1–2), he responded by going to Nineveh and preaching (3:3–4). After the king and people repented and believed (3:5–9), God relented from His threat to destroy them (3:10). Jonah was angry because God showed mercy toward the hated foreigners (4:1–2). The prophet was so angry he prayed to die, but God asked him if he had the right to be angry (4:3–4). Jonah settled down outside the city to see what would happen (4:5). God prepared a vine that pleased Jonah with its shade; then God prepared a worm to destroy the vine; and finally God sent a hot wind to add to Jonah's discomfort (4:6–8). Jonah asked again to die. God asked if he had a right to be angry about the vine; Jonah said he did (4:9). Reminding Jonah of his concern about the fate of a vine, God asked if He didn't have the right to be concerned about the fate of people and cattle (4:10–11).

I. Jonah's Preaching and Nineveh's Repentance (Jonah 3:1–10)

1. God's second call to Jonah (3:1–2)

1 And the word of the Lord came unto Jonah the second time, saying,

2 Arise, go unto Nineveh, that great city, and preach unto it the preaching that I bid thee.

After the fish vomited Jonah out on dry land, the Lord called Jonah a second time. Jonah had gone through all the experiences of chapters 1–2 and found himself back where he began-listening to God's call. By now, Jonah must have realized that God was trying to tell him something. The wording of the second call is almost the same as the first call (1:2). The main difference is that the first call emphasized Nineveh's wickedness and the second stressed that the prophet was to speak what the Lord told him.

2. Jonah's obedience (3:3–4)

3 So Jonah arose, and went unto Nineveh, according to the word of the Lord. Now Nineveh was an exceeding great city of three days' journey.

4 And Jonah began to enter into the city a day's journey, and he cried, and said, Yet forty days, and Nineveh shall be overthrown.

Verse 3a stresses Jonah's obedience to the word of the Lord when it came the second time. He arose and went to Nineveh. Verse 3b shows something of the size of Nineveh. If the words "three days' journey" refer to the time it took to walk straight across Nineveh, it was a city about sixty miles across. If this is the meaning, the Bible is doubtlessly referring to Nineveh and all its surrounding area. The "three days' journey" may refer to the time it took to travel through Nineveh stopping and moving about to preach to the people.

Verse 4 shows the message God gave Jonah to preach. The later responses of the king and people of Nineveh mention God; therefore, they had some idea that Jonah represented God. Unless they repented within forty days, God would overthrow the city. The word *overthrow* is the same word used of God's overthrowing Sodom and Gomorrah (Gen. 19:29).

3. Nineveh's repentance (3:5–9)

5 So the people of Nineveh believed God, and proclaimed a fast, and put on sackcloth, from the greatest of them even to the least of them.

Earlier, the heathen sailors had worshiped God after the storm ceased (1:16). Now the wicked people of this huge Gentile city believed in God and repented of their sins. Their repentance was expressed by fasting and wearing sackcloth. All the people repented—from the greatest to the least of them.

In fact, the king and nobles issued a decree calling on all to fast, wear sackcloth, and cry fervently to God (3:6–8). Jonah's message had said nothing about the possibility of the city being spared if the people repented, but the decree declared that perhaps God would turn from His purpose of destruction and spare the city (3:9).

4. God's response (3:10)

10 And God saw their works, that they turned from their evil way; and God repented of the evil, that he had said that he would do unto them; and he did it not.

Two very different kinds of repentance are described in verse 10. The sinful people of Nineveh turned from their moral and spiritual acts of evil. God responded by relenting from the threatened judgment against Nineveh. The word *evil* was used to refer to both the sins of Nineveh and to the destructive judgment threatened by God. Thus the verse definitely does not teach that God is guilty of evil from which He repents. It means that when people repent, He turns from the purpose of judgment and bestows His mercy and grace on the repentant, believing sinners.

The word translated "repented" in verse 10 is derived from the idea of "breathing heavily" in grief or in relief. In other words, it was as if God breathed a sigh of relief when Nineveh repented and He could withhold His judgment. The revelation of Scripture is clear that God's deep desire is to show mercy to sinners, not to destroy them (see Ezek. 33:11; 2 Pet. 3:9).

II. Jonah's Anger and God's Response (Jonah 4:1–11)

1. The reason for Jonah's anger (vv. 1–3)

1 But it displeased Jonah exceedingly, and he was very angry.

2 And he prayed unto the Lord, and said, I pray thee, O Lord, was not this my saying, when I was yet in my country? Therefore, I fled before unto Tarshish: for I knew that thou art a gracious God, and merciful, slow to anger, and of great kindness, and repentest thee of the evil.

How revealing these verses are! First, we are shocked by Jonah's response to the repentance of Nineveh and to God's sparing them. We wonder what kind of evangelist or missionary gets mad because the people repent and believe as a result of his message. Isn't that what preachers hope and pray will happen? We expect Jonah to rejoice; instead, he was exceedingly angry.

Then Jonah's words to God reveal his reason for being angry. In verse 2, Jonah revealed why he had fled to Tarshish when God called him the first time. He knew that God was a merciful God, who forgave repentant sinners. He knew because he knew the revelation God had given to Moses in Exodus 34:6–7. I like to call this passage the John 3:16 of the Old Testament. It was one of the earliest and clearest revelations of God's love, and it was quoted repeatedly by later generations. Jonah clearly had Exodus 34:6–7 in mind in his prayer of verse 2 (see also Pss. 86:5,15; 103:8–9; Joel 2:13; Mic. 7:18).

Although Israelites usually applied Exodus 34:6–7 only to the chosen people, Jonah feared that God's love might include the hated Ninevites. Because of this fear, Jonah had tried to evade God's call. Finally, God led him to go and preach; and Jonah's worst fears were realized: Nineveh repented and God spared them.

2. God's response to Jonah's anger (vv. 3–4)

3 Therefore now, O Lord, take, I beseech thee, my life from me, for it is better for me to die than to live.

4 Then said the Lord, Doest thou well to be angry?

Verse 3 shows the depth of Jonah's feelings. He was so angry that he prayed to die. He thought of living in a world where the hated Ninevites were fellow believers as a result of his preaching! The prospect was so distasteful to him that he asked the Lord to take his life. The Lord's simple response was a question, "Have you any right to be angry?" (NIV). At this point, Jonah ignored the question; but the Lord came back to the question after dealing further with Jonah (see v. 9).

3. Jonah waiting outside the city (v. 5)

5 So Jonah went out of the city, and sat on the east side of the city, and there made him a booth, and sat under it in the shadow, till he might see what would become of the city.

Jonah camped outside the city. He seems to have thought that God might change His mind and destroy Nineveh after all. If that happened, the angry prophet wanted a seat on the 50-yard line. The booth provided some shade from the blazing sun.

4. God dealing with Jonah (vv. 6–8). Verses 6–8 use the same word that was used in Jonah 1:17 when God prepared a great fish to swallow Jonah. Now God prepared a gourd vine that provided shade. Jonah was glad for the vine (v. 6). Then God prepared a worm that destroyed the vine (v. 7). Finally God prepared a scorching east wind. The wind with the sun was so hot that Jonah repeated his earlier prayer to die (v. 8)

5. Jonah's continuing anger (v. 9). God asked Jonah if he had any right to be angry about the vine, and the prophet replied that he did.

6. What God tried to teach Jonah (vv. 10–11). God responded by telling Jonah that he was concerned about a vine that he had neither planted nor made to grow and that had a life-span of one day (v. 10).

11 And should not I spare Nineveh, that great city, wherein are more than sixscore thousand persons that cannot discern between their right hand and their left hand; and also much cattle?

Jonah was concerned about a vine; didn't God have the right to be concerned about multitudes of people? Who were the 120,000 people who couldn't tell their right hand from their left? Some Bible students think this was a reference to the morally and spiritually benighted people of Nineveh. Many Bible students think this was a reference to children, who were not accountable for the plight of their city. In other words, God was reminding Jonah that even if He disregarded the repentance of the adult sinners of Nineveh and destroyed the city, 120,000 children would also be destroyed. God even mentioned the cattle. Cattle are a higher form of life than a gourd vine; yet if Jonah had his way, they too would be destroyed. Jonah had been concerned about the destruction of a gourd vine; God asked if He didn't have the right to care about the destruction of children and cattle?

The Book of Jonah ends with God's question hanging in the air like an invitation. God was calling Jonah and his fellow countrymen to change their attitudes and actions to reflect their God who loves all people, not just them.

APPLYING THE BIBLE

1. The preacher's business. G. Campbell Morgan (1863–1945) was a noted English preacher, the son of a Baptist minister. "The preacher must catch the spirit of the age," he was once told. "God forgive him if he does," Morgan responded. "The preacher's business is to correct the spirit of the age."[1]

2. The preacher's life. John Wesley once remarked: "There are some men who preach so well when in the pulpit, that it is a shame they ever come out of it; and when they are out of it, they live so illy that it is a shame they should ever enter it."[2]

3. He didn't even know her name. Sir Wilfred T. Grenfell (1865–1940) was a medical doctor-missionary who served heroically and under severe hardships in the cold north of Labrador. Once aboard a ship bound from England for New York, Grenfell met a young woman and proposed to her, not even knowing her name. The following November, he and Miss Anne Elizabeth Caldwell MacClanahan were married. Soon thereafter they sailed to their new home where she served faithfully for many years by the side of her husband and bore him three children.

Jonah, unlike Grenfell, knew the hated name of the people God called him to warn. And it was a bitter pill for Jonah to swallow as our lesson today clearly shows.

We may not know the names or condition of the people who live near us, but still he calls us to love them in Christ and be a light to guide them to the Light of the world.

4. To feel unloved. Both Henry Stanley and Charles Dickens, as youths, felt unloved. Their younger days were bleak and cheerless days, but they rose above their misfortune and lived meaningfully.

Stanley (1841–1904) was an orphan who spent most of his youth in a workhouse. In March 1871, Stanley started his successful search for missionary doctor David Livingstone of Africa whom the world thought was dead. In 1874, he returned to Africa to continue Livingstone's work.

Charles Dickens (1812–1870) was one of England's greatest novelists. Dickens had an unhappy childhood, and it furnished the background for some of his novels.

But out of his dark background of sadness, Dickens rose to become one of England's greatest literary luminaries. Who could ever forget his *A Tale of Two Cities*, *David Copperfield*, or his magnificent *A Christmas Carol*?

To be unwanted and unloved is surely one of the most grievous burdens one can bear. Although the cruel Assyrians did not know God and did not know how much He wanted them for Himself, still they were divinely loved. That was the message God called Jonah to preach to them, and that's the message the world needs today.

5. God's knock is answered. Not long ago, I stood in St. Paul's Cathedral in London, admiring Holman Hunt's majestic painting of Jesus, *The Light of the World*, standing and knocking before a closed door. Beneath the picture are inscribed the words, "Oh, do not pass me by."

The closed door, symbolizing the human heart closed against God, has no handle on the outside, for it must be opened from within. Through Jonah's preaching, God stood before the hearts of the Ninevites and knocked to be admitted by faith. They responded with open hearts and "believed." They then proved by their actions that their repentance was genuine (3:5). As a result, the wrath of God was turned from them (3:10).

TEACHING THE BIBLE

▶ *Main Idea:* God's mercy toward the Ninevites demonstrates His great love for all people.
▶ *Suggested Teaching Aim:* To lead adults to describe Jonah's response to God's mercy toward the Ninevites, and to examine their own attitudes toward others who have not believed.

A TEACHING OUTLINE

1. Use an illustration to introduce the lesson.
2. Use a chart to examine God's two calls to Jonah.
3. Use group discussion and questions to examine Jonah's anger and God's response.
4. Use a chart to examine our response to God's call.

Introduce the Bible Study

Share the following: There is an old story about a woman who brought some proofs back to the photographer. She slammed them down on the counter and said: "These do not do me justice." The photographer looked up at the hard, bitter lines of the woman's face and said: "Madam, what you need is mercy, not justice."

This photographer expressed a great spiritual thought. We cannot stand before God without His mercy.

Search for Biblical Truth

Prepare the following chart but omit the italicized answers. Leave room for a third column to be added (see "Give the Truth a Personal Focus").

Jonah's Calls

	First	Second
God's Call	Arise, go, cry	Arise, go, preach
The Place	Nineveh	Nineveh
Jonah's Response	Fled	Went
Jonah's Attitude	Angry	Angry
God's Attitude	Loved Ninevites	Loved Ninevites

To summarize last week's lesson, ask members to provide answers for Jonah's first call. (Their answers may be phrased somewhat differently.)

IN ADVANCE, enlist a reader to read Jonah 3–4, possibly in a modern translation. Then ask members to fill in the information about Jonah's second call. Point out that about the only difference between it and his first call is that Jonah went to Nineveh. Very little had changed. He was still angry toward God and did not want God to show mercy to the Ninevites.

DISCUSS: What evidence do you see that Jonah was a reluctant prophet?

Ask members to look at 3:10. Point out the two different types of repentance (Ninevites and God's) in the verse. Use "Studying the Bible" to explain the difference between the two.

Ask members to look at 4:1–4. Ask: What was Jonah's response to the Ninevites' repentance? (Anger.) What do Jonah's words reveal about God? (See 4:2.) What reveals the depth of Jonah's anger? (Wanted God to take his life.)

DISCUSS: Do you feel somewhat angry when a notorious criminal or otherwise great sinner makes a late-in-life confession and claims salvation just before death? How does that differ from Jonah's feelings?

Ask members to look at 4:5–9 and describe (1) Jonah's actions (built booth, waited to see God's response), and (2) God's reaction (provided vine; provided worm; provided scorching east wind.)

Ask members to look at 4:10–11. Ask: What lesson did God try to teach Jonah? (Jonah was concerned about a vine; God was concerned about multitudes of people.)

DISCUSS: How would you compare your attitudes toward non-Christians with Jonah's? Are they alike? similar? different? Do you feel God's mercy should be withheld from certain people to pay them back for their sins? Should God withhold His mercy from you to pay you back for your sins?

Give the Truth a Personal Focus

Add a third column to the chart: My Call. Ask members how God's call to them differs from His call to Jonah. (Only the place is different.) Give members a piece of paper and ask them to complete their response to God's call to them by writing on it what they feel God has called them to do. End in prayer that members will not repeat Jonah's actions.

---

1. Walter B. Knight, *Knight's Master Book of New Illustrations* (Grand Rapids: William B. Eerdmans Pub. Co., 1956), 495.

2. Ibid., 498.

The Loyalty of Ruth

Basic Passage: Ruth 1
Focal Passages: Ruth 1:1–8,16–18

T he Book of Ruth, like Jonah, has only four chapters. It is basically a love story: the love of Ruth and Naomi, and the love of Ruth and Boaz. The theme is similar to the Book of Jonah, but the point is made in a more subtle way. The book keeps before the reader the fact that Ruth was not a native Israelite, but was from Moab (1:22; 2:2, 6, 10, 21; 4:5,10). Yet this foreigner became the great-grandmother of David (4:22). This book, like Jonah, challenged those in Israel who wanted to exclude Gentiles from the blessings of faith in the Lord. Ruth 1 reveals the love of Naomi for her family, including her daughters-in-law, and contains the famous pledge of loyal love by Ruth for Naomi.

▶ ▶ ▶ ▶ **Study Aim:** *To identify expressions of love and loyalty between Naomi and Ruth*

STUDYING THE BIBLE

LESSON OUTLINE
I. In Moab (Ruth 1:1–18)
 1. Sojourning in Moab (Ruth 1:1–2)
 2. Tragedy strikes (Ruth 1:3–5)
 3. Naomi's love for her daughters-in-law (Ruth 1:6–13)
 4. Different choices (Ruth 1:14–18)
II. Return to Bethlehem (Ruth 1:19–22)
 1. Naomi's bitterness (Ruth 1:19–21)
 2. Glimmer of a new beginning (Ruth 1:22)

Because of a famine, a man moved from Bethlehem to Moab with his wife Naomi and two sons (vv. 1–2). The man died; his two sons married Orpah and Ruth, Moabite women; later the two men died (vv. 3–5). With a hope that the Lord would deal kindly with her daughters-in-law, Naomi urged the young women. To return to their childhood homes (vv. 6–13). Although both at first refused, Orpah left, but Ruth expressed undying loyalty to Naomi (vv. 14–18). When Naomi returned to Bethlehem, she bitterly complained that she had left full but returned empty (vv. 19–21). Naomi and Ruth arrived in Bethlehem at the beginning of barley harvest (v. 22).

I. In Moab (Ruth 1:1–18)
1. Sojourning in Moab (vv. 1–2)
 1 Now it came to pass in the days when the judges ruled, that

there was a famine in the land. And a certain man of Beth-
lehem-judah went to sojourn in the country of Moab, he, and his
wife, and his two sons.

2 And the name of the man was Elimelech, and the name of
his wife Naomi, and name of his two sons Mahlon and Chilion,
Ephrathites of Beth-lehem-judah. And they came into the country of Moab, and continued there.

The setting of the book was in the time of the judges. While various
judges were struggling with enemies within and without, the Book of
Ruth tells of one family's times of hardship and sorrow, love and joy.
This particular family was from Bethlehem in Judah. Since the district
was also sometimes called Ephrathah, they were also called Ephrathites
(see Mic. 5:2).

A famine in Judah caused a man named Elimelech to take his family
to Moab. The word "sojourn" implies that he didn't intend to settle permanently in this foreign land, but only to stay until conditions changed
in Bethlehem. Moab was not too far away, just on the other side of the
Dead Sea. The people of Moab originally descended from Abraham's
nephew Lot (Gen. 19:36–37); but in later years they worshiped idols,
not the God of Abraham.

2. Tragedy strikes (vv. 3–5)

3 And Elimelech Naomi's husband died; and she was left, and
her two sons.

4 And they took them wives of the women of Moab; the name
of the one was Orpah, and the name of the other Ruth: and they
dwelled there about ten years.

5 And Mahlon and Chilion died also both of them; and the
woman was left of her two sons and her husband.

Keep in mind two factors about the world in which Naomi lived.
For one thing, it was a man's world. A woman alone had no rights and
was dependent on the charity of the community just to survive. Men of
the family were expected to care for the women. Before marriage, a female was cared for by her father, then by her husband; if her husband
died, she was cared for by her sons.

The other factor to keep in mind was the importance of male children to continue the family line. Losing her husband was a terrible
blow for Naomi; but as long as she had her two sons, she could be assured of someone to take care of her; and she had the hope of grand-
children to continue their line. The latter seemed likely when her sons
married two young women of Moab, Orpah and Ruth. But then her two
sons also died. Within a few years, Naomi lost her husband and her two
sons.

3. Naomi's love for her daughters-in-law (vv. 6–13)

6 Then she arose with her daughters in law, that she might return from the country of Moab: for she had heard in the country
of Moab how that the Lord had visited his people in giving them
bread.

7 Wherefore she went forth out of the place where she was,
and her two daughters in law with her; and they went on the

way to return unto the land of Judah.

8 And Naomi said unto her two daughters in law, Go, return each to her mother's house: the Lord deal kindly with you, as ye have dealt with the dead, and with me.

When Naomi heard that the famine was ended in Judah, she headed home. Orpah and Ruth were with her. At some point in the journey, perhaps as they reached the border, Naomi told her daughters-in-law to return to their own homes. Verse 9 makes clear the reason for this: By returning home, these women, who were still young, might remarry and find security in the house of a husband.

She told each to return to "her mother's house." This was not because their fathers were dead, for Ruth 2:11 shows that Ruth's father was alive. The "mother's house" in the society of that day referred to the women's quarters.

The last part of verse 8 reveals some important qualities of Naomi, Orpah, and Ruth. The words "deal kindly" express both Naomi's faith in the Lord and her love for Orpah and Ruth. The Hebrew word from which "deal kindly" is translated was used to describe the mercy or kindness of the Lord (Exod. 34:7; Ruth 2:20) or of people (Hos. 6:6; Ruth 3:10). On several occasions, Naomi expressed her feelings that the Lord had dealt harshly with her (see 1:13, 20); however, her words to Orpah and Ruth show that she still believed in the mercy of the Lord.

Her words also show that she prayed that her daughters-in-law would experience His loving care. Naomi prayed that the Lord would deal kindly with them as they had dealt with their husbands and with her. These two young women had showed kindness and support to Naomi during their times of shared grief.

Naomi kissed them and wept as she told them to return to their own people. They had helped her; but they needed to think about their own futures, which would be more hopeful back with their own families (v. 9). Both Orpah and Ruth protested Naomi's advice to return home; they both said they would return with her to her own people (v. 10). Naomi was thinking of them, but they were thinking of her. They knew they could be of further help to her.

The only way to understand verses 11–13 is to be aware of the custom of levirate marriages. According to this custom, a man was expected to marry the widow of his deceased brother if the widow was childless. In this way, the dead brother's name and heritage would be continued (see Deut. 25:5–10). Naomi told Orpah and Ruth that the only way either of them could marry her husband's brother would be for Naomi to remarry and have sons. Naomi said she was too old to remarry and have sons. Even if she did, Orpah and Ruth were themselves too old to wait for any other sons of Naomi to grow up.

4. Different choices (vv. 14–18). Orpah and Ruth wept. Orpah kissed Naomi and headed back to her mother's house, but Ruth clung to her mother-in-law (v. 14). Naomi told Ruth to join her sister-in-law in returning to her own people and her own gods (v. 15).

16 And Ruth said, Intreat me not to leave thee, or to return

from following after thee: for whither thou goest, I will go; and where thou lodgest, I will lodge: thy people shall be my people, and thy God my God:

17 Where thou diest, will I die, and there will I be buried: the Lord do so to me, and more also, if ought but death part thee and me.

18 When she saw that she was stedfastly minded to go with her, then she left speaking unto her.

Ruth 1:16–17 are the most famous verses in the book. Over the centuries, people have been impressed by the love, loyalty, and faith expressed by these words. Many couples have incorporated these words in their wedding ceremony. No words could express any better the total commitment of one person to another.

The words clearly express Ruth's determination to remain with Naomi. She would go with her wherever she went. She would live wherever she lived. She would live her life there and be buried where Naomi was buried. Ruth knew that Naomi was right that Ruth's own prospects of remarriage were better back where she grew up. Ruth also knew that she would be a foreigner in Judah, and she realized this would make her lot all the harder and more hazardous. However, Ruth also believed that Naomi would need help; and Ruth was willing to provide what help she could. The rest of the book bears out that fact. Thus, Ruth displayed the kind of unselfishness that marks true love.

Ruth's words also constitute a confession of faith in the Lord God of Israel. In her vow, she used not only the word for *God* that was common for many religions; she also used the personal name of the Lord of the Hebrews. She had lived with Naomi and her family long enough to see evidences of their faith in the Lord. When she decided to go with Naomi, she openly declared her determination to serve Naomi's God.

One of the strong themes in the Book of Ruth is the interaction between human decisions and divine providence. The doctrine of God's providence means that He works in our lives toward a purpose of ultimate good. Throughout the book is the interplay of human decisions and divine providence. In verse 1, we saw the decision of Elimelech to move to Moab because of a famine. Later in the book we will see other decisions and their results that some people might call coincidences. People of faith see the hand of God working in the background to achieve His purpose of good. At this point, Naomi was having a hard time believing this because she was concentrating on the bad things that had happened to her. But Ruth's decision was the beginning of great good that God had for both of them.

II. Return to Bethlehem (Ruth 1:19–22)

1. **Naomi's bitterness (vv. 19–21).** When the two women arrived in Bethlehem, the people asked, "Is this Naomi?" (v. 19). She replied that her name, which means "pleasant" should be changed to "Mara," which

means "bitter" (v. 20). She felt that she had left Bethlehem full but was returning empty because the Lord had afflicted her (v. 21).

2. Glimmer of a new beginning (v. 22). Verse 22 contains a subtle clue that better days were ahead. The two women returned just at the beginning of the barley harvest.

APPLYING THE BIBLE

1. Benjamin Franklin on Ruth. When Benjamin Franklin was living in Paris, he joined a literacy society made up mostly of infidels. From time to time they would meet, read papers they had written, and discuss them.

On one occasion it was Franklin's time to present a paper. Copying the Book of Ruth, Franklin read the Old Testament love story without revealing its identity. When he had finished, the chairman of the group asked Franklin for permission to publish it.

"I am sorry, sir, but the story has already been printed. You will find it in the Bible, which you claim to despise," Franklin replied.[1]

2. Dwight L. Moody's godly mother. D. L. Moody, one of the world's greatest and best-known evangelists, had a hard life as a boy. His father died when Moody was only four years old, leaving a widowed wife with nine children to rear. The family lived in a modest but mortgaged home, and Moody's mother struggled in poverty to rear and educate her family. The family was in debt and the creditors were unbelievably cruel, taking everything she owned "including the wood from the woodpile," but she refused to give up. This brave, sturdy woman gave the world a son, who through his preaching, shook two continents for Christ and founded Christian schools, and another son who became president of a great college.[2]

Such a woman was Naomi. Her life as a widow was hard, and her faith was severely tested. But this godly woman was the most singular influence on Ruth, a Moabite who did not know God. Ruth became the great-grandmother of David, from whom came the Messiah. Life's sweetest fruit is often produced under the most trying circumstances.

3. "Sweet are the uses of adversity" (Shakespeare). American poet Sidney Lanier wrote: "The dark is full of nightingales, of dreams and of heavenly muse [inspiration]."

One sees that in Naomi, the mother-in-law of Ruth. In a strange land, far from her home in Bethlehem, Naomi's husband died, and all looked so dark. But out of that darkness God brought light, meaning, and blessings. As the iceberg that sank the Titanic passed on to melt in warmer waters after it had created such a grave tragedy, so our sorrows pass by, leaving us refined, sweeter, better, and more useful to God if we accept them in faith and commit them in confidence to our caring Savior.

4. Sweet songs come out of trials. Hardships and sorrow, such as that experienced by Naomi and Ruth, were used by God to give the world a Savior.

God uses sorrow to produce the greatest blessings that have blessed our world. Handel wrote the *Messiah* under circumstances most trying. Disappointed in love and disillusioned by friends, Franz Schubert transferred his sorrow into the beautiful song "Ave Maria." Johann Goethe's mother said that whenever her son had a sorrow, he always turned it into a poem. And Goethe is remembered today as Germany's greatest writer.

5. Ruth's loyalty. Near the post office on Broadway in New York City stands a bronze statue of a young man whose arms and feet are tied and whose shirt collar is open. Beneath the statue are etched the words, "I regret that I have but one life to give for my country. Nathan Hale."

Hale (1755–1776) was an American Revolutionary War patriot who was hanged at the age of twenty-one by the British as an American spy. His courage in the face of death, and his loyalty to a great cause that consumed him, made Hale one of America's great heroes.

Captain Hale served George Washington in a group called the Rangers. When Washington asked the commander of the Rangers to select a man to pass through the British lines and obtain information for the Americans, Hale volunteered. Posing as a Dutch schoolmaster, Hale crossed the British lines, got the information needed but was captured by the British on September 21, 1776, as he was returning to the American lines. He was condemned to be hanged by British General William House.

Loyalty is an attitude most noble, and in Scripture one will find no better human example of it than in Ruth's loyalty to Naomi.

6. Abraham Lincoln and divine providence. The late news commentator Lowell Thomas once told how divine providence guided in giving America her noblest president.

A farmer was working in his Kentucky field in 1784 with his two sons when he was shot down by Indians. The elder son saw his father fall, ran to the cabin for his gun, and shot the Indian who had snatched up the younger son and was hurrying him toward the woods. When the Indian fell, the little boy ran to the cabin and safety.

The boy saved was Thomas Lincoln who later became the father of Abraham Lincoln, America's great emancipator.

As our lesson writer states today, "One of the strong themes in the Book of Ruth is the interaction between human decisions and divine providence." We must not fail to see in this lesson about Naomi and Ruth the hand of God at work to give the world a Savior through David, whose great grandmother was Ruth, a converted Moabitess.

TEACHING THE BIBLE

▶ *Main Idea:* Ruth's love and loyalty for Naomi models the kind of family loyalty we should have.

▶ *Suggested Teaching Aim:* To lead adults to describe Ruth's love and loyalty for Naomi, and to commit themselves to strengthen their family relationships.

A TEACHING OUTLINE

1. Use an illustration to introduce the Bible study.
2. Use a series of questions to describe the setting of the Book of Ruth.
3. Use member-prepared reports to involve members in the study.
4. Identify five expressions of Ruth's love and loyalty for Naomi and their result.
5. Identify how this study can lead members to strengthen their family relationships.

Introduce the Bible Study

Introduce the lesson by summarizing "Benjamin Franklin on Ruth" in "Applying the Bible." Read the "Suggested Teaching Aim."

Search for Biblical Truth

Use the introduction (the first paragraph) to "Studying the Bible" to compare Ruth and Jonah. IN ADVANCE, enlist a member to prepare a two- to three-minute report on Ruth, using the article in the *Holman Bible Dictionary* or another Bible dictionary. Call for the report at this time.

Ask members to share their concept of the time of the judges. (It was a violent time.) Point out that it was a violent time, but that this lovely book takes place in that same time.

On a chalkboard or a large sheet of paper write the following questions. The answers in parentheses are suggestions only; members answers may differ some.

Who was involved? (Elimelech, Naomi, Mahlon, Chilion, Orpah, Ruth.)

What happened? (Family moved to escape famine.)

When did this occur? (During the time of the judges.)

Where did this take place? (Bethlehem, Moab; locate Bethlehem and Moab on a map.)

Why did all this take place? (Because of a famine that may have been caused by invading forces taking the food supply.)

Either make five group assignments and let the groups answer these questions or work together as a class to answer them. Briefly summarize the events in 1:3–5, emphasizing the position of women in a male-dominated society who were widowed and left without sons to care for them.

Ask a volunteer to read 1:6–13. IN ADVANCE, ask a member to define "Levirate Marriage," based on information in the *Holman Bible Dictionary* or another Bible dictionary. Call for the report at this time. Ask a volunteer to read 1:14–18. Ask the class to find at least five expressions of love and loyalty between Ruth and Naomi: (1) I will go where you go; (2) I will live where you live; (3) I will make your people my people (would convert to Judaism); (4) I will worship your God; (5) and I will stay with you till you die.

Ask members to share how they feel each of these expressions helped Naomi. (See "Studying the Bible" for additional information.)

Give the Truth a Personal Focus

Ask members to work with others near them to write suggestions based on these verses as to how they can strengthen their family relationships. Let groups share their ideas with the whole class.

Close in prayer for strength and wisdom to carry out their suggestions.

---

1. J. B. Fowler, Jr., *Living Illustrations*; (Nashville Broadman Press, 1985), 18.

2. Benjamin P. Browne, *Illustrations for Preaching* (Nashville: Broadman Press, 1977), 167.

The Kindness of Boaz

Basic Passage: Ruth 2–4
Focal Passages: Ruth 2:1, 8–12; 4:13–17

A s we have already noted, the Book of Ruth is a love story: the love of Ruth and Naomi, and the love of Ruth and Boaz. The book also shows how a young woman from Moab became a worshiper of the Lord and how the community of faith accepted her. Woven throughout the story are evidences of God using human actions and circumstances to work out His good purpose.

▶ ▶ ▶ ▶ **Study Aim:** *To explain the circumstances and significance of Ruth's marriage to Boaz*

STUDYING THE BIBLE

LESSON OUTLINE
  I. Gleaning in the Field of Boaz (Ruth 2:1–23)
    1. Boaz notices Ruth (Ruth 2:1–7)
    2. Boaz shows kindness to Ruth (Ruth 2:8–17)
    3. Ruth reports to Naomi (Ruth 2:18–23)
  II. At the Threshing Floor of Boaz (Ruth 3:1–18)
    1. Ruth carries out Naomi's plan (Ruth 3:1–9)
    2. Boaz responds to Ruth (Ruth 3:10–15)
    3. Naomi responds to Ruth's report (Ruth 3:16–18)
  III. Boaz at the City Gate (Ruth 4:1–12)
    1. Boaz confronts the other kinsman (Ruth 4:1–8)
    2. Elders attest the marriage of Boaz and Ruth
      (Ruth 4:9–12)
  IV. Joy in the Birth of a Son (Ruth 4:13–22)
    1. A son born to Ruth and Boaz (Ruth 4:13)
    2. The women rejoice (Ruth 4:14–15)
    3. Naomi cares for the new baby (Ruth 4:16–17)
    4. A royal line (Ruth 4:18–22)

When Ruth came to glean in his field, Boaz noticed her (2:1–7). He showed special kindness for her because of her kindness to Naomi (2:8–16). When Ruth reported what had happened, Naomi rejoiced because Boaz was a kinsman of her husband (2:17–23). Ruth carried out Naomi's plan for confronting Boaz with his duty as kinsman redeemer (3:1–9). Boaz promised to fulfill this role if a closer kinsman refused (3:10–15). When Ruth reported, Naomi said they would wait and see what happened (3:16–18). When Boaz confronted the other kinsman, the man declined to marry Ruth (4:1–8).

Before ten elders, Boaz said he would act as kinsman (4:9–12).

When a child was born to Ruth and Boaz (4:13), the women praised God for changing the fortunes of Naomi through a daughter-in-law, who was better than seven sons (4:14–15). Naomi cared for the baby; and in God's time, the child became the grandfather of David (4:16–17). Thus, Ruth the Moabitess bore a son who was in the royal line (4:18–22).

I. Gleaning in the Field of Boaz (Ruth 2:1–23)
1. Boaz notices Ruth (vv. 1–7)

1 And Naomi had a kinsman of her husband's, a mighty man of wealth, of the family of Elimelech; and his name was Boaz.

The key factor about Boaz was that he was a kinsman of Elimelech. This was important because of Jewish law and custom about the role of a kinsman in a situation like that of Naomi and Ruth. The word translated "kinsman" in 2:1 is not the usual word for kinsman found later in Ruth for the kinsman redeemer. The latter word is found in Ruth 2:20; 3:9, 12, 13; 4:1, 3, 6, 8, 14.

For one thing, a kinsman was responsible for redeeming ancestral land that had been lost to the family through sale or debt. More important for the story of Ruth, a kinsman had the duty of a levirate marriage for a childless widow of the dead kinsman. In comments on Ruth 1:11–13, we noted that this custom called for a man to marry the childless widow of his deceased brother (Deut. 25:5–10). The Book of Ruth shows that sometimes a kinsman other than a brother fulfilled that responsibility.

Gleaning was the practice of allowing the poor to pick up grain and fruit left by the harvesters. This was one of the ways the community provided for widows like Naomi and Ruth. Deuteronomy 24:19–21 commanded harvesters to leave some for the gleaners. Ruth went into the fields to glean and ended up gleaning in the field of Boaz (vv. 2–3). Boaz noticed Ruth and found out that she was the Moabitess who came back with Naomi (vv. 4–6). The servant of Boaz told him how long and hard Ruth had been working (v. 7).

2. Boaz shows kindness to Ruth (vv. 8–16)

8 Then said Boaz unto Ruth, Hearest thou not, my daughter? Go not to glean in another field, neither go from hence, but abide here fast by my maidens:

9 Let thine eyes be on the field that they do reap, and go thou after them: have I not charged the young men that they shall not touch thee? and when thou art athirst, go unto the vessels, and drink of that which the young men have drawn.

10 Then she fell on her face, and bowed herself to the ground, and said unto him, Why have I found grace in thine eyes, that thou shouldest take knowledge of me, seeing I am a stranger?

11 And Boaz answered and said unto her, It hath fully been shewed me, all that thou hast done unto thy mother in law since the death of thine husband: and how thou hast left thy father and thy mother, and the land of thy nativity, and art come unto a people which thou knewest not heretofore.

12 The Lord recompense thy work, and a full reward be given thee of the Lord God of Israel, under whose wings thou art

come to trust.

Boaz's words to Ruth in verses 8–9 show his special kindness toward her. Humbly falling on her face before Boaz, Ruth asked why he had taken special notice of her. She was especially amazed that he would be so kind to a stranger or foreigner. Boaz explained that he had heard of the young woman from Moab who had chosen to return with her mother-in-law even though it meant leaving behind her father, mother, and native land.

Boaz was a man of faith. He believed that the Lord would reward such commitment as Ruth showed, and Boaz felt called to be God's instrument in providing part of the reward. The last part of verse 12 testifies to the faith of Ruth as well as Boaz. He said that Ruth had found refuge under the wings of the Lord God.

Boaz also told Ruth to eat lunch with his servants (v. 14). He ordered his servants to leave grain for Ruth (vv. 15-16). At the end of the day, she had about an ephah of barley (v. 17).

3. Ruth reports to Naomi (vv. 18–23). When Ruth reported to Naomi (vv. 18–19), Naomi said, "Blessed be he of the lord, who hath not left off his kindness to the living and to be dead." She rejoiced because she knew that Boaz was a kinsman and might be their hope for the future (v. 20). Naomi instructed Ruth to continue to glean as Boaz had told her (vv. 21–23).

II. At the Threshing Floor of Boaz (Ruth 3:1–18)

1. Ruth carries out Naomi's plan (vv. 1–9). Naomi proposed a plan to confront Boaz with his duty as their kinsman (vv. 1–4). Ruth agreed (v. 5). After Boaz was asleep, Ruth uncovered his feet and lay down at his feet (vv. 6–7). When Boaz woke up and asked who was there, Ruth answered, "I am Ruth thine handmaid: spread therefore thy skirt over thine handmaid; for thou art a near kinsman" (vv. 8–9).

2. Boaz responds to Ruth (vv. 10–15). Boaz commended Ruth for her kindness in choosing him rather than a younger man (v. 10). He promised to do as she asked (v. 11); however, he told her that another man was a closer kinsman than he (v. 12). Boaz promised to confront the other kinsman, so that one of the two would act as their kinsman redeemer (v. 13). Boaz sent Ruth away before others realized she had been there (v. 14). He gave her grain as she left (v. 15).

3. Naomi responds to Ruth's report (vv. 16–18). After Ruth reported (vv. 16–17), Naomi said that they should now wait quietly to see what happened (v. 18).

III. Boaz at the City Gate (Ruth 4:1–12)

1. Boaz confronts the other kinsman (vv. 1–8). Boaz waited at the city gate for the other kinsman (v. 1). When the man arrived, Boaz asked ten elders to witness their negotiations (v. 2). Then Boaz told him about Naomi and some land that needed to be redeemed (v. 3). When Boaz asked the man if he would purchase it, the man said that he would (v. 4). Then Boaz told him that the kinsman who purchased the field also would need to claim Ruth as wife (v. 5). The man refused because this would affect his inheritance; he told Boaz to act as kinsman redeemer (v. 6). According to the custom of the day, the agreement was made in the presence of the elders (vv. 7–8).

2. Elders attest the marriage of Boaz and Ruth (vv. 9–12). Boaz called on the elders to witness his purchase of the lands of Elimelech (v. 9). Boaz also publicly declared that he would act as kinsman redeemer by marrying Ruth, the widow of Mahlon, so that Mahlon's heritage would be preserved (v. 10). The elders publicly declared that they were witnesses. They also asked the Lord to make Ruth like Rachel and Leah, to whom many sons were born, and like Tamar, to whom twins were born (vv. 11–12).

IV. Joy in the Birth of a Son (Ruth 4:13–22)

1. A son born to Ruth and Boaz (v. 13)

13 So Boaz took Ruth, and she was his wife: and when he went in unto her, the lord gave her conception, and she bare a son.

God answered their prayer in the birth of a son. The child was considered the descendant of Mahlon, to carry on his line. Since the later genealogy includes the name of Boaz, not Mahlon, possibly Boaz had no other sons; and the firstborn also was considered the son of Boaz, as well as the son of Mahlon.

2. The women rejoice (vv. 14–15)

14 And the women said unto Naomi, Blessed be the Lord, which hath not left thee this day without a kinsman, that his name may be famous in Israel.

15 And he shall be unto thee a restorer of thy life, and a nourisher of thine old age: for thy daughter in law, which loveth thee, which is better to thee than seven sons, hath born him.

The women of Bethlehem praised God for not leaving Naomi without a kinsman redeemer. They asked God to make the name of Boaz famous in Israel.

The "he" in verse 15 refers to the new son of Ruth and Boaz. The women prayed that the child would restore life and hope to Naomi. After Naomi lost her sons before they had sons of their own, she had felt that the future was bleak. Now with the birth of a son to carry on the line of Elimelech and Mahlon, Naomi had new hope and new reason for living.

The women paid tribute to Ruth's loyal love for Naomi. The women said that Ruth was better than seven sons for Naomi. Seven is the perfect number. Job had seven sons before and after his trials (Job 1:2; 42:13).

3. Naomi cares for the new baby (vv. 16–17)

16 And Naomi took the child, and laid it in her bosom, and became nurse unto it.

17 And the women her neighbours gave it a name, saying, There is a son born to Naomi; and they called his name Obed: he is the father of Jesse, the father of David.

Naomi reached the pinnacle of joy as she held the baby. She was more than a hired nurse for the child. Notice that the women said, "There is a son born to Naomi." Because Obed was born of a levirate marriage to carry on the line of Naomi's son, wasn't Obed then her grandson according to the customs of the day?

They named the baby Obed, which means "servant." In time he became the father of Jesse, one of whose sons became Israel's famous king David. This fact is strong affirmation for the inclusion of Gentiles in God's love.

4. A royal line (vv. 18–22). This brief genealogy supplements verse 17, showing the inclusion of Ruth's son in David's royal line (see Matt. 1:1–17).

APPLYING THE BIBLE

1. The finger of God. A minister once told about a man in a prayer meeting praying earnestly that God's finger would touch a certain man for whom the man was concerned. Suddenly, he stopped praying. When asked why he had stopped, he said God had just spoken to his heart, saying, "You are my finger!"

God would put his hands upon Ruth to care for her and bless her, but Boaz was to be the hand God would use to preserve Ruth and her lineage.

2. How would you use your wealth, if you had it? Andrew Carnegie, the late multimillionaire steel magnate, once said, "Millionaires seldom smile." And John D. Rockefeller once told a minister that great wealth is a burden that destroys one's zest for life and peace of heart. Both statements, I suppose, are true, but surely if one uses wealth properly it would put a smile on one's face and bring peace in one's heart.

Boaz was wealthy (2:1), and from the Scripture account he used his wealth wisely. Surely, there was a smile on his face and peace in his heart!

How would you use your wealth if you had it? Would you clutch it greedily to your bosom and become senile and selfish, or would you invest it in the work of God in helping the less fortunate?

3. Kindness comes back to us. Do you remember George Bernard Shaw's story about "Androcles and the Lion"? In the legend, Shaw tells about Androcles, who was a Greek Christian and a lover of animals.

While he and his wife Megaera were traveling through Africa, they encountered a savage lion with a thorn in its paw. Androcles removed the thorn and went on his way.

Years later, Androcles was arrested along with other Christians and thrown to the wild beasts. As the Christians prayed and sang hymns, one of the lions, which was the one from which Androcles removed the thorn, spared Androcles' life. The emperor was so impressed that he pardoned Androcles and the other Christians.

The moral of the story is simple: kindness expressed comes back to bless us.

It was so with Boaz. He treated Ruth kindly and permitted her to gather grain from around the edges and corners of his field, fell in love with her, and enjoyed a full and happy life.

4. Love flavors life. A king, so the story goes, once asked his three daughters how much they loved him. The first two declared that they loved him more than silver or gold. The youngest said, "I love you more than salt."

Her statement puzzled the king. "Salt?" What did she mean by salt? he wondered. "She is just immature," he thought to himself. But the cook overheard the young girl's confession, and deliberately left the salt out of the king's food she was preparing.

When he took the first bite, he exclaimed, "The salt is missing, and the food doesn't taste good." Then, suddenly, he realized what his daughter meant: nothing tastes good without salt (as you readers with high blood pressure well know!).

Boaz had wealth, but surely he was lonely, for something was missing in his life. When he found Ruth, she brought joy immeasurable into his life.

Remember: everybody needs your love. Few need your criticism.

5. Ruth gets her man! All kinds of strange love potions have been used through the centuries to catch and keep husbands. For example, the ancient Greeks believed that if a girl walked with the udder of a hyena under her left arm she would get her man! Emperor Caligula was thrown into a fit, so it is told, by a love potion brewed by his wife that was too strong! Hippocrates, the father of modern medicine, said that a brew of donkey's milk and honey would work every time! Marigolds, in sixteenth-century England would do the trick, it was believed! And when the potato was introduced into Spain in 1534, they fetched up to $1,250 a pound as love food!

Naomi and Ruth tried none of this foolishness to get the attention of Boaz, but the method they used was ingenious and innocent. And Ruth got her man!

TEACHING THE BIBLE

▶ *Main Idea:* Boaz's marriage to Ruth demonstrates how God can repay kindness.
▶ *Suggested Teaching Aim:* To lead adults to describe the result of Boaz's kindness to Ruth, and to identify acts of kindness they will perform to members of their family.

A TEACHING OUTLINE

1. Use an illustration to introduce the lesson.
2. Use word definitions to explain the setting.
3. Use group activity to summarize the Scripture.
4. Use group discussion to examine the significance of the birth of Ruth and Boaz's son.
5. Lead members to identify one family member to whom they will show kindness this week.

Introduce the Bible Study
Use the illustration, "Kindness comes back to us," in "Applying the Bible" to introduce the lesson.

Search for Biblical Truth

Use the first paragraph under "Studying the Bible" to summarize the Scripture passage.

On a chalkboard or large sheets of paper, write the following words printed in bold:

Important Concepts in Ruth

Kinsman: relative.

Kinsman redeemer: relative who had the responsibility of redeeming ancestral land and of levirate marriage for a kinsman's childless widow.

Glean: the poor gathering grain or other crops that had been dropped or left by the reapers.

Levirate marriage: provision requiring a dead man's brother or near relative (kinsman redeemer) to marry his childless widow and produce a son who would be considered the dead man's son.

Present a brief lecture on Ruth 2:1–7 in which you explain the four concepts above (see last week's lesson for information on levirate marriage). After your lecture, ask members to define each of the terms; write their definitions opposite the appropriate word. Members' answers may differ from the suggested answers given above.

Assign each of the five verses in 2:8–12 to five people or five groups. Give each group a large strip of paper and ask them to summarize their verse in one statement. Allow two to three minutes for study and then ask groups to place their posters on the focal wall and summarize their verses.

Present a three- to four-minute lecture in which you summarize the highlights of 2:18–4:12.

Ask members to read silently 4:13–17. Ask:
(1) What was significant about Ruth's pregnancy (4:13)? (The Lord gave her conception after being childless in her previous marriage.)
(2) What was the reaction of the women of Bethlehem to the birth (4:14)? (Praised God and asked God to make the baby famous.)
(3) How was Ruth better to Naomi than seven sons (4:15)? (Ruth had cared for her and now presented her with a grandchild.)
(4) How could the women of Bethlehem say that a son had been born to Naomi (4:17)? (Because of the levirate marriage, the son was considered Mahlon's; apparently, it was considered Boaz's as well.)
(5) What is the significance of this son (4:17)? (Grandfather of David, ancestor of Jesus.)

Give the Truth a Personal Focus

Point out how God had rewarded Ruth's kindness to Naomi and Boaz's kindness to Ruth. Distribute paper and pencils to all members. Ask them to write on the paper the name of one family member to whom they will show kindness this week. Point out that although God often rewards kindness by special blessings, to perform these acts of kindness to earn a blessing would defeat the purpose. Point out, too, that the joy of performing the act may well be the blessing.

Teachings of Jesus

MARCH
APRIL
MAY
1996

INTRODUCTION

This quarter focuses on key teachings of Jesus.

Unit I, "Teachings About the Kingdom of Heaven," is a five-year session study of parables from Matthew and Luke. The following parables will be studied: sower (soils), unforgiving servant, vineyard workers, three servants (talents), and the great feast.

Unit II, "Teachings About God," contains four sessions from Luke and John focusing on the nature of God the Father and Jesus Christ, His Son. The Easter session tells of the appearance of the risen Lord to two of His followers on the road to Emmaus. The stories of the lost sheep and lost coin reveal the seeking love of God for sinners. The image of the Good Shepherd portrays Jesus' love for people and His sacrifice for them. The teachings of the vine and branches show how Christ's followers can abide in Him and thus bear fruit.

Unit III, "Teachings About Living," contains four sessions from the Sermon on the Mount in Matthew 5–7. The Beatitudes describe qualities of life that God approves and that bring fulfillment to followers of Christ. Jesus' teachings about loving our enemies stand in striking contrast to the human tendency to get even with those who hurt us. Studying about the danger of loving offers a challenge for Christians living in an affluent society. Jesus' teachings about prayer emphasize its importance as well as provide help in knowing how to pray.

Parable of the Sower

Basic Passage: Matthew 13:1-23
Focal Passages: Matthew 13:1-9,18-23

Matthew 13 is known for its parables of the kingdom of heaven. The first and most famous is the parable of the sower, sometimes called the parable of the soils. This parable has a twofold application: (1) First, it challenges each of us to be sure that we are like the seed sown in good soil, which bears fruit. (2) Second, it encourages believers to sow the seed of God's Word. Not all the seed bears good fruit, but some of it does.

▶ ▶ ▶ ▶ ▶ ▶ ▶ **Study Aim:** *To characterize the kinds of hearers represented by each of the four kinds of soil*

STUDYING THE BIBLE

I. Parable of the Sower (Matt. 13:1–9)
   1. Sowing the seed (Matt. 13:1–3)
   2. Seed on hard soil (Matt. 13:4)
   3. Seed in shallow soil (Matt. 13:5–6)
   4. Seed among thorns (Matt. 13:7)
   5. Seed in good soil (Matt. 13:8)
   6. Listen (Matt. 13:9)
II. Why Jesus Taught in Parables (Matt. 13:10–17)
   1. Insiders and outsiders (Matt. 13:10–12)
   2. Closed eyes and ears (Matt. 13:13–15)
   3. Open eyes and ears (Matt. 13:16–17)
III. Jesus Explains the Parable (Matt. 13:18–23)
   1. Not understanding (Matt. 13:18–19)
   2. Not persevering (Matt. 13:20–21)
   3. Worries and wealth (Matt. 13:22)
   4. Fruitful lives (Matt. 13:23)

As Jesus taught the crowds in parables, He told of a sower who went forth to sow (vv. 1-3). Some seed fell on the hard path and was eaten by birds (v. 4). Some fell on shallow soil, sprang up quickly, but soon withered (vv. 5–6). Some fell into thorns and never bore fruit (v. 7). Some fell in good soil and bore much fruit (v. 8). Jesus called on His listeners to truly hear (v. 9). When the disciples asked Jesus why He taught in parables, He explained that it was given to the disciples to know the mysteries of the kingdom, but it was not given to others (vv. 10–12). Some have eyes, but do not see; and ears, but do not hear (vv. 13–15). Those who do see and hear are experiencing what earlier people of faith yearned to see and hear (vv. 16–17). The seed on the path are people who don't understand the word (vv. 18–19). The seed on shallow soil are people who quickly accept the word but fail to persevere (v. 20–21). The seed among thorns are people who allow worries and riches to choke out their fruitfulness (v. 22). The seed in good soil are people who receive the word and bear much fruit (v. 23).

I. Parable of the Sower (Matt. 13:1-9)

1. Sowing the seed (vv. 1–3)

1 The same day went Jesus out of the house, and sat by the sea side.

2 And great multitudes were gathered together unto him, so that he went into a ship, and sat; and the whole multitude stood on the shore.

3 And he spake many things unto them in parables, saying, Behold, a sower went forth to sow.

Jesus was in the midst of His ministry. Opposition to Him among the religious leaders was growing, but He was still popular with the multitudes. He taught them in parables, which were short stories or analogies that He used to illustrate what He was teaching. The parables of Jesus are often defined as earthly stories with a heavenly meaning. Most of the parables of Jesus were taken from life. This was surely true of the parable of the sower. Jesus lived in a mostly rural country, where nothing was so common as a farmer sowing his field with seed.

2. Seed on hard soil (v. 4)

4 And when he sowed, some seeds fell by the way side, and the fowls came and devoured them up.

Most farmers scattered their seed in all directions over the field. The parable of Jesus described four kinds of soil into which some of the seed fell. Between each field was a footpath, which was made hard by the pounding of feet. Some seed fell on the hard path. The ever vigilant birds ate these seeds, which lay in the open on the hard path.

3. Seed in shallow soil (vv. 5–6)

5 Some fell upon stony places, where they had not much earth: and forthwith they sprung up, because they had no deepness of earth:

6 And when the sun was up, they were scorched; and because they had no root, they withered away.

The word "stony" refers to a large formation of rock just under the surface. Thus Jesus was describing a thin layer of soil that looked deep, but was actually shallow. Some seed fell into such shallow soil. Notice the three things that happened: (1) it sprang up quickly; (2) it was scorched; (3) it withered. Jesus explained that there was "no deepness of earth," and the sprouted seed "had no root."

4. Seed among thorns (v. 7)

7 And some fell among thorns; and the thorns sprung up, and choked them.

As the farmer scattered the seed, some fell into soil that was infested with weeds and weed seeds. Most of these areas were in the corners of the field. The soil was deep enough to take root, but the plants never bore fruit. The thorns were so thick and strong that the thorns choked the young plants.

5. Seed in good soil (v. 8)

8 But other fell into good ground, and brought forth fruit, some an hundredfold, some sixtyfold, some thirtyfold.

If all the seed fell into one of the first three kinds of soil, the farmer would soon starve. Fortunately, some seed fell into good soil. Such soil was not hard but broken so as to receive the seed. It was not shallow soil on a ridge of rock, but it was rich and deep. It was not infested with thorns, but free of weeds so that the young plants could grow and bear fruit. When the harvest came, the good seed yielded many more seed than were planted—some as much as one hundred times as many; some, sixty; and some, thirty.

6. Listen (v. 9)

9 Who hath ears to hear, let him hear.

Hearing and responding to the word of God call for a special kind of hearing. Some have ears and hear the sounds, but they do not hear with faith and obedience. Verse 9 prepares the way for verses 10–17, where Jesus explained the difference between closed and open eyes and ears.

II. Why Jesus Taught in Parables (Matt. 13:10–17)

1. Insiders and outsiders (vv. 10–12). The disciples asked Jesus why He spoke to the people in parables (v. 10). Jesus spoke about the mysteries of the kingdom, which insiders understand and outsiders do not understand (vv. 11–12). Those who had experienced the kingdom for themselves were the insiders, whose faith enabled them to understand.

2. Closed eyes and ears (vv. 13–15). Outsiders see with their eyes and hear with their ears, but they neither truly see nor hear (v. 13). Jesus said that the words of Isaiah 6:9–10 were fulfilled in the closed eyes and ears of those who rejected Christ (vv. 14–15).

3. Open eyes and ears (vv. 16–17). Those who truly see and hear are blessed, for they see and hear what earlier people of faith had yearned to see and hear.

III. Jesus Explains the Parable (Matt. 13:18–23)

1. Not understanding (vv. 18–19)

18 Hear ye therefore the parable of the sower.

19 When any one heareth the word of the kingdom, and understandeth it not, then cometh the wicked one, and catcheth away that which was sown in his heart. This is he which received seed by the way side.

The first clause in verse 19 makes clear two things that apply to all four kinds of soils in the parable: (1) The seed represents the word of the kingdom. (2) All four groups represent people who hear the word of God.

Jesus described two distinctive things about the first group of hearers: (1) They did not understand the word. (2) Satan then took away the word sown in their heart. The word "understandeth" refers to more than an intellectual understanding. Verses 9–17 make this clear. They heard the Word of God, but they were not really open for the word to find a place in their hearts. Their hearts belonged to another; therefore, when the word was heard, Satan eliminated the possibility of a lasting impact of the word.

2. Not persevering (vv. 20–21)

20 But he that received the seed into stony places, the same is he that heareth the word, and anon with joy receiveth it;

21 Yet hath he no root in himself, but dureth for a while: for when tribulation or persecution ariseth because of the word, by and by he is offended.

Unlike the first kind of hearers, the second kind receive the word with joy right away. Like the seed sown in shallow soil, they show almost immediate evidence of life. However, also like the seed in shallow soil, they soon wither. The problem in both cases is that they have no root. The seed in shallow soil, therefore, represents those who make what appears to be a genuine profession of faith; however, when the troubles of life test their profession, they turn aside from Christ and His way. The meaning of the doctrine of perseverance of faith is that true faith perseveres. We are not saved by persevering; but if faith is real, it will persevere.

3. Worries and wealth (v. 22)

22 He also that received seed among the thorns is he that heareth the word; and the care of this world, and the deceitfulness of riches, choke the word, and he becometh unfruitful.

The seed that fell into the thorny soil took root, but weeds choked out its fruitfulness. Some professing believers have a genuine experience of faith, but their lives never become fruitful. Anxiety about possessions and the quest for wealth choke out moral and spiritual fruitfulness. The quest for wealth is deceitful because our lives do not consist in the abundance of our possessions (Luke 12:15). Those who spend their lives laying up earthly treasures often lose them in life and always lose them in death (Matt. 6:19–21; Luke 12:13–21).

Some Bible students think that Jesus intended to describe professing believers whose unfruitfulness shows that their faith is not genuine. If so, the third kind of hearer is similar to the second. Other Bible students believe Jesus was describing genuine believers whose lives never are as fruitful as the Lord intends (1 Cor. 3:11–15). If so, their condition is still serious. They miss the real purpose of their relationship with the Lord.

4. Fruitful lives (v. 23)

23 But he that received seed into the good ground is he that heareth the word, and understandeth it; which also beareth fruit, and bringeth forth, some an hundredfold, some sixty, some thirty.

This is the kind of hearer that each person ought to be. This hearer responds with faith and obedience. The seed of the word takes root in this person's life. This person's faith perseveres through the trials of life. This person's faith is focused on the Lord, not on worldly things. This person's faith bears fruit.

Looking at the parable from the point of view of those who sow the Word of God, this fourth kind of hearer is the reason for us to remain faithful. Sunday School teachers—like preachers, missionaries, and witnesses of all kinds—sometimes grow discouraged because many of our hearers fall into one of the first three groups. Don't lose heart. Some of the seed falls into good soil and bears fruit for the Lord.

An Arab farmer near Bethlehem sowing seeds on his land. Credit: *Biblical Illustrator*, Ken Touchton.

APPLYING THE BIBLE

1. What is a parable? In Sunday School as a boy, I was taught that "a parable is an earthly story with a heavenly meaning." That's a pretty good definition. In his *A Harmony of the Gospels*, A. T. Robertson lists fifty-two parables spoken by Jesus. The number differs with different authors, for some count allegories and metaphors separately. *Holman's Bible Dictionary* records that "Jesus could turn people's ears into eyes, sometimes with a still picture and then again with a moving picture. . . . As Jesus proclaimed through parables, God was bursting into history, the hinge of history had arrived."[1]

2. The importance of little things. In 1987, a young man in Chicago named Mike Hayes figured out a way to finance his college education. He estimated it would take $28,000 for a four-year college education, so he wrote *Chicago Tribune* columnist Bob Greene requesting that he ask each of his readers to send Hayes one penny—just one cent. Breaking his estimate down in pennies, he figured it would take 2.8 million pennies to do it. And Greene wrote about it in his column.

Money came in from everywhere,—the fifty states as well as from many foreign nations. And Hayes got more than he needed! In fact, he got an extra thousand dollars which he put in a scholarship fund to help another struggling student.

Little things, such as pennies or seeds—as our lesson today points out—are extremely important. Talking to His hearers about a thing as common or ordinary or small as a seed, Jesus taught a great truth about the kingdom of God.

3. The purpose of the parables. In Hamburg, Germany, some years ago, there was a contest sponsored by an art museum to determine what piece of their collection of modern art was the finest. The piece that was named the best was a bewildering, confusing, bizarre "splashing" of bright colors across a canvas that made no sense at all. And it was not until after the award had been made that the judges discovered it had been hanging upside down all the while. Apparently, turning it right side up would not have improved its quality any!

To the people of His day—or our day, for that matter—understanding and knowing God was bewildering and impossible. But in this flesh Jesus shows us what God is like, and through His parables He teaches us what God is like. That's the basic purpose of any of the parables of Jesus.

4. Royalty is speaking. It is told that once, when Queen Elizabeth of England was a little girl, she was trying to say something but nobody would listen. Her father and mother were entertaining guests, but no one would pay little Elizabeth any attention. Going to the middle of the room she stamped her foot and exclaimed amid the silence, "Royalty is speaking!"

We need to pay close attention to the words of Jesus as they are recorded in Scripture, for royalty is speaking!

5. Jesus fills the empty heart. Pascal, the great French physicist and philosopher, said: "There is a God-shaped vacuum in the heart of every man which cannot be filled by any created thing, but only by God the creator, made known by Jesus Christ."

God, the heavenly Father knew that, and that is the reason He sent Jesus. Jesus, too, knew it, and that's the reason He wrapped all His eternal truth about God in simple stories so the people could know Him (Mark 4:34).

6. Who hath ears to hear, let him hear (v. 9). George Whitefield (1714–1770), a native of England who preached on numerous occasions in the American colonies, had a profound effect upon early American Christianity.

A New England infidel had heard much about Whitefield and wanted to see him, but he was determined not to listen to what the preacher would say.

Climbing a tree so that he could clearly see Whitefield, who was preaching in the open air, the infidel put his hands over his ears so that he would not hear Whitefield's message. But a fly lighted on the man's face, and just as he moved a hand from an ear to brush the fly away, Whitefield exclaimed, "He that hath ears to hear, let him hear." And the Holy Spirit used those words of Jesus to convict the unbeliever so deeply that he was wonderfully saved.

▶ *Main Idea:* Jesus' parable of the sower illustrates that people receive the Word differently.

▶ *Suggested Teaching Aim:* To lead adults to identify the four kinds of soil Jesus described, and to determine what kind of soil their lives represent.

A TEACHING OUTLINE

1. Use an illustration and a poster to introduce the lesson.
2. Use a poster to identify the four types of soil and the meaning of the four types.
3. Share an illustration of the viability of God's Word.
4. Ask members to identify what kind of soil they have been this past week.

Introduce the Bible Study

Use "What is a parable?" from "Applying the Bible" to introduce the lesson. IN ADVANCE, write on a large sheet of paper the definition of parable used in this illustration and place it on the wall where all can see it. As you share the illustration, call attention to this definition. Save this poster for the rest of the lessons on parables.

Search for Biblical Truth

IN ADVANCE, enlist a member to summarize the introduction of the quarter's lessons as an overview of the lesson. Suggest the member make a lesson outline poster as a teaching aid for the report.

DISCUSS: Why did Jesus teach in parables? If He spoke in our church today, do you think He would teach in parables? Why?

Share the information in 13:1–3. IN ADVANCE, write the following on a chalkboard or a large sheet of paper:

Soil	Meaning
13:4	13:19
13:5–6	13:20–21
13:7	13:22
13:8	13:23

Enlist a reader to read 13:4–9. Either working as a class or forming four groups, ask members to identify the four types of soil Jesus mentioned (hard, shallow, thorny, good). Write these four words (or similar words) under *Soil.* Use "Studying the Bible" to explain the agricultural practices Jesus described.

Enlist a reader to read 13:19–23. Either working as a class or forming four groups, ask members to identify the meanings of the four types of soil and write these on the poster under *Meaning.* Ask members to identify current conditions that would make the their lives hard, stony, or thorny. List these on a chalkboard or a large sheet of paper.

Give the Truth a Personal Focus

Share the following illustration that happened to this writer as he was working on this lesson: "A friend of mine from a church I had served nearly thirteen years ago called to tell me that a former church member had died. The woman was not very active, and her husband was not a member. At the funeral home her husband expressed great appreciation for my ministry and remembered when I had shared some garden produce with him. When my friend shared this with me, I had no recollection at all of having shared the abundance of my garden, but the man remembered it approximately fifteen years later. As I thought of this experience and this lesson, I wondered how many other seed I had sown that I would never know about."

Remind members that the seed is the Word of God and that it is always good seed. The results of the harvest depend on the type of soil God's Word falls on.

Ask them to look at the four types of soil on the poster and determine what kind of soil they have been this week. Close in prayer that this next week all will be open to the planting of God's Word in their lives.

---

1. *Holman Bible Dictionary,* Trent C. Bulter, ed., (Nashville: Holman Bible Publishers, 1991), 1072–73

Parable of the Unforgiving Servant

Basic Passage: Matthew 18:21–35
Focal Passage: Matthew 18:21–35

T he Bible emphasizes a right relationship with God, but it also insists that our relationship with God affects our relationship with other people. The parable of the unforgiving servant teaches that God offers to forgive the enormous debt of our sins. This forgiveness from God should be reflected in forgiveness of those who sin against us. A heart that is open to receive divine forgiveness is also open to forgive others. A heart that is closed to forgive others is closed to receive God's forgiveness.

▶ ▶ ▶ ▶ ▶ ▶ ▶ ▶ ▶ **Study Aim:** To forgive others as God has forgiven us

STUDYING THE BIBLE

I. **A Question About Forgiveness (Matt. 18:21–22)**
    1. Peter's question (Matt. 18:21)
    2. Jesus' answer (Matt. 18:22)
II. **A Forgiving King and an Unforgiving Servant (Matt. 18:23–35)**
    1. An enormous debt (Matt. 18:23–25)
    2. Generous forgiveness (Matt. 18:26–27)
    3. A smaller debt (Matt. 18:28)
    4. Unforgiving servant (Matt. 18:29–30)
    5. Judgment on the unforgiving servant (Matt. 18:31–34)
    6. The lesson of the parable (Matt. 18:35)

Peter asked Jesus if disciples should forgive others as often as seven times (v. 21). Jesus refused to place limits on the number of times to forgive others (v. 22). Jesus told of a king whose servant owed him an enormous debt that he couldn't pay (vv. 23–25). When the servant pleaded for patience, the king forgave the debt (vv. 26–27). Someone owed the forgiven servant a much smaller debt, which the servant demanded be paid (v. 28). Although the debtor pleaded for patience, the servant had him thrown into prison (vv. 29–30). When this was reported to the king, the angry king pointed out that being forgiven the enormous debt should have made the servant compassionate toward his fellow servant (vv. 31–34). Jesus said that the heavenly Father would deal harshly with those who are unwilling to forgive their brothers (v. 35).

I. A Question About Forgiveness (Matt. 18:21–22)

1. Peter's question (v. 21)
    21 Then came Peter to him, and said, Lord, how oft shall my

brother sin against me, and I forgive him? till seven times?

Jesus had just taught the disciples how to deal with a brother who had sinned (Matt. 18:15–20). This led Peter to ask how often he should forgive someone who sinned against him. He asked specifically if he should forgive someone as many as seven times.

Peter was the one who often put into words questions that were in the minds of the disciples. Often his questions showed his own limited understanding. In this case, for example, he was trying to place limits on forgiveness. However, two things should be said in Peter's defense: (1) Peter's questions often gave Jesus the opportunity to clarify and re-inforce what He was trying to teach. (2) By the standards of the day, forgiving the same person as many as seven times was considered more than generous. At least one Jewish source suggested that three times was a reasonable limit to such forgiveness.

2. Jesus' answer (v. 22)

22 Jesus saith unto him, I say not unto thee, Until seven times: but, Until seventy times seven.

Some ancient copies of the Bible have "seventy-seven times" (NIV). Actually the point of Jesus is the same whether He said "seventy times seven" or "seventy-seven." Jesus was saying that no limits should be placed on forgiveness. His point was not that we should keep count until we count 77 or 490 times, and then refuse any further forgiveness.

Possibly Jesus had in mind the story of Lamech in Genesis 4. God had said that if any one killed Cain, sevenfold vengeance would be taken on him (Gen. 4:15). Lamech was a brutal man who boasted of murdering those who harmed him (Gen. 4:23). He said sarcastically, "If Cain shall be avenged sevenfold, truly Lamech seventy and sevenfold" (Gen. 4:24). Lamech was the father of all those who seek to retaliate against others for real or imagined wrongs. Instead of the endless revenge of sinful humans, Jesus taught unlimited forgiveness.

II. A Forgiving King and an Unforgiving Servant (Matt. 18:23–35)

1. An enormous debt (vv. 23–25)

23 Therefore is the kingdom of heaven likened unto a certain king, which would take account of his servants.

24 And when he had begun to reckon, one was brought unto him, which owned him ten thousand talents.

25 But forasmuch as he had not to pay, his lord commanded him to be sold, and his wife, and children, and all that he had, and payment to be made.

Jesus compared the kingdom of heaven to a king who was settling accounts with his servants. One servant owed the king an enormous debt. A talent was the highest denomination of money known in the first-century world, and "ten thousand" was the largest number for which the Greek language had a single word. It was an amount of money far beyond the ability of the average person of that day to conceive of, much less to pay. Because money values change, it is impossible to say exactly what the dollar value would be today, but it would be like saying that a debtor owed an amount approaching the national debt.

Jewish law forbade the kind of harsh treatment that was to be meted out to the debtor. No Jewish creditor was allowed to torture a debtor or sell his family into slavery. Therefore, the king in the parable was probably a foreign king. Such harsh measures, however, were common in the ancient world. The theory was to reclaim as much of the debt as possible by selling the debtor and his family into slavery and by selling all he owned.

2. Generous forgiveness (vv. 26–27)

26 The servant therefore fell down, and worshipped him, saying, Lord, have patience with me, and I will pay thee all.

27 Then the lord of that servant was moved with compassion, and loosed him, and forgave him the debt.

The desperate debtor pleaded for the king to be patient. He promised to pay back all he owed. Although the king knew that the debtor could never pay off his debt, he had compassion on the humbled man. The king canceled his punishment and forgave him the enormous debt.

Jesus did not intend that every point in this parable have an application for people's relationship with God. However, some clear applications in verses 23–27 are taught elsewhere in the Bible: (1) Sin is an enormous debt that none of us can pay. (2) God is compassionate with sinners. (3) When we repent, God cancels our punishment. (4) God not only saves us from punishment for our sin; He forgives our sin and thus makes reconciliation with Him possible.

3. A smaller debt (v. 28)

28 But the same servant went out, and found one of his fellowservants, which owed him an hundred pence: and he laid hands on him, and took him by the throat, saying, Pay me that thou owest.

The servant who had been forgiven the enormous debt was himself a creditor for a much smaller amount. A fellow servant owed him "a hundred denarii" (NIV). A denarius was the amount earned for a day's labor in the fields (Matt. 20:2). Thus one hundred denarii would be equal in our terms to what a laborer could earn in one hundred days at minimum wages. This was not a trivial amount, especially for laborers; however, it was a trivial amount compared to the unpayable debt of ten thousand talents that the king had forgiven. Yet the first servant grabbed the second servant around the throat and demanded that he pay what he owed.

4. Unforgiving servant (vv. 29–30)

29 And the fellowservant fell down at his feet, and besought him, saying, Have patience with me, and I will pay thee all.

30 And he would not: but went and cast him into prison, till he should pay the debt.

The second servant's pleas in verse 29 are almost word for word the same as the earlier pleas of the first servant to the king in verse 26. Each servant pled for patience and promised to repay the debt. The second servant, however, responded differently to the pleas of his debtor. He sent the unfortunate man to prison.

5. Judgment on the unforgiving servant (vv. 31–34)

31 So when his fellowservants saw what was done, they were very sorry, and came and told unto their lord all that was done.

32 Then his lord, after that he had called him, said unto him, O thou wicked servant, I forgave thee all that debt, because thou desiredst me:

33 Shouldest not thou also have had compassion on thy fellowservant, even as I had pity on thee?

34 And his lord was wroth, and delivered him to the tormentors, till he should pay all that was due unto him.

Other servants of the king were aware of this harsh action toward a debtor. They doubtlessly had rejoiced at the compassion of the king in forgiving the first servant. They were disturbed by the opposite action of the first servant toward his debtor. Since many of them were debtors, they probably imagined themselves in the place of each of the two debtors. They much preferred the king's compassion to the servant's harshness.

When the other servants reported what had happened to the king, the monarch called the first servant back into his presence. He reminded the servant how he had forgiven him an enormous debt when the servant pleaded for mercy. He asked the servant why he didn't show similar compassion on the servant who owed him a much smaller amount. Then the king ordered that the unforgiving servant be tortured until he paid his debt. This was comparable to life imprisonment at hard labor, because the servant would never be able to work off the enormous debt.

6. The lesson of the parable (v. 35)

35 So likewise shall my heavenly Father do also unto you, if ye from your hearts forgive not every one his brother their trespasses.

Every point in a parable should not be pressed. Jesus was not saying that God our Father is like the pagan king in every way. The main point of comparison is the expectation by God that those whom He forgives should forgive those who sin against them. Paul expressed the lesson in a positive way: "Be ye kind one to another, tenderhearted, forgiving one another, even as God for Christ's sake hath forgiven you" (Eph. 4:32). The Model Prayer that Jesus gave His disciples includes the words, "Forgive us our debts, as we forgive our debtors" (Matt. 6:12). The prayer assumes that we seek God's forgiveness and show a forgiving spirit to others.

On the negative side, the parable warns of judgment against those who display an unforgiving spirit toward others. Jesus spelled this out in Matthew 6:14: "For if ye forgive men their trespasses, your heavenly Father will also forgive you: But if ye forgive not men their trespasses, neither will your Father forgive your trespasses" (Matt. 6:14–15). Jesus was not teaching that a forgiving spirit merits divine forgiveness. He was teaching that forgiveness is a two-way street. If a heart is open to receive God's forgiveness, it is open to forgive others. If a heart is closed to forgive others, it is closed to receive God's forgiveness.

1. Forgiveness accepted/rejected. It has been estimated by our government that ninety-three thousand American servicemen went AWOL—absent without leave–during the Vietnam War era. Another thirteen thousand deliberately dodged the draft by fleeing to Canada and other countries.

When the war ended in 1973, President Gerald Ford offered to grant amnesty to the 13,000 draft dodgers on the condition that they do so much community service. Some accepted the amnesty, while others rejected it.

Then President Jimmy Carter offered complete and unconditional amnesty in 1977. Again, some accepted the government's forgiveness while others rejected it.

The same is true of the forgiveness God offers. Some accept it in Christ, and others reject it although refusing it is the most foolish choice one will ever make. As our lesson points out today, forgiveness is available, and when we repent of our sins God cancels and forgives them. But the choice is up to us (v. 27).

2. We ought to forgive much. Jesus put no limitation on forgiveness—either God's forgiveness or our forgiveness of others. God's forgiveness is infinite and our forgiveness of others is to be habitual.

Why should we forgive so much and so often? Because we need so much of it ourselves both from God and from others.

When John Wesley was serving as a missionary in the American colony of Georgia, he pleaded the case of an offending colonist before the governor. "I never forgive," replied the governor, to which Wesley responded, "Let us hope, then, that you never offend!"

Our lesson today reminds us that we cannot be forgiven by God unless and until we forgive others. Even in His Model Prayer, Jesus taught us to pray: "And forgive us our debts, as we forgive our debtors" (6:12).

3. How much is a billion dollars? "It's more than I will ever see," we all answer! Yes, but there are a few billionaires around.

If you had a billion dollars, and spent $1,000 a day from the time Christ was born, you still would not have spent a billion dollars. You might be interested to know that when Neil Armstrong took his historic two-hour-and-forty-minute walk on the moon, it cost us taxpayers twenty-four billion dollars! For that walk, he received his regular pay: thirty-three dollars!

The greedy man in the parable Jesus told did not owe a billion dollars, but he had a sizable debt, and he did not have the money to pay it (v. 25).

4. Lincoln's compassion. Of all the words that might characterize Abraham Lincoln, perhaps the best is compassion. His last public act before his tragic assassination was one of compassion.

Just before Lincoln left for Ford's Theater on the night of April 14, 1865, Senator J. B. Henderson brought to Lincoln the plea of condemned Confederate soldier and spy George Vaughn that his life be spared. His plea for mercy to Secretary of War Edwin M. Stanton had been denied, and Lincoln was Vaughn's last hope. When Lincoln was told about Stanton's refusal to show mercy, Lincoln shook his head sadly. He then sat down at his desk and wrote out an unconditional pardon for the condemned Confederate soldier.

Unlike the compassion showed by Lincoln was the hardness of heart demonstrated by the man in Jesus' parable whose great debt had been canceled, but who was unwilling to forgive the man with the lesser debt.

Unfortunately, we are too often like the unforgiving servant of the parable, and too little like Lincoln.

5. Jesus' prayer. On the cross Jesus prayed for all of us whose sin debt was too great to pay: "Father, forgive them; for they know not what they do" (Luke 23:34). It is remarkable that Jesus prayed for our forgiveness when no one had asked for it. Must this not also be our attitude? We must be eager and ready to forgive, even when no remorse for having wronged us is evident or no forgiveness from us has been asked.

TEACHING THE BIBLE

▶ *Main Idea:* The parable of the unforgiving servant demonstrates that God wants us to forgive others as He has forgiven us.

▶ *Suggested Teaching Aim:* To lead adults to describe how God has forgiven them, and to identify ways they can forgive others.

A TEACHING OUTLINE

1. Use posters and an illustration to introduce the Bible study.
2. Use a lesson outline to study the text.
3. Encourage members to forgive those who have wronged them.

Introduce the Bible Study

IN ADVANCE, make several posters that contain the equation: 7 x 70 = 490 and place them around the room.

Use "Lincoln's compassion" from "Applying the Bible" to introduce the lesson. Point out that the equations around the room are a reminder of the compassion God had for us and that we should have for others. Read the "Main Idea" of the lesson.

Search for Biblical Truth

IN ADVANCE, copy the eight sentences in the first paragraph under the heading, "Studying the Bible," along with the verse references. Number them (1–8), and tape them to the backs of eight chairs. Ask the eight people to read them in order to set the context for the lesson.

On a chalkboard or a large sheet of paper, write Peter's Question and Jesus' Answer. Ask a volunteer to read Peter's question in Matthew 18:21. Under Peter's Question write the number 7. Share the two points made in Peter's defense in "Studying the Bible." Ask a volunteer to read Jesus' answer in Matthew 18:22. Under Jesus' Answer write 490. Explain that some translations have "seventy-seven" instead of "seventy times seven." Share the information in "Studying the Bible" about Lamech and point out that Jesus may have been contrasting His kingdom people with Lamech in Genesis 4.

IN ADVANCE, prepare the following poster on a chalkboard or a large sheet of paper:

A Forgiving King and an Unforgiving Servant
(Matt. 18:23–35)

1. An Enormous Debt (18:23–25)
2. Generous Forgiveness (18:26–27
3. A Smaller Debt (18:28)
4. Unforgiving Servant (18:29–30)
5. Judgment on the Unforgiving Servant (18:31–34)
6. The Lesson of the Parable (18:35)

Cover each of the points in the outline with paper until you are ready to teach them.

Call attention to the definition of a parable from March 3. Point out that in this parable, Jesus taught that forgiveness was a requirement of kingdom people.

Uncover the first point on the outline and ask a volunteer to read 18:23–25. Use "Studying the Bible" to explain "ten thousand talents" and the practice of selling creditors into slavery. Point out the extraordinary size of the debt.

Uncover the second point on the outline and ask a volunteer to read 18:26–27. Use "Studying the Bible" to point out the four applications of these verses.

Uncover the third point on the outline and ask a volunteer to read 18:28. Explain the meaning of "hundred pence."

Uncover the fourth point on the outline and ask a volunteer to read 18:29–30. Point out the similarity of the two servants' pleas.

Uncover the fifth point on the outline and ask a volunteer to read 18:31–34. Explain the king's judgment on the unforgiving servant.

Uncover the sixth point on the outline and ask a volunteer to read 18:35. Use "Studying the Bible" to explain the main point of the parable as being the expectation by God that those whom He forgives should forgive those who sin against them.

Give the Truth a Personal Focus

Ask members to bow their heads and think of people they need to forgive. Point out that the person may not deserve the forgiveness, but that they need to forgive to keep from destroying themselves. Close in prayer that all will forgive those they need to forgive.

Parable of the Vineyard Workers

Basic Passage: Matthew 19:27–20:16
Focal Passage: Matthew 20:1–16

T he parable of the vineyard workers was based on the common practice of hiring day laborers to do seasonal work, but the manner of payment provided a surprise to those who heard Jesus tell the parable. The meaning and application of this parable have been debated over the centuries since Jesus told it.

▶ ▶ ▶ ▶ **Study Aim:** *To explain how the parable of Matthew 20:1–16 related to the question and answer in Matthew 19:27–30*

STUDYING THE BIBLE

I. A Question and Answers About Rewards (Matt. 19:27–30)
    1. Peter's question (Matt. 19:27)
    2. Jesus' answers (Matt. 19:28–30)
II. A Generous Employer and His Workers (Matt. 20:1–16)
    1. Agreement with the first workers (Matt. 20:1–2)
    2. Promise to later workers (Matt. 20:3–7)
    3. Equal pay for all (Matt. 20:8–10)
    4. Complaints from the early workers (Matt. 20:11–12)
    5. The employer's fairness and generosity (Matt. 20:13–15)
    6. The lesson of the parable (Matt. 20:16)

Peter asked Jesus what the apostles would receive for forsaking all to follow Him (19:27). Jesus replied that the apostles and others would receive far more than they gave up (19:28–29). Then Jesus said that the first would be last, and the last first (19:30). Jesus told a parable of a vineyard owner who agreed to pay an early group of workers a denarius ("penny") for a day's work (20:1–2). Returning to the marketplace several times later in the day, the employer hired other unemployed workers, promising to pay them what was right (20:3–7). At the end of the day, each worker received a denarius (20:8–10). The early workers complained that treating all the workers alike was unfair, because they had worked all day in the heat (20:11–12). The employer said that the early workers were paid what was agreed, and he asked if he didn't have the right to be generous even if they were envious (20:13–15). Then Jesus said that the last shall be first and the first last (20:16).

I. A Question and Answers About Rewards (Matt. 19:27–30)

1. Peter's question (v. 27). Peter's question came right after the rich young ruler refused the invitation of Jesus to sell all that he had and come follow Him (see Matt. 19:16–26). Peter asked, "Behold, we have forsaken all, and followed thee; what shall we have therefore?"

2. Jesus' answers (vv. 28–30). Jesus' first response was to assure Peter that he and the other apostles would be judges over the twelve tribes of Israel in the coming regeneration of all things (v. 28). Jesus then broadened the assurance to include all who had made sacrifices to follow Him; they would be rewarded a hundredfold as well as inherit eternal live (v. 29). Then Jesus spoke these enigmatic words: "But many that are first shall be last; and the last shall be first" (v. 30).

II. A Generous Employer and His Workers (Matt. 20:1–16)

1. Agreement with the first workers (vv. 1–2)

1 For the kingdom of heaven is like unto a man that is an householder, which went out early in the morning to hire labourers into his vineyard.

2 And when he had agreed with the labourers for a penny a day, he sent them into his vineyard.

The first two verses contain no surprises. This scene was repeated over and over in the time of Jesus. A "householder" was not only master of his house but owner of a large vineyard. His vineyard was so large that he had to hire workers to pick the grapes. When the time came for the work to be done, the employer went to the marketplace. This is where day laborers went looking for work. The man went early in the morning so that the workers could get an early start. He agreed to pay each a "penny a day." The word "penny" translates the Greek word *denarius*. This parable along with some other sources shows that a denarius was the customary payment for a day's work by laborers.

2. Promise to later workers (vv. 3–7)

3 And he went out about the third hour, and saw others standing idle in the marketplace.

4 And he said unto them; Go ye also into the vineyard, and whatsoever is right I will give you. And they went their way.

5 Again he went out about the sixth and ninth hour, and did likewise.

6 And about the eleventh hour he went out, and found others standing idle, and saith unto them, Why stand ye here all the day idle?

7 They say unto him, Because no man hath hired us. He saith unto them, Go ye also into the vineyard; and whatsoever is right, that shall ye receive.

The Jews divided the day, from sunrise to sunset, into twelve parts. Thus "about the third hour" would be about 9:00 A.M.. "About the sixth hour" would be around noon. "About . . . the ninth hour" would be about 3:00 P.M. "About the eleventh hour" would be about 5:00 P.M. At each of these times, the employer returned to the marketplace and hired more workers. Jesus did not explain why the man didn't hire all he needed early in the day.

Two facts are emphasized about these other workers: (1) The word "idle" doesn't mean lazy, but unemployed. When the employer asked the final group why they had been standing there all day, they replied, "Because no man hath hired us." (2) Nothing was agreed about specific pay. The employer simply promised to pay what was right.

3. Equal pay for all (vv. 8–10)

8 So when even was come, the lord of the vineyard saith unto his steward, Call the labourers, and give them their hire, beginning from the last unto the first.

9 And when they came that were hired about the eleventh hour, they received every man a penny.

10 But when the first came, they supposed that they should have received more; and they likewise received every man a penny.

Part of these verses reflects the common practice of paying workers at the end of the day's work (Deut. 24:15). The owner of the vineyard, however, had given two unusual instructions to the steward in charge of paying workers: (1) Begin with those who were hired latest in the day. (2) Give each worker a denarius. Jesus was not leading a seminar on management of a vineyard. He was teaching something about the kingdom of heaven. Therefore, he used the surprising actions of the employer in the story to teach something about God.

4. Complaints from the early workers (vv. 11–12)

11 And when they had received it, they murmured against the goodman of the house,

12 Saying, These last have wrought but one hour, and thou hast made them equal unto us, which have borne the burden and heat of the day.

The early workers may have wondered at being paid last; but when they realized that the late workers were each paid a denarius, they began to calculate how much more they would be paid. They reasoned like this: "These worked only one hour late in the day, and they were paid a full denarius. Since we worked all day, surely we will be paid more than what they received."

When they received only a denarius, they murmured against their employer. They complained because the employer had made them equal to those who worked only one hour. They felt their employer was unfair to pay late and early workers the same. After all, they had borne the heat of the sun all day.

5. The employer's fairness and generosity (vv. 13–15)

13 But he answered one of them, and said, Friend, I do thee no wrong: didst not thou agree with me for a penny?

14 Take that thine is, and go thy way: I will give unto this last, even as unto thee.

15 Is it not lawful for me to do what I will with mine own? Is thine eye evil, because I am good?

The vineyard owner addressed himself to one of the complainers. Perhaps he was a spokesman for the others. The employer first addressed the complaint that he had not paid the early workers enough. He pointed out that he had done them no wrong. He had agreed to pay them a denarius. He paid them a denarius (v. 2). He advised the spokesman to take his denarius and go his way.

Then the employer addressed the implied complaint that he had paid the late workers too much by paying them the same as the early workers. The employer had no agreement with the later workers except to pay them what was right. He asked the spokesman for the complainers if he as vineyard owner didn't have the right to pay them whatever he chose.

The last question in verse 15 contrasts their "evil" eye with his goodness. In this context, an eye that is "evil" referred to a spirit that is grudging and envious. The word "good" in this context referred to an open, generous spirit. Thus verse 15 may be translated: "Don't I have the right to do what I want with my own money? Or are you envious because I am generous?" (NIV).

Given human nature, the response of the early workers was predictable. Nothing can so upset any group of workers as to discover the salaries of fellow employees. A person may be perfectly content with what is paid until the person discovers that someone else receives a higher salary, especially if the latter person works shorter hours. Jesus told the parable not as a model for employers, but in order to teach something about how God deals with people.

6. The lesson of the parable (v. 16)

16 So the last shall be first, and the first last: for many be called, but few chosen.

The first part of verse 16 is the same as the enigmatic reply to Peter's question in Matthew 19:30. The only difference is that verse 16 starts with the last who become first rather than the first who become last. Jesus told the parable of the vineyard workers to illustrate the truth in Matthew 19:30 and 20:16. All of this was part of the answer of Jesus to the question of Peter in Matthew 19:27. Jesus gave a twofold answer to Peter's question. First, He acknowledged that those who leave all to follow Him shall receive far more than they ever give up (Matt. 19:28–29). Then Jesus reminded the apostles that all rewards are actually gifts of God's grace.

Bible students have suggested a variety of applications of the parable. Some apply it to the apostles, who may have expected greater rewards for being the first to follow Jesus. Others apply it to the arguments among the apostles about which of them was the greatest (see Matt. 20:21–28; Mark 10:35–45; Luke 22:24). The parable is broad enough to apply to anyone who thinks that he deserves first place with God because of his own efforts. Our relationship with God is not based on our efforts, but on His grace.

Paul often had to defend his call as an apostle. His critics charged that Paul was not an apostle because he was not one of the first twelve. If Paul was an apostle, they considered him less an apostle that the original ones. At times, Paul was tempted to point out how hard he had worked and how much he had sacrificed, but in his better moments Paul reminded himself and others that only by God's grace was he anything: "By the grace of God I am what I am: and his grace which was bestowed upon me was not in vain; but I laboured more abundantly than they all: yet not I, but the grace of God which was with me" (1 Cor. 15:10).

APPLYING THE BIBLE

1. The Suffering of Polycarp. Polycarp (c. 70–156) was, apparently, a disciple of John the beloved apostle. Polycarp was the pastor of the church at Smyrna, one of the seven churches to which John addressed the Revelation. His martyrdom, described in a letter from the church at Smyrna to the church of Philomelium, is the earliest "extant" (still existing) Christian martyrology, according to J. D. Douglas in *Who's Who in Christian History*.[1]

Polycarp, who was eighty-six when he was martyred, was urged by the Roman authorities to recant his faith in Christ. By doing so, Polycarp's life would be spared. But Polycarp refused: "I have served Christ eighty-six years and He has done me no wrong. How can I blaspheme my king? I am a Christian."[2]

One can only imagine with what glory the old martyr was received into heaven. For him who had served so faithfully and sacrificed so much, the blessed words of Jesus had a marvelous fulfillment (19:27–30; esp. v. 29).

2. Rewards in heaven. Jesus spoke of preparing a place for us in His Father's house of many mansions (John 14:2–3). In Henry Van Dyke's story "The Mansions," he describes a man entering heaven and asking to be shown his mansion. The angel sadly told the man there was no mansion for him. "We make mansions out of the good material believers send up to us from earth. You did not send us any building material," the angel said.

In answer to Peter's question (19:27), Jesus told him that one's reward in heaven shall be based on one's service to Christ on earth (vv. 29-30).

3. On questioning God. When some crisis, sorrow, or setback happens we have often heard some devout believer say, "But we must not question God!"

Why not? He has created us, loves us, and saved us. He is our Father and loves us more than any father loves his children. Have we not questioned the things our earthly father has done without being rebuked by him? Do we suppose that our questioning God will shake His sovereignty or decrease His love for us? No! God will deal patiently with our questions. But having done so, accept what has come and move on with a deeper faith in our Father-God.

4. God, Friend or Foe? G.A. Studdert-Kennedy was an English chaplain and poet. One dark night he stood on the cliffs of Dover, peering out into the darkness, asking the question asked so often by so many: "Is there a God? If there is, does He really care about us?" Recalling his days as a military chaplain, he seemed to hear the sentry calling out in the darkness to an approaching form, "Who goes there, friend or foe?" What a relief it is, Kennedy thought to himself, when the answer comes back, "Friend."

That dark night at Dover, Kennedy asked the same question of God he said, and the answer came back clearly and strongly to his anxious heart, "Friend."

Although the workers in Christ's parable concluded that the master who had hired them was more foe than friend, they were wrong. In Jesus Christ, God acts as our friend, and always does for us what is right and fair although we don't always understand His dealings with us. [3]

5. We are to be faithful servants. Lord Viscount Palmerton (1784–1865) was prime minister of Great Britain during the reign of Queen Victoria. On one occasion, so it is told, he was crossing Westminster Bridge when a little girl ahead of him dropped and broke the bottle of milk she was carrying. Immediately, she burst into tears, and Palmerton, who had no money with him, dried her tears and told her to return to the bridge at the same time the next day and he would give her money for another bottle of milk. The next morning, during a cabinet meeting, he suddenly remembered his promise. Excusing himself, he hurried to the bridge where the little girl was waiting, gave her the money, and returned to the cabinet meeting.

Whatever our work for God may be, we must be faithful in the doing of it. And as we are, God will reward us fairly.

TEACHING THE BIBLE

▶ *Main Idea:* The parable of the vineyard demonstrates that God rewards people as He deems best.

▶ *Suggested Teaching Aim:* To lead adults to identify principles of the kingdom in this parable, and to determine their response to God's grace.

A TEACHING OUTLINE

1. Read a newspaper article to create interest.
2. Organize in five groups to study the Bible passage.
3. Encourage members to respond to and live in God's grace.

Introduce the Bible Study
Read the following:
Local Union Strikes Area Business
"A local union struck its employer this last week. When workers were interviewed on the picket line, they expressed grave dissatisfaction over the way the company had been paying hourly employees. They refused to go back to work until management had agreed to remedy the situation. 'Absolutely not!' replied one worker when asked if he would return to his job, 'not until they start treating us right.'

"When asked what the company had done, the unnamed worker said the company had been paying half-time employees the same amount as they had been paying employees who worked a full eight-hour shift."

Point out that no company, union or nonunion, could survive with this kind of policy, but that this is the situation Jesus described in His parable.

Search for Biblical Truth

Set the context by sharing the information about Peter's question (Matt. 19:27–30).

Organize the class in five groups (groups may have no more than one person) and make the following assignments (without answers). If you prefer not to organize groups, you can work on these assignments as a class.

Group 1

Read Matthew 20:1–2. Answer the following questions and be prepared to share them with the rest of the class.

1. What was Jesus' purpose in sharing this parable? (To tell what the kingdom of heaven is like.)
2. Who does the "householder" represent? (God.)
3. Who do the workers represent? (People.)
4. How much did the householder agree to pay? (A denarius a day which was the customary wage for a laborer.)

Group 2

Read Matthew 20:3–7. Answer the following questions and be prepared to share them with the rest of the class.

1. Explain how the Jews divided the day. (Twelve divisions from 6:00 A.M. to 6:00 A.M.)
2. What does the word *idle* (v. 6) mean? (Unemployed.)
3. What agreement for payment was made with these workers? (Only what was right.)

Group 3

Read Matthew 20:8–10. Answer the following questions and be prepared to share them with the rest of the class.

1. When did the owner pay the workers? (Each evening.)
2. What two commands did the owner give to the steward? (Pay the last hired first; give each a denarius.)

Group 4

Read Matthew 20:11–12. Answer the following questions and be prepared to share them with the rest of the class.

1. What was the reaction of the first workers to their pay? (Complained because they had worked in sun all day.)
2. Why would this policy not work in the job market?
3. What lesson was Jesus trying to teach?

Group 5

Read Matthew 20:13–15. Answer the following questions and be prepared to share them with the rest of the class.

1. Why had the owner not wronged the first workers? (He gave them the agreed-on wage.)
2. What right does an employer have to pay whatever he wants?
3. What right does God have to bless anyone who comes to Him?

Point out that Jesus' purpose was to show something about God's kingdom, not the labor force. Ask members to suggest why Jesus needed to tell this parable. (To teach apostles a lesson.)

Give the Truth a Personal Focus

Ask, how do you feel about death-bed confessions? Somewhat cheated? Happy that someone just barely made it into heaven? Other?

Point out that all of us enter heaven only by God's grace, not by our great labor. Encourage members to accept and live in God's grace.

---

1. J. D. Douglas, *Who's Who in Christian History* (Wheaton, Ill.: Tyndale House Publishers, Inc., 1992), 572-37.

2. Ibid., 573.

3. Robert J. Dean, *God's Big Little Words* (Nashville: Broadman Press, 1975), 36

The Parable of the Three Servants

Basic Passage: Matthew 25:14–30
Focal Passage: Matthew 25:14–30

Matthew 24 and 25 form a unit. Matthew 24 tells of Christ's future coming. Matthew 25 records three parables that describe how people ought to respond to the hope of the Lord's return. The parable of the three servants, usually called the parable of the talents, concentrates on the need for faithful stewardship as we await the coming of the Lord.

▶ ▶ ▶ ▶ **Study Aim:** *To evaluate our faithfulness in the use of what the Lord has entrusted to us*

STUDYING THE BIBLE

I. Varying Responses to the Master's Trust (Matt. 25:14–18)
   1. The trust (Matt. 25:14–15)
   2. Varying responses (Matt. 25:16–18)
II. The Master's Accounting (Matt. 25:19–30)
   1. Faithfulness rewarded (Matt. 25:19–23)
   2. An unfaithful servant (Matt. 25:24–25)
   3. Rebuke of the unfaithful servant (Matt. 25:26–27)
   4. Results of unfaithfulness and faithfulness
     (Matt. 25:28–30)

Before traveling to a distant country, a man entrusted five talents to one servant, two to another, and one to yet another in accordance with their abilities (vv. 14–15). The first two servants doubled their investment, but the other servant dug a hole and buried his talent (vv. 16–18). When the man returned, he praised the faithful servants (vv. 19–23). The third servant explained that his actions were due to his belief that his master was a hard man (vv. 24–25). The master said that if the third servant believed that he was a hard man, he should at least have put the talent into the bank to draw interest (vv. 26–27). The master gave the unused talent to the first servant and consigned the unfaithful servant to outer darkness (vv. 28–30).

I. Varying Responses to the Master's Trust (Matt. 25:14–18)

1. The trust (vv. 14–15)

   14 For the kingdom of heaven is as a man travelling into a far country, who called his own servants, and delivered unto them his goods.

   15 And unto one he gave five talents, to another two, and to

another one; to every man according to his several ability; and straightway took his journey.

As we saw in the lesson on Matthew 18:21–35, a talent was the largest denomination of currency in the ancient world. A talent would be comparable to several thousand dollars today. The parable itself doesn't spell out what the servants were to do with the talents entrusted to them. The larger context shows that they were expected to be faithful and wise servants while they awaited the master's return (Matt. 24:45–46).

Each of the three servants was entrusted with something that belonged to the master. While he was away, they were expected to handle his possessions in the way he would do himself. As applied to our Lord, we are His stewards, who are entrusted with what is His. Paul summed up what is expected of stewards: "Moreover it is required in stewards, that a man be found faithful" (1 Cor. 4:2).

Since the talents in the parable were money, our use of the Lord's money is a clear application. Money is often the acid test of stewardship. Those who are faithful stewards of money are usually, but not always, faithful stewards in other areas. Our English word *talent* has its roots in this parable. Thus our ancestors recognized that the principles of the parable applied to the use of our abilities, aptitudes, and spiritual gifts.

Verse 15 points to another basic biblical principle of stewardship. The master entrusted different amounts to different people, since each person has different capacities. Five talents went to one man; two to another; and one to yet another: "each according to his ability" (NIV).

2. Varying responses (vv. 16–18)

16 Then he that had received the five talents went and traded with the same, and made them other five talents.

17 And likewise he that had received two, he also gained other two.

18 But he that had received one went and digged in the earth, and hid his lord's money.

The first two servants "traded with" what they had been given. In other words, each "put his money to work" (NIV). We are not told what specific investments were involved, but we are told that each doubled the original investment by putting it to work. Therefore, we know that an element of risk was involved. Likewise, an element of risk is involved in faithful use of what the Lord has entrusted to us.

The third servant took a very different course. He simply dug a hole and buried the master's money.

II. The Master's Accounting
(Matt. 25:19–30)

1. Faithfulness rewarded (vv. 19–23)

19 After a long time the lord of those servants cometh, and reckoneth with them.

20 And so he that had received five talents came and brought other five talents, saying, Lord, thou deliveredst unto me five tal-

ents: behold, I have gained beside them five talents more.

21 His lord said unto him, Well done, thou good and faithful servant: thou hast been faithful over a few things, I will make thee ruler over many things: enter thou into the joy of thy lord.

In the context of Matthew 24–25, the return of the master after a long time represents the Lord's future coming. The reckoning with the servants was a time of settling accounts. In terms of the Lord's dealings with people, it is the time of judgment. As Paul wrote, "Every one of us shall give account of himself to God" (Rom. 14:12; see also 2 Cor. 5:10).

When the servant with five talents reported, he was commended by his master. The commendation included an evaluation of his work: "well done." It included personal affirmation: "good and faithful." It included two rewards. For one thing, the faithful servant was rewarded by a larger area of responsibility. He had proved faithful over a few things; in the future, he would be put in charge of many things. The second reward was to enter into the joy of his master. This may be translated "share your master's happiness" (NIV).

Verse 21 can be directly applied to the commendation and rewards that the Lord will give to His faithful servants. What could sound sweeter to a true servant of God than the words: "Well done, thou good and faithful servant"! Faithful servants will receive the same twofold reward as in verse 21, but our limited experience keeps us from fully understanding the heavenly aspects of these rewards. We know in this life how the principle of larger responsibility works; we do not yet know exactly what "ruler over many things" will mean in the future life. For one thing, it surely affirms that the future life will include continuing service. Faithful servants already have experienced some of what is meant by entering into the joy of the Lord, but the full experience lies ahead.

22 He also that had received two talents came and said, Lord, thou deliveredst unto me two talents: behold, I have gained two other talents beside them.

23 His lord said unto him, Well done, good and faithful servant; thou hast been faithful over a few things, I will make thee ruler over many things: enter thou into the joy of thy lord.

The master's words to the second servant are almost the same as to the first servant. Verse 15 shows that the Lord assigns responsibility according to individual capabilities. Verse 23 shows that He judges and rewards on the basis of faithfulness. The servant with two talents was not criticized because he gained only two talents while the first servant gained five. He was rewarded on the basis of what the Lord had entrusted to him.

2. An unfaithful servant (vv. 24–25)

24 Then he which had received the one talent came and said, Lord, I knew thee that thou are an hard man, reaping where thou hast not sown, and gathering where thou hast not strawed:

25 And I was afraid, and went and hid thy talent in the earth: lo, there thou hast that it thine.

The third servant explained his actions as based on what he believed about the character of his master. The servant explained that he thought his master was the kind of man who harvested what he did not plant. Because the servant believed his master was a hard man, his primary feeling toward his master was fear. The servant said that he dug a hole and buried the master's talent because he was afraid of his master.

3. Rebuke of the unfaithful servant (vv. 26–27)

26 His lord answered and said unto him, Thou wicked and slothful servant, thou knewest that I reap where I sowed not, and gather where I have not strawed:

27 Thou oughtest therefore to have put my money to the exchangers, and then at my coming I should have received mine own with usury.

The master said that if the servant really believed he was a hard man, the servant should have put the money in the bank at the safest level of risk. If he had done that, at least the talent would have earned some interest, however small. By saying what he did in verse 26, the master in the parable was neither denying nor affirming that he was a hard man. We certainly know that verse 26 is a distortion of the character of the divine Lord. Many people have a view of God that is like the servant's view of his master. These people do not know God as the loving heavenly Father, but as a heavenly tyrant who demands what they cannot give. Their attitude toward God is somewhere between fear and indifference.

Notice the sin of the unfaithful servant. He didn't steal the talent and flee to another land. His sin was that he simply did nothing with what the Lord had entrusted to Him. The lord called him a "wicked, lazy servant" (NIV) because he dug a hole and buried the talent entrusted to him by his master.

Everything we have has come from God. He has entrusted us with the gift of life and our own particular gifts and possessions. What we do with what God has entrusted to us determines whether we are judged faithful or unfaithful by the Lord.

4. Results of unfaithfulness and faithfulness (vv. 28–30)

28 Take therefore the talent from him, and give it unto him which hath ten talents.

29 For unto every one that hath shall be given, and he shall have abundance: but from him that hath not shall be taken away even that which he hath.

30 And cast ye the unprofitable servant into outer darkness: there shall be weeping and gnashing of teeth.

Faithful servants of the Lord enter into the joy and light of eternal fellowship. Those whose unfaithfulness shows no love or trust in the Lord face the pain of outer darkness.

This parable illustrates the principle expressed in Matthew 16:25: "Whosoever will save his life shall lose it: and whosoever will lose his life for my sake shall find it." People who trust and love God are willing to take the risks called for by their Lord. The third servant is typical of those whose lack of trust and love in God causes them to misuse or neglect what the Lord has entrusted to them. Unfaithful servants lose their lives in seeking to save them. Faithful servants find their lives because they are willing to risk all for the Lord.

APPLYING THE BIBLE

1. Prepared for the Lord's return. There is an old and often-told story of a traveler who happened upon a beautiful home on a lake in Switzerland. Everything was green, trimmed, and well-kept. The traveler complimented the gardener on the beautiful grounds and gardens and then asked if the master of the house were home.

"Oh, no," the old gardener replied. "He does not live here. He lives far away."

"Does he often come to stay in this beautiful home?" asked the traveler. "No, he has been here only four times in twenty-four years," replied the traveler. "But the grounds are so well-kept it appears as though you are expecting him tomorrow."

"I work the gardens and grounds as though he will return today," the old gardener replied.

Our lesson writer today tells us that chapters 24 and 25 are a unit. In chapter 24, Jesus tells us He is coming again, and in the parable of the talents He tells us how we are to serve and live as we await His coming: as though He would come today.

2. Don't stoop to become a king. The great English preacher Charles Haddon Spurgeon once said: "If God calls you to be His worker, don't stoop to become a king."

3. Are we doing our best for Christ? A salesman was trying to persuade a farmer to buy some books that would teach him how to be a better farmer.

"But son," the old farmer replied. "I know more about farming right now than I am doing!"

That, no doubt, can be said of most of us. God has given each of us a gift, or several gifts, and we surely know more about how to use them than we are doing.

4. Each of us has a talent we can use. Robert Henri (1865–1929) was a well-known American portrait and landscape painter. Once he was attending a private art showing in a New York gallery, admiring the work of John Singer Sargent (1856–1925), one of the best-known French artists of his day. Standing nearby was another man who was admiring the same canvas, and Henri overheard the man saying to himself, "They have given me a place at last."

Henri knew the painting was by Sargent, and he said to the man, "Are you also in this line of work?"

"Oh, yes," said the man, "I have been in it for years."

When Henri asked the man where his painting was hanging, he pointed to the work of Sargent.

"Why Sargent painted that," Henri exclaimed in disgust.

"Oh, yes, I know," said the man, "but I made the frame!"

Like the three men of Jesus' parable, to each of us has been given a divine gift to use in His service. It may not be much, but each of us must use what gift we have for the glory of God.

5. Not much, but enough. Christ is good at using what we have, though it may be not much, for his glory: He used a donkey to ride into Jerusalem; a boy's lunch to feed the multitudes; a once-cursing, backslidden preacher to preach on the day of Pentecost and open the door of grace to the Gentile word; a poor woman's mites to teach us the value of faithful stewardship; a borrowed boat in which to preach to multitudes; and an adulterous woman to bring the glorious gospel to the Samaritans.

God expects us to use faithfully what He has given us although it may not seem to be much. Blessing and multiplying it is up to Him. Of us, He only requires our being faithful.

TEACHING THE BIBLE

▶ *Main Idea:* The parable of the three servants illustrates that we should be faithful with what the Lord has entrusted to us.

▶ *Suggested Teaching Aim:* To lead adults to examine the three responses of the servants, and to identify how they can be faithful with what the Lord has entrusted to them.

A TEACHING OUTLINE

1. Begin the lesson by asking a thought question.
2. Use a chart or handout to guide the Bible study.
3. Ask members to formulate principles to apply the Scripture.
4. Lead members to apply these principles to their lives.

Introduce the Bible Study

Ask members to think about their checkbook record. Ask, If a biographer were to use your checkbook record to determine what you considered important in your life, what would it reveal?

Suggest that the lesson today will help us determine how we use our money that has been loaned to us by God.

Search for Biblical Truth

IN ADVANCE, prepare the following chart or make individual copies for each member (omit italicized answers in both cases):

The Parable of the Three Servants
Matthew 25:14–30

	Amount Given	Servant's Action	Master's Response
First Servant	5 talents	Invested	Praised
Second Servant	2 talents	Invested	Praised
Third Servant	1 talent	Buried	Condemned

Organize the class in three groups (or work together as a class) and ask each group to fill in the chart for one servant. Allow about three to four minutes for study, and then call for responses. If you decide to work as a class, give each member a copy of the poster as a note-taking help. They will remember better what they have written down.

After the groups have reported and filled in the chart, write the words *Financial Stewardship* on a chalkboard. Ask members to examine the parable and find principles that would apply to their financial stewardship. Write these on the chalkboard.

Now write *Christian Service* on the chalkboard. Ask members to examine the parable and find principles that would apply to their Christian service. Write these on the chalkboard.

Give the Truth a Personal Focus

Read the "Main Idea" of the lesson and ask members to identify ways they can be faithful with what the Lord has entrusted to them.

Distribute pencils and paper to members. (If you gave members copies of the chart, ask them to turn it over.) Ask them to look at the list of principles and select one from each list (Financial and Service) and apply it to their lives. Ask them to list one or two ways these principles would apply to their lives and how they can be more faithful in their financial stewardship and in their Christian service. Close in prayer for the courage to practice their ideas.

NOTE: Next week's lesson calls for advanced assignments. Check to see if you want to make those assignments. This will help you involve members of the class in the Bible study.

The Parable of the Great Feast

Basic Passage: Luke 14:1–24
Focal Passage: Luke 14:15–24

L uke 14:1–24 records what happened when Jesus ate a Sabbath meal with a Pharisee. He healed a sick man, and he taught in parables. One of these parables was about a great feast.

▶ ▶ ▶ ▶ ▶ ▶ ▶ ▶ ▶ **Study Aim:** *To explain why some people use excuses to avoid accepting God's invitation*

STUDYING THE BIBLE

I. Miracle and Teachings at a Sabbath Meal (Luke 14:1–14)
    1. Healing on the Sabbath (Luke 14:1–6)
    2. A parable to guests (Luke 14:7–11)
    3. Instruction to the host (Luke 14:12–14)
II. Parable of the Great Feast (Luke 14:15–24)
    1. A pious comment (Luke 14:15)
    2. Summoned to a great feast (Luke 14:16–17)
    3. Making excuses (Luke 14:18–20)
    4. Broadening the invitation (Luke 14:21)
    5. Extending the invitation to outsiders (Luke 14:22–23)
    6. A sobering warning (Luke 14:24)

At a Sabbath meal in a Pharisee's house, Jesus healed a sick man (vv. 1–6). He told a parable about not seeking the best places at a wedding feast (vv. 7–11). Jesus told His host that when he had a feast, he should invite not his rich friends, but the poor and handicapped (vv. 12–14). Someone at the feast spoke of the blessedness of those who eat bread in the kingdom of God (v. 15). Jesus told a parable of a man whose servant went out to summon those who had been previously invited to a great feast (vv. 16–17). Everyone offered an excuse for not coming (vv. 18–20). The man then told his servant to go into the streets and lanes of the city and to bring in the outcasts (v. 21). Then he sent his servant into the highways and hedges to invite others to come (vv. 22–23). Jesus said that none of those who rejected the invitation would partake of the feast (v. 24).

I. Miracle and Teachings at a Sabbath Meal (Luke 14:1–14)

1. Healing on the Sabbath (vv. 1–6). When Jesus accepted an invitation to eat a Sabbath meal in the home of a chief Pharisee, He was watched closely (v. 1). When a man with dropsy came in (v. 2), Jesus asked the lawyers and Pharisees if healing on the Sabbath was lawful

(v. 3). After they gave no answer, Jesus healed the man (v. 4). Jesus asked them if they wouldn't pull one of their animals out of a pit on the Sabbath (v. 5), but they didn't answer (v. 6).

2. A parable to guests (vv. 7–11). Noticing that the guests had sought out places of honor at the table, Jesus told a parable (v. 7). When people are invited to a wedding feast, they shouldn't choose the places of honor (v. 8). If they do, the host may ask them to move if someone more distinguished arrives (v. 9). Instead, the guests should choose the lowest places; so that if they are asked to move, it will be to a better place (v. 10). Those who exalt themselves will be humbled, and those who humble themselves will be exalted (v. 11).

3. Instructions to the host (vv. 12–14). Jesus told His host not to invite his relatives and rich friends to a meal. If he did, these would invite him in return to eat with them (v. 12). Instead, he should invite the poor, crippled, lame, and blind (v. 13). Although such people cannot repay their host, God will reward such generosity at the resurrection of the just (v. 14).

II. Parable of the Great Feast
(Luke 14:15–24)

1. A pious comment (v. 15)

> **15 And when one of them that sat at meat with him heard these things, he said unto him, Blessed is he that shall eat bread in the kingdom of God.**

One of the other guests, probably a Pharisee, heard what Jesus said in verse 14. He spoke the words in verse 15. He was right in describing the future life as being like a great feast. Jesus Himself did the same in verses 16–24. The man was also right that the one who partakes of the heavenly feast will be blessed. However, he was wrong to glibly assume that he and those like him would be among those who partake of the heavenly feast.

2. Summoned to a great feast (vv. 16–17)

> **16 Then said he unto him, A certain man made a great supper, and bade many:**

> **17 And sent his servant at supper time to say to them that were bidden, Come; for all things are now ready.**

In great feasts of that time, a two-part invitation was given. First, the guests were invited to come to a feast at a future date. Then when the feast was ready, a summons was sent to those who had accepted the first invitation.

Jesus was describing God's invitation to share in the joys of His kingdom. Verse 17 is one of many Bible invitations that use the word "come" (see Isa. 1:18; 55:1; Matt. 11:28; Rev. 22:17). God's grace is seen in His gracious invitation for sinners to come to Him and find life. Anyone who has accepted God's invitation can testify to the joys that we have already received, and we know that this is only a foretaste of the glory of heaven.

3. Making excuses (vv. 18–20)

> **18 And they all with one consent began to make excuse.**

The first said unto him, I have bought a piece of ground, and I must needs go and see it: I pray thee have me excused.

19 And another said, I have bought five yoke of oxen, and I go to prove them: I pray thee have me excused.

20 And another said, I have married a wife, and therefore I cannot come.

Strangely enough, many people make excuses to avoid accepting God's invitation to life and joy. Such excuses are depicted in verses 18–20 of Jesus' parable. Keep in mind that all these people earlier had said that they would attend the feast; but when the actual invitation to come was extended, they all offered excuses. Jesus cited three excuses that were typical.

One of the invited guests told the servant that he had bought a field, and he had to go and see it. Another said that he had purchased five yoke of oxen, and he was on his way to try them out. Each of these two asked to be excused from going to the feast. There is a kind of grim humor in these first two excuses. Who buys a field that he hasn't seen or oxen that he hasn't tried out? Jesus was portraying people who were using lame excuses to try and hide the fact that they didn't want to attend the feast.

The third man felt that he had a reason, not an excuse. He didn't ask to be excused. He simply announced that he had gotten married and, therefore, couldn't come. The Old Testament excused a man from business or military service for one year after he was married (Deut. 24:5). This exemption did not extend to social occasions. He could have gone if he had wanted to go; his excuse shows that he didn't want to go.

When we accept God's invitation and experience the joys of knowing Him, we have a hard time understanding those who resist the invitation to life, love, joy, and peace. We can only conclude that those who offer such lame excuses just don't want to accept the invitation. Why not? They obviously believe that God is trying to rob them of life, rather than to give life.

In the original context, the people who excused themselves were people like the Pharisees. God's chosen people Israel had originally accepted the divine invitation; but when God sent His servants John the Baptist and Jesus, many found various pretexts for rejecting the message through John or through Jesus (see Luke 7:31–35). The Pharisee who spoke the pious beatitude of verse 15 assumed that he and those like him were already included among those who would eat the heavenly feast. Jesus was telling them that they were excluding themselves by their rejection of the message of the Father through the Son.

4. Broadening the invitation (v. 21)

21 So that servant came, and shewed his lord these things. Then the master of the house being angry said to his servant, Go out quickly into the streets and lanes of the city, and bring in hither the poor, and the maimed, and the halt, and the blind.

These were the same groups that Jesus had mentioned in his earlier words to his host (see v. 13). The fact that they were in the lanes and streets of the city implies that they had no comfortable homes of their own. They were the "street people" of Jesus' day. These groups represented the kinds of people whom the Pharisees didn't invite to their feasts and whom the Pharisees assumed would not be included in the heavenly feast. They included outcasts of all kinds. The parable mentions the poor and handicapped. Although the words are not used in verse 21, they also represented the moral outcasts of the day—the tax collectors and sinners whom the Pharisees despised, but whom Jesus sought and accepted (Luke 5:27–32; 7:36–50; 15; 19:1–10).

In the parable, the master told his servant to go out to these people and to bring the outcasts into his feast. This represents the love of God for all kinds of people. It also represents the truth that people who are aware of their sins often repent and enter the kingdom of heaven, while the self-righteous refuse to acknowledge their need (see Matt. 21:31; Luke 18:9–14).

The broadening of the invitation in the parable sounds as if this was an afterthought of the master when the original guests refused to come. However, no parable can illustrate every truth. God's plan has always been to include moral, physical, and social outcasts in His invitation.

5. Extending the invitation to outsiders (vv. 22–23)

22 And the servant said, Lord, it is done as thou hast commanded, and yet there is room.

23 And the lord said unto the servant, Go out into the highways and hedges, and compel them to come in, that my house may be filled.

The groups in verse 21 were within the city; the people in verse 23 were outside the city. Those in verse 21 represented Jewish people who were considered outcasts by Pharisees. Those in verse 23 represented Gentiles, who also were excluded by the Pharisees. Again the parable itself presents their inclusion as an afterthought of the master. However, that was not the point Jesus was making. Including Gentiles has always been God's plan. Recently we have studied some Old Testament books—Isaiah, Jonah, and Ruth—that make this clear. We also saw how this plan came to fruition in the events recorded in the Book of Acts. During the lifetime of Jesus, the emphasis was on reaching Jews. However, in teachings like the parable of the great feast, Jesus anticipated the commission to world evangelism that He gave to His followers after His death and resurrection (see Matt. 28:18–20; Acts 1:8).

At times in Christian history, the word "compel" from verse 23 has been quoted to justify the use of force in compelling people to become Christians. Nothing more distorts the biblical way of evangelism. The word is used to describe the servant's ability to persuade them to come, not his ability to force them to come. People participate in divine salvation only when they voluntarily choose to do so. The invitation is to all, but only those who accept the invitation actually enter.

6. A sobering warning (v. 24)

24 For I say unto you, That none of those men which were bidden shall taste of my supper.

Jesus spelled out the grim warning of the parable. People like the man who spoke the pious words of verse 15 assumed that he and others like him would share in the joys of the heavenly feast. The parable of Jesus showed that many like him actually turned down God's invitation by rejecting God's Son. No matter what credentials they might claim as a basis for entering, they will be excluded by their own refusal of God's gracious invitation.

APPLYING THE BIBLE

1. The Jewish Sabbath versus the Christian Sunday. Some of the severest criticism of Jesus was leveled at Him because, according to the Pharisees, Jesus misused the Sabbath day. Such is the case in our lesson today (v. 2).

Perhaps this would be a good time for us to consider why the Jews keep the seventh day holy (Sabbath), and we Christians observe the Lord's Day (Sunday) as our day of worship.

The Jews observed the Sabbath because God rested from His creative work on the seventh day (Gen. 2:2). Also, in the Ten Commandments, given to Moses, God commanded: "Remember the sabbath day to keep it holy (Exod. 20:8; also 9–11). But Jesus fulfilled the law and the prophets (Matt. 5:17) and is greater than they are. He was raised from the dead on the first day of the week and made at least eleven postresurrection appearances in the forty days between His resurrection and ascension. At least six of these were on the resurrection Sunday (five) and on the following Sunday (one). The other days He appeared are not certain, but some interpreters have suggested they, too, may have been on Sunday. Gradually, therefore, the early church began to break away from Sabbath observance and to assemble on the first day of the week to celebrate Christ's victory over death.

2. Feeding the poor. Nothing is more the work of Jesus than feeding the poor and hungry. I know a Baptist man who has built a great ministry doing just that. A man of means, he has dedicated himself and his resources to ministering to the needy and has taken it upon himself, with the help of financially able businessmen, to build a large and adequate building where hundreds from off the streets are fed each week. Also, showers are provided for them and a job placement ministry also seeks to help them find work and get on their feet.

In his parable, Jesus stresses the importance of our feeding those truly in need (vv. 23–24). When we do so, we put bread in the mouth of Jesus Himself (Matt. 25:35, 40, 45).

3. We are all invited to the feast. The parable, it appears, had a dual application: the Jews were first invited to come into the kingdom of God, but they refused the invitation. Then the Gentiles—the outcasts— were invited.

The feast symbolizes the privilege of becoming a part of God's family and participating in the joys of the kingdom of God. The invitation is given to all to come, and take of the water (and bread) of life freely (John 4:10–11). Many accept God's invitation of grace but, regrettably, many refuse the gift of salvation and die in their sins.

Multitudes of educated, wealthy, socially prominent, and powerful people have accepted His invitation. But, thank God, so have the outcasts, the diseased, the broken, and the morally bankrupt! Indeed, it is a glorious invitation that opens up a glorious opportunity!

4. One excuse is as good as another. The Tehran Conference held in Tehran, Iran, in 1943, was the first meeting of President Franklin Roosevelt, British Prime Minister Winston Churchill, and Russian Premier Joseph Stalin. In the meeting, the three superpowers bound themselves together to crush Germany's military might.

During their meeting, Stalin told a story that put Roosevelt "in stitches." The neighbor of an Arab sheik asked to borrow a rope and the other sheik replied, "I cannot lend it, for I have milk tied up in it." The first sheik exclaimed, "Surely, you don't tie your milk with a rope." And the second sheik replied, "Brother, when you don't want to do something, one excuse is as good as another."

TEACHING THE BIBLE

▶ *Main Idea:* Jesus' parable of the great feast warns us not to reject God's offer of salvation.
▶ *Suggested Teaching Aim:* To lead adults to examine the parable of the great feast, and to identify excuses that are keeping them from accepting God's invitation.

A TEACHING OUTLINE

1. Use a graffiti wall to create interest.
2. Make six advanced assignments to study the focal passage.
3. Use the graffiti wall to help members see the ridiculousness of their excuses.

Introduce the Bible Study

Place a large sheet of paper on a wall and provide marking pens. As members enter, ask them to go to the wall and write some of the ridiculous excuses they have heard (or possibly used!) for not coming to church.

As you begin class, read some of these excuses. As an alternate approach, enlist two people to role play a person using some of these excuses when invited to church.

Search for Biblical Truth

IN ADVANCE, make the following strip posters:
Parable of the Great Feast
Luke 14:15–24
1. A Pious Comment (Luke 14:15)
2. Summoned to a Great Feast (Luke 14:16–17)
3. Making Excuses (Luke 14:18–20)
4. Broadening the Invitation (Luke 14:21)
5. Extending the Invitation to Outsiders (Luke 14:22–23)
6. A Sobering Warning (Luke 14:24)

A WEEK IN ADVANCE, give six different people one of the above strips. Ask them to study the passage and be prepared to share its meaning with the rest of the class. If you choose not to make the advance assignments, you can do these as a class by means of a lecture.

Call for the first person to tape the strip poster on the wall and share the information about the verse. Be sure the glibness of the speaker at the dinner is noted.

Call for the second person to tape the strip poster on the wall and share the information about the verses. Be sure the following are noted: (1) the method of summoning guests, and (2) that Jesus is describing God's invitation to His kingdom.

Call for the third person to tape the strip poster on the wall and share the information about the verses. Be sure the following are pointed out: (1) the ridiculousness of the excuses, (2) who the original people were who made such excuses.

Call for the fourth person to tape the strip poster on the wall and share the information about the verse. Be sure the following are pointed out: (1) who these people represented, and (2) God's plan has always included everyone.

Call for the fifth person to tape the strip poster on the wall and share the information about the verses. Be sure the following are pointed out: (1) who the people in the highways and hedges represented, and (2) what the word *compel* means.

Call for the sixth person to tape the strip poster on the wall and share the information about the verse. Be sure the following are pointed out: (1) only those accepting Jesus will share in the great feast, and (2) those who are excluded have excluded themselves.

Give the Truth a Personal Focus

Refer to the graffiti wall. Ask members silently to identify how many of the excuses they have used themselves or what excuse they are using to refuse to accept God's gracious invitation. Suggest that regardless of how "good" their excuse may be, they will still miss God's kingdom if they reject God's Son.

Spend some time in silent prayer to allow members to consider their own situations. If you have members in your class who need to accept God's offer of salvation, encourage them to do so and let them know that you will be available after class to speak with them.

The Living Lord

Basic Passage: Luke 24:1–36
Focal Passage: Luke 24:13–27

T
he heart of the Christian good news is that Jesus died for our sins
and was raised from the dead (1 Cor. 15:3–4). The message of
the cross and resurrection are inseparable. This is made clear in
Luke's account of the risen Lord's conversation with the two disciples
on the road to Emmaus.

► ► ► ► **Study Aim:** *To explain how the resurrection of Jesus validated
His suffering and death as God's plan*

STUDYING THE BIBLE

I. The Empty Tomb (Luke 24:1–12)
   1. The women's discovery (Luke 24:1–3)
   2. The angels' words (Luke 24:4–7)
   3. The women's report (Luke 24:8–10)
   4. The apostles' response (Luke 24:11–12)
**II. Appearance to Two on the Emmaus Road
   (Luke 24:13–22)**
   1. Jesus unrecognized (Luke 24:13–16)
   2. Sad disciples (Luke 24:17–21)
   3. Reports of the empty tomb (Luke 24:22–24)
   4. Christ's suffering and glory (Luke 24:25–27)
   5. Recognizing the risen Lord (Luke 24:28–32)
III. Other Appearances (Luke 24:33–36)

Women went to Jesus' tomb early on the first day of the week, but
they found an empty tomb (vv. 1–3). Two angels told them that Jesus
was risen and reminded them of Jesus' words predicting His resurrection (vv. 4–7). Remembering the words of Jesus, the women reported
to the apostles and to the other followers (vv. 8–10). The men didn't
believe the words of the women (vv. 11–12). While two followers
walked and talked together on the way to Emmaus, Jesus joined them;
but they didn't recognize Him (vv. 13–16). The two sad disciples described the ministry and crucifixion of Jesus, and said that they had
hoped that He would redeem Israel (vv. 17–21). They also told of the
women's report about the empty tomb and the words of the angels, and
they said that some of the apostles had gone to the tomb and found it
empty (vv. 22–24). Jesus rebuked them and explained from the Scriptures how Christ was to suffer and enter into His glory (vv. 25–27).
When they stopped to eat, the two disciples recognized Jesus as He
broke bread and blessed it (vv. 28–32). Returning to Jerusalem, the two
disciples were told by the apostles that Jesus had appeared to Simon
(vv. 33–35). As the two disciples reported what had happened to them,
Jesus suddenly appeared in their midst (v. 36).

I. The Empty Tomb (Luke 24:1–12)

1. The women's discovery (vv. 1–3). Some women came with spices to the tomb early on the first day of the week (v. 1). They found the stone rolled away; and when they went in, they found the tomb empty (vv. 2–3).

2. The angels' words (vv. 4–7). Two angels asked the women why they sought the living among the dead (vv. 4–5). The angels announced that Jesus was not there, but was risen (v. 6a). They reminded the women of Jesus' predictions of His crucifixion and resurrection (vv. 6b–7).

3. The women's report (vv. 8–10). The women remembered Jesus' words and returned to report to the apostles and to the rest of Jesus' followers (vv. 8–9). The report was given by Mary Magdalene, Joanna, Mary the mother of James, and other women (v. 10).

4. The apostles' response (vv. 11–12). Because the words of the women seemed to the apostles to be like the talk of crazy people, the apostles didn't believe them (v. 11). Later, some of the apostles went to the tomb and confirmed that it was empty (v. 12).

II. Appearance to Two on the Emmaus Road (Luke 24:13–32)

1. Jesus unrecognized (vv. 13–16)

13 And, behold, two of them went that same day to a village called Emmaus, which was from Jerusalem about threescore furlongs.

14 And they talked together of all these things which had happened.

Two followers of Jesus were walking that day on the road from Jerusalem to Emmaus, a distance of about seven miles. The two men were not apostles, but were from the larger group of disciples called the "rest" in verse 9. The name of one disciple was Cleopas (v. 18). We aren't told the name of the other. The time was in the afternoon of the first day of the week (v. 29).

15 And it came to pass, that, while they communed together and reasoned, Jesus himself drew near, and went with them.

16 But their eyes were holden that they should not know him.

As they were concentrating on their conversation with each other, a third person joined them as they walked. The third person was none other than Jesus, but the two disciples didn't recognize Him at first. Remember His appearance to Mary Magdalene, related in John 20:11–18. Mary didn't recognize Jesus at first. How can we account for these failures of followers to recognize the risen Lord?

One factor was that they were not expecting Jesus to be raised from the dead. Jesus had predicted His death and resurrection (Luke 9:22; 18:31–33); however, Jesus' followers were not expecting Him to be raised from the dead. Even after the tomb was found empty, they didn't conclude that Jesus had been raised from the dead. Mary thought someone had taken His body (John 20:13).

When Jesus had predicted His suffering, death, and resurrection, the disciples had not understood. The idea of the Messiah suffering and dying was foreign to what they expected. Peter even rebuked Jesus when the Lord first predicted His suffering and death (Mark 8:31–33). Because the disciples didn't understand what Jesus predicted about suffering and death, they didn't really hear what He said about resurrection.

Another factor in the failure of the two disciples to recognize Jesus was that His resurrection body was in some ways different. However, we need to emphasize that the body of the risen Lord also still bore the prints of the spear and the nails (John 20:27). He could be touched, and He could eat with His followers (Luke 24:39–43). After His appearances, Jesus' followers were convinced that they had seen the Lord.

The primary factor for Cleopas and his companion was that at first "they were kept from recognizing him" (NIV). Only later were their eyes opened to recognize Jesus (v. 31).

2. Sad disciples (vv. 17–21)

17 And he said unto them, What manner of communications are these that ye have one to another, as ye walk, and are sad?

18 And the one of them, whose name was Cleopas, answering said unto him, Art thou only a stranger in Jerusalem, and hast not known the things which are come to pass there in these days?

19 And he said unto them, What things? And they said unto him, Concerning Jesus of Nazareth, which was a prophet mighty in deed and word before God and all the people:

20 And how the chief priests and our rulers delivered him to be condemned to death, and have crucified him.

21 But we trusted that it had been he which should have redeemed Israel: and beside all this, to day is the third day since these things were done.

Jesus used questions to get their thoughts out into the open. They were amazed that their traveling companion knew nothing of what had been happening in Jerusalem. They concluded that He must be a stranger. Their words provide insight into what the followers of Jesus believed during the time between His death and their awareness of His resurrection. They still remembered the ministry of Jesus. They spoke of His power in word and deed before God and the people.

What they couldn't understand was why Jesus, who had such power, was condemned and crucified. They were looking for a Messiah who would use His power to redeem Israel from the Roman yoke and restore the glory of the days of King David. When they saw the evidences of divine power in the ministry of Jesus, they had hoped that He was that Messiah. Their words show that the Christian gospel includes not only the cross but also the resurrection. Before they were aware that God had raised Jesus from the dead, His followers saw the cross only as a puzzling defeat. Only in light of His resurrection did they see divine salvation in the suffering and death of Jesus.

3. Reports of the empty tomb (vv. 22–24)

22 Yea, and certain women also of our company made us astonished, which were early at the sepulchre;

23 And when they found not his body, they came, saying, that they had also seen a vision of angels, which said that he was alive.

24 And certain of them which were with us went to the sepulchre, and found it even so as the women had said: but him they saw not.

The two disciples also told of the strange reports they had heard earlier in the day. Remember that the men had not believed the women's report of seeing angels who announced that Jesus was alive (vv. 9–11). Even when some of the men went and found the tomb empty, the men did not believe. Note that verse 24 ends by saying, "Him they saw not." These verses show again that the followers of Jesus were not expecting the resurrection of Jesus. Even when they found the tomb empty, they still did not believe that Jesus was alive. Their faith in the resurrection was based not on the fact that the tomb was empty; it was based on the fact that later the Lord appeared to them alive.

4. **Christ's suffering and glory (vv. 25–27)**

25 Then he said unto them, O fools, and slow of heart to believe all that the prophets have spoken:

26 Ought not Christ to have suffered these things, and to enter into his glory?

27 And beginning at Moses and all the prophets, he expounded unto them in all the scriptures the things concerning himself.

Jesus rebuked the two disciples for failing to see what the Scriptures taught about the suffering as well as the glory of the Messiah. Not many weeks ago, we studied Isaiah 52:13–53:12. At the time, we noted that the passage tells of both the suffering and the victory of the Servant. He entered into His victory through His suffering and death for our sins. This was no doubt one of the passages that Jesus used to stress this truth to the two on the Emmaus Road (see also v. 44).

Verses 25–27 show that the suffering and death of Jesus was not an afterthought of God, but was part of His plan of redemption all along. But the early believers saw this only in light of the resurrection.

5. **Recognizing the risen Lord (vv. 28–32).** The two travelers asked Jesus to stop and eat with them (vv. 28–29). As Jesus blessed the bread, they recognized Him (vv. 30–31). After He vanished, they talked of how their hearts had burned as He had opened the Scriptures to them (v. 32).

III. Other Appearances (Luke 24:33–36)

The two disciples returned to Jerusalem and found the apostles and others together (v. 33). The apostles said that the Lord was risen and had appeared to Simon (v. 34). Then the two told of the Lord's appearance to them (v. 35). As they were speaking, the Lord appeared among them (v. 36).

The Garden Tomb is one site offered by tradition as the the burial place of Jesus' body. Credit: Thomas B. Brisco, Professor of Biblical Backgrounds and Archeology, Southwestern Baptist Theological Seminary, Fort Worth, Texas.

APPLYING THE BIBLE

1. Women and Jesus. America's first woman in space was a thirty-one-year-old astrophysicist with a Ph.D. from Stanford University named, appropriately, Sally P. Ride. Out of eight thousand astronaut applicants, male and female, she was chosen as one of the thirty-five in the 1978 class of astronauts. NASA officials chose her as America's first woman in space because, they said, she "had the right stuff."

Among the "firsts" for women are many significant accomplishments. But the most significant of all is that women were first to come to the tomb of Joseph to anoint the dead body of Jesus (vv. 1–3) and the first to announce the good news of His resurrection to the world (vv. 8–10).

Is it not significant that a woman was the first to sin (Gen. 3:1–6) and women were the first to announce that redemption for sinful humanity had been provided through the death, burial and resurrection of Jesus Christ?

2. Sharing the good news. Each of us has had some experience that was just too good to keep. What was yours? Your conversion? Your first love? Your engagement? Your first job? Your first child? Grandchild? Life is sweetened and elevated, from time to time, for each of us with news that is simply too good to keep. We must share it with someone, and on our first opportunity it just explodes from us in a burst of joy and excitement.

In our lesson today, some news was shared with some people that was just too good to keep: the woman (vv. 9–10); Peter (v. 12); Cleopas and his companion (vv. 32, 35); and the eleven disciples, excluding Thomas who was absent (vv. 33–40).

What about us? Have we experienced in our hearts the glory and wonder of the news too good to keep? If so, what are we doing with it? It is not just our good news to be hoarded selfishly, but the good news that Christ has called us to share with the world (v. 48).

3. News too good to keep. When our first son was born, before the days when fathers were permitted in the delivery room, I was waiting in an adjoining room while my wife was giving birth. The room had a small pink light and a blue light, to announce to the anxious father waiting there whether he had a son or a daughter. Suddenly, the pink light flashed on, and I rushed off down the hospital corridor to announce to all who would listen that I was the father of a little girl. But, lo and behold, when I returned to the waiting room the pink light was off, and the blue light was on.

"What's going on?" I wondered. Twins? "Oh, no, surely not! Oh, yes, maybe so," my heart reasoned. But the attendant had erred and pushed the wrong button. It was a boy! The first news—the pink light—was too good to keep. I was eager and excited to share it with everyone. But the announcement was a mistake, and soon I was on my way, red-faced, to confess that my initial announcement was wrong. Nevertheless, all rejoiced with me that our first son had been born. I am ashamed to say that too often through the years I have not been as eager to announce to others that, as Paul says, "Christ died for our sins" and "was buried and that he arose the third day" to save us from our sins (1 Cor. 15:3–4). This is truly news too good to keep.

TEACHING THE BIBLE

▶ *Main Idea:* Jesus' resurrection shows how His suffering and death were a part of God's plan.
▶ *Suggested Teaching Aim:* To lead adults to examine the evidence for Jesus' resurrection, and to explain how Jesus' resurrection influences our daily lives.

A TEACHING OUTLINE

1. Introduce the lesson by asking two questions.
2. Visually emphasize Jesus' resurrection by making six posters.
3. Examine the Focal Passage by using a brief lecture and discussion questions.
4. Relate the lesson to members' lives by using discussion groups and reporting to class.

Introduce the Bible Study

Ask: What significance did the resurrection have for your life yesterday? What significance does the resurrection have for your life tomorrow? Encourage members to be honest in their responses. List these responses on a chalkboard or a large sheet of paper. You will use them again in "Give the Truth a Personal Focus."

Search for Biblical Truth

IN ADVANCE, make six posters approximately 8 1/2 by 11 inches. On one side write: Jesus is dead. One the other side write: Jesus is alive! Place these around the front of the room with the words *Jesus is dead* showing.

Briefly summarize the material from I. The Empty Tomb (Luke 24:1–12) in "Studying the Bible." When you finish with your summary, turn over one of the posters so it reads *Jesus is alive!*

DISCUSS: Why didn't Jesus' followers expect Him to rise?

Call for a volunteer to read Luke 24:13–16. Use a map to point out Emmaus and summarize the material related to these verses in "Studying the Bible." Turn over another poster.

DISCUSS: Why didn't the two disciples recognize Jesus? Why do you think Jesus chose these two to spend so much time with on the first day of His resurrection? Why did they fail to understand why Jesus was crucified?

Call for a volunteer to read Luke 24:17–21. Summarize the material in "Studying the Bible" for these verses. Turn over another poster.

DISCUSS: What convinced the disciples that Jesus had risen?

Call for a volunteer to read Luke 24:22–24. Summarize the material in "Studying the Bible" for these verses. Turn over another poster.

DISCUSS: What is the significance of women being first at the tomb of Jesus?

Call for a volunteer to read Luke 24:25–27. Summarize the material in "Studying the Bible" for these verses. Turn over another poster.

DISCUSS: How does Isaiah 52:13–53:13 relate to Jesus' suffering and victory?

Briefly summarize the remaining material in the background passage and turn over the last poster.

DISCUSS: Why were Jesus' appearances more helpful in proving His resurrection than was the empty tomb? Which means most to you today?

Give the Truth a Personal Focus

Ask members to look at the list compiled in "Introduce the Bible Study." Organize the class into groups of two or three persons and ask them to consider ways the resurrection can influence their lives this coming week. Let a representative of each group share their ideas. List these on the same chalkboard or large sheet of paper next to the previous list. Encourage members to make this Easter a significant one by letting Christ's resurrection become a part of their lives.

Close in prayer for a resurrection victory in the life of each member.

The Loving God

Basic Passage: Luke 15:1–10
Focal Passage: Luke 15:1–10

I f a number of people were asked to name some of their favorite chapters of the Bible, many would include Luke 15. It tells three famous parables: the lost sheep, the lost coin, and the prodigal son. In this study, we will focus on the first two parables.

▶ ▶ ▶ ▶ ▶ ▶ ▶ ▶ **Study Aim:** *To describe what Luke 15:1–10 reveals about the love of God*

STUDYING THE BIBLE

I. Friend of Sinners (Luke 15:1–2)
    1. Sinners attracted to Jesus (Luke 15:1)
    2. Jesus criticized by Pharisees (Luke 15:2)
II. The Lost Sheep (Luke 15:3–7)
    1. A parable (Luke 15:3)
    2. Search for the lost sheep (Luke 15:4)
    3. Joy in finding the sheep (Luke 15:5–6)
    4. Joy in heaven (Luke 15:7)
III. The Lost Coin (Luke 15:8–10)
    1. Search for a lost coin (Luke 15:8)
    2. Shared joy (Luke 15:9)
    3. God's joy (Luke 15:10)

Tax collectors and sinners flocked to hear Jesus (v. 1). The Pharisees and scribes criticized Jesus for receiving sinners and eating with them (v. 2). Jesus told three parables to illustrate God's love for sinners (v. 3). Jesus said that a man with one hundred sheep would search for one lost sheep until he found it (v. 4). He would ask others to join him in rejoicing over the lost sheep that had been found (vv. 5–6). Jesus said that heaven rejoices more over one repentant sinner than over ninety-nine righteous people who need no repentance (v. 7). Jesus also said that a woman with ten coins would search diligently until she found one lost coin (v. 8). When she found it, she would ask friends and neighbors to rejoice with her (v. 9). Jesus said that angels in heaven share in the joy over one repentant sinner (v. 10).

I. Friend of Sinners (Luke 15:1–2)
1. Sinners attracted to Jesus (v. 1)
1 Then drew near unto him all the publicans and sinners for to hear him.

"Publicans" were tax collectors. In a land under Roman rule, tax collectors were considered to be collaborators with the enemy. Many tax collectors also abused their power by extorting money from helpless people (see Luke 3:12–13). The Pharisees had an Aramaic term they used to describe "sinners." The Pharisees' definition of sinners included all the people of the land who didn't follow the religious rules of the Pharisees.

"Publicans and sinners" were often mentioned together because the Pharisees considered them moral and social outcasts (see Luke 5:30). They were also often mentioned because they were attracted to Jesus. Matthew (Levi), a tax collector, followed Jesus and gave a banquet for Him to which many tax collectors and sinners came (Matt. 9:9–11; Luke 5:27–30). Zacchaeus, a chief tax collector, was drawn to see Jesus and followed Him (Luke 19:2–8).

2. Jesus criticized by Pharisees (v. 2)

2 And the Pharisees and scribes murmured, saying, This man receiveth sinners, and eateth with them.

Jesus' attitude toward tax collectors and sinners explains why they were attracted to Him. He treated them with respect and compassion. He accepted them as friends and associated with them in social situations. Eating with someone is an act of friendship and fellowship, and Jesus did not hesitate to eat with tax collectors and sinners.

One of the criticisms of Jesus by the Pharisees was that He was a friend of sinners. To their way of thinking, Jesus could not associate with sinners without Himself becoming tainted with their sins. Thus they called Him "a glutton, and a drunkard, a friend of tax collectors and 'sinners'" (Matt. 11:19, NIV). At the very least, they felt that His associating with moral outcasts showed that He was no prophet (Luke 7:39).

II. The Lost Sheep (Luke 15:3–7)

1. A parable (v. 3)

3 And he spake this parable unto them, saying,

The key to understanding Luke 15 is to recognize that the parables Jesus told in this chapter were directed against the criticism of verse 2. He told three parables to make His point. The first two: lost sheep (vv. 4–7) and lost coin (vv. 8–10) are similar in structure and teaching. The third parable, usually called the parable of the prodigal son, would more aptly be called the parable of the loving father. The father had two lost sons—one lost in the far country like the sinners of Jesus' day and the other lost at home like the Pharisees (vv. 11–32).

2. Search for the lost sheep (v. 4)

4 What man of you, having an hundred sheep, if he lose one of them, doth not leave the ninety and nine in the wilderness, and go after that which is lost, until he find it?

Jesus asked His critics if they would not search diligently for one lost sheep even if they had ninety-nine others that were in safe pastures. The "wilderness" referred to the open country where sheep grazed, not a waterless desert. A truly concerned owner or shepherd would search for the one lost sheep until he found it.

Jesus was explaining His own actions with regard to tax collectors and sinners. As Matthew 9:36 puts it: "When he saw the multitudes, he was moved with compassion on them, because they fainted, and were scattered abroad, as sheep having no shepherd." To put it another way, He saw them through the eyes of the One from whom the sheep had gone astray (Isa. 53:6).

As a result of such love, He went after sinners and associated with them wherever He could find them. After the conversion of Zacchaeus, Jesus explained, "The Son of man is come to seek and to save that which was lost" (Luke 19:10). How far would Jesus go in His search for the lost sheep? Like the shepherd of the parable, He searches for it until He finds it. In other words, there is no limit to how far Jesus was willing to go to save even one lost sinner. This kind of love led Him to go all the way to Calvary, where He laid down His life.

3. Joy in finding the sheep (vv. 5–6)

5 And when he hath found it, he layeth it on his shoulders, rejoicing.

6 And when he cometh home, he calleth together his friends and neighbours, saying unto them, Rejoice with me; for I have found my sheep which was lost.

These words were a strong rebuke to the Pharisees. Jesus was like the shepherd who had found a lost sheep and called on others to rejoice with him. Instead of rejoicing with Jesus over the salvation of lost sinners, the Pharisees criticized Him for associating with the sinners.

The Pharisees were willing to receive repentant sinners if the sinners came to the Pharisees and showed proper remorse, but the Pharisees would not go out seeking sinners. When Jesus sought and saved sinners, however, the Pharisees were so angry at Jesus that they overlooked the results of His evangelistic approach.

4. Joy in heaven (v. 7)

7 I say unto you, that likewise joy shall be in heaven over one sinner that repenteth, more than over ninety and nine just persons which need no repentance.

The Pharisees might not join in rejoicing over repentant sinners whom Jesus sought and found, but heaven rings with joy over one repentant sinner. Joy in heaven means that God Himself rejoices over one sinner who is sought and found. This is the main point of the three parables in Luke 15. *God Himself is the One who seeks sinners and rejoices over one that repents.* The saving work of Jesus Christ, the Son of God, is the saving work of God Himself. The mission of Jesus to seek and to save the lost reveals the heart of God. This kind of divine love for sinners was seen even in the Garden of Eden when God came seeking Adam and Eve after they had sinned (Gen. 3:9). He could have destroyed them for their sins; instead, He set in motion His plan to seek and to save what was lost.

The Pharisees could defend their position of waiting for sinners by quoting Old Testament passages that call on sinners to seek the Lord (Isa. 55:6–7). Both sets of passages are true. God seeks sinners, but sinners must seek the Lord by responding to His presence. The parable of the lost sheep shows the seeking love of God. The parable of the prodigal son shows that sinners must respond to such love. In order to find a lost sheep, a shepherd needs only to locate it and carry it home. The loving father in the parable of the prodigal is not pictured as going to the far country and dragging his son home by force. Instead, He is pictured as waiting for the boy to come home (Luke 15:20).

Who were "the ninety and nine just persons, which need no repentance"? Jesus could have been referring to those who previously had come to God and were living changed lives. More likely, Jesus was using irony to describe people who considered themselves to be righteous. Jesus pointed out to the Pharisees that moral outcasts were quicker to repent than the self-righteous Pharisees (Matt. 21:32). This is the point in the parable of the publican and the Pharisee (Luke 18:9–13).

III. The Lost Coin (Luke 15:8–10)
1. Search for a lost coin (v. 8)

8 Either what woman having ten pieces of silver, if she lose one piece, doth not light a candle, and sweep the house, and seek diligently till she find it?

The coin was a Greek drachma, which had about the same value as a Roman denarius. As we noted in the study of Matthew 20:1-16, a denarius was a day's wages for a laborer. For a wealthy person, this would not be a lot of money; however, for a poor person, it would be. This woman was from the working class, who often lived from day to day. She had managed to save an amount equal to about ten days' wages. Losing one of these coins would be a great loss to her. Therefore, she did what the shepherd did about his lost sheep; she sought it diligently until she found it.

2. Shared joy (v. 9)

9 And when she hath found it, she calleth her friends and her neighbours together, saying, Rejoice with me; for I have found the piece which I had lost.

The woman's joy in finding her coin was the same as the shepherd's in finding his sheep. Like the shepherd, the woman called together her friends and neighbors to rejoice with her.

3. God's joy (v. 10)

10 Likewise, I say unto you, there is joy in the presence of the angels of God over one sinner that repenteth.

Who is rejoicing in the presence of the angels? Jesus was saying that God is like the woman who calls in her friends and neighbors to rejoice with her over her lost coin. God calls together the angels of heaven to rejoice with Him over one lost sinner that repents.

The theme of all three parables in Luke 15 is God's joy over the salvation of lost sinners. It is implied in verse 7. It is implied even more strongly in verse 10. It is spelled out in the response of the loving father to the return of his prodigal son (vv. 22–24). The elder brother did not share in this joy. The parable closes with the father inviting the elder brother to join in the celebration (vv. 25–32). Something is seriously wrong with people who share none of the Father's concern for the lost or His joy in their salvation!

1. The friend of sinners. What word means more to us than the word *friend*? A friend, according to Mr. Webster, is "one that seeks the society or welfare of another whom he holds in affection. . . . " Our lesson today beautifully pictures Jesus as the Friend of "the publicans and sinners," i.e., the social outcasts despised by others.

Will Rogers said he never met a man he didn't like. I have often wondered about that! To my shame, and perhaps you would include yourself in my confession, I have met a good many people I didn't like! But thank God for the great and compassionate love of Jesus. He loved all people, and the social outcasts were especially at ease around Him. Surely, this says a great deal about His gentle love.

2. "Christ Receiveth Sinful Men." The old hymn we often sing describes the attitude of Jesus toward sinners:

> *Sinners Jesus will receive:*
> *Sound this word of grace to all*
> *Who the heav'nly pathway leave,*
> *All who linger, all who fall.*
> *Sing it o'er and o'er again;*
> *Christ receiveth sinful men;*
> *Make the message clear and plain:*
> *Christ receiveth sinful men.*[1]

Because Christ associated with "sinners" He was severely criticized by the religious leaders of His day who were long on orthodoxy and short on love.

3. What is your favorite verse or verses? In a prayer meeting one night, each person was asked to quote his or her favorite Bible verse. One good brother, who was not up-to-date on his Scripture memorization, was considerably concerned about what he would say. The woman next to him quoted her favorite verse, "Jesus wept," and then it was the good brother's turn. His mind was absolutely blank, but he muttered barely audibly, "She got mine!"

What is your favorite Bible verse or passage? Many, no doubt, would reply, "John 3:16." And others of us might say, "Romans 8:28." But one of the passages best-known and most-loved by believers is this passage we are studying today which tells about a lost sheep, a lost coin, and a lost son (actually two lost sons).

4. "A" parable. Verse 3 says, "And he spake this parable unto them." Although most people think of Luke 15 as three parables, I like to think of them as one parable with three dramatic stories or acts because "this parable" is singular. Did Jesus intend to include all three as one—"this"—parable? But, I suppose, it doesn't really matter.

In the story about the lost sheep, 1 percent of the sheep were lost. In the story of the lost coins, 10 percent of the coins were lost. And in the story of the lost son, 50 percent were lost. It would probably be more accurate to say that 100 percent were lost!

5. Seeking a lost boy. When I was a young pastor, still in the seminary, someone rushed into town one day telling that Charles, a six-year-old boy who lived in a nearby natural gas camp, had wandered away from home and was lost in the adjoining ranchland. Men left their work. Women left their household chores. The community organized to find the boy who was lost.

The ranchland was rough and covered with mesquite bushes, and the search was long and hard. The searchers looked urgently for the boy because night was beginning to fall. Finally, the boy was found, returned to his father and mother, and there was great rejoicing in the community because the little boy who was lost had been found! But the greatest rejoicing of all was in his home that night, where a worried mother held to her breast her son, who had been lost but was found.

Does it not put us to shame that we can be so concerned about a child who is lost, and rightly so, but so unconcerned about the lost around us who are dying and going to hell without a Savior?

TEACHING THE BIBLE

▶ *Main Idea:* God in His love searches for those who are lost.
▶ *Suggested Teaching Aim:* To lead adults to identify how God searches for the lost, and to identify at least one lost person with whom they will share God's love.

A TEACHING OUTLINE

1. Use an illustration to introduce the lesson.
2. Use two study groups and a study guide to search for biblical truth.
3. Encourage members to identify persons with whom they can share God's love.

Introduce the Bible Study

Use "Seeking a lost boy" from "Applying the Bible" to introduce the lesson.

Search for Biblical Truth

Ask members if they would agree or disagree with the following statement: Birds of a feather flock together. Ask members to explain their reasons.

Call for a volunteer to read Luke 15:1–2 and point out that the adage about birds is not true in Jesus' case. Ask: Why do you think publicans and sinners flocked to Jesus? What made Him so attractive to them? Why did the Pharisees and scribes object to Jesus' associating with the publicans and sinners?

Organize the class in two groups: the coins and the sheep. IN ADVANCE prepare the following study guides without answers. Give each group the appropriate study guide. If you choose not to organize in groups, you can use the study guides with the whole class.

Group 1—Sheep
Luke 15:4–7

1. Who was this parable directed against? *(Pharisees and scribes.)*

2. What does this parable reveal about God? *(He will search for the lost.)*

3. What does this parable say about the limits of God's love? *(No limit to God's love; He will search until He finds the lost sheep.)*

4. Who would the lost sheep symbolize in Jesus' day? *(Tax collectors and sinners.)*

5. Who would the ninety-nine sheep symbolize? *(Jesus may have ironically been referring to self-righteous Pharisees who thought of themselves as being within the fold.)*

6. What does this parable say about the thrust of Jesus' ministry? *(Jesus sought those who were lost, not those who considered themselves saved.)*

7. What one word describes the owner's attitude when he found his lost sheep? *(Joy.)*

8. Write the main idea of this parable.

Group 2—Coins
Luke 15:8–10

1. Why do you think Jesus told this parable? *(To silence the Pharisees and scribes who were grumbling about Jesus' association with outcasts.)*

2. How much did the lost coin represent? *(A day's wage.)*

3. What would this parable say about God's love and patience? *(God never gives up in seeking us.)*

4. Why do you think the woman invited her friends and neighbors to celebrate with her?

5. Who rejoices in heaven when one sinner repents? *(God's angels.)*

6. What one word describes the woman's attitude when she found her lost coin? *(Joy.)*

7. Write the main idea of the parable.

Give the Truth a Personal Focus

Ask groups to consider people with whom they can share God's love. Ask them to write these persons' names on the back of their study guide and list three or four steps they will take to reach them.

---

1. *The Baptist Hymnal* (Nashville: Convention Press, 1991), 563.

The Good Shepherd

Basic Passage: John 10:1–30
Focal Passage: John 10:1–18

John's Gospel contains the famous "I am" statements of Jesus (6:35; 8:12; 10:9, 11; 11:25–26; 14:6; 15:1). Two of these are found in the passage for today's study: "I am the door" and "I am the good shepherd."

▶ ▶ ▶ ▶ **Study Aim:** *To describe what Jesus taught about Himself as the Good Shepherd*

STUDYING THE BIBLE

I. A Parable of Sheep and Shepherds (John 10:1–6)
    1. Entering by the door (John 10:1–2)
    2. Calling and guiding the sheep (John 10:3–5)
    3. The disciples' failure to understand (John 10:6)
II. I Am the Door (John 10:7–10)
    1. True and false shepherds (John 10:7–8)
    2. Door to salvation and abundant living (John 10:9–10)
III. I Am the Good Shepherd (John 10:11–18)
    1. Shepherd, not a hired man (John 10:11–13)
    2. Mutual knowledge (John 10:14–15)
    3. One Shepherd (John 10:16)
    4. Laying down His life (John 10:17–18)
IV. True and False Sheep (John 10:19–30)
    1. A division of opinion (John 10:19–21)
    2. Unbelievers who are not His sheep (John 10:22–26)
    3. Security and characteristics of true sheep
      (John 10:27–30)

Jesus told how only the shepherd could enter the door of a sheepfold (vv. 1–2). He also described how sheep know their shepherd and follow only his voice (vv. 3–5). Although His followers were familiar with shepherds and sheep, they didn't understand the application of Jesus' words (v. 6). Jesus said that He was the door through which true undershepherds themselves must pass; others were thieves, not true shepherds (vv. 7–8). Jesus also is the door for the sheep to find salvation and abundant life (vv. 9-10). Jesus said that He was the Good Shepherd who laid down His life for the sheep, in contrast to a hired person who would flee personal danger (vv. 11–13). Jesus and His sheep know one another with the kind of personal knowledge that exists between Father and Son (vv. 14–15). Jesus will be the Shepherd of one flock from all nations and groups (v. 16). Jesus' life was not taken from Him; instead, He gave His life in accordance with the Father's will. Jesus had power to lay down His life and to take it up again (vv. 17–18). A division of opinion arose about Jesus (vv. 19–21). When some people demanded that Jesus tell them whether He was the Messiah, He said their unbelief showed they were not His sheep (vv. 22–26). His sheep follow Him and are secure in the hand of Jesus, which is the same as being in the Father's hand (vv. 27–30).

I. A Parable of Sheep and Shepherds (John 10:1–6)

1. Entering by the door (vv. 1–2)

1 Verily, verily, I say unto you, He that entereth not by the door into the sheepfold, but climbeth up some other way, the same is a thief and a robber.

2 But he that entereth in by the door is the shepherd of the sheep.

Chapter 10 begins with a situation familiar to Jesus' hearers. He described a typical sheepfold. This was an enclosure with one opening. Jesus said that the shepherd entered through the door. Those who climbed the walls were thieves and robbers.

2. Calling and guiding the sheep (vv. 3–5)

3 To him the porter openeth; and the sheep hear his voice; and he calleth his own sheep by name, and leadeth them out.

4 And when he putteth forth his own sheep, he goeth before them, and the sheep follow him: for they know his voice.

5 And a stranger will they not follow, but will flee from him: for they know not the voice of strangers.

A special relationship existed between sheep and shepherd. In some parts of the world, shepherds drive their sheep; but in Palestine, a shepherd called and led his sheep. A shepherd knew his sheep and had a special call for them. They knew him and recognized his distinctive call. Thus after the doorkeeper allowed him into the fold, the shepherd called his sheep and led them out. They followed him; but they would not follow a stranger, whose call was not that of the shepherd.

3. The disciples' failure to understand (v. 6)

6 This parable spake Jesus unto them: but they understood not

An Arab shepherd tends his herd in the Judean hills. Credit: *Biblical Illustrator*, Ken Touchton.

what things they were which he spake unto them.

The disciples were familiar with what Jesus said about sheep, shepherds, sheepfolds, and doorkeepers. However, they did not understand what application Jesus intended to make.

II. I Am the Door (John 10:7–10)

1. True and false shepherds (vv. 7–8)

7 Then said Jesus unto them again, Verily, verily, I say unto you, I am the door of the sheep.

8 All that ever came before me are thieves and robbers: but the sheep did not hear them.

We might expect Jesus to immediately compare Himself with the shepherd; however, he first compared Himself to the door. Some Bible students think that verses 7 and 9 refer to the shepherd, who sometimes guarded the entrance to the fold by lying down in the opening. However, in the fold that Jesus described, a doorkeeper guarded the door. Therefore, Jesus apparently intended to compare Himself to the door in verses 7 and 9.

In verses 7–8, Jesus was speaking about human shepherds. Old Testament passages like Ezekiel 34 compared the leaders of the people to false shepherds, who exploited the people. Those who are charged with the care of others are to be shepherds of their flock. The first requirement for a true undershepherd is that he has entered into the fold by the door. In other words, a true undershepherd must have entered salvation through faith in Christ, the door.

In his opening parable, Jesus had said that those who seek to enter by climbing the walls are thieves and robbers. Verse 8 builds on that fact. Many religious leaders in Jesus' day refused to believe in Jesus. They were representative of false shepherds in every generation who do not know the Good Shepherd because they have not entered through Him who is the door.

2. Door to salvation and abundant living (vv. 9–10)

9 I am the door: by me if any man enter in, he shall be saved, and shall go in and out, and find pasture.

10 The thief cometh not, but for to steal, and to kill, and to destroy: I am come that they might have life, and that they might have it more abundantly.

Verse 9 refers to the door to salvation through which the sheep enter. The door was the only way into the safety of the fold and out into the pastures. Jesus is the door to salvation and to abundant living. He gives eternal life that extends beyond death (v. 28) and abundant life in the here and now. The exploiters of our age claim to offer happiness and fulfillment, but they actually offer only broken lives and hopes. Only He who is the way offers true life—abundant and eternal.

III. I Am the Good Shepherd (John 10:11–18)

1. Shepherd, not a hired man (vv. 11–13)

11 I am the good shepherd: the good shepherd giveth his life for the sheep.

12 But he that is an hireling, and not the shepherd, whose own the sheep are not, seeth the wolf coming, and leaveth the sheep, and fleeth: and the wolf catcheth them, and scattereth the sheep.

13 The hireling fleeth, because he is an hireling, and careth not for the sheep.

In verses 11–18, Jesus called Himself the Good Shepherd. Several themes run through these verses, but the strongest theme is that the Good Shepherd came to lay down His life for the sheep. This theme is repeated in verses 11, 15, 17, and 18.

Jesus contrasted a shepherd-owner to a person hired to protect a flock of sheep. When danger threatened, the shepherd-owner defended his sheep. By contrast, a hired person would flee in the face of danger. In one crucial respect, the Good Shepherd went far beyond what even shepherd-owners normally did. A shepherd sometimes had to defend his flock; however, rarely did a shepherd actually lose his life. By contrast, the Good Shepherd came to lay down His life for the sheep.

2. Mutual knowledge (vv. 14–15)

14 I am the good shepherd, and know my sheep, and am known of mine.

15 As the Father knoweth me, even so know I the Father: and I lay down my life for the sheep.

In the opening parable, Jesus had described the kind of relationship that existed between shepherd and sheep (vv. 3–5). As a first-century shepherd knew his sheep and they knew him, so does the Good Shepherd know His sheep and they know Him. Jesus compared this kind of knowledge to the relationship between Father and Son. It is a personal knowledge of acquaintance with someone, not an indirect knowledge of facts about the person.

3. One Shepherd (v. 16)

16 And other sheep I have, which are not of this fold: them also I must bring, and they shall hear my voice; and there shall be one fold, and one shepherd.

Jesus looked beyond the time of His earthly mission to the time when His Spirit would lead in carrying the good news to all people— Gentiles as well as Jews. God's plan is to include all the sheep into one flock under one Shepherd.

4. Laying down His life (vv. 17–18)

17 Therefore doth my Father love me, because I lay down my life, that I might take it again.

18 No man taketh it from me, but I lay it down of myself. I have power to lay it down, and I have power to take it again. This commandment have I received of my Father.

Verses 17–18 provide the strongest emphasis on Jesus laying down His life. Laying down His life is presented as the will of the Father and an expression of the love of the Father for the Son. These verses also clearly present the death of Jesus as a voluntary sacrifice on His part.

His life was not taken from Him against His will; instead, He willingly offered His life. Jesus predicted not only His sacrificial death but also His victorious resurrection. He had the power to give His life and the power to take it up again.

IV. True and False Sheep
(John 10:19–30)

1. A division of opinion (vv. 19–21). A division of opinion arose about Jesus (v. 19). Some said that He was demon-possessed (v. 20). Others, however, said that a demon-possessed person couldn't open the eyes of the blind (v. 21; see the healing of the man born blind in John 9).

2. Unbelievers who are not His sheep (vv. 22–26). These events took place during the Feast of Dedication in the winter (v. 22). As Jesus walked in the temple, some Jews asked Jesus to tell them plainly whether He was the Messiah (vv. 23–24). Jesus said they had not believed His works and words, and their unbelief showed they were not His sheep (vv. 25–26).

3. Security and characteristics of true sheep (vv. 27–30). As Jesus had said earlier, one characteristic of His sheep is that they know and follow Him (v. 27; see vv. 3-5, 14–15). Jesus gives eternal life to His sheep. Nothing can pluck His sheep from His hand, because being in the hand of Jesus is the same as being in the hand of the Father, and no one can snatch the sheep from the Father's hand (vv. 28–29). This fact is one illustration of the unity that exists between Father and Son (v. 30).

APPLYING THE BIBLE

1. One door. I still remember a song I learned in Sunday School as a child about Jesus being the door to heaven. Do you remember it?

> *One door and only one*
> *And yet the sides are two;*
> *I'm on the inside,*
> *On which side are you?*

In our lesson today, Jesus not only tells us that He is the good Shepherd, but that He also is the only door—the only way—to the Father, safety, and eternal life.

2. No other way. Former baseball commissioner Bowie Kuhn said it takes five hundred thousand dollars to prepare a baseball player for the major leagues. If you had one-half million dollars and spent it all in an attempt to be saved and go to heaven when you die, it would all be in vain. Jesus tells us in our lesson today He is the only door to heaven.

3. The Shepherd who leads His sheep. For many years I lived in the West where sheep and goats abound. I don't know too much about either, but I have observed that goats can be driven, but sheep must be led. Jesus says that He leads His sheep out to pasture. His actions toward us are gentle, like those of a good shepherd. Jesus does not drive His sheep in anger with a stick. Rather, He leads us gently along life's way (v. 3).

4. False shepherds. One who keeps up with what is going on in the world knows full well that religious charlatans and false teachers abound. I am thinking of one such false shepherd who is now serving time in a federal prison for fleecing the sheep, and another false shepherd of national prominence whose multimillion dollar religious empire crumbled under the weight of his lust. As the Old Testament instructs us, our sins have a way of finding us out. Add to these two examples the large number of religious leaders whose homosexual abuse has affected the lives of scores of boys under their care, who have taken the wicked shepherds to court for justice. False shepherds abound, but Jesus is the one dependable, Good Shepherd who never abuses His sheep.

5. Christ's "other sheep." One of the most memorable and moving experiences of my life took place one morning in London's Westminster Abbey, where scores of England's notable leaders are buried.

Near the entrance to the Abbey I found, in the floor, the grave of the great missionary-physician-explorer Dr. David Livingstone. When he died in Africa in 1873, at his request his heart was cut from his body and buried in the soil of Africa where he had toiled for three decades. His body was then embalmed, carried nine hundred miles overland by natives who loved him, and put on a ship to be returned to England and buried in Westminster.

I pulled a chair up in front of Livingstone's grave in the Abbey as other people shuffled by, never knowing or caring that they were in the presence of such a great man. I sat alone and wept unashamedly as I read his epitaph: "Other sheep I have, which are not of this fold: them also I must bring" (v. 16).

These are the words of Jesus. Not only were the Jews to be included in his fold, but the Gentile world as well. Thank God that Jesus included us too!

6. More valuable than silver or gold. On the very day I wrote these illustrations for *Broadman Comments*, our local paper, the *San Antonio Express-News*, told about an exhibit of treasures from the Spanish galleon Nuestra Señora de Atocha being put on exhibition in our city. The treasures, estimated to be worth more than $400 million, is one of the greatest recoveries of sunken treasures in history.

The ship, bound from the new world for Spain was lost at sea, off the Florida Keys, in 1622, after a fierce hurricane in the Caribbean. Among the treasures recovered by Mel Fisher and his crew in 1986 are thousands of "pieces of eight (Spanish silver dollars), uncut emeralds, artifacts, and gold and silver bullion—eighty tons of silver, two hundred bars of gold, five thousand emeralds, more than one hundred thousand "pieces of eight"—which were headed for the Spanish crown.

It is, without doubt, one of the greatest treasures ever discovered—

but not the greatest. The greatest treasure one will ever discover, and which lies at our very feet, is forgiveness and eternal life through Jesus Christ. He is the "Pearl of Great Price," and He has laid down His life for His poor, lost sheep (vv. 17–18).

TEACHING THE BIBLE

▶ *Main Idea:* Jesus' description of Himself as the Good Shepherd describes Jesus' care for His followers.
▶ *Suggested Teaching Aim:* To lead adults to describe Jesus as the Good Shepherd, and to identify what their response to Him will be.

A TEACHING OUTLINE

1. Introduce the Bible study by having a member present a research assignment.
2. Use an acrostic to identify qualities of Jesus.
3. Use discussion questions to guide the Bible study.
4. Lead members to determine what their response to Jesus will be.

Introduce the Bible Study

IN ADVANCE, enlist a member to read "Shepherd" in the *Holman Bible Dictionary* (p. 123) or other Bible dictionary and prepare a report on the role of shepherd in the Bible to begin the class session.

Search for Biblical Truth

ASK: What one point do you think Jesus was trying to make when He referred to Himself as the Good Shepherd? Write the word Shepherd on a chalkboard or a large sheet of paper and let members suggest characteristics of Jesus that contain the letters of the word. The following are only suggestions:

S ecurity
H elper
Fri **E** nd
P rotector
Punis **H** er
F **E** eder
Ca **R** etaker
D efender

Now, ask members to search John 10:1–18 to find verses that support their word.

On a chalkboard or a large sheet of paper write *Good Shepherd* and *False Shepherds.* Ask members to contrast these two. (You will use many of the same words listed above.) DISCUSS: How can you identify false shepherds today? What is the primary difference between Jesus and the false shepherds?

Ask a member to read John 10:9–10. Ask: What did Jesus mean by saying that He was the door? What basis does He have for claiming that He is the only door to eternal life? What does abundant life mean?

Ask a member to read John 10:11–13. Ask: What qualities make Jesus the Good Shepherd? If Jesus were speaking to us today, what image do you think He would use instead of Good Shepherd?

Ask a member to read John 10:16. Ask: What did Jesus mean by "other sheep"? What specific application does this have to us today?

Ask a member to read John 10:17–18. Ask: What is the greatest act Jesus performs as the Shepherd for the sheep? Why do you think this was necessary?

Give the Truth a Personal Focus

ASK: What difference has Jesus' laying down His life made in your life? Have you accepted it for your salvation?

Encourage all members to accept Jesus' sacrifice as the Shepherd/Lamb of God. Close in prayer that all members will accept Jesus' sacrifice.

The True Vine

April

28

1996

Basic Passage: John 15:1–17
Focal Passage: John 15:1–17

I n the preceding lesson, we looked at two of the "I am" statements of Jesus in John's Gospel. In this lesson, we will look at the final "I am" statement: "I am the true vine." This is in a passage from Jesus' farewell discourse to His disciples, found in John 13–17.

▶ ▶ ▶ ▶ **Study Aim:** *To describe the characteristics of those who abide in Christ as branches of the true Vine*

STUDYING THE BIBLE

I. Vine, Branches, and Fruit (John 15:1–6)
　　1. The True Vine (John 15:1)
　　2. Two kinds of branches (John 15:2–3)
　　3. Abiding and bearing fruit (John 15:4–5)
　　4. Dead branches (John 15:6)
II. Marks of True Disciples (John 15:7–11)
　　1. Prayer (John 15:7)
　　2. Glorifying the Father (John 15:8)
　　3. Abiding in Christ's love (John 15:9–10)
　　4. Christ's joy and ours (John 15:11)
III. Love One Another (John 15:12–17)
　　1. "As I have loved you" (John 15:12–15)
　　2. The purposes of God's choice (John 15:16)
　　3. Christ's commandment (John 15:17)

Jesus called Himself the true Vine and His Father the vinedresser (v. 1). Branches without fruit are taken away; fruitful branches are cleansed (vv. 2–3). Following Christ involves abiding in Him and bearing fruit (vv. 4–5). Branches without fruit are burned (v. 6). Those who abide in Christ have their prayers answered (v. 7). God is glorified when disciples bear much fruit (v. 8). Abiding in Christ involves abiding in Christ's love and keeping His commandments (vv. 9–10). Christ wants His followers to share His joy (v. 11). He commands us to love one another as He has loved us—a love shown by laying down His life for us (vv. 12–15). Christ has chosen His followers to bear fruit and promised to give what we ask in His name (v. 16). Christ repeated His command to love one another (v. 17).

I. Vine, Branches, and Fruit (John 15:1–6)
1. The True Vine (v. 1)
1 I am the true vine, and my Father is the husbandman.
A number of Old Testament passages refer to Israel as a vine. God

pronounced judgment on Israel as a vine that produced evil fruit (see Isa. 5:2; Jer. 2:21; Hos. 10:1–2). By contrast, Jesus is the true Vine. As in the Old Testament, God Himself is the Vinedresser.

2. Two kinds of branches (vv. 2–3)

2 Every branch in me that beareth not fruit he taketh away: and every branch that beareth fruit, he purgeth it, that it may bring forth more fruit.

3 Now ye are clean through the word which I have spoken unto you.

Verse 2 describes the work of God as keeper of the vineyard. He finds two kinds of branches. One kind bears no fruit; the other bears fruit. The branches that don't bear fruit are taken away. Verse 6 describes what happens to them (see comments on v. 6). God cleanses the fruitful branches so they may bear more fruit.

Judas had already left to do his evil work (John 13:30). He was like a fruitless branch that had been taken away (v. 2a). The other apostles were like fruitful branches that were pruned or cleansed (v. 2b). Verse 3 reassured them that they had already been cleansed by Christ's word (compare John 13:10–11).

3. Abiding and bearing fruit (vv. 4–5)

4 Abide in me, and I in you. As the branch cannot bear fruit of itself, except it abide in the vine; no more can ye, except ye abide in me.

5 I am the vine, ye are the branches: He that abideth in me, and I in him, the same bringeth forth much fruit: for without me ye can do nothing.

To abide in Christ means basically to maintain a vital relationship with Christ. Just as a vine draws its life and strength from the vine, so do we draw our life and strength from Christ. A branch can bear fruit only when it is attached to the vine. Whoever abides in Christ will bear fruit. Whoever does not abide in Christ will not bear fruit.

The word "fruit" occurs six times in John 15:1-17. What kind of fruit did Jesus mean? Was He thinking of the qualities of Christlikeness described by Paul as "the fruit of the Spirit" (Gal. 5:22–23). Or was Jesus speaking of new converts? The emphasis in verses 4–5 seems to be on the fruit of the Spirit. The emphasis in verse 16 seems to be on winning others to Christ.

4. Dead branches (v. 6)

6 If a man abide not in me, he is cast forth as a branch, and is withered; and men gather them, and cast them into the fire, and they are burned.

Verse 6 refers to the fate of the branches in verse 2a. Because they did not bear fruit, they were taken away. Jesus used the vine analogy to emphasize fruitfulness from abiding in Him, not to teach that true believers can lose their relationship with Him. If we had only this passage, we might take it that way; but we have too many passages that emphasize the security of true disciples (for example, see John 10:27–29).

II. Marks of True Disciples
(John 15:7–11)

1. Prayer (v. 7)

7 If ye abide in me, and my words abide in you, ye shall ask what ye will, and it shall be done unto you.

Prayer is the normal language of those who abide in Christ. What they ask out of this vital relationship will be given. Some people mistakenly think that promises like verse 7 provide a blank check for anyone who wants to use prayer to get what he wants. Such prayer promises are not unconditional. The condition is that we abide in Christ and are seeking to do His will.

2. Glorifying the Father (v. 8)

8 Herein is my Father glorified, that ye bear much fruit; so shall ye be my disciples.

God is glorified in the Son (John 1:14; 12:28; 13:31–32; 17:4).

Verse 8 shows that one way the Father is glorified is as disciples abide in Christ and bear fruit. We show ourselves to be true disciples as we bear fruit that glorifies God.

3. Abiding in Christ's love (vv. 9–10)

9 As the Father hath loved me, so have I loved you: continue ye in my love.

10 If ye keep my commandments, ye shall abide in my love; even as I have kept my Father's commandments, and abide in his love.

Christ loves us with the kind of love the Father has for Him. Our assurance is based on the assurance of His love for us. The expression of our awareness of His love for us is that we keep His commandments (see John 14:15).

Verse 10 is another verse that is sometimes misunderstood. Does verse 10 imply that abiding in Christ is dependent on keeping His commandments? This is not the point. God loves all people and wants to reveal His love to them, but people must receive God's love to experience the full benefits of that love. Those who experience God's love show it by keeping His commandments.

4. Christ's joy and ours (v. 11)

11 These things have I spoken unto you, that my joy might remain in you, and that your joy might be full.

Too many people think of Christ as a killjoy rather than the joy-giver. Jesus knew joy and wanted His followers to know joy. Jesus found joy in doing the will of the Father. His joy was in finishing the task God had given Him (Heb. 12:2). Likewise, Jesus spoke of faithful servants receiving the commendation of their Lord and entering into His joy (Matt. 25:21, 23). Joy and peace are Christ's legacy to His followers (see John 14:27).

III. Love One Another (John 15:12–17)

1. "As I have loved you" (vv. 12–15)

12 This is my commandment, That ye love one another, as I have loved you.

13 Greater love hath no man than this, that a man lay down his life for his friends.

14 Ye are my friends, if ye do whatsoever I command you.

15 Henceforth I call you not servants; for the servant knoweth not what his lord doeth: but I call you friends; for all things that I have heard of my Father I have made known unto you.

Love is a strong theme in the writings of John. John 3:16 is one of many passages that refers to God's love for us. During the teachings of Jesus to His disciples on the eve of His death, He gave special emphasis to the need for His disciples to love one another. John 15:12 echoes John 13:34: "A new commandment I give unto you, that ye love one another; as I have loved you." These verses show that the model, motivation, and power for that kind of love came from the disciples' experience of His love for them.

Verses 13–15 describe Christ's love for the apostles. He referred to them as His "friends." He had called them "servants," but now He called them friends. A master is under no obligation to explain himself to his servants. A friend shares himself with his friends. Thus Jesus took His followers into His confidence and explained to them His purpose.

No greater expression of love is possible than giving one's life for others. Jesus said that He was going to give His life for His friends. Of course, Jesus died for more than this small group. He died for all people. In Romans 5:6–8, Paul described the depth of Christ's love because He died for His enemies as well as His friends.

2. The purposes of God's choice (v. 16)

16 Ye have not chosen me, but I have chosen you, and ordained you, that ye should go and bring forth fruit, and that your fruit should remain: that whatsoever ye shall ask of the Father in my name, he may give it you.

Some people believe that these and similar words teach that God chooses some people to be lost and others to be saved, regardless of their response. Some passages could be interpreted this way, but what about the "whosoever will" passages (like John 3:16; Rom. 10:13; Rev. 22:17)? Verse 16 expresses the biblical doctrine of election. It emphasizes that our salvation is rooted in God's eternal plan and His saving grace. When believers track their salvation to its source, it leads back to the eternal love in the heart of God. We are not responsible for our salvation. God is.

The disciples had not sought out Jesus. He had sought them out. This does not mean that they had no choice in whether to follow Him. It does mean that their call to salvation and service came from Christ, not from their own doing. Christ chose them—and He chooses us—not just for salvation but also for service. He chose them and appointed them to bear fruit for Him.

The strength to fulfill this high calling comes from Christ. Thus, whatever we ask in His name will be given to us. Praying in Jesus' name is more than saying a magical formula at the end of a prayer. "In His name" means that we are living and serving as Christ's representatives. As we do, we can ask Him to give us whatever we need to do what He wants us to do.

3. Christ's commandment (v. 17)

17 These things I command you, that ye love one another.

As noted earlier, this theme is emphasized throughout Jesus' farewell discourse (John 13:34–35; 15:12, 17). Jesus wanted His followers to remember that their love for one another provided the foundation for their mission to the world in Christ's name. Jesus said, "By this shall all men know that ye are my disciples, if ye have love one to another" (John 13:35).

APPLYING THE BIBLE

1. Good advice. As a young pastor, I went through a grave crisis that sorely tried my faith. Returning to my college town, I went to the home of a trusted, retired Bible professor who had greatly influenced me during my college days. Explaining to him my concern, I asked him what to do, and he simply replied, "Abide in Jesus."

In our lesson today. Jesus gives us the same advice. When life's problems weigh us down and we don't know which way to turn, we must abide in Jesus—cling to Him obediently, refusing to let go—until the answer comes and the burden is lifted (vv. 4-7). Abiding in Jesus is the key to the victorious, fruitbearing Christian life (v. 5).

2. Died from inactivity. Several years ago, the newspaper carried the sad story of a man, identified only as "Patient X," who died after having been in a coma for nine years. He had been injured in an accident, and in an attempt to remove a bloodclot from his brain the cells were damaged beyond repair. For nine years he was only kept alive by machines. When he died, his death certificate did not read "died from brain injury," but "died from brain inactivity." Day after day, he died a little more from deterioration until there was no longer life.

Christians have spiritual life and will bear spiritual fruit. According to Galatians 5:22–26, the Holy Spirit living in a believer will produce the fruit of the Spirit. But we do not always produce the quality of fruit we should because we do not abide in Christ as we should (v. 5). Abiding in Jesus is the key to abundant fruit bearing.

We need to remember, however, that both the sweet, 100-pound black diamond watermelon is a fruit, as is the grape. But a professing Christian who bears no fruit is all profession and no possession. And Jesus tells us what the end of the pretenders is (v. 6).

3. Someone who knows how to pray. Has some crisis been so great or some burden so heavy that you have sought out someone you knew who really knew how to pray and humbly said to that friend, "Please pray for me"?

As a minister for more than forty years, I have often done it, as I am sure you have. In the churches I have served, I have known great prayer warriors who knew how to get through to God in prayer. More than once I have gone to the home of one of those in whose prayers I believed, unburdened my heart, and asked them to pray for me.

I remember one woman in a church I served who loved Jesus deeply, but who was generally misunderstood in the community, and even in the church, because of her devotion and zeal. I knew she knew how to take hold on God, so I went to her with a special prayer request. It was not long before the answer—plain and victorious—came, and I was grateful for and blessed by her prayers.

The secret to answered prayer is seeking God's will and how He would have us pray. And the secret to that is abiding obediently in Jesus (v. 7).

4. The importance of prayer. Great Christians testify to the importance and power of prayer.

Early American missionary Adoniram Judson said: "Be resolute in prayer. Make any sacrifice to maintain it." American evangelist Dwight L. Moody said about prayer: "Every great movement of God can be traced to a kneeling figure." George Whitefield, an English preacher whose ministry helped shape the religious life of the American colonies, wept in prayer for the unsaved: "O Lord, give me souls or take my soul." David Brainerd, a colonial missionary to the American Indians, burned his life out at an early age in prayer for and service to the Indians. Englishman George Muller knelt by his chair day and night praying England's orphanage ministry into existence. At one time, in his sixty-plus-year ministry, through prayer and faith alone, never asking anyone for a shilling's worth of help, Muller cared for more than two thousand orphans.[1]

TEACHING THE BIBLE

▶ *Main Idea:* Jesus' statement that He is the true Vine shows that those who abide in Him should bear fruit.

▶ *Suggested Teaching Aim:* To lead adults to describe characteristics of Jesus as the true Vine, and to describe characteristics of those who abide in Christ as branches of the true Vine.

A TEACHING OUTLINE

1. *Use an illustration to introduce the Bible study.*
2. *Draw a poster to use in studying the Bible passage.*
3. *Enlist a reader to read the Scripture.*
4. *Use a drawing/writing activity to apply the Bible.*

Introduce the Bible Study
Use "Good advice" from "Applying the Bible" to introduce the lesson.

Search for Biblical Truth
IN ADVANCE, enlist a member to prepare a report on the symbolic use of *vine* in the Bible. Suggest the person use the article "Vine" in *Holman Bible Dictionary* or another Bible dictionary. Call for the report at this time.

IN ADVANCE, draw a stump of a grape vine on a chalkboard or a large sheet of paper. IN ADVANCE, enlist a reader to read all the

Scripture passage. Call for the reading of 15:1. Write, The True Vine, under the drawing.

Call for 15:2–3, 6 to be read. Draw thirteen branches on the stump. Point out that Jesus spoke of two types of branches: those that bear fruit and those that do not. Erase three of the branches to symbolize the pruning.

Call for the reading of 15:4–5. Point out that the emphasis in these verses suggests that the fruit refers to the "fruit of the Spirit." Ask a volunteer to read Galatians 5:22–23. Write the nine fruits of the Spirit on nine of the remaining branches. (The remaining branch will be used later.) Point out that the fruit comes because we abide in Jesus; we do not produce this as a result of our own strength.

Call for 15:7–11 to be read. Around the outside of the vine write: Prayer (v. 7), Glorifying the Father (v. 8), Abiding in Christ's love (vv. 9-10), and Christ's joy and ours (v. 11) as the reader reads these verses. Use the material in "Studying the Bible" to explain each of these verses.

Call for 15:12–15 to be read. Above the vine poster write "Love one another." Organize the class in groups of two to four members and ask them to discuss these questions: What does it mean to love one another as Christ has loved us? What evidence do you see that we are doing this? that we are not? Ask members to share the results of their discussion with the rest of the class. (You can do this with the whole class, but the small groups likely will yield more ideas because they have not heard each other's ideas.) Call for group reports.

Call for 15:16 to be read. Ask: What difference do you see in the "fruit" in this passage and in 15:5? (This passage seems to indicate that the fruit those abiding in Christ are to bear is winning others to Christ; write Winning Others on the remaining branch.) For what has Christ chosen us? (Salvation and service.) Where does the strength come from to fulfill our high calling? (Christ.) How does He give it to us? (Through prayer.) What do we need to do to claim more of Jesus' power?

Call for 15:17 to be read. Share the information about this verse in "Studying the Bible."

Give the Truth a Personal Focus

Give members a piece of paper and ask them to draw a vine similar to the one you have drawn. Ask them to look at the vine on the chalkboard and identify characteristics they have in their lives and to write these characteristics on the branches of their vine. Ask them to identify one "fruit" they want to cultivate and to write that on a branch. Ask, Where will the strength come to produce that fruit? (By abiding in Jesus and letting Him provide the strength.)

---

1. J. B. Fowler, Jr., *Illustrating Great Words of the New Testament* (Nashville: Broadman Press, 1991), 135.

Teachings About Happiness

Basic Passage: Matthew 5:1–12
Focal Passage: Matthew 5:1–12

D uring March, April, and May, we are studying "Teachings of Jesus." No study of His teachings would be complete without including some passages from His famous Sermon on the Mount in Matthew 5–7. During May we will be looking at four themes from the Sermon on the Mount. The first study is the Beatitudes.

▶ ▶ ▶ ▶ ▶ ▶ ▶ ▶ ▶ **Study Aim:** *To explain how the Beatitudes present descriptions of happiness different from those in today's society*

STUDYING THE BIBLE

I. The Sermon on the Mount (Matt. 5:1–2)
II. The Beatitudes (Matt. 5:3–12)
    1. Poor in spirit (Matt. 5:3)
    2. Mourn (Matt. 5:4)
    3. Meek (Matt. 5:5)
    4. Hunger and thirst after righteousness (Matt. 5:6)
    5. Merciful (Matt. 5:7)
    6. Pure in heart (Matt. 5:8)
    7. Peacemakers (Matt. 5:9)
    8. Persecuted (Matt. 5:10–12)

Jesus taught His disciples the Sermon on the Mount (vv. 1–2). He pronounced a series of eight Beatitudes on people with the following qualities: the poor in spirit (v. 3), those who mourn (v. 4), the meek (v. 5), those who hunger and thirst after righteousness (v. 6), the merciful (v. 7), the pure in heart (v. 8), peacemakers (v. 9), and the persecuted (vv. 10–12).

I. The Sermon on the Mount (Matt. 5:1–2)

1 And seeing the multitudes, he went up into a mountain: and when he was set, his disciples came unto him:

2 And he opened his mouth, and taught them, saying,

Some people think the Sermon on the Mount is only a collection of commonsense rules for everyone to practice. Such people say: "My religion is the Sermon on the Mount. I don't need Christ and salvation to practice His simple teachings." The rest of us wonder if such people have ever read what Jesus actually said, especially His many hard sayings.

Other people are so aware of the hard sayings in the Sermon on the Mount that they conclude it must have been for some future age. Most of us realize that Jesus spoke these words to His disciples—not just the twelve, but the larger group of followers. He intended for His followers to take seriously the hard sayings of the Sermon on the Mount. Because Jesus spoke to disciples, He was speaking to people who had experienced God's grace. His grace and power are with us as we seek to live by His perfect standards. When we fail—as we sometimes do—He continues to encourage and help us to do better.

II. The Beatitudes (Matt. 5:3–12)

The Beatitudes describe the qualities of people who know the blessedness of God's favor. The kind of blessedness Jesus described is not primarily something we feel, but something we are. Thus, if we use the word *happiness* to describe the Beatitudes, we need to realize Jesus was describing us from God's point of view. Any joy that comes as a result of God's blessedness is a fruit of what He is doing in and through us.

The eight qualities in the Beatitudes present a totally different standard of values from the world in which we live. Jesus is calling us to seek to be the kind of people who win the smile of God rather than the approval of the world.

1. Poor in spirit (v. 3)

3 Blessed are the poor in spirit: for theirs is the kingdom of heaven.

The world's version of this says, "Blessed are the rich and famous, for they will be recognized as important people." Jesus deliberately began His list by pronouncing God's blessing on the poor in spirit. He said that the kingdom of heaven is made up of the poor in spirit. It doesn't matter whether they are rich or poor, famous or unknown. As a rule, the world's rich and famous are seldom among the poor in spirit (Matt. 19:24; Rev. 3:17).

Jesus was talking about our recognition that we are spiritually destitute and desperately need the grace of God. In a sense, this is the first quality necessary to enter the kingdom. Remember Jesus' parable about the proud Pharisee and the contrite tax collector in the temple (Luke 18:9–14).

2. Mourn (v. 4)

4 Blessed are they that mourn: for they shall be comforted.

Could there be a more obvious contrast to the world's view of happiness than this blessing on mourners. The world's version says, "Blessed are those who party, for they will enjoy life to the fullest." By contrast, true followers of Christ mourn over their sins and over the plight of others. Jesus was a person of joy, and He wants us to know joy (John 15:11). Jesus was also "a man of sorrows, and acquainted with grief" (Isa. 53:3). He knew nothing of sorrow over His own sins, for He had no sins. But He wept over the moral and spiritual plight of others (Luke 19:41).

3. Meek (v. 5)

5 Blessed are the meek: for they shall inherit the earth.

This Beatitude is the exact opposite from what our world says, "Blessed are the aggressive, for they shall inherit the earth." The word *meek* means "gentle." It is the opposite of those who greedily lay claim to everything for themselves. The meek are those who claim nothing for themselves. How shall such people ever inherit the earth? They shall inherit it because God rewards gentleness and unselfishness. The paradox was stated by Jesus: "Whosoever will save his life shall lose it: and whosoever will lose his life for my sake shall find it" (Matt. 16:25).

4. Hunger and thirst after righteousness (v. 6)

6 Blessed are they which do hunger and thirst after righteousness: for they shall be filled.

How many people do you know who hunger and thirst after righteousness? Hunger and thirst are the strongest possible words to describe a deep yearning and search for something. Anyone who has ever been dying of hunger or thirst knows that satisfying these basic human needs consumes one's total attention.

By contrast, the world says, "Blessed are those who do their own thing, for they will find personal fulfillment." By the world's standards, anyone striving to please God is a religious fanatic. Worldly people are intent on finding personal satisfaction. They assume that this is found by doing their own thing, certainly not by seeking God and His kingdom.

5. Merciful (v. 7)

7 Blessed are the merciful: for they shall obtain mercy.

God is loving and merciful in His dealings with people. He expects His children to treat other people with mercy and understanding. Micah said that the Lord expects us "to do justly, and to love mercy, and to walk humbly with thy God" (6:8). Jesus told of a good Samaritan who showed compassion toward a needy person. By contrast, a priest and a Levite "passed by on the other side" (Luke 10:31–32). The world's version of this Beatitude is, "Blessed are those who take care of number one, for they don't need to worry about anyone else."

6. Pure in heart (v. 8)

8 Blessed are the pure in heart: for they shall see God.

The world's version says, "Blessed are those who have just enough religion to get by, for they will have the best in this life and hedge their bets about the hereafter." The words of Jesus stand in striking contrast to this self-serving attitude. The pure in heart are people with a single-minded devotion to God that is reflected in a life of moral purity. Jesus may have had in mind Psalm 24:3–4: "Who shall ascend into the hill of the Lord? or who shall stand in his holy place? He that hath clean hands, and a pure heart."

Many have no desire to see God, for they shall see Him only as Judge. However, the pure in heart who walk with God in this life yearn to see Him face to face (1 Cor. 13:12).

7. Peacemakers (v. 9)

9 Blessed are the peacemakers: for they shall be called the children of God.

God Himself is the great Peacemaker. Through Jesus Christ, He calls sinners to find peace with God (Rom. 5:1). Christ also reconciles people to one another, thus making peace (Eph. 2:14). God also promises a future age of peace (Isa. 2:4). Those who know the Lord have a ministry of reconciliation as peacemakers in His name. Those who serve as peacemakers are recognized as children of God.

By contrast, the world's advice is, "Blessed are those who don't get involved in other people's quarrels, for they will avoid getting caught in the middle." This reminds us that true peacemaking is risky and costly. It cost Jesus His life to reconcile sinners to God and believers to one another.

8. Persecuted (vv. 10–12)

10 Blessed are they which are persecuted for righteousness' sake: for theirs is the kingdom of heaven.

11 Blessed are ye, when men shall revile you, and persecute you, and shall say all manner of evil against you falsely, for my sake.

12 Rejoice, and be exceeding glad: for great is your reward in heaven: for so persecuted they the prophets which were before you.

Jesus knew that the clash of two irreconcilable value systems produced persecution. He knew that His own mission would end in rejection and crucifixion. He also knew that His followers would be subject to misunderstanding and sometimes worse. He pronounced the blessing of God on those who were persecuted for righteousness' sake. He wasn't talking about obnoxious people who develop a martyr complex because people don't like them. He was talking about true disciples whose faithfulness to Christ produces a clash with those opposed to Christ.

The world's version of this is, "Blessed are those who don't rock the boat, for they will be liked by all." Jesus warned, "Woe unto you when all men shall speak well of you! for so did their fathers unto the false prophets" (Luke 6:26). Those who are persecuted can rejoice because they are following in the steps of the prophets of God, whose stand for truth often brought rejection and abuse.

Jesus said that those who are persecuted can rejoice and be glad. In other words, in times of trouble, followers of Christ can dare to rejoice. This amazing paradox found expression in the lives and teachings of His followers. It is reflected in passages like Romans 5:1–5; 1 Peter 1:3–9; and James 1:2–3. Paul, Peter, and James all taught that Christians can rejoice in trouble. Where did they learn that? They learned it from the life and teachings of Jesus. When Paul and Silas were in the Philippian jail, they sang songs at midnight, even though they had been beaten, were confined in stocks, and had an uncertain future (Acts 16: 19–25).

This final Beatitude, like the others, shows the striking contrast between the joy that comes from Christ and the kind of happiness sought by people who don't know Christ. Worldly people assume that happiness depends on outward circumstances. Christ said that joy is dependent only on being in the center of God's will. Such people seek first the kingdom of God and His righteousness (Matt. 6:33). One fruit of this is a joy that comes as a result of being led by the Spirit of the Lord (Gal. 5:22–23).

1. What is your religion? A lady said to me recently, "My conscience is clear. I keep the Ten Commandments." Wrong! Her conscience was more dead than clear, for no one keeps the Ten Commandments. According to James, to break even one of them is to break all of them (James 2:10). Others are quick to reply that their religion is the Beatitudes, or "I live by the Golden Rule." But keeping the Beatitudes, the Ten Commandments, or the Golden Rule is impossible because of our sinful nature (1 Cor. 2:14). Christ alone is our righteousness. Apart from accepting Christ by faith, we have no righteousness at all that is acceptable to God (Isa. 64:6; Rom. 10:4; Rom. 3:20–22).

2. "The Religion of the Towel. Jesus "humbled Himself, and became obedient unto death, even the death of the cross" (Phil. 2:8). It was He who, as the late Henry Alford Porter wrote, practiced "The Religion of the Towel," humbling Himself on the night before His crucifixion and washing the feet of the disciples (John 13:4–5). This is the attitude of those who are "poor in spirit" (v.3). They are humble, serving followers of Jesus.

3. Broken to the bit and bridle. The late Dr. Ray Summers, who taught New Testament at Southwestern Seminary for many years, told us in class one day that the word *meek* (v. 5) was used in ancient, secular Greek to describe a magnificent horse broken to the bit and bridle. All his strength was still there, but under control. Summers' description of meekness made a lasting impression upon me. To be meek is not to be a spineless person who bends with every wind that blows. Rather, it describes a believer—man, woman, or child—full of zest for life, whose strength is under the Lord's control.

4. "I'll do it my way." The song, "I Did It My Way," is offensive to me. We who are followers of the lowly Shepherd of Galilee are not to approach life and handle it our way. That's the way of a proud, unregenerate world. Rather, we are to do it Christ's way, for He is our Master. We are, as Jesus taught us, to "hunger and thirst after righteousness" (v. 6). This describes an intense desire to please God rather than ourselves.

5. "I thought I was nobody's boy." Walter B. Knight tells about a businessman who took the ferry each day into New York City. One day he spoke kindly to the little shoe-shine boy as the boy was polishing the man's shoes. After that, the little boy would watch for the man daily, carry his bundles, brush his coat, and dust off his shoes.

When the man asked the boy about his attentiveness, he replied: "The first time you met me you called me, 'my boy.' Until then, I thought I didn't belong to anybody."[1]

"Blessed are the merciful; for they shall obtain mercy" (v. 7). That is to be our attitude because of the One to whom we belong.

6. The pursuit of happiness. Thomas Jefferson headed up the committee charged to draw up a Declaration of Independence for the colonies. The work was largely the effort of Jefferson, but contributions to the document were made by Patrick Henry, George Mason, George Washington, and others. In an earlier statement, Congress had claimed the right of the colonists to "life, liberty, and prosperity." But Jefferson, who was a man of means, struck out the word *prosperity* and replaced it with "the pursuit of happiness." In doing so, Jefferson made the declaration's hope available to all—rich and poor alike.

TEACHING THE BIBLE

▶ *Main Idea:* The Beatitudes' description of happiness demonstrates that the happiness of believers differs from that of the world.
▶ *Suggested Teaching Aim:* To lead adults to evaluate Jesus' description of happiness in the Beatitudes, and to identify ways they can apply the Beatitudes to their lives

A TEACHING OUTLINE

1. Use an illustration to introduce the Bible study.
2. Use group assignments that include Bible study, paraphrasing, and creative writing to search for biblical truth.
3. Use group assignments to apply the Beatitudes to members' lives.

Introduce the Bible Study

Use "What is your religion?" in "Applying the Bible" to introduce the lesson.

Search for Biblical Truth

IN ADVANCE, write each of the eight Beatitudes on a large sheet of paper; leave room for members to write the world's version. Organize the class into eight groups and assign each group one of the following Beatitudes and Scriptures: 5:3; 5:4, 5:5; 5:6; 5:7; 5:8; 5:9; 5:10–12. (One or more persons can make a group; if you have fewer than eight members, you can assign more than one Beatitude to a group.)

IN ADVANCE, make eight copies of the following group assignment and give one to each group. Allow about five minutes for study and then call for reports.

Group Assignment

1. Read your Beatitude in as many different translations as you can.
2. Discuss its meaning with the group.
3. Paraphrase the Beatitude.
4. Explain how Jesus fulfilled this Beatitude in His life.
5. On the poster on which the Beatitude is written, write the world's version of the Beatitude—one that is completely opposite to Jesus' statement. Place this on the wall for all to see when you make your report.
6. Prepare to share the above information with the whole class.
7. If you obeyed this Beatitude completely, how would your life change?

After study time, call for groups to share the results of their study on assignments 1 through 6. Use the material in "Studying the Bible" to explain the Beatitude more fully.

From "Applying the Bible," use "Broken to the bit and bridle" to illustrate 5:5 and "I thought I was nobody's boy" to illustrate 5:7.

Give the Truth a Personal Focus

Ask groups to look at Jesus' Beatitudes and the world's version. Ask members to think silently about which version is closer to their behavior. Ask groups to share their response to question 7.

Challenge members to choose one Beatitude and seek to live it fully this coming week. Allow time for members to write down some ways they will do this.

Close in a prayer of commitment for courage for members to follow through on their decisions.

---

1. Walter B. Knight, *Knight's Master Book of New Illustrations* (Grand Rapids, Mich.: Wm. B. Eerdmans Pub. Co., 1956), 355.

Teachings About Loving Your Enemies

Basic Passages: Matthew 5:38–48; Luke 10:25–37
Focal Passage: Matthew 5:38–48

Jesus told His followers that their righteousness had to exceed the righteousness of the scribes and Pharisees (Matt. 5:17–20). In Matthew 5:21–48, He gave six examples of what He meant. First He stated the rules the Pharisees followed; then He set forth His teachings in these six areas: murder (vv. 21–26), adultery (vv. 27–30), divorce (vv. 31–32), oaths (vv. 33–37), retaliation (vv. 38–42), enemies (vv. 43–48). This session focuses on the last two examples.

▶ ▶ ▶ ▶ **Study Aim:** *To evaluate our treatment of others in light of Jesus' teachings about loving enemies*

STUDYING THE BIBLE

I. Avoid Retaliation (Matt. 5:38–42)
    1. An eye for an eye (Matt. 5:38)
    2. Avoid getting even (Matt. 5:39–42)
II. Love Your Enemies (Matt. 5:43–48)
    1. Hate your enemies (Matt. 5:43)
    2. Love your enemies (Matt. 5:44)
    3. God's kind of love (Matt. 5:45)
    4. World's kind of love (Matt. 5:46–47)
    5. Be perfect (Matt. 5:48)
II. Love Your Neighbor (Luke 10:25–37)
    1. The teaching (Luke 10:25–29)
    2. Parable of good Samaritan (Luke 10:30–37)

The Old Testament law placed restrictions on the human tendency to seek to hurt our enemies more than they have hurt us (Matt. 5:38). Over against that, Jesus taught that His followers should not seek revenge of any kind; and He gave four examples of what He meant (Matt. 5:39–42). The people of Jesus' day knew that the Scriptures commanded love for neighbors, but they did not include enemies among those they should love (Matt. 5:43). Jesus taught His followers to love their enemies (Matt. 5:44). He said that this was God's kind of love (Matt. 5:45). Jesus also pointed out that even unbelievers love those who love them (Matt. 5:46–47). God expects nothing less than perfection from His children (Matt. 5:48). Jesus talked with a lawyer who wanted to exclude many people from his definition of "neighbor" (Luke 10:25–29). Jesus told the parable of the good Samaritan to show that God expects us to love all people (Luke 10:30–37).

I. Avoid Retaliation (Matt. 5:38–42)

1. An eye for an eye (v. 38)

38 Ye have heard that it hath been said, An eye for an eye, and a tooth for a tooth.

Jesus quoted the Old Testament provision for measured retaliation (see Ex. 21:23–25; Lev. 24:19–21; Deut. 19:21). When someone was injured, the law provided that the injured party could retaliate in kind. If an eye was lost, for example, the offender's eye could be put out. The purpose of the law was to put limits on the desire for revenge. When people were injured, they often wanted to hurt their enemy as much as possible. The law of measured retaliation limited what could be done.

2. Avoid getting even (vv. 39–42)

39 But I say unto you, That ye resist not evil: but whosoever shall smite thee on thy right cheek, turn to him the other also.

Over against the Old Testament law of limited retaliation, Jesus set His way of not retaliating at all. The word "evil" refers not to evil in general, but to an evil person. Jesus was speaking about not trying to get even with people who hurt us. Our natural tendency is to try to hurt them as they have hurt us. Jesus expects His followers to show love, not to seek revenge.

We need to be careful how we understand the meaning of "resist not evil." At times, we must resist evil. James used the same word to say, "Resist the devil" (James 4:7). At times, we must resist evil people. Jesus drove the money changers out of the temple (see Matt. 21:12–13; Mark 11:15–18; Luke 19:45–46). Thus Jesus was not saying that we should never resist evil or evil people; He was speaking about seeking personal vengeance: "Do not take revenge on someone who wrongs you" (GNB).

After stating His expectation, Jesus gave four illustrations from life in the first century. These four examples are not commandments that can be literally practiced in every situation; they are illustrations that provide guidance as we seek to apply the teaching of Jesus to a variety of situations.

The first example had to do with handling personal insults. Striking a person on the right cheek suggests a backhanded slap by a right-handed person. This was a form of insult in Jesus' land and day. Turning the other cheek, therefore, means to accept personal insults without seeking to strike back at the one who has insulted us. We should not strike back either with blows, with words, or in any other way.

40 And if any man will sue thee at the law, and take away thy coat, let him have thy cloak also.

The second example had to do with a lawsuit. Jesus spoke of a situation in which one of His followers was being sued for damages. The follower was being asked to give up his coat or inner garment. Jesus said that the follower of His should voluntarily give up also his cloak or outer garment. In our day, it would be like saying, "If someone takes you to court to sue you for your shirt, let him have your coat as well" (GNB).

41 And whosoever shall compel thee to go a mile, go with him twain.

The land of Jesus was under Roman occupation. Roman soldiers were allowed to compel a Jew to carry their pack or baggage for one mile, but they were not allowed to force a Jew to carry it beyond a mile. Jesus used this as an illustration of His teaching about not getting even. When a Jew was forced to carry a Roman's equipment for a mile, the Jew's normal reaction was anger and resentment. The Jew certainly would not carry the baggage beyond what was required. Jesus, however, said that His followers should voluntarily carry the load a second mile.

42 Give to him that asketh thee, and from him that would borrow of thee turn not thou away.

The fourth example is not specifically related to a desire for revenge. The situation is of someone asking for financial help, either as a gift or as a loan. Jesus said that His followers should give to those who ask for such help.

II. Love Your Enemies (Matt. 5:43–48)
1. Hate your enemies (v. 43)

43 Ye have heard that it hath been said, Thou shalt love thy neighbour, and hate thine enemy.

The Old Testament contains the words, "Thou shalt love thy neighbour as thyself" (Lev. 19:18). The Old Testament contains passages in which the writer asked God to destroy their enemies (see Ps. 137:7–9). It also contains passages in which God destroyed the enemies of Israel (see Deut. 25:17–19). However, it never said to Israel, "Hate your enemies." In fact, some passages showed God's love for enemy nations and challenged Israel to share such love (see Jon. 4).

Thus the last part of verse 43 was not a quotation from the Old Testament, but it was an expression of how some people in Jesus' day thought about their enemies. They tried to limit their neighbors to people of their own kind. Jesus consistently defined "neighbor" to include all people (see below for comments on Luke 10:25–37).

2. Love your enemies (v. 44)

44 But I say unto you, Love your enemies, bless them that curse you, do good to them that hate you, and pray for them which despitefully use you, and persecute you.

Matthew 5:44 clearly shows that Jesus intended for His followers to love their enemies. Verse 44 and its companion verses, Luke 6:27–28, describe enemies as doing such things as cursing us, hating us, despitefully using (mistreating) us, or persecuting us. Love for enemies is described as blessing them, doing good for them, and praying for them.

We need to remember that Christian love is primarily an action, not an emotion. Loving our enemies does not mean that we must first have a warm affection for them before acting on their behalf. The fact that they are enemies means that we have hard feelings toward them. The beginning point for Christian love is doing good for others. Jesus calls His followers to do good for our enemies, whatever are our feelings toward them. Often our feelings change as we bless our enemies, do good for them, and pray for them. However, the actions usually precede the emotions.

3. God's kind of love (v. 45)

45 That ye may be the children of your Father which is in heaven: for he maketh his sun to rise on the evil and on the good, and sendeth rain on the just and on the unjust.

Jesus was not saying that we become children of God by loving our enemies. He was saying that we show ourselves to be children of God when we do good for our enemies. This is God's kind of love. He loves all people. He provides sunshine and rain for all kinds of people. This teaching has two implications: (1) When we experience God's love, this inspires and empowers us to love others as He has loved us. (2) When we practice God's kind of love for all people, even enemies, this bears testimony to our faith in the heavenly Father.

4. World's kind of love (vv. 46–47)

46 For if ye love them which love you, what reward have ye? do not even the publicans the same?

47 And if ye salute your brethren only, what do ye more than others? do not even the publicans so?

"Publicans" were tax collectors, a group whom pious Jews considered no better than pagans. Jesus taught that loving our own is no different from the love of an unbelieving world. Each of us naturally loves those who love us. Jesus expected more of His followers than what unbelievers do. They love their friends. The followers of Jesus have a strong love for friends and family, but they also seek to do good for those who are enemies.

5. Be perfect (v. 48)

48 Be ye therefore perfect, even as your Father which is in heaven is perfect.

Verse 48 concludes the entire section of Matthew 5:21–48. It provides a summary of what God expects of His children. His expectations are high. He expects us to live by the standard of heaven while we are still on earth. Loving enemies is only one of six examples of God's high expectations. Actually, Jesus said, God expects us to be perfect.

None of us, of course, is perfect; but perfection remains our goal. It is what the Father expects of His children. If you are a parent, do you expect anything less than the best of your children? They sometimes don't measure up to your expectations; but rather than lowering your standards, you provide forgiveness and encouragement to your children. The heavenly Father calls each of us to the highest and best. When we fail, He forgives and encourages us. Paul's testimony in Philippians 3:12-14 shows that he realized he was not perfect, but he was pressing on toward God's goal for him.

III. Love Your Neighbor (Luke 10:25–37)

1. The teaching (vv. 25–29). A lawyer's question to Jesus revealed that he was looking for a way to limit those whom he was expected to love.

2. Parable of the good Samaritan (vv. 30–37). Jesus told a parable which showed that all people are our neighbors, whom we are to love.

1. The old cowboy's interpretation of the principle. A cowboy of the Old West had been converted from his wild and unruly ways. He had been a hard drinker and a fighter, and people knew better than to cross him.

After he was saved, he still had a real problem with his temper. He still couldn't stand idly by and not defend himself from abuse.

Once he got into a fight with a man who stopped him on the street. An argument ensued, tempers flared, and before the cowboy knew it he was flat on the ground—with a hard fist to his jaw! Getting up slowly, he wasn't on his feet but a minute when a left to the jaw laid him out in the dust again.

He remembered what his new Master taught: "But whoever shall smite thee on thy right cheek, turn to him the other also" (v. 39). Getting back to his feet the second time, the cowboy drawled: "You know I am a Christian and a member of the church. Jesus told me that if I were attacked, I should turn the other cheek. I have done that, but the Good Master didn't say what to do next." With that, he quickly make short work of his antagonist and left him sprawled out in the dusty street!

That isn't exactly what Jesus meant by turning the other cheek! He meant that our lives should be ruled by love and compassion and that revenge should be left to God.

2. Should fellow believers sue one another in court? That's a hard question and there is no easy answer. Based on the principle laid down by Jesus, the answer is "no." There are, perhaps, some exceptions when that is the only recourse. But it is a poor example to set before a nonbelieving world.

A classic example of the harm this does to the name of Christ and the Christian community is the Louisiana lawsuit against Jimmy Swaggart, the evangelist, by another minister who charged Swaggart with destroying his ministry. This multimillion-dollar lawsuit made headlines in newspapers around the country.

Is there not a better way for believers to settle their differences than by going before worldly courts and working feverishly to destroy one another? There must be. Reconciliation and a just settlement worked out behind closed doors through binding mediation is a much better way.

3. The second mile. The late C. Roy Angell said that carrying the baggage of a Roman soldier was one of the most distasteful things imaginable to a Jew. It was not uncommon for a hated Roman soldier to commandeer a Jew on his way to the field or to the city and force that Jew to carry the soldier's heavy gear. Angell said it was common for a Jew to have a mile marked off in every direction from his house, knowing that the law forbade the soldier from forcing the Jew to go farther. At the end of the mile, Angell said, the Jew would throw down the gear of the despised soldier and declare, "There! I have done it! You cannot force me to go farther."

Jesus taught His followers to do more than the law demands: to return good for evil; to go the second mile; and in so doing show those who treat us unkindly that following Jesus makes better people of us.

The late professor of New Testament at Southwestern Seminary, Ray Summers, was fond of saying: "To return evil for evil is manlike. To return evil for good is animal-like. But to return good for evil is Godlike."

4. Hate hurts everyone. In his little book *God's Psychiatry*, Methodist minister Charles Allen related an incident out of the old radio program, *Amos and Andy*.

There was a big man who would always hit Andy on the chest when they met. Having taken all he could, Andy said to Amos, "I'll fix him good. I put a stick of dynamite in my pocket, and the next time he does that he will blow his hand off!" What Andy was overlooking was that when the dynamite exploded, it would also blow Andy up!

Hate is like that. It hurts the hater and the hated. No one wins with a hateful attitude, for hate hurts everyone. Because of this, Jesus tells us even to love those who hate us. That's hard, but the results are much sweeter than harboring hate in our hearts (v. 44).

TEACHING THE BIBLE

▶ *Main Idea:* Jesus' teachings about loving our enemies demands that we love those who wrong us instead of retaliating against them.

▶ *Suggested Teaching Aim:* To lead adults to examine Jesus' teachings about loving enemies, and to list ways they will deal with a broken relationship.

A TEACHING OUTLINE

1. Use an illustration from "Applying the Bible" to introduce the Bible study.

2. Use small groups to develop and present role plays, skits, case studies, or life situations as you study the Bible.

3. Use a lecture.

4. Guide members to list ways of dealing with a broken relationship.

Introduce the Bible Study

Introduce the lesson by using "The second mile" in "Applying the Bible."

Search for Biblical Truth

IN ADVANCE, make the following two strip posters:

I. Avoid Retaliation (Matt. 5:38–42)
II. Love Your Enemies (Matt. 5:43–48)

Summarize the first background paragraph under "Studying the Bible" to set the context. Place the first strip poster on the wall. Call for a volunteer to read Matthew 5:38–42. Use the information in "Studying the Bible" to explain the following: (1) The Old Testament law was an improvement over previous practices and limited what could be done. (2) Jesus' way is not to retaliate at all.

DISCUSS: Does a Christian ever have a right to go against Jesus' statement about retaliation?

Organize the class in four groups. Make the following assignments: Group 1—Matthew 5:39; Group 2—Matthew 5:40; Group 3—Matthew 5:41; Group 4—Matthew 5:42. Ask the groups to plan a modern presentation that would illustrate Jesus' examples in these verses. Their presentation may be a role play, skit, case study, or life situation (where the story is stopped and members are asked to complete the story). Stress that their presentations should reflect current activities. Call for their presentations when ready.

Place the second strip poster on the wall and ask a volunteer to read Matthew 5:43–48.

Ask: Would you agree with the statement from "Studying the Bible": "Christian love is primarily an action, not an emotion?" Why?

Give a brief lecture in which you cover the following points from "Studying the Bible": (1) God's response to "enemies" in the Old Testament. (2) The last part of 5:43 is not from the Bible. (3) Loving our enemies does not mean having a warm affection for them.

DISCUSS: Can we obey Jesus' command if we do good to people we do not like, but perform our deeds without warmth of feeling for the person(s)?

(4) We do not become God's children by loving our enemies; we only demonstrate our relationship to God by our actions.

DISCUSS: Can people be children of God if they do not act like it?

(5) God empowers us to love our enemies. (6) If we do not love our enemies, we are acting no better than pagans. (7) God's standard is perfection and that should be our goal.

DISCUSS: What happens when we fall short of God's perfection?

Give the Truth a Personal Focus

Distribute paper and pencils. Ask members to think of a broken relationship in their lives. Then ask them to write on one side of the paper what they would like to do about the relationship from a human standpoint. On the reverse side, write the ideal response based on the Scripture passage today.

ASK: What steps can you take to bring the relationship in line with Jesus' teachings?

Teaching About Riches and Anxiety

Basic Passages: Matthew 6:19-21,24–34; Luke 12:13–21
Focal Passages: Matthew 6:19–21,24–34

S ome people don't like sermons and Sunday School lessons about money. They complain that churches spend too much time on this sensitive subject. However, Jesus had a lot to say about money and possessions. This Bible study focuses on what He taught about riches and anxiety in Matthew 6.

▸ ▸ ▸ ▸ ▸ ▸ ▸ ▸ ▸ **Study Aim:** *To evaluate personal attitudes and actions about possessions in light of what Jesus taught*

STUDYING THE BIBLE

I. Treasures (Matt. 6:19–21)
II. God and Mammon (Matt. 6:24)
III. Anxiety (Matt. 6:25–34)
    1. Don't be anxious (Matt. 6:25)
    2. Look at the birds (Matt. 6:26)
    3. Futility of worry (Matt. 6:27)
    4. Look at the lilies (Matt. 6:28–30)
    5. Pagan anxiety (Matt. 6:31–32)
    6. First things first (Matt. 6:33)
    7. Day by day (Matt. 6:34)
IV. Covetousness (Luke 12:13–21)
    1. Beware covetousness (Luke 12:13–15)
    2. The parable of the rich fool (Luke 12:16–21)

Jesus told people to lay up treasures in heaven, not treasures on earth (Matt. 6:19–21). He said that no one can serve God and mammon (Matt. 6:24). Jesus warned against anxiety about food and clothing (Matt. 6:25). If God feeds the birds, surely humans can trust Him to provide daily bread (Matt. 6:26). Worry adds nothing to life (Matt. 6:27). If God clothes the lilies of the field so beautifully, surely people can trust Him for clothing (Matt. 6:28–30). Anxiety is a mark of pagan unbelief, not of trust in a caring heavenly Father (Matt. 6:31–32). Those who put God's kingdom first are promised God's adequate provision of needs (Matt. 6:33). Believers should not worry about tomorrow, because each day has troubles of its own (Matt. 6:34). Jesus warned against covetousness (Luke 12:13–15). He told the parable of the rich fool to illustrate the danger of greed (Luke 12:16–21).

I. Treasures (Matt. 6:19–21)
19 Lay not up for yourselves treasures upon earth, where

moth and rust doth corrupt, and where thieves break through and steal:

20 But lay up for yourselves treasures in heaven, where neither moth nor rust doth corrupt, and where thieves do not break through nor steal:

21 For where your treasure is, there will your heart be also.

Jesus warned against storing up valuables "for yourselves. . . upon earth." The two sins were that (1) the valuables were solely for themselves and (2) they were confined to earthly valuables. Jesus said earthly valuables do not last. No matter how carefully we store and protect them, they are constantly in danger.

Jesus said to lay up treasures in heaven because these are the only secure treasures. Our earthly lives and all we call our own are temporary; however, we can invest time, money, and other resources in God's eternal kingdom.

Our treasures make a difference in how we live and think. Our hearts are where our treasures are. If our only treasures are on earth, we live for ourselves and leave out God and others. If our treasures are in heaven, we live for God and others.

II. God and Mammon (Matt. 6:24)

24 No man can serve two masters: for either he will hate the one, and love the other; or else he will hold to the one, and despise the other. Ye cannot serve God and mammon.

Jesus was speaking of slaves and masters. A person today can work at more than one job and have more than one boss. However, a slave belonged totally to the master. In such a relationship, a slave could not serve more than one master. Jesus applied this to people's relationship to God and mammon. The latter was the name of a money-god worshiped by many ancient people. Jesus taught that we cannot serve the true God and the money-god.

III. Anxiety (Matt. 6:25-34)

1. Don't be anxious (v. 25)

25 Therefore I say unto you, Take no thought for your life, what ye shall eat, or what ye shall drink; nor yet for your body, what ye shall put on. Is not the life more than meat, and the body than raiment?

The words "take no thought" sound as if Jesus was warning against planning for the future. However, Jesus was warning against anxiety. He was not forbidding future planning. Anxiety is the theme of Matthew 6:25-34. The warning against anxiety is found six times in the passage (see vv. 25, 27-28, 31, 34).

Notice that Jesus warned about anxiety concerning food and clothing. Few people in Jesus' day were rich; many were poor. The poor spent their time struggling to put bread on the table, clothes on their back, and a roof over their heads. The poor were preoccupied with food and clothing; the rich were preoccupied with their quest for wealth. Jesus warned both that life is more than possessions (see Luke 12:15).

2. Look at the birds (v. 26)

26 Behold the fowls of the air: for they sow not, neither do they reap, nor gather into barns; yet your heavenly Father feedeth them. Are ye not much better than they?

Jesus told His followers to look at the birds. They neither sow nor reap, yet God takes care of them. Since humans are created in God's image, how much more will God care for us? This is not an argument for idleness, for the birds forage for food. Jesus, however, was pointing out that their food was a gift from God. So is ours. We may feel that we have earned our own bread, but God is the giver of every good and perfect gift (James 1:17). Thus, we should give thanks to God for our daily bread (Matt. 6:11).

3. Futility of worry (v. 27)

27 Which of you by taking thought can add one cubit unto his stature?

The word *stature* can refer either to height or to time. Thus the verse is often translated like this: "Who of you by worrying can add a single hour to his life?" (NIV). Worry does not increase either our height or our life span. In fact, many studies show that anxiety contributes to all kinds of emotional and physical ailments. Thus, anxiety can actually shorten life.

4. Look at the lilies (vv. 28–30)

28 And why take ye thought for raiment? Consider the lilies of the field, how they grow; they toil not, neither do they spin:

29 And yet I say unto you, That even Solomon in all his glory was not arrayed like one of these.

30 Wherefore, if God so clothe the grass of the field, which to day is and to morrow is cast into the oven, shall he not much more clothe you, O ye of little faith?

Jesus had used the birds as examples of creatures whom God feeds. He used the lilies of the field as examples of living things that God clothes. Jesus reminded those who were anxious about clothing that Solomon in all his glory was never clothed with such beautiful clothes as the lilies.

The lilies and other vegetation have short growing seasons. They sprout, grow, and flourish, only to wither and die all too soon. Although the Bible at times compares the shortness of human life to the brief life of the flowers and grass (Ps. 103:15–16), the point in verse 30 is the difference between the lilies and human beings. Humans are created in the image of God and capable of knowing God in eternal life. Thus if God clothes the flowers, how much more will He supply our needs for clothing?

5. Pagan anxiety (vv. 31–32)

31 Therefore, take no thought, saying, What shall we eat? or, What shall we drink?, or, Wherewithal shall we be clothed?

32 (For after all these things do the Gentiles seek:) for your heavenly Father knoweth that ye have need of all these things.

Anxiety about material things is typical of those who do not know the love and care of the heavenly Father. They do not believe in or trust in Him. Jesus told His followers that they were acting like pagan unbelievers when they became anxious and preoccupied with material things.

Jesus assured His followers that their heavenly Father knows what they need. He was encouraging them to replace anxiety with trust in the loving care of the heavenly Father. Jesus was not saying that His followers would be free from trouble and conditions that lead others to be fearful and anxious. He was saying that believers should live their lives and face their problems with a firm reliance on the goodness of God.

6. First things first (v. 33)

> 33 But seek ye first the kingdom of God, and his righteousness; and all these things shall be added unto you.

This is a key verse in the passage and in the Bible. Everyone's life is focused around something. Jesus had already said that some people focus their lives around money. They allow their concern for things to dominate their lives. Their ambitions are determined by the fact that they put their own material needs and wants before other things. As Jesus said, a person cannot build his life around God and also build it around mammon.

Thus Jesus called His followers to seek first the kingdom of God. Such people honor God as King, live by the righteous standards of His realm, and give themselves to advance His cause. This priority shapes all their attitudes and actions. Jesus made a promise to those who put first things first. He promised, "All these things will be given to you as well" (NIV). In the context of Matthew 6:25–34, "these things" are food, clothing, and other material needs. What does this promise mean? It means that God promises to give us what we need to do His will. It is not a blank check to become wealthy. One of His gifts is the ability to be content with what we have (see Phil. 4:11–13).

7. Day by day (v. 34)

> 34 Take therefore no thought for the morrow: for the morrow shall take thought for the things of itself. Sufficient unto the day is the evil thereof.

As Jesus closed this subject, He repeated His theme from verse 25. The new thought in verse 34 is that since each day has troubles enough of its own, we shouldn't spend valuable time and energy fretting about the future. One way to translate verse 34 is this: "Therefore do not worry about tomorrow, for tomorrow will worry about itself. Each day has enough trouble of its own" (NIV). People who worry about the future are less prepared to handle what comes up each new day. Although Jesus does not say it in so many words, many of our worst fears never happen.

IV. Covetousness (Luke 12:13–21)

1. Beware covetousness (vv. 13–15). Jesus was interrupted in His teaching by a man angry about his inheritance (vv. 13). Jesus told the man and others to beware of covetousness, for life is not the same thing as possessions (vv. 14–15).

2. The parable of the rich fool (vv. 16–21). Jesus told a parable of a rich farmer who became so preoccupied with success that he lost his soul. The farmer was not portrayed as a dishonest man, but as a covetous man.

APPLYING THE BIBLE

1. No earthly treasure is safe. When I was pastor in Lubbock, Texas, a thief broke into the parsonage and stole some things that were very precious to me. My mother sold milk, butter, and eggs during the depression and bought my father a Browning pump 20-gauge shotgun for his thirty-third birthday. As a boy, my father and I spent many happy late afternoons squirrel hunting on Sand Creek with his new shotgun. And the thief stole it! Also, my father gave me a gold pocket watch he had bought as a young man. And the thief stole that, too! In addition, several credit cards were stolen, and the thief used them, for a short while, living it up. He had good taste, for he stayed in the best motels!

The gun was never recovered, but the crushed watchcase was found, and I still have that. These were not priceless possessions so far as value were concerned, but they were priceless to me. And the thief stole the heirlooms I highly prized.

It was a sober reminder to me of the truth Jesus spoke when he warned about our earthly treasures that "thieves [would] break through and steal [them]" (v. 19). But it also reminded me of a truth I have never forgotten. Although our earthly treasures will disappear, treasures stored up in heaven will be safe forever.

2. No U-Haul trailers behind hearses. I have conducted hundreds of funeral services of all kinds. But I have never seen one of those orange U-Haul trailers being pulled to the cemetery behind a black hearse! Whatever we accumulate on this earth will be left behind when we depart. We came naked and empty-handed into the world, and we will leave the same way. Therefore, while we are here it behooves us to be good stewards of what God has loaned us for a brief season.

3. Till the end of the line. Once I heard Dr. Carl Bates, a former pastor in Amarillo, Texas, and North Carolina, define a *steward*. Bates said he was riding a train one day and fell into conversation with one of the train's stewards.

"What is a steward, and what is he supposed to do?" Bates asked his new friend.

"A steward is one who takes care of the bossman's goods until he gets to the end of the line," the steward replied. Could you put it any better? We are God's stewards, loaned certain things from Him that belong to Him to take care of for Him "till we get to the end of the line" (see 1 Cor. 4:1–2).

4. Paying too much for too little. Guy deMaupassant (Mo-pas-saw), a popular French author of the last century, wrote an interesting story which he called, "The Necklace."

A French couple of moderate means was invited to a lavish party. Mathilde, the wife, wanted to impress the other quests, so she borrowed what she supposed to be a very expensive necklace. They had a grand time, and she was proud of the necklace, but the evening was spoiled when she got home and discovered she had lost it.

In order to pay for the necklace, the couple moved into a cheap, run-down apartment, and both of them worked at whatever jobs were available. It took them ten long years to save enough money, but finally, old and worn, Mathilde took the money to her friend from whom she had borrowed the necklace. Great was her shock when her friend Jeannie told Mathilde the necklace was only cheap glass—an imitation—worth only a few cents.

It is a parable of life. Too many of us pay too much for too little, only to learn too late in life how foolish we have been (vv. 24–25).[1]

5. How to worry scientifically. In a light vein, someone has given some steps to help us in our scientific age to worry scientifically: worry about only one problem at a time; set a definite time to worry, but never in bed, the dining room, the kitchen, when you are out-of-doors, or in church; always worry in an air-conditioned room as you sit in your easy chair; set a time limit for worry, and give yourself credit for time and one-half if you worry longer.

Also: never frown when you worry—always smile, sing, or whistle; never worry if you are tired, depressed, sick or angry; never worry when you are working, playing, or gossiping; never worry about things you can't help or things you can help; and never worry alone—ask your family and friends to join you!

And I would add: never worry when you can pray!

TEACHING THE BIBLE

▶ *Main Idea:* Jesus' teachings about riches and anxiety remind us that we should not be anxious about the future.
▶ *Suggested Teaching Aim:* To lead adults to identify reasons why worry is useless, and to outline steps they can take to reduce anxiety in their lives.

A TEACHING OUTLINE

1. *Use an illustration to introduce the study.*
2. *Use a lesson outline to identify five reasons worry is useless.*
3. *Use discussion groups to describe steps members can take to identify ways they can combat worry.*

Introduce the Bible Study

Ask members to think of one thing that causes them the most anxiety. Then on a chalkboard or a large sheet of paper, write money/security. Ask how many of their anxieties revolve around money/security.

Share "How to worry scientifically" from "Applying the Bible."

Search for Biblical Truth

Ask members to open their Bibles to Matthew 6:19. Ask for a volunteer to read 6:19–21. Using "Studying the Bible," point out the two sins about accumulating wealth. Share "No earthly treasure is safe" in "Applying the Bible."

Call for a volunteer to read 6:24. Identify mammon and ask: Why can we not serve God and mammon at the same time?

IN ADVANCE, make six strip posters with the following heading and five points. Tape the heading to the focal wall and tape the five points to the backs of five chairs.

Don't Worry, Because . . .
(1) Life is more important than food and clothing (6:25).
(2) God provides for the birds (6:26).
(3) Worry can't make us live longer or grow taller (6:27).
(4) God makes the common flowers beautiful (6:28–30).
(5) Worry is essentially pagan (6:31–32).

Read the heading and suggest that Jesus gave five reasons why we should not worry. Ask the person with the first point to read it and place it on the focal wall under the heading. Ask a volunteer to read Matthew 6:25.

DISCUSS: How can worrying about food and clothing occupy either the poor or the wealthy?

Ask the person with the second point to read it. Call for a volunteer to read 6:26. Suggest that another reason why we should not worry is that if God provides for birds, He surely will provide for those made in His image.

Ask the person with the third point to read it. Call for a volunteer to read 6:27. Use "Studying the Bible" to explain how the word *stature* can refer either to height or time.

Ask the person with the fourth point to read it. Call for a volunteer to read 6:28–30. Ask: What lesson can we learn from this point? (Basically the same as point 2.)

Ask the person with the fifth point to read it. Call for a volunteer to read 6:31–32.

DISCUSS: Ask: How does worry make us act like pagans?

Call for a volunteer to read 6:33–34. Ask members to turn to people around them and discuss the question, How does seeking God's kingdom first keep us from worrying? Call for responses from the groups.

Give the Truth a Personal Focus

Ask members to stay in the same groups and, based on the lesson, suggest one step they can take to reduce their worry. Allow about three to four minutes for discussion and then ask groups to share these. Write these on a chalkboard or a large sheet of paper. After all groups have reported, let members share other ideas they may have thought of. Challenge members to take one idea and incorporate it into their actions this week.

---

1. Robert Hastings, *A Word Fitly Spoken* (Nashville: Broadman Press, 1962), 43-44.

Teaching About Prayer

Basic Passages: Matthew 6:5–15; 7:7–14; Luke 11:1–13
Focal Passage: Matthew 6:5–15

T he Gospels bear testimony to two realities about prayer: (1) the prayer life of Jesus and (2) the teachings of Jesus about prayer. On one occasion after Jesus had been praying, His disciples asked, "Lord, teach us to pray?" (Luke 11:1). Among His richest teachings about prayer is the focal passage for this Bible study.

► ► ► ► **Study Aim:** *To commit to practicing what Jesus taught about prayer*

STUDYING THE BIBLE

I. When You Pray (Matt. 6:5–8)
    1. Avoid hypocrisy (Matt. 6:5)
    2. Private prayer (Matt. 6:6)
    3. Avoid empty words (Matt. 6:7–8)
II. The Model Prayer (Matt. 6:9–15)
    1. Praise (Matt. 6:9)
    2. Commitment (Matt. 6:10)
    3. Petition (Matt. 6:11)
    4. Confession (Matt. 6:12)
    5. Guidance (Matt. 6:13)
    6. Action (Matt. 6:14–15)
III. Promised Answer to Prayer (Matt. 7:7–14)
    1. Ask, seek, knock (Matt. 6:7–11)
    2. Loving actions and total commitment (Matt. 6:12–14)
IV. "Lord, Teach Us to Pray" (Luke 11:1–13)
    1. Teach us how to pray (Luke 11:1–4)
    2. Teach us the need to pray (Luke 11:5–13)

When you pray, don't do it in order to be seen and praised (Matt. 6:5). Build your life on private communion with the Father (Matt. 6:6). Instead of using lots of empty words, pray with trust in God's goodness (Matt. 6:7–8). The Model Prayer in Matthew 6:9–15 teaches the elements of true prayer: praise, commitment, petition, confession, guidance, and action. When we ask, God will answer (Matt. 7:7–11). Real prayer assumes loving actions and total commitment (Matt. 7:12–14). When Jesus was asked to teach His followers to pray, He used the Model Prayer to teach them what to say (Luke 11:1–4). He also taught them the need to keep on praying (Luke 11:5–13).

I. When You Pray (Matt. 6:5–8)

1. Avoid hypocrisy (v. 5)

5 And when thou prayest, thou shalt not be as the hypocrites are: for they love to pray standing in the synagogues and in the corners of the streets, that they may be seen of men. Verily I say unto you, They have their reward.

Matthew 6:1–18 is about doing good in order to receive human praise. Jesus cited three examples: giving alms (vv. 2–4), praying (vv. 5–15), and fasting (vv. 16–18). Each of these was a good thing to do, but Jesus warned about doing these good things to be seen and praised by people. Thus in verse 5 Jesus was not warning against praying in public—He was warning against praying in order to receive human praise. If we pray in order to receive human praise, such praise will be our only reward.

2. Private prayer (v. 6)

6 But thou, when thou prayest, enter into thy closet, and when thou hast shut thy door, pray to thy Father which is in secret; and thy Father which seeth in secret shall reward thee openly.

The foundation of a person's prayer life must be private prayer. Jesus taught His followers to practice the discipline of private prayer. Find a place where you can be alone. This enables one to shut out distractions and to be aware of God's presence.

3. Avoid empty words (vv. 7–8)

7 But when ye pray, use not vain repetitions, as the heathen do: for they think that they shall be heard for their much speaking.

8 Be not ye therefore like unto them: for your Father knoweth what things ye have need of, before ye ask him.

Jesus warned against empty words. Every religion has its forms of prayer. Many religions believe that the repetition of certain words and phrases constitutes prayer. These religions assume that fervent praying will move their gods to do their bidding. Jesus warned against adopting pagan forms of praying. He came to reveal a different God from the false gods of pagans. What a low view of God, to assume that we must get His attention and win His favor by repeating formulas that we call prayers!

Jesus taught that the heavenly Father knows our needs before we ask. Instead of having to be convinced to help us, He is aware of our needs and eager to care for us. You may ask: "If God knows our needs, why do we need to pray at all? Why doesn't He just give us what we need?" The answer is that He does give us many good gifts apart from prayer (Matt. 5:45). However, His best gifts depend on our awareness of need and openness to receive. Can parents give a child a college education? They can provide the financial means to attend college, but the child has to want the education and do what is required to be educated. So it is with the best of God's blessings.

II. The Model Prayer (Matt. 6:9–15)

1. Praise (v. 9)

9 After this manner therefore pray ye: Our Father which art in

heaven, Hallowed be thy name.

We generally call Matthew 6:9-13 the Lord's Prayer or the Model Prayer. Jesus gave it as a model for the elements of prayer. It begins with praise.

The striking difference between Christian praying and pagan praying is the God to whom we pray. Jesus taught us to pray to the eternal God who created heaven and earth, who is also our loving heavenly Father. The "name" of God stands for who and what He is. Believers pray that God will be hallowed or honored.

2. Commitment (v. 10)

10 Thy kingdom come. Thy will be done in earth, as it is in heaven.

A worldly person is concerned about seeing his own name in lights, in seeking his own petty kingdoms, in his own selfish interests. A believer in God seeks first the kingdom of God and His righteousness (Matt. 6:33). One expression of seeking first the kingdom of God is praying that God's kingdom, not our own, will come to pass. This means that God's will shall be done. In order to pray "thy will be done," one must also pray—as Jesus did—"not my will, but thine, be done" (Luke 22:42).

3. Petition (v. 11)

11 Give us this day our daily bread.

Most people think of prayer only as asking for things. True prayer includes many other elements, but prayer does include petition. Rather than being anxious about material needs, believers ask God for daily bread and thank Him for providing it. Arrogant unbelievers think that they provide their own food through their own work. Believers know that life itself is a gift and so is every good thing in life. They also know that the ability to work is not contradictory to our dependence on the Heavenly Father for our life and sustenance.

4. Confession (v. 12)

12 And forgive us our debts, as we forgive our debtors.

This is one part of the Model Prayer that the Lord Jesus Himself never prayed. Since He had no sin, He did not pray for forgiveness. However, the rest of us are sinners who need forgiveness. Thus confession of sins is part of all true prayer. Jesus gave this Model Prayer to committed followers. They had already confessed their sins and been forgiven. However, Jesus taught that they needed to continue to confess sins. This doesn't mean that they were not forgiven when they were saved; it means that believers continue to fall short of the glory of God. Because of this, we need to confess our sins in order to maintain our communion with God and be instruments of His will (see 1 John 1:8–10).

Jesus also said that seeking God's forgiveness for our own sins means that we also forgive those who have sinned against us. (See comments on verses 14–15.)

5. Guidance (v. 13)

13 And lead us not into temptation, but deliver us from evil: For thine is the kingdom, and the power, and the glory, for ever.

Amen.

James 1:13–15 teaches that God is not the author of temptation. On the surface, this seems to contradict Matthew 6:13. The truth is that God allows us to pass through experiences that test our faith, but His is a good purpose. Satan, however, turns these tests into temptations to do evil.

Some of the Pharisees in Jesus' day challenged God to put them to the test. They were so confident of their moral strength that they felt that they were immune from giving in to temptation. We are never so vulnerable as when we are confident of our own strength. As Paul said, "Let him that thinketh he standeth take heed lest he fall" (1 Cor. 10:12). In verse 13, Jesus taught His followers to be aware of their own weaknesses and of the strength of the evil one. Instead of asking to be tested, we should ask God that we not be put to the test. We also should ask God to deliver us from the power of evil when we are tempted.

6. Action (vv. 14–15)

14 For if ye forgive men their trespasses, your heavenly Father will also forgive you:

15 But if ye forgive not men their trespasses, neither will your Father forgive your trespasses.

These verses are not part of the Model Prayer, but they clarify the meaning of verse 12. Specifically, they teach that our prayers for divine forgiveness will not be answered if we do not forgive those who have hurt us. The general principle is that all our prayers must be accompanied by appropriate actions. If we praise God with our lips, we must praise Him with our lives. If we pray for His kingdom to come, we must be willing to do our part. If we ask for daily bread, we must be willing to work for it and share it. If we pray for deliverance from evil, we must not expose ourselves unnecessarily to temptation; and we must be willing to resist it with God's help.

Several weeks ago (March 10), we studied the parable of the unforgiving servant from Matthew 18:21–35. That story illustrates the meaning of Matthew 6:14–15. Jesus did not mean that forgiving others is a good work that merits the forgiveness of God. His point was that if we have received God's forgiveness, we will be willing to forgive others.

III. Promised Answer to Prayer
(Matt. 7:7–14)

1. Ask, seek, knock (vv. 7–11). Those who ask God will receive (vv. 7–8). If parents give good things to their children, how much more will the heavenly Father give good things in response to the requests of His children (vv. 9–11).

2. Loving actions and total commitment (vv. 12–14). A life of real prayer to God is also a life that practices the Golden Rule (v. 12). It is also a life that has chosen the straight and narrow way of total commitment to God (vv. 13–14).

IV. "Lord, Teach Us to Pray"
(Luke 11:1-13)

1. Teach us how to pray (vv. 1-4). Jesus gave the Model Prayer in answer to the disciples' request to teach them to pray.

2. Teach us the need to pray (vv. 5-13). Jesus also answered their request by telling the parable of the friend at midnight, which shows that real needs will keep being expressed in prayer (vv. 5-8). Jesus also said that if a father gives his children good things, how much more will the heavenly Father (vv. 9-13).

APPLYING THE BIBLE

1. "Mother, that was a good sermon, wasn't it?" Once I called on a retired pastor who was visiting our morning worship service to offer the benediction. I guess he had not preached for some time, for he prayed and prayed, telling God a great many things He already knew! When the good brother finished praying, I heard a little boy in the congregation say to his mother: "That was a good sermon, wasn't it, Mother?" And the boy was not talking about the sermon I had just preached either!

We have a bad tendency when we pray, it seems, to try to impress both God and man. But Jesus says that is not the way to pray (vv. 7-8). As someone has put it, when we pray we are to approach God humbly, as hungry beggars asking for bread.

2. "A wish turned heavenward." Phillips Brooks, a noted preacher of the last century best known for his Christmas hymn "O Little Town of Bethlehem," said that prayer, in its simplest definition, is merely "a wish turned heavenward." And poet James Montgomery wrote about prayer:

> *Prayer is the soul's sincere desire,*
> *Uttered or unexpressed;*
> *The motion of a hidden fire,*
> *that trembles in the breast.*

3. How to address God in prayer. Jesus tells us to address God as "Our Father" when we pray.

Perhaps it is just one of my hang-ups, but it concerns me when I hear a pastor or a church leader: "O God" this, and "Almighty God" that. But I really don't believe it is just a personal hang-up with me, for Jesus taught us how to address God: He is our heavenly Father, and we ought to pay attention to how Jesus taught us to pray. If He had not intended for us to address God as Father, why then did He tell us to do so? Look at the times in chapter 6 that Jesus addressed God as Father. When one speaks to his or her earthly father about a personal matter, he or she does not do so in a stilted, formal way: "Mr. Jones, or Mr. Smith." Rather, we address him personally as "Father" or "Daddy." So we are to address God in the same way a child addresses a loving earthly father.

4. How to pray. Jesus tells us how we are to pray. It is not a liturgical formula that is set in concrete, but it is an excellent guide. That's why we call it "The Model" prayer:

(1) We are to pray unselfishly—"Thy kingdom come. Thy will be done"(v. 10).

(2) We are to pray humbly and for our personal needs—"Give us this day our daily bread."(v. 11)

(3) We are to confess our sins and ask for divine forgiveness—"And forgive us our debts"(v. 12).

(4) We are to forgive others as awe pray—"As we forgive our debtors "(v. 12).

(5) We are to pray for power over temptation and sin—"Lead us not into temptation; but deliver us from evil"(v. 12).

(6) And we are to praise God in prayer—"For thine is the kingdom, and the power, and the glory for ever. Amen." (v. 13).

This is a simple guideline for us as we pray. Our prayers ought to include each of these elements.

5. Forgiving others. One of America's greatest evangelists was Dwight L. Moody (1837–1885). He was to his day what Billy Graham is to our day. Once, in an evangelistic service, Moody told Ira Sankey, the music director who was playing the organ: "Excuse me, I see a friend I offended today downtown and I must go to him and ask for his forgiveness." The man saw Moody coming, they were reconciled, and a great service followed.

About prayer and forgiving others those who have offended us or those whom we have offended, Jesus gives some strong teaching in verses 14–15. Jesus' words about forgiveness in the previous chapter (5:23–24) instruct us to make forgiveness a priority. It must take precedence over everything, including worship. Heaven's channel of blessings to us is blocked until we, from our hearts, truly forgive others.

TEACHING THE BIBLE

▶ *Main Idea:* Jesus' teachings about prayer show us that we should come to God as a Father with our concerns.

▶ *Suggested Teaching Aim:* To lead adults to describe elements in Jesus' teaching about prayer, and to commit themselves to a new level of prayer.

A TEACHING OUTLINE

1. Use an illustration to introduce the study.
2. Use Scripture search to identify three principles or guidelines for prayer.
3. Use an acrostic to identify six elements in the Model Prayer.
4. Lead members to identify the strongest and weakest elements in their prayer life and commit to improve the weakest.

Introduce the Bible Study

Use "Mother, that was a good sermon, wasn't it?" ("Applying the

Bible") as an illustration to begin the lesson.

Search for Biblical Truth

On a chalkboard or a large sheet of paper, write *Three Guidelines for Prayer.* Call for a volunteer to read 6:5 and let members suggest a principle or guideline for prayer that this verse suggests. (*Avoid hypocrisy or some similar statement.*) Write the guideline on the board.

Ask a volunteer to read 6:6 and let members suggest a principle or guideline for prayer that this verse suggests. (*Pray privately and God will hear.*) Write the guideline under the heading on the board.

Ask a volunteer to read 6:7-8 and let members suggest a principle or guideline for prayer that these verses suggest. (*Avoid empty words.*) Write the guideline under the heading on the board.

DISCUSS: If God knows our needs, why do we need to pray? Why doesn't God just give us what we need? (*His best gifts depend on our awareness of need and openness to receive.*)

Write the words LORD'S PRAYER down the center of a chalkboard or a large sheet of paper. Using "Studying the Bible," point out six elements in the Model Prayer. As you mention each one, write it on the chalkboard to form the following acrostic:

L

A C T I**O** N (6:14–15)

P **R** A I S R E (6:9)

D

C O N F E S **S** I O N (6:12)

P E T I T I O N (6:11)

R

G U I D **A** N C E (6:13)

Y

C O M M I T M **E** N T (6:10)

R

Discuss the following as you deal with each verse:

6:9—What is the most striking difference between Christian and pagan praying?

6:10—What does praying for God's will to come to pass mean to you?

6:11—What difference does it make whether we ask for our bread from God?

6:12—If we do not forgive those who have wronged us, can we be forgiven?

6:13—Why should we ask God to lead us away from temptation?

6:14-15—Why do you think Jesus added these two verses to what He had already said?

Give the Truth a Personal Focus

Ask members to look at the six words on the acrostic. Ask: Which one of these words represents the strongest element in your prayer life? the weakest?

Suggest that members write one thing they will do this week to strengthen the weakest area of their prayer life. Encourage them to call someone this week and share their need and covenant to pray together this week for each other.

A Practical Religion (James)

INTRODUCTION

The Book of James is one of the General Letters. The book begins like a letter but reads like a sermon or series of sermons. The theme is practical religion. The five sessions focus on five of the main subjects dealt with by James.

The first session, "Faith and Faithfulness," deals with faithfulness in trials and with being doers of the Word of God. The second session, "Faith and Relationships," deals with the practice of impartial love and with refusing to pass judgment on others. The third session, "Faith and Action," deals with a faith that shows itself in good works and Christian fellowship. The fourth session, "Faith and Wisdom," deals with the wisdom that comes from God and is expressed in speech and actions. The fifth session, "Faith and Righteousness," deals with the difference between Christian righteousness and worldly strife and materialism.

Faith and Faithfulness

Basic Passage: James 1
Focal Passages: James 1:2–4,12–15,19–27

T he overall theme of James 1 is faithfulness. This faithfulness is expressed by faithfulness in trials and temptations (vv. 1–15) and by doing as well as hearing God's Word (vv. 16–27).

▸ ▸ ▸ ▸ ▸ ▸ ▸ ▸ ▸ **Study Aim:** *To evaluate personal faithfulness in light of the teachings in James 1*

STUDYING THE BIBLE

LESSON OUTLINE
I. Faithful in Trials (James 1:1–15)
    1. Rejoicing in trails (James 1:1–4)
    2. Asking for wisdom (James 1:5–8)
    3. Glorying in true riches (James 1:9–11)
    4. Receiving the crown of life (James 1:12)
    5. Seeing temptation for what it is (James 1:13–15)
II. Doers of the Word (James 1:16–27)
    1. Receiving life through the Word (James 1:16–18)
    2. Responding to the implanted Word (James 1:19–21)
    3. Hearing and doing the Word (James 1:22–25)
    4. Practicing true religion (James 1:26–27)

James called on people of faith to rejoice in times of trial (vv. 1–4). He encouraged them to ask God for wisdom to live right (vv. 5–8). Believers can glory in the true riches that do not fade away (vv. 9–11). Those who are faithful are blessed with the crown of life (v. 12). God doesn't tempt, but each person is tempted by deadly desires (vv. 13–15). One evidence of God's goodness is the Word of truth, which brings a new birth (vv. 16–18). People should be patient and responsive hearers, especially of God's implanted Word (vv. 19–21). Those who truly hear the Word of God will also be doers of the Word (vv. 22–25). Some people who profess to be religious show by their actions that their religion is worthless; the test of true religion is a clean life and service to the needy (vv. 26–27).

I. Faithful in Trials (James 1:1–15)
1. Rejoicing in trials (vv. 2–4)
    2 My brethren, count it all joy when ye fall into divers temptations.

After a brief greeting (v. 1), James launched right into his subject. The word translated "temptations" can also be translated "trials" (NIV).

The same experience can be both a trial and a temptation. God allows trials, but He has a purpose of good in allowing them (see Rom. 8:28). As James later makes clear, God never tempts anyone to do evil (see vv. 13–15).

The message of verse 2 is that believers can rejoice in different kinds of trials. Paul (Rom. 5:3–4) and Peter (1 Pet. 1:6–7) taught the same thing. Paul, Peter, and James got this teaching from Jesus Himself. A month ago we studied the Beatitudes and were reminded of what Jesus taught about being blessed in persecution (Matt. 5:10–12).

3 Knowing this, that the trying of our faith worketh patience.

4 But let patience have her perfect work, that ye may be perfect and entire, wanting nothing.

Jesus and the others did not teach that trials are a joy; instead, they taught that believers can rejoice in trials. Verses 3–4 explain that trials are tests. Endurance (the meaning of "patience" in vv. 3–4) is one of the results of passing the test of trials. The end result of enduring trials is that God enables us to move toward the goal He has for us. This seems to be the force of the word "perfect" in verse 4. The word suggests the idea of fulfilling a desired end (see Phil. 3:12–14).

2. Asking for wisdom (vv. 5–8). God promised wisdom to those who ask in faith (see comments on vv. 5–8 in the lesson for June 23).

3. Glorying in true riches (vv. 9–11). Poor and rich believers can rejoice in the blessings of true riches. By contrast to true riches, earthly wealth will pass away like the withering of flowers.

4. Receiving the crown of life (v. 12)

12 Blessed is the man that endureth temptation: for when he is tried, he shall receive the crown of life, which the Lord hath promised to them that love him.

James used the form of Jesus' Beatitudes (Matt. 5:3–12) to declare the blessedness of those who endure trials and temptations. The "crown of life" stresses the lasting quality of the reward in contrast to the temporary wealth of those who seek earthly crowns and riches. This does not mean that Christians enter into heaven by their own good works. It means that those who have been saved by grace enter the heavenly life that God has promised at the end of a life of faith and faithfulness.

5. Seeing temptation for what it is (vv. 13–15)

13 Let no man say when he is tempted, I am tempted of God: for God cannot be tempted with evil, neither tempteth he any man.

Some people make God the direct cause of everything that happens. Since God is Creator of all things, He is blamed for all the evils that happen. Some people even blame God for their temptations and thus for their sins. James denied that God is responsible for temptation and sin. The holy God is not tempted, and He does not tempt anyone else. He does allow trials as tests through which our faith can be strengthened. Trials that are intended by God for our good, however, can become occasions for temptations to evil thoughts and actions.

14 But every man is tempted, when he is drawn away of his

own lust, and enticed.

15 Then when lust hath conceived, it bringeth forth sin: and sin, when it is finished, bringeth forth death.

The Bible teaches that we are responsible for our own actions. Since the time of Adam and Eve, people have tried to blame someone other than themselves. When confronted with their sin by God, Adam blamed Eve, and by implication the God who had given Eve to him (Gen. 3:12). Eve blamed the tempter (Gen. 3:13). James insisted that each of us is tempted "by his own evil desire" (NIV). James did not mean to exclude the work of the devil (see James 4:7), but he did intend to show that individuals are accountable for their own sins.

Being tempted is not the same thing as committing sin. Sin happens when we yield to temptation. Verse 15 shows what happens when people yield to temptation and continue in their sins. This is pictured as three generations of evil. First, lust enters into illicit union with temptation and conceives sin. Second, sin is born of this illicit union. Then when sin becomes full-grown, it spawns its own evil child, death.

II. Doers of the Word (James 1:16–27)

1. Receiving life through the Word (vv. 16–18). People should not err in thinking that God is the author of evil (v. 16). To the contrary, God is the giver of every good and perfect gift (v. 17). Among His best gifts is new birth through the Word of truth (v. 18).

2. Responding to the implanted Word (vv. 19–21)

19 Wherefore, my beloved brethren, let every man be swift to hear, slow to speak, slow to wrath:

20 For the wrath of man worketh not the righteousness of God.

Before concentrating on hearing the Word of God, James dealt in general with the need to be good listeners. He urged that believers be careful in exercising the gift of speech. Elsewhere he had a lot to say about the sins of the tongue (see 1:26; 3:1–12). Here he seems to have in mind the sins committed with angry words. Believers should control their tempers and their tongues, and listen to what others are saying.

21 Wherefore lay apart all filthiness and superfluity of naughtiness, and receive with meekness the engrafted Word, which is able to save your souls.

This verse addresses the proper attitude for hearing the Word of God. One must lay aside sins in order to receive God's Word. A person also must receive the Word with a humble spirit. This is the way a sinner first responds to the Word that produces salvation from sin's guilt. It is the way believers continue to receive the Word of God as He continues His saving work in us.

3. Hearing and doing the Word (vv. 22–25)

22 But be ye doers of the Word, and not hearers only, deceiving your own selves.

James had just written of the importance of listening to God's Word; in verses 22–25 he stressed the need to be doers as well as hearers of the Word. The last part of verse 22 warns against the self-deception that comes to people who convince themselves that they have fulfilled their duty merely by hearing the Word.

23 For if any be a hearer of the Word, and not a doer, he is like unto a man beholding his natural face in a glass:

24 For he beholdeth himself, and goeth his way, and straightway forgetteth what manner of man he was.

At the end of the Sermon on the Mount, Jesus told a parable of two men who built houses. One built on the sand; the other, on a rock. The storms swept away the house on the sand, but the house on the rock stood. Jesus said that the difference between the men was that the latter practiced what he heard from God (see Matt. 7:24–27). Verses 23–24 provide another illustration of the difference between those who hear only and those who hear and do the Word. Those who merely hear are like people who look at themselves in a mirror but quickly forget what they see. If their face is dirty, they don't wash it. If their hair is a mess, they don't comb it. They are like the multitudes who hear God's Word, but never act on what they hear.

25 But whoso looketh into the perfect law of liberty, and continueth therein, he being not a forgetful hearer, but a doer of the work, this man shall be blessed in his deed.

Verse 25 describes the Word, the way people should respond, and the result of a positive response. God's Word is described as perfect in its truth and liberating in its results. The proper response is not to be a forgetful hearer, but to be one who looks intently into the Word and who acts on what he sees.

4. Practicing true religion (vv. 26–27)

26 If any man among you seem to be religious, and bridleth not his tongue, but deceiveth his own heart, this man's religion is vain.

Think of the kind of person described in verse 26. He faithfully performs the outward requirements of public worship. As a result, he considers himself a religious person. However, the same person doesn't control his tongue. Verse 26 doesn't identify specific sins of the tongue. Elsewhere, James spoke of angry words (1:19–20), cursing people while blessing God (3:9), slander (4:11–12), and swearing (5:12). James said that the person who seems to be religious but who doesn't control his tongue has an empty and worthless religion.

27 Pure religion and undefiled before God and the Father is this, To visit the fatherless and widows in their affliction, and to keep himself unspotted from the world.

James described two characteristics of true religion: (1) Such religion ministers to needy groups like orphans and widows. (2) It results in a clean life that is committed to God and His way, not the world and its ways. James stood in line with the Old Testament prophets and with Jesus in denouncing empty religion that makes no difference in how one lives and treats others. James along with Jesus and the prophets called for a life of service and of purity (see Isa. 1:10–17; Amos 5:21–24; Mic. 6:6–8; Luke 10:25–37).

APPLYING THE BIBLE

1. Thankfulness in trials. Years ago I was pastor of a church where an elderly deacon taught me an unforgettable lesson on prayer. Highly respected by the congregation, the deacon, when called upon to pray, would always conclude his prayer with the words, "And, Lord, we thank You that all is as well with us as it is."

It so impressed me that in my next pastorate I regularly included it in my pastoral prayer in the morning worship service. If I omitted it, invariably someone—often several people—would say to me at the door as I shook hands with the people, "Pastor, you forgot 'our prayer' this morning."

Life may lie heavily upon us as James points out (vv. 1–4), but things could be a lot worse. We can always rejoice, therefore, that "all is as well with us as it is."

2. Believers can rejoice in trials. Our writer points out that "Jesus and the others did not teach that trials are a joy; instead, they taught that believers can rejoice in trials." We can do this because of the sweet fruits adversity produces in our lives (vv. 3–4). Often the sweetest saints carry the heaviest burdens.

I know the father of an adult woman who has lived most of her life in an iron lung, but her Christian testimony is radiant; her writing skills are extraordinary and have made a significant contribution to Baptist work. She carries a heavy burden, but her life is producing magnificent, sweet fruit. Indeed, she has cause to rejoice—not in her limitations but in the fruit they have produced (v. 1).

3. True wealth. In September 1857, the U.S.S. Central America encountered a hurricane while en route from the California gold fields to New York City. The ship and its treasure were recently discovered off the coast of South Carolina. When she sailed from California, on board were five hundred passengers and a cargo of three tons of gold nuggets, assay bars, and coins worth an estimated one billion dollars.

For three days the passengers and crew bailed water hoping to save the vessel, but they were unsuccessful. Of the five hundred people on board, four hundred and twenty-five perished. Survivors told of passengers jumping overboard fatally weighed down with gold.[1]

Their greed killed them! There is nothing wrong with wealth if we use it properly, but there is a greater wealth about which James speaks and this wealth must be our chief concern and pursuit (vv. 9–12 and Matt. 6:19–21).

4. Being tempted is no sin. Being tempted is no sin, but succumbing to temptation is. Jesus was tempted, "yet without sin," the Scriptures declare.

What are we to do about temptation? We are to pray about it (Matt. 6:13), asking to be delivered from it; we are not to blame God for it (v. 13); we are to identify its source (Luke 4:13); we are to shun lust that draws us into temptation (v. 14); and we are to cultivate a strong faith in God, believing His power is sufficient to keep us from sin even in the midst of the severest temptation (1 Cor. 10:13).

5. Two ears but one tongue. Why do you suppose God gave us two ears and one tongue? Could it be because He wants us to listen more than talk? James says we ought to be quick to hear but slow to speak (v. 19–20).

Winston Churchill once listened patiently as he was belittled and crucified by a ranting, raving political opponent. When the man had finished making a fool of himself, Churchill rose and said: "Our honorable colleague should, by now, have trained himself not to generate more indignation than he has the capacity to hold!"[2]

Good advice according to James (vv. 19–20). Uncontrolled anger is an indication of arrested development.

6. How true Christianity expresses itself. In the Christian life, a genuine relationship to Christ will express itself in ways that are obvious: a controlled tongue (v. 26); a clean life (v. 27); and a compassionate attitude (v. 27).

TEACHING THE BIBLE

▶ *Main Idea:* James's description of faith and faithfulness demands that we live out our faith in the world.

▶ *Suggested Teaching Aim:* To lead adults to describe James's teachings about faith and faithfulness, and to describe what they can do to be more faithful to Christ.

A TEACHING OUTLINE

1. *Use an illustration to introduce the session.*
2. *Use a research report to introduce the Book of James.*
3. *Use a session outline to move through the Bible study.*
4. *Use discussion questions and small groups to explore the Bible passage.*
5. *Use small groups to identify ways of being faithful to Christ.*

Introduce the Bible Study

Use "Thankfulness in trials" from "Applying the Lesson" to introduce the Bible study.

Search for Biblical Truth

IN ADVANCE, enlist a member to read the article in the *Holman Bible Handbook* on "James" and give a two- to three-minute report to introduce the book.

On a chalkboard or a large sheet of paper write *I. Faithful in Trials (James 1:1–15)*. Ask members to open their Bibles to James 1:1. Call for a volunteer to read 1:2–4. Ask members to react to this statement from "Studying the Bible": "Jesus and the others did not teach that trials are a joy; instead, they taught that believers can rejoice in trials."

Ask, Based on 1:2–4, why do we have to endure trials? Define the following words: *temptations* (trials), *patience* (endurance), *perfect* (mature).

Call for a volunteer to read 1:12–15.

DISCUSS: Since withstanding temptation cannot earn us heaven, it makes little difference whether we avoid it or not.

Ask members to examine 1:13 to find why we can't blame our temptation on God. Point out the "three generations of evil" in 1:15.

DISCUSS: What role does the priesthood of the believer have in determining our responsibility for our sin?

On the chalkboard or the large sheet of paper, write *II. Doers of the Word (James 1:16–27)*. Ask a volunteer to read 1:19–27. Organize the class in four groups (one person can be a group) and make the following assignments: 1:19–20; 1:21; 1:22–25; 1:26–27. Ask: Based on these verses, how should believers act in the world? Ask members (1) to identify the ways their verses answer the question, and (2) to write a brief case study or role play that illustrates their answer. Allow three or four minutes for study and then call for reports.

Give the Truth a Personal Focus

Read the "Suggested Teaching Aim." Ask members to continue in their same groups and ask them to identify what they can do to be more faithful to Christ. Give each group markers and large sheets of paper and ask them to make a poster listing their ideas. Allow five minutes for study and then call for reports. Ask groups to place their posters on the focal wall and explain their ideas.

After all the groups have reported, ask members to find one suggestion and to adopt that suggestion for this week. Ask them to return to their groups and to let each other help them in writing steps they can take to achieve this suggestion.

Ask members to conclude the study session with prayer in their groups. Ask them to pray for each other this week and to make contact to encourage faithfulness.

---

1. Jack Gulledge, *Proclaim* (July–September 1992); adapted from *The Tennessean* (September 8, 1990).

2. J. Wallace Hamilton, *Ride the Wild Horses* (Old Tappan N.J.: Fleming H. Revell Company, 1952), 116.

Faith and Relationships

Basic Passages: James 2:1–13; 4:11–12
Focal Passages: James 2:1–13; 4:11–12

O ur relationship with God is inseparable from our relationships with other people. We cannot have a right relationship with God and practice wrong relationships with other people. James made this point by stressing the need for impartial love (2:1–13) and by condemning slander and judgment toward others (4:11–12).

▶ ▶ ▶ ▶ **Study Aim:** *To practice impartial love and avoid speaking evil of others*

STUDYING THE BIBLE

LESSON OUTLINE
I. Practice Impartial Christian Love (James 2:1–13)
    1. Faith and impartiality (James 2:1)
    2. An example of partiality (James 2:2–4)
    3. Denying God's love for the poor (James 2:5–7)
    4. Violating the royal law (James 2:8–11)
    5. Judged by the law of liberty (James 2:12–13)
II. Avoid Speaking Against or Judging Others (James 4:11–12)

Partiality or prejudice is inconsistent with faith in Christ (2:1). James gave an example of partiality toward a rich man and a poor man who came to church (2:2–4). Partiality is wrong because it denies God's love (2:5–7), violates the royal law (2:8–11), and will be judged by God (2:12–13). Christians should not speak evil against others or pass judgment on them (4:11–12).

I. Practice Impartial Christian Love (James 2:1–13)

1. Faith and impartiality (v. 1)
    1 My brethren, have not the faith of our Lord Jesus Christ, the Lord of glory, with respect of persons.
On the surface, the English words "respect of persons" sound like showing respect for persons. The Greek word translated "respect of persons" has its background in an Old Testament word that means "to lift up the face of a person." Originally, the word had a positive meaning of lifting up a person's face in order to help. The word came to be used in the negative sense of showing favoritism to some people based on their wealth or appearance and showing prejudice against the poor and unlovely.

Thus Old Testament judges were warned, "Ye shall not respect persons in judgment; but ye shall hear the small as well as the great" (Deut. 1:17). The Greek word was used by Peter when he made the great declaration of Acts 10:34, "Of a truth I perceive that God is no respecter of persons." In other words, God is impartial and fair in His dealings with people.

James 2:1 says that partiality or prejudice is inconsistent with faith in the Lord Jesus Christ. To put it positively, God expects us to treat others with the same impartiality and fairness that He shows toward people.

2. An example of partiality (vv. 2–4)

2 For if there come into your assembly a man with a gold ring, in goodly apparel, and there come in also a poor man in vile raiment;

3 And ye have respect to him that weareth the gay clothing, and say unto him, Sit thou here in a good place; and say to the poor, Stand thou there, or sit here under my footstool:

4 Are ye not then partial in yourselves, and are become judges of evil thoughts?

James gave an example of what he meant. He presented the example as a situation that might occur. Verse 6 shows that such things actually happened in James's day. Unfortunately, similar things have happened many times throughout Christian history.

James described two men who came into one of their meetings. One man was well dressed and had on a gold ring, such as only rich people wore. The other man was a poor man in shabby clothes. The two men were treated very differently. The rich man was given a warm welcome and a choice seat. The poor man was snubbed and told to stand or to sit on the floor.

This example illustrates partiality and prejudice. The people who saw the two men knew nothing about either one, but they judged each purely on the basis of his appearance. On that basis, they immediately decided the well-dressed man was a good prospect to be treated with extra courtesy. They also decided that the poor man was not the kind of person who could do anything for them. To the contrary, his plight meant that he likely would become a drain on their resources.

3. Denying God's love for the poor (vv. 5–7)

5 Hearken, my beloved brethren, Hath not God chosen the poor of this world rich in faith, and heirs of the kingdom which he hath promised to them that love him?

James stressed God's gracious action in seeking those who are poor. This does not deny that God's love reaches out to all—rich and poor alike. However, James was dealing with a situation in which the church showed partiality toward the rich. Over against this, James stressed that God's love was directed toward the poor. When Jesus described His mission, He said, "The Spirit of the Lord is upon me, because he hath anointed me to preach the gospel to the poor" (Luke 4:18).

James also stressed that the poor are often responsive to God's love for them. He wrote of those who were "rich in faith and heirs of the kingdom." Often the word *poor* is used in the Bible to describe the pious poor (see Ps. 70:5; Luke 6:20).

6 But ye have despised the poor. Do not rich men oppress you, and draw you before the judgment seats?

7 Do not they blaspheme that worthy name by the which ye are called?

James accused the believers of despising the poor, whom God loves. At the same time, James accused them of fawning over a man purely because he was rich. In so doing, they were forgetting that the rich often dragged believers before the courts and even blasphemed the name of the Lord. James was not condemning all rich people, but he was reminding his readers of how rich people often treated Christ and His people.

The Bible reflects many examples in which rich people used their wealth and power to exploit the poor. Ezekiel condemned the powerful people of his day who had "oppressed the alien and mistreated the fatherless and widows" (Ezek. 22:7, NIV). Jesus accused the Pharisees of using their positions of trust to "devour widows' houses" (Mark 12:40). James wrote of wealthy landowners who exploited the poor by withholding their wages (5:1–5).

4. Violating the royal law (vv. 8–11)

8 If ye fulfil the royal law according to the scripture, Thou shalt love thy neighbour as thyself, ye do well.

The royal law came from Leviticus 19:18. Jesus quoted it along with Deuteronomy 6:4–5 when He was asked to name the greatest commandment of the law (Mark 12:28–31). Thus, love for neighbors is the royal law of the King and His kingdom.

Verse 8 helps correct a possible misunderstanding of verses 6–7. Some people might have thought James was condemning any positive actions toward rich people. That was not what James meant as he described the sins of the rich in general. If Christians acted in love toward their neighbors, they would show the same love toward rich and poor alike. The problem in verses 2–4 was not the good treatment of the rich man, but the bad treatment of the poor man.

9 But if ye have respect to persons, ye commit sin, and are convinced of the law as transgressors.

10 For whosoever shall keep the whole law, and yet offend in one point, he is guilty of all.

11 For he that said, Do not commit adultery, said also, Do not kill. Now if thou commit no adultery, yet if thou kill, thou art become a transgressor of the law.

Showing partiality is a sin against the royal law. One does not have to break all the Commandments to be a transgressor of the law. A murderer doesn't have to break the other Commandments to be considered a transgressor of God's law. A person who shows partiality may not be either a murderer or an adulterer, but he is a sinner who has transgressed God's royal law.

Some read this passage and conclude, "If I'm already a sinner because of my few sins, I may as well go ahead and break all God's laws."

This is certainly not the point James was trying to make. Anyone who uses one sin as an excuse to commit another is heading for moral and spiritual ruin. James was dealing with self-righteous people who didn't think that their prejudice was a sin. James was trying to warn them that it is a violation of God's royal law.

5. Judged by the law of liberty (vv. 12–13)

12 So speak ye, and so do, as they that shall be judged by the law of liberty.

Verses 12–13 state another reason why believers should avoid the sin of partiality. We shall be judged for this and other sins that show a lack of Christian love. Some people are disturbed at the idea of Christians having to face judgment. The Bible clearly teaches that Christians will be judged according to their words and deeds (see 1 Cor. 3:13; 2 Cor. 5:10; 1 Pet. 1:17). This does not mean that our eternal destiny is at stake.

We shall be judged by the law of liberty. James used the same terms in 1:25. Christians understand God's demands in terms of love, not keeping a list of rules. This royal law of love is a law of liberty because the compulsion for obedience is internal, not external. Such a law of love makes deeper demands than rules ever could.

13 For he shall have judgment without mercy, that hath shewed no mercy; and mercy rejoiceth against judgment.

Verse 13 echoes the teachings of Jesus about mercy and forgiveness. The merciful will receive mercy (Matt. 5:7). Those who show no mercy will receive no mercy (Matt. 18:21–35). Jesus and James were not presenting mercy as a good work that merits salvation. They were showing that people who have experienced God's mercy will show mercy to others.

The last part of verse 13 refers to the triumph of mercy over judgment. Christians who show mercy to others demonstrate that they have received divine mercy, which overcomes judgment.

II. Avoid Speaking Against or Judging Others (James 4:11–12)

11 Speak not evil one of another, brethren. He that speaketh evil of his brother, and judgeth his brother, speaketh evil of the law, and judgeth the law: but if thou judge the law, thou art not a doer of the law, but a judge.

12 There is one lawgiver, who is able to save and to destroy: who are thou that judgest another?

Speaking evil against others refers to tearing them down with words, usually when they are not present to defend themselves. Peter used the same Greek word to describe the slander that persecutors used against Christians (1 Pet. 2:12; 3:16). James used the word to describe what Christians were doing to one another. Gossip is more than a harmless indoor sport; it is a vicious habit that hurts and destroys.

Closely related is judging others. When we pass judgment on others, we usually express our judgment by speaking against them. When we pass judgment, we place ourselves above the law by presuming to do what only God can do. He alone is qualified to be the Judge. The question at the end of verse 12 echoes the words of Paul in Romans 14:4: "Who are you to judge someone else's servant? To his own master he stands or falls. And he will stand, for the Lord is able to make him stand" (NIV).

APPLYING THE BIBLE

1. The cross is both vertical and horizontal. As our lesson writer points out, one cannot be right with God and wrong with others. The very symbolism of the cross reveals this: the vertical portion of the cross reaches up to God while the horizonal arms reach out to embrace others. To be rightly related to God means to love others unconditionally and impartially (2:1–13) and to refuse to judge or slander others (4:11–12).

2. Pride and prejudice. Pride and prejudice are made from the same cloth. One is the inside and the other is the outside of the same garment. Like Siamese twins, they always go together. But we who bear the name of Christ are to be like Him. The life of Jesus is a rebuke to every kind of pride: pride of birth and standing—"Is not this the carpenter's son?" (Matt. 13:55); pride of wealth—"The Son of man hath not where to lay his head" (Matt. 8:20); pride of heritage—"Can there any good thing come out of Nazareth?" (John 1:46); pride of appearance—"When we shall see him, there is no beauty that we should desire him" (Isa. 53:2); pride of social position—"A friend of publicans and sinners" (Matt. 11:19).

Also: pride of education.—"How knoweth this man letters, having never learned?" (John 7:15); pride of superiority—"I am among you as he that serveth" (Luke 22:27); pride of success—"His own received him not" (John 1:11); and pride of ability—("I can of mine own self do nothing" (John 5:30).[1]

This consuming sense of pride in oneself is not only opposed to the attitude of Jesus, but it also produces every form of human prejudice (see vv. 1–7).

3. Prejudice toward the wise and wealthy. There is a great emphasis in America today to "dress appropriately," move in the right circles, make the proper contacts in order to move up the ladder, and drive the car that will make the right impression. In other words, there is a prejudice toward (not against) the affluent and well educated. Look at our justice system in America. Is it easier for an affluent and wealthy person indicted for some crime to get a fair trial than it is for a poor person or a minority person?

And in the church it isn't any different. Well-liked, affluent people of "standing" in the community are easily elected to powerful positions in the church while the poor and uneducated are overlooked. And more than one pastor has been accused of catering to wealthy members while others are neglected. In no uncertain words James rebukes this prejudice in the church (vv. 2–4; 5–7; 9).

4. The royal law. American poet Edwin Markham (1852–1940) is well remembered by lovers of poetry for his poem, "The Man with the Hoe." In preparing for retirement, Markham trusted a friend to invest his (Markham's) life's savings. Too late, Markham discovered his friend had absconded with the money. Old and broke, Markham pondered his plight. Finally, he concluded he could only start writing again with the hope he could build up his assets. But his heart was so filled with hate that the inspiration was blocked. As he doodled on the paper before him, Markham cried out to God to help him forgive his friend who had wounded him. It was then that the inspiration returned and he wrote the little piece of poetry which, many believe, was his finest work:

> He drew a circle that shut me out—
> heretic, rebel, a thing to flout.
> But Love and I had the wit to win;
> We drew a circle and took him in.

That's it! That's the "royal law" about which James speaks in verse 8 of our lesson today. *Love* is more than a four-letter word. It expresses itself in actions. And love is never love until it also includes the unlovely.

5. Get as much on the altar as you can. The late Tennessee pastor Dr. R. G. Lee once told about a person (whether man or woman I, fortunately, do not know!) who came down the aisle at invitation time and confessed that he or she had been guilty of gossiping about others. Of course, everyone was well aware of it. "Pastor, today I want to lay my tongue on the altar," the repentant said. "God bless you," the pastor said. "Put as much of it on the altar as you can and let the rest lap off in the aisle!"

TEACHING THE BIBLE

▶ *Main Idea:* Faith and relationships demand that we practice impartial love and avoid speaking evil of others.

▶ *Suggested Teaching Aim:* To lead adults to describe the relationship between loving God and loving others, and to identify one or two principles they will apply to their lives this week.

A TEACHING OUTLINE

1. Introduce the study by using an illustration from "Applying the Bible."

2. Give an illustrated lecture using a poster and discussion questions.

3. Lead members to identify guidelines to govern their lives.

Introduce the Bible Study
Use "The royal law" from "Applying the Bible" to introduce the session.

Search for Biblical Truth

On a large sheet of paper write the following from the introduction to "Studying the Bible": "Our relationship with God is inseparable from our relationships with other people. We cannot have a right relationship with God and practice wrong relationships with other people."

On a large sheet of paper write the following lesson outline. After each point leave ample space to write the principles suggested below. Cover the three points until you are ready to teach them.

Faith and Relationships

I. Prohibition Against Prejudice (2:1–7)

II. Prevention of Prejudice (2:8–13)

III. Prohibition Against Judging (4:11–12)

Uncover the first point and call on a volunteer to read James 2:1–7. Present a lecture using "Studying the Bible" in which you cover the following:

(1) Explain "respect of persons" (2:1).

(2) Point out the danger of judging between well-dressed persons and poorly dressed persons (2:2–4) (or any other criteria) is that our decisions are based on appearance rather than the real value of the person.

(3) Emphasize God's concern for the poor (2:5) and the dangers of showing favoritism to the rich (2:6–7).

DISCUSS: Can persons claim to be believers if they do not have a genuine concern for the poor?

Ask members to suggest principles these verses suggest that would govern their actions toward people today. Write these below the outline point.

Uncover the second outline point. Give a lecture in which you cover the following points:

(1) Explain the source of the "royal law" (2:8).

(2) Point out that we should avoid showing partiality because it is a sin against the royal law (2:9–11).

(3) Point out that we should avoid showing partiality because we will be judged for this and other sins that show a lack of Christian love (2:12–13).

(4) Emphasize the relationship between persons showing mercy to others and having received it themselves (2:13).

DISCUSS: If we are already sinners because of a few sins, what difference would it make if we broke all of God's laws?

Ask members to suggest principles these verses suggest that would govern their actions toward people today. Write these below the outline point.

Uncover the third outline point. Present a lecture in which you cover the following points:

(1) Explain what speaking evil against another person means (4:11).

(2) Explain what judging others means (4:12).

Share "Get as much on the altar as you can" from "Applying the Bible."

DISCUSS: When do we have a right as believers to judge another person?

Ask members to suggest principles these verses suggest that would govern their actions toward people today. Write these below the outline point.

Give the Truth a Personal Focus

Ask members to review the principles and suggest how their lives would change if they applied them. Ask them to choose one or two they will seriously seek to fulfill this week. Distribute paper and pencils and ask them to suggest one or two specific steps they will take in fulfilling these guidelines.

---

1. Adapted from Walter B. Knight, *Knight's Master Book of New Illustrations* (Grand Rapids: Eerdmans, 1956), 516.

Faith and Action

Basic Passages: James 2:14–26; 5:7–20
Focal Passages: James 2:14–26; 5:13–16

ames stressed practical religion. Probably the most familiar and controversial part of James is his insistence that faith must be accompanied by good works. Many people see this as a contradiction of the teaching of Paul that we are saved by faith.

▶ ▶ ▶ ▶ **Study Aim:** *To compare the teaching of James about faith and works with what Paul taught about faith and works*

STUDYING THE BIBLE

LESSON OUTLINE
I. Faith and Works (James 2:14–26)
   1. Faith without works (James 2:14–17)
   2. Faith and works (James. 2:18–19)
   3. Old Testament examples (James 2:20–26)
II. Christian Actions (James 5:7–20)
   1. Patient endurance (James 5:7–11)
   2. Swear not (James 5:12)
   3. Life in the Christian fellowship (James 5:13–20)

James insisted that faith without works is dead (2:14–17). Faith and works belong together (2:18–19). James gave two Old Testament examples of people justified by faith and works: Abraham and Rahab (2:20–26). People of faith practice patient endurance (5:7–11). They do not swear (5:12). They worship, pray, confess their sins, and restore those who go astray (5:13–20).

I. Faith and Works (James 2:14–26)
1. Faith without works (vv. 14--17)
   14 What doth is profit, my brethren, though a man say he hath faith, and have not works? can faith save him?

Notice that James was writing about people who "say" they have faith. With their words they claimed to have faith, but their actions called in question their profession of faith. The word "faith" in the original language has a definite article in front of it. Thus the last part of verse 14 can be translated, "Can such faith save him?" (NIV). James was not calling in question the saving power of faith. He was calling in question a claim to an empty faith, which is not expressed in actions.

   15 If a brother or sister be naked, and destitute of daily food,
   16 And one of you say unto them, Depart in peace, be ye warmed and filled; notwithstanding ye give them not those things which are needful to the body; what doth it profit?
   17 Even so faith, if it hath not works, is dead, being alone.

James asked his readers to suppose that a Christian brother or sister needed food and clothing. James concentrated on the failure of fellow Christians to help the needy brother or sister. The needy people received only pious words, without any action to provide help. James was not denying the importance of words. Words are often used by God to help people. The problem was not with the words. The problem was that the situation called for action, but all the needy got were words.

Verses 15–16 help us understand what James meant when he used the word *works*. These verses show that works included helping brothers and sisters (see Matt. 25:31–46; 1 John 3:17–18). When James wrote of "works," he had in mind such actions as: helping the needy, living a pure life (1:27), showing impartial love (2:1–13), controlling the tongue (3:1–12), avoiding selfish strife (3:13–4:10), avoiding worldly presumption (4:13–17), patiently enduring persecution (5:1–7), and expressing Christian worship and fellowship (5:13–18).

Verse 17 expresses James's conclusion from verses 14–16, a conclusion he repeated in verse 26. Faith without works is dead. At no point does James play down the importance of true faith. He considered faith to be crucial (see 1:3, 6; 2:1, 5). James had nothing but good to say about real faith. However, he insisted that true faith shows itself in works.

2. Faith and works (vv. 18–19)

18 Yea, a man may say, Thou hast faith, and I have works: shew me thy faith without thy works, and I will shew thee my faith by my works.

James introduced an imaginary person who was claiming that faith and works can be separated. Over against this, James stressed that they belong together. A possible translation is: "But someone will say, 'One person has faith, another has actions.' My answer is, 'Show me how anyone can have faith without actions. I will show you my faith by my actions'" (GNB). The main point is that faith and works belong together. True faith shows itself in good works.

19 Thou believest that there is one God; thou doest well: the devils also believe, and tremble.

James was writing to people who professed to believe in one God, but their lives were barren of any fruit of true faith. James reminded them that the demons believe in one God in the sense of believing that God exists. James was showing that true faith must be more than believing that something is true. The demons believe that God exists, but they are still demons. They do not trust God. They do not worship and serve God.

3. Old Testament examples (vv. 20–26)

20 But wilt thou know, O vain man, that faith without works is dead?

James continued the style of addressing an imaginary person who said that faith alone is all that God expects. He asked if the person needed further evidence that faith without works is dead. Then in verses 21–25, James gave two Old Testament examples of faith that was fulfilled in works: Abraham and Rahab.

21 Was not Abraham our father justified by works, when he had offered Isaac his son upon the altar?

22 Seest thou how faith wrought with his works, and by works was faith made perfect?

23 And the scripture was fulfilled which saith, Abraham believed God, and it was imputed unto him for righteousness: and he was called the Friend of God.·

24 Ye see then how that by works a man is justified, and not by faith only.

Verses 21–24 seem on the surface to contradict what Paul taught. Paul cited Abraham as an example of one who was justified by faith. Paul even quoted Genesis 15:6, the same verse James quoted in verse 23. For Paul's teaching, see especially Romans 4:9–25 and Galatians 3:6–9. The word "justified" comes from the law court and means "to be declared righteous." James and Paul used the same word to make different points. Paul referred to what happens when a sinner exercises faith in Christ. God acquits the sinner and accepts the sinner on the basis of the death of Jesus and the sinner's faith in Christ. James used the word to describe God's pronouncement that a person has become righteous.

James was not denying Abraham's faith, which was proverbial. His point was that Abraham's faith was not "faith without works." Rather, James wrote, "His faith and his actions were working together, and his faith was made complete by what he did" (2:22, NIV). James pointed to Abraham's willingness to offer Isaac as evidence that his faith was made complete by his actions.

Paul stressed that sinners can be saved only by God's grace, not by anything they do to atone for their sins. A repentant sinner can only trust God's grace to be acquitted from sin's guilt. But Paul, no less than James, stressed that real faith leads to a transformed life. He didn't state it the same way as James, but he stated it nonetheless. See, for example, Ephesians 2:8–10; Romans 6:1–14; 8:1–8; Galatians 5:13–26.

25 Likewise also was not Rahab the harlot justified by works, when she had received the messengers, and had sent them out another way?

26 For as the body without the spirit is dead, so faith without works is dead also.

Rahab was different from Abraham in many ways. She was a woman, a prostitute, and a Gentile. But she and Abraham were both people who put their faith into action. Both were declared righteous by God. Rahab's confession of faith is found in Joshua 2:8–13. She showed her faith by hiding the Israelite spies.

II. Christian Actions (James 5:7–20)

1. Patient endurance (vv. 7–11). People of faith are patient as they await the coming of the Lord (vv. 7–9). Their patience has the kind of endurance exemplified by the prophets and by Job (vv. 10–11).

2. Swear not (v. 12). James repeated the teaching of Jesus against swearing (see Matt. 5:33–37).

3. Life in the Christian fellowship (vv. 13–20)

> **13 Is any among you afflicted? let him pray. Is any merry? let him sing psalms.**
>
> **14 Is any sick among you? let him call for the elders of the church; and let them pray over him, anointing him with oil in the name of the Lord:**
>
> **15 And the prayer of faith shall save the sick, and the Lord shall raise him up; and if he have committed sins, they shall be forgiven him.**

James described life in the church as a shared life of worship and mutual help. In times of trouble, Christians should pray. In times of joy, they should sing hymns of praise. In times of sickness, they are to pray for one another.

The Bible teaches that God knows our needs before we ask, but God uses our prayers to help and heal. In the first century, oil was used as a healing ointment (see Luke 10:34). People of faith prayed for the sick and did what they could to provide healing. They saw no contradiction.

The promise in verse 15 should be interpreted in light of other Bible teachings about answers to prayers for the sick. Some prayers for the sick are not answered by healing the sick. No less a person than Paul prayed for the removal of his thorn in the flesh. His prayer was answered but not by the removal of the thorn (see 2 Cor. 12:7–9). Faith includes not only the belief that God can heal, but also the trust to allow God to work out His good purpose (see Rom. 8:28).

Verse 15 also brings up the issue of sin and sickness. All sickness is not the result of sin (John 9:2–3), although some is. In either case, sickness is always an appropriate time to confess one's sins. Thus the last part of verse 15 assumes that the sick person has prayed for forgiveness.

> **16 Confess your faults one to another, and pray one for another, that ye may be healed. The effectual fervent prayer of a righteous man availeth much.**

The theme of confessing sins continues in verse 16. We should confess our sins not only to God but also to one another. This includes the sins we commit against one another. It also includes other sins. We confess sins to one another so that we can encourage and pray for one another.

Verse 16 is one of many New Testament examples of the shared life of the church. Christians constitute a family of faith and love. Some of this in done in the entire church; often, especially in large churches, the Sunday School class is where people confess their sins to one another and pray for one another.

The last part of verse 16 is illustrated in the prayer life of Elijah (vv. 17–18). Verses 19–20 provide another example of life in the family of faith and love: helping to restore someone who has strayed.

APPLYING THE BIBLE

1. Faith without works. A French magician named Blondin once stretched a cable across Niagara Falls and rolled a wheelbarrow across to the cheers of the great multitude that had gathered to watch him. He then asked the people if they thought he could do it again, and the people cheered their affirmation of Blondin's skill and shouted, "Yes! Yes! We believe." But it grew deathly quiet and no one stepped forward when Blondin challenged them: "If you believe in Blondin, who will be the first one to ride in my wheelbarrow?" The people "said" they had faith, but they didn't prove they had faith.

That's what James refers to in 2:14 of our study today. Merely to say we have faith in Christ is not enough. Faith is alive and active and expresses itself in good works.

2. Luther's faith led to action. Genuine faith leads us to action. We demonstrate or act out our faith in Christ in daily life.

An example of this is the life of Martin Luther. Hauled before King Charles V on orders from the Pope, Luther was commanded to retract his teachings against the authority and doctrines of the Roman Catholic Church (1521). But Luther answered: "My conscience is bound in the Word of God; I cannot and will not recant anything." He was then imprisoned in the castle at Wartburg, Germany, for ten months and the Protestant Reformation was born. Luther's song —"A Mighty Fortress Is Our God," first published in 1523—has been called "the battle hymn of the Reformation."

You see, our faith will express itself. If it doesn't, James says it is dead (2:17). It may express itself in a dangerous and threatening situation as in Luther's case. But it most certainly expresses itself in simple, compassionate acts that characterize the Savior (2:15–17).

3. Even Satan believes. According to verse 19, even Satan believes. He and his demons believe there is one God and tremble. But there is a serious flaw revealed here: the demons believe there is one God, but no one is saved simply by believing that (John 3:16–18). Satan fears God, but no one is saved by that. Satan "believes," but his belief is simply the acceptance of a truth not even he can deny or refute: he knows there is one God; his belief is simply intellectual affirmation of a truth, such as two and two equal four. It is not heart commitment to Christ that manifests itself in a changed life (Eph. 2:8–10; Rom. 10:9–10).

4. Waiting, working until Jesus comes. The late William Barclay relates in his book *The King and the Kingdom*, that years ago a deep and dreadful darkness, probably an eclipse of the sun, fell over America. People thought the end of the world had come. The Senate was in session when the darkness fell like a dark shroud over the land and many wished to abandon all businesses and prepare for the end. But one senator, who was wiser than the others, insisted that candles be lighted and that business proceed. "How could we better meet our Lord than by doing the work He has appointed us to do?" the senator insisted.

James insists in 5:7–9 that we are to do just that. Unlike some foolish Christians of the past, we are not to sell our homes and businesses, move to some remote area cut off from the world and sit idly by as we wait for Jesus. No! We are to keep busily engaged in His work, patiently waiting and doing what He has called us to do.

5. God is the healer. All who are sick and get well are healed by God. He may use doctors, medicine, time, and the loving care of the family, but God alone heals.

Prayer and healing go hand in hand (5:14–16), but not all who pray to be healed are healed in this life. Every suffering believer shall be healed, however, when Jesus comes. As our writer points out, not even Paul was healed although he prayed fervently (2 Cor. 12:7–9).

A man hobbled on crutches into a revival service where I was preaching. After the service, the pastor told me that the man's picture had been on the cover of *Life* magazine, which was doing a story about a well-known healing evangelist. The camera caught the man throwing his crutches in the air. He was healed, he said! But was he? When I saw him, he was still on his crutches.

God can and often does heal suddenly and miraculously. None of us denies this. But we cannot corner God, even in prayer, and expect Him to obey us. He is God. He acts sovereignly—as He chooses—according to His will, not according to ours.

Should we pray for healing? Certainly! But also we should pray, as Jesus taught us, "Thy kingdom come. Thy will be done."

TEACHING THE BIBLE

▶ *Main Idea:* Faith and action both are essential to the Christian life.
▶ *Suggested Teaching Aim:* To lead adults to describe James's description of the relationship of faith and words, and to help adults put their faith into action by doing good deeds.

A TEACHING OUTLINE

1. Use an illustration to create interest.
2. Use discussion questions/group discussion to move through the focal passage.
3. Use brainstorming to identify ways members can put their faint in action.

Introduce the Bible Study

Use "Faith without works" from "Applying the Bible" to introduce the study.

Search for Biblical Truth

Point out that this lesson is related to last week's lesson because James used "speak" and "do" (2:12), and it triggered his thinking about speaking and doing.

On a chalkboard or a large sheet of paper, write:
"I. Faith and Works."
Call for a volunteer to read 2:14–17.
Use the following DISCUSSION QUESTIONS:
- What does "faith" mean in 2:14? (All the doctrines of belief.)
- What is the proper balance between faith and works?

Share "Luther's faith led to action" in "Applying the Bible."
Call for a volunteer to read 2:18–19. Use the following DISCUSSION QUESTIONS:
- What is the point of James's mentioning the demons? (Show that belief is not enough.)
- How do we act like the demons when we say we believe but do not act like it?

Share "Even Satan believes" from "Applying the Bible."
Call for a volunteer to read 2:20–26. Use the following DISCUSSION QUESTIONS:
- How does Paul's mention of Abraham further his argument?
- How do we know the proper balance of faith and works?
- How does Paul's mention of Rahab further his argument?
- Do we really believe this?

On the chalkboard or large sheet of paper write:
"II. Christian Actions."
Call for a volunteer to read 5:13–16. Point out that these verse describe life in the Christian fellowship.
Use the following DISCUSSION QUESTIONS:
- What is the relationship between prayer and the practice of medicine? (People of faith prayed for the sick and did what they could to provide healing.)
- How do we know when sickness is or is not the result of sin?
- What is the relationship between prayer and healing?
- What should be our practice of confessing our faults to one another?

Share "God is the healer" from "Applying the Bible."

Give the Truth a Personal Focus

Read the last part of the "Teaching Aim" and ask members to suggest ways they can put their faith into action by doing good deeds. List these one a chalkboard or a large sheet of paper without comment. Encourage members to list ideas all ideas that come to their minds.

After all the ideas have been listed, ask members to choose one of these suggestions and seek to apply it to their lives this week.

Close in prayer for the determination to put this into practice.

Faith and Wisdom

Basic Passages: James 1:5–8; 3:1–5a,13–18
Focal Passages: James 1:5–8; 3:1–5a, 13–18

Wisdom is prominent in certain Bible books. The Book of Proverbs is the most obvious example. Wisdom is not the same as knowledge; instead, it is insight into God's will and its application to daily life. James stressed wisdom in several passages.

▶ ▶ ▶ ▶ ▶ ▶ ▶ ▶ **Study Aim:** *To identify characteristics of the kind of wisdom advocated in the Book of James*

STUDYING THE BIBLE

LESSON OUTLINE
I. Asking for Wisdom (James 1:5–8)
    1. Praying for wisdom (James 1:5)
    2. Praying in faith (James 1:6–8)
II. Wisdom in Speech (James 3:1–5a)
    1. A word of warning to teachers (James 3:1)
    2. Watching what we say (James 3:2–4)
    3. Sins of the tongue (James 3:5a)
III. True and False Wisdom (James 3:13–18)
    1. True wisdom (James 3:13)
    2. Worldly wisdom (James 3:14–16)
    3. Wisdom from above (James 3:17–18)

James wrote that believers should ask God for wisdom, and a generous and merciful God will answer the prayer (1:5). The prayer should be prayed in single-minded faith, not with doubts of either God's goodness or His power (1:5–8). Those who aspire to be teachers should recognize their accountability (3:1). People who can control what they say show great self-control; for although the tongue is small, it exerts great influence (3:2–4). Although small, the tongue boasts great things (3:5a). True wisdom is seen in a good life and a humble spirit (3:13). Worldly wisdom is of the devil, and is seen in such sins as envy and strife (3:14–16). God's wisdom shows itself in such things as purity, gentleness, humility, mercy, good works, impartial love, sincerity, and peacemaking (3:17–18).

I. Asking for Wisdom (James 1:5–8)
1. Praying for wisdom (v. 5)
    5 If any of you lack wisdom, let him ask of God, that giveth to all men liberally, and upbraideth not; and it shall be given him.
    Since wisdom is not the same as knowledge, one doesn't get wisdom by studying. Wisdom is a gift of God to those who ask in faith. In addition to wisdom, verse 5 stresses two other themes in James: the goodness of God (1:16–17) and prayer (4:2–3; 5:13–18).

God's character is the assurance that our prayers will be answered. He is a loving, generous God. His generosity is immeasurable. "Liberally" can be translated "generously." The words "upbraideth not" further explain the goodness of God. He does not look for ways to avoid giving us what we ask. God could keep bringing up our past sins and failures. He could point out that we have already received far more than we deserve. Since His blessings are gifts of grace, He continues to give generously.

2. Praying in faith (vv. 6–8)

> **6 But let him ask in faith, nothing wavering. For he that wavereth is like a wave of the sea driven with the wind and tossed.**
>
> **7 For let not that man think that he shall receive any thing of the Lord.**
>
> **8 A double minded man is unstable in all his ways.**

God is ready to answer our prayers, but our prayers must be real prayers. One condition of true prayer is faith. Faith involves trusting God's goodness to give us what we need and believing in God's power to meet our needs.

The opposite of this kind of faith is described in the last part of verse 6 and in verses 7–8. Doubting either the goodness or power of God is the opposite of faith. Doubters are compared to waves of the sea. The waves are constantly changing because they are subject to the power of the wind. Faith has a quality of constancy and perseverance like that described in verses 2–4.

Verse 8 describes such people as "double minded" and "unstable." This sheds further light on what James meant when he contrasted faith and doubt. Faith is single-minded commitment to the Lord. Doubt is trying to serve God and also live for ourselves, something Jesus said was impossible (see Matt. 6:24).

II. Wisdom in Speech (James 3:1–5a)

1. A word of warning to teachers (v. 1)

> **1 My brethren, be not many masters, knowing that we shall receive the greater condemnation.**

The word translated "masters" means "teachers." James wrote, "Not many of you should presume to be teachers, my brothers, because you know that we who teach will be judged more strictly" (NIV). In first-century church life, teachers were honored members of the community. They instructed believers in what to believe and how to live the Christian life. Judging from what James said, some people aspired to be teachers for the wrong reasons. They wanted the honor of the position, but they failed to be faithful stewards of the responsibility. James said that such people should not presume to be teachers.

God holds teachers more accountable for fulfilling their responsibility. James used "we," showing that he included himself among this highly accountable group. Teachers are accountable for speaking and living the truth. Their own daily words and deeds must be consistent with what they teach.

The words of James should not discourage any of us teachers from fulfilling what we believe to be God's calling for us. However, this verse from God's Word reminds us of our great responsibility to God and to those we teach.

2. Watching what we say (vv. 2–4)

2 For in many things we offend all. If any man offend not in word, the same is a perfect man, and able also to bridle the whole body.

Notice that James continued to use "we." He was aware that he and his fellow believers were not perfect. They continued to fall short in many ways. They were especially liable to fall short in the way they used words. James had teachers especially in mind, but he broadened his application to how any group uses the gift of speech. In many ways, controlling what we say is the supreme test. Whoever is able to control his tongue is usually able to exercise self-control over other areas of life. James did not use the word *perfect* in the sense of being without any sin. He used it in the sense Paul did in Philippians 3:12–14—pressing on toward God's purpose for us.

3 Behold, we put bits in the horses' mouths, that they may obey us; and we turn about their whole body.

4 Behold also the ships, which though they be so great, and are driven of fierce winds, yet are they turned about with a very small helm, whithersoever the governor listeth.

James gave two examples of something small that exercises control over something much larger. A rider controls a horse with a small bit in the horse's mouth. A pilot of a large ship steers the ship with a small rudder. James's point is not that the tongue controls the whole body, but that if a person could control his tongue, he would have the discipline to control all his actions.

3. Sins of the tongue (v. 5a)

5 Even so the tongue is a little member, and boasteth great things.

In verses 2–4, James wrote that people who can control what they say are people of exceptional self-discipline. In verse 5, James noted that although the tongue is a small part of the human body, this small member is loud in its boasting and great in its influence for evil. Verse 5 introduces a discussion on sins of the tongue. Verses 5b–12 are not part of this lesson, but you may want to read these verses to remind yourself of the evil power of an uncontrolled tongue.

III. True and False Wisdom (James 3:13–18)

1. True wisdom (v. 13)

13 Who is a wise man and endued with knowledge among you? let he shew out of a good conversation his works with meekness of wisdom.

The question in verse 13 implies that some of James's readers thought of themselves as especially wise. However, James pointed out that true wisdom is not shown by boasting. Instead real wisdom is shown by a way of life that doesn't need to boast of its accomplishments. The word translated "conversation" means "behavior" or "way of life." Thus verse 13 repeats a familiar theme in James: true wisdom, like true religion and faith, shows itself in good works (see 1:26–27; 2:14–26).

2. Worldly wisdom (vv. 14–16)

14 But if ye have bitter envying and strife in your hearts, glory not, and lie not against the truth.

15 This wisdom descendeth not from above, but is earthly, sensual, devilish.

16 For where envying and strife is, there is confusion and every evil work.

What about people who boast of being wise, but who practice envy and strife? They are lying when they claim to have true wisdom. The wisdom they have is not from above, but from below. James used three words in verse 15 to describe this false wisdom: it is earthly, not heavenly; sensual, not spiritual; of the devil, not of God. The inward selfishness of such people results in confusion, strife, and every evil work. Compare what James said about worldly wisdom with what Paul wrote about the works of the flesh in Galatians 5:19–21. Some of the same sins are on both lists because both James and Paul were describing the same thing—living by the standards of a world without God.

3. Wisdom from above (vv. 17–18)

17 But the wisdom that is from above is first pure, then peaceable, gentle, and easy to be intreated, full of mercy and good fruits, without partiality, and without hypocrisy.

18 And the fruit of righteousness is sown in peace of them that make peace.

Just as earthly wisdom is from the devil, so true wisdom is from God. James used several descriptions of heavenly wisdom. The words show that this wisdom does not relate to our IQ. James's list reminds us of similar lists elsewhere in the Bible. It reminds us of the Beatitudes of Jesus in Matthew 5:3–12 (see the session for May 5.) It is also like Paul's list of the fruit of the Spirit in Galatians 5:22–23.

The characteristics of true wisdom reflect what James wrote in other parts of his letter. James 1:26 warns of hypocrisy. Purity is mentioned is 1:27. Impartiality is the theme of 2:1–13. Acts of mercy are stressed in 1:27 and in 2:15–16. James 4:1–10 warns against strife and calls for humility and peaceful living. Thus, true wisdom includes a sincere commitment to God that is seen in how we live, especially in how we treat other people.

Verse 18 is not easy to translate. The point seems to be that those who love peace (v. 17) will also be those who seek to make peace. Jesus said, "Blessed are the peacemakers: for they shall be called the children of God" (Matt. 5:9). One way to translate verse 18 is, "Peacemakers who sow in peace raise a harvest of righteousness" (NIV). The efforts of peacemakers result in both peace and righteousness.

APPLYING THE BIBLE

1. Wisdom from above. As our lesson points out today, "'Wisdom' is not the same as knowledge; instead, it is insight into God's will and its application to daily life."

In a Keswick Week message, Paul Rees stated several things about this wisdom that comes from above: It is a gift (1:5); it is a gift for Christians (1:2—"brethren"); it is a gift for all believers who ask (1:5—"Any of you"); it is given liberally and sufficiently (1:5—"liberally"); it is a grace gift given by the Holy Spirit (1 Cor. 12:8); it is a gift given to help us live well the Christian life (1:2—"when ye fall into divers temptations"); and it is a gift whose first and all-inclusive quality is purity (3:14–16).[1]

2. Why John Milton kept his life pure. English poet and writer John Milton (1608–1674) was one of England's greatest writers. Perhaps he is best remembered for his "Paradise Lost" and "Paradise Regained." On a masterful passage written by Milton, he said that he was kept clean from the vices and immoralities that stained the lives of many of his young friends at college by two things: he recognized that he was created in God's image and did not want to sin against himself or God; and he knew what a great price Jesus had paid for his redemption.

This is an excellent example of how the wisdom of God reveals itself. It changes our priorities and strengthens our character. Our lesson shows how the wisdom of God reveals itself in the life of a believer: purity, gentleness, humility, mercy, good works, impartial love, sincerity, and peacemaking (3:17–18). Compare these attributes with the fruit of the Spirit of God (Gal. 5:22–23).

3. Caring for His regular customers. When the late Dr. Roy Angell was pastor of Central Baptist Church in Miami, Florida, a terrible hurricane struck the city. Angell told of a woman who called her pastor claiming that she had prayed her home would be protected. Instead, it was a total loss. The woman, who was not a regular churchgoer, asked the pastor why. And his answer was straight and simple: "I guess He was taking care of His regular customers!"

Prayer ought to be the regular, daily habit of our lives. We must cultivate the daily presence of God so that we can come boldly into His presence with our petitions (Heb. 4:14–16). Prayer is neither some kind of holy rabbit's foot nor a parachute to be used only in emergencies (1:6–8).

4. A proud, young preacher taught an embarrassing lesson. Henry Ward Beecher (1813–1887) was a powerful, dynamic preacher—nationally known in his day. Stranded one night in the Middle West, he decided to attend a revival service in the town. When he arrived at the church, the young, cocky pastor and all the congregation immediately recognized Beecher. Surrounded by a group of people, the pastor asked, "Dr. Beecher, how did you like my sermon? Did you get anything out of my sermon?"

"I did," Beecher confessed. "Three weeks ago I heard Phillips

Brooks (who wrote "O Little Town of Bethlehem") preach, and his message was so powerful I went away vowing never to preach again. But after hearing you, I have changed my mind!"

It was a rebuke said with tongue in cheek, but perhaps it sufficiently deflated the young preacher's pride that he went on to become an effective minister.[2]

Our lesson (3:1) points out that teachers in the first century churches were held in high regard. But James warns that "masters" (teachers) must aspire to teach from the right motives: to honor Christ, teach His word to new converts, and glorify the Savior. To teach from the desire to bring honor to oneself (pride) only brings "greater condemnation."

5. "Into the book it goes." Long ago, on a sailing vessel, the first mate got drunk and, although it was his first offense, the captain entered it into the ship's logs. The mate protested that this was his first offense, and the entry would cost him his job. But the captain wouldn't budge. "It's a fact and into the log it must go!"

Some days later, the mate had to make an entry into the log, and when he had completed his entry he wrote, "Captain sober today!" The captain was outraged because he was not a drinking man. But the mate insisted: "It is a fact and into the log it must go!"

James warns us about the terrible power of the tongue (3:2–12), or in this case any communication of any kind. And a half-truth can do as much damage as a full-fledged lie. Before we speak, we should test our words by this threefold test: Is it true? Is it necessary? And is it kind?

TEACHING THE BIBLE

▶ *Main Idea:* James's description of wisdom teaches that true wisdom comes from God.

▶ *Suggested Teaching Aim:* To lead adults to describe the characteristics of wisdom taught in James, and to commit themselves to seeking God's wisdom.

A TEACHING OUTLINE

1. *Use a graffiti wall to introduce the lesson.*
2. *Use a chart to define true wisdom.*
3. *Use a chart to identify characteristics of true and false wisdom.*
4. *Use a chart to encourage members to seek God's wisdom.*

Introduce the Bible Study

Place a large sheet of paper on a wall. As members enter, ask them to go to the graffiti wall and write either wise sayings or a definition of wisdom.

Read several of the wise sayings and then read some of the definitions of wisdom.

Search for Biblical Truth

IN ADVANCE, make the following poster except do not add the information in italics.

Faith and Wisdom

Wisdom: *"Wisdom is a gift of God to those who ask in faith."*
What is true wisdom: *Pure, peaceable, gentle, submissive, full of mercy and good fruits.*
In what does this true wisdom result? *Free from hypocrisy (1:26); purity (1:27); impartiality (2:1–13); acts of mercy (1:27; 2:15–16).*
What is false wisdom: *Earthly, sensual, devilish.*
In what does this false wisdom result? *Confusion, strife, every evil work.*

Ask a volunteer to read James 1:5–8. Based on this passage and on the definitions already read, ask members to formulate a definition of wisdom that would describe what James is talking about. Your definition should be similar to the one in the chart.

DISCUSS: What do we have to do to gain wisdom? (Ask God through prayer.) What is a person like who doubts God's goodness? (A wave of the sea, unstable.)

Ask a volunteer to read James 3:1–5a in a modern translation or define "masters" as teachers. Lecture briefly as you point out the following: (1) Teachers were honored members of the community. (2) God holds teachers more accountable for fulfilling their responsibility. (3) Those who control their speech usually exercise control over the rest of their lives. (4) Though the tongue is small, it controls something much larger—as does a bit and a rudder.

DISCUSS: Why would you agree or disagree with this statement: "Whoever is able to control his tongue is usually able to exercise self-control over other areas of life."

Ask a volunteer to read James 3:13–18. Ask members to listen for what true wisdom is and what false wisdom is. Then have them suggest what this passage says what false wisdom is. (Earthly, sensual, devilish.) Write these on the chart. Ask, In what does this false wisdom result? (Confusion, strife, every evil work.) Write these on the chart.

Ask, What are the characteristics of true wisdom? (Pure, peaceable, gentle, submissive, full of mercy, and good fruits.) Write these on the chart. In what does this true wisdom result? (Many things but consider: free from hypocrisy [1:26]; purity [1:27]; impartiality [2:1–13]; acts of mercy [1:27; 2:15–16].) Write these on the chart.

DISCUSS: How would you compare true wisdom with the Beatitudes of Jesus in Matthew 5:3–12 and Paul's list of the fruit of the Spirit in Galatians 5:22–23?

Give the Truth a Personal Focus

Ask members to look at the characteristics of true wisdom and to determine how many of these characteristics they have in their lives. Suggest that they choose one characteristic they do not have or one that is not strong in their lives to ask God for this week. Close in prayer that they may all have true wisdom.

---

1. Adapted from Paul Rees, *The Keswick Week* (London: Marshall, Morgan and Scott, Ltd., 1958), 19–21.

2. Adapted from Edgar DeWitt Jones, *Sermons I Love to Preach* (New York: Harper & Brothers, 1953), 158–159.

Faith and Righteousness

Basic Passages: James 4:1–10, 13–17
Focal Passages: James 4:1–10, 13–17

I n our studies in James, we have seen how he repeatedly called for practical applications of faith to daily life. In chapter 4, he analyzed the causes of human strife, issued a call to humble worship, and warned of forgetting that life is a fragile gift.

▶ ▶ ▶ ▶ ▶ ▶ ▶ ▶ ▶ **Study Aim:** *To identify three practical applications of Christian faith in the focal passages*

STUDYING THE BIBLE

LESSON OUTLINE
I. Causes of Strife (James 4:1–5)
    1. Selfishness, covetousness, and fighting (James 4:1–2a)
    2. Prayerlessness and selfish praying (James 4:2b–3)
    3. Friendship with the world (James 4:4–5)
II. Call to Worship (James 4:6–10)
    1. Grace to the humble (James 4:6)
    2. Submitting to God (James 4:7)
    3. Prescription for worship (James 4:8–10)
III. Making Plans Without God (James 4:13–17)
    1. Planning or presuming (James 4:13–16)
    2. Sins of omission (James 4:17)

Strife is caused by selfish desires and a covetous spirit (vv. 1–2a). Selfish people either do not pray, or they pray selfishly (vv. 2b–3). They are friends of the world because they are unfaithful to their God (vv. 4–5). God gives grace to the humble (v. 6). Those who submit to God are able to resist the devil's temptations (v. 7). James called people to cleanse their hands and purify their hearts in order to worship God (vv. 8–10). James warned people who make future plans without reference to God (v. 13). They forget that life is a fragile gift of God to be lived according to His will (vv. 14–16). Whoever fails to do what he knows to be good is guilty of sin (v. 17).

I. Causes of Strife (James 4:1–5)

1. Selfishness, covetousness, and fighting (vv. 1–2a)

1 From whence come wars and fightings among you? come they not hence, even of your lusts that war in your members?

2 Ye lust, and have not: ye kill, and desire to have, and cannot obtain: ye fight and war.

Strife is part of life at every level of society. If you look in any day's newspaper, you will read of battles between warring nations and groups. You will read of strife in our own country. You will read of strife within families, and perhaps you may even read about a church fight. Where does all this strife come from? James said that it begins with selfish desires. This selfishness is expressed in covetousness, which in turn leads to strife. If people are self-centered, they want more and more for themselves. They see others with things they want. They try to take those things for themselves, and they cling tightly to what they already claim as their own. When selfish, covetous people or groups come in contact, the result is strife.

2. Prayerlessness and selfish praying (vv. 2b–3)

    2 Yet ye have not, because ye ask not.

    3 Ye ask, and receive not, because ye ask amiss, that ye may consume it upon your lusts.

The kind of living that includes selfish desires, covetousness, and strife is life without a right relation with God. A person's prayer life reveals a person's relation with God. Verses 2b–3 set forth two faults of the prayer life of selfish people: (1) prayerlessness and (2) selfish praying. Many people simply never really pray. Because they have no real relation with God, they see no need to pray. However, at times worldly people do try to get something from God through prayer. They approach prayer as if God is a genie and prayer is a magic lamp.

3. Friendship with the world (vv. 4–5)

    4 Ye adulterers and adulteresses, know ye not that the friendship of the world is enmity with God? whosoever therefore will be a friend of the world is the enemy of God.

James may have been condemning people who were guilty of sexual adultery, a sin clearly condemned in God's Word (Exod. 20:14; 1 Cor. 6:9; Heb. 13:4; James 2:11). More likely, James was referring to the spiritual unfaithfulness of people to their God. The Bible uses marriage to describe the relation of God to His people (Isa. 54:1-6; Jer. 2:2; Eph. 5:22–32). Unfaithfulness to God is spiritual adultery (Jer. 3:20; Hos. 2:5, 7).

The "world" is not used in verse 4 to describe the good earth created by God (Gen. 1; Ps. 19). Nor was James referring to the world that God so loved when He gave His only Son (John 3:16). James was writing of the world of selfish desires, covetousness, and strife. Those who choose to live for this world set themselves against God (1 John 2:15–17).

    5 Do ye think that the scripture saith in vain, The spirit that dwelleth in us lusteth to envy?

The last part of verse 5 is not a quotation from the Bible, but an expression of a teaching found throughout the Bible. The human spirit tends to be selfish and envious of others. Often when we speak of worldliness, we think only of sins like drunkenness and sexual immorality. We forget that the sins of the flesh include sins like selfishness, envy, and strife (see James 3:14–16).

II. Call to Worship (James 4:6–10)

1. Grace to the humble (v. 6)

6 But he giveth more grace. Wherefore he saith, God resisteth the proud, but giveth grace unto the humble.

Over against the sins of humanity, James set the grace of God. Every good gift is from God, and His best gift is the gift of grace. He freely offers His grace to those caught in sin's deadly grasp. James quoted Proverbs 3:34 to illustrate his point. Proud people are not looking for God's grace. By contrast, humble people know they are dependent on God and His grace. This spirit of openness enables God to pour out His grace on them.

2. Submitting to God (v. 7)

7 Submit yourselves therefore to God. Resist the devil, and he will flee from you.

Some people try to resist temptation in their own strength. They are doomed to fail. Before people can successfully resist the devil, they must submit themselves to God. Then they can resist the devil, and he will flee from them.

3. Prescription for worship (vv. 8–10)

8 Draw nigh to God, and he will draw nigh to you. Cleanse your hands, ye sinners; and purify your hearts, ye double minded.

This could serve as an evangelistic invitation, but James used it as a call to come to worship. People of faith sometimes neglect the most important aspect of their lives—their relation to God. James called them to draw near to God. He promised that if they drew near to God, He would meet them in worship.

In the last part of verse 8, James seems to have had in mind Psalm 24:3–4. The psalm asked who was able to go up to the temple to worship. The answer was, "He that hath clean hands, and a pure heart." James called on believers to cleanse their hands and to purify their hearts so that they might worship God.

9 Be afflicted, and mourn, and weep: let your laughter be turned to mourning, and your joy to heaviness.

Verse 9 is reminiscent of Joel 2:12. Joel and James called would-be worshipers to weep and mourn. They were addressing people who had allowed their sins to dull their moral and spiritual sensitivity. Such people needed to see themselves as God saw them. If they did, they would see their callous hearts and be moved to repent. When James mentioned "laughter" and "joy," he was thinking of the superficial pleasure of worldly living, not the true joy of walking with the Lord.

10 Humble yourselves in the sight of the Lord, and he shall lift you up.

Humility is the opposite of the worldly strife and pride described in James 3:14–16 and 4:1–5. Humility recognizes that God and His will are what count, not me and my wants. Humility recognizes that God has a large family of children of whom I am only one. Because God loves all His children, I must seek to live with and love my brothers and sisters.

III. Making Plans Without God
(James 4:13–17)

1. Planning or presuming? (vv. 13–16)

13 Go to now, ye that say, To day or to morrow we will go into such a city, and continue there a year, and buy and sell, and get gain:

This verse sounds like a sales meeting in a modern business. Notice the aspects of their plan: when the plan would be launched, where they would go, how long they would stay, and what they would do. The planners also took for granted that the venture would produce a profit.

What's wrong with that? Shouldn't business people make such plans? Shouldn't they do their best to make the business profitable? For answers, read on.

14 Whereas ye know not what shall be on the morrow. For what is your life? It is even a vapour, that appeareth for a little time, and then vanisheth away.

James was not against long-range planning. He was reflecting a consistent biblical warning against the dangers of forgetting that life is a fragile gift. James described life as a mist that soon disappears. Elsewhere the Bible compares life to a breath (Ps. 39:5), a cloud (Job 7:9), and a shadow (Ps. 102:11). When James wrote verse 14, he may have had in mind Proverbs 27:1, "Boast not thyself of to morrow; for thou knowest not what a day may bring forth." James was not suggesting that all future planning is wrong because life is short and uncertain. He was not advocating a passive fatalism that waits around for sure death. He was condemning worldly presumption that falsely assumes that life is under human control.

15 For that ye ought to say, If the Lord will, we shall live, and do this, or that.

16 But now ye rejoice in your boastings: all such rejoicing is evil.

James warned against leaving out God and His will. Verses 15–16 show that this was the problem with the business meeting in verse 13. The planners in verse 13 were like the rich farmer in the parable of Luke 12:16–21. The farmer was not condemned as dishonest or as one who exploited others. He was condemned because he was so preoccupied with his possessions that he left God out of His life and His plans.

Verse 15 calls people to recognize that life is the gift of God. He gives us life, and we become accountable for how we use this fragile gift. We can forget God and assume that life is ours to do with as we please. Verse 16 says that this kind of blind pride is deadly and evil. The proper way to live is to recognize God as the giver of life and to seek His direction about how to use this precious gift.

2. Sins of omission (v. 17)

17 Therefore to him that knoweth to do good, and doeth it not, to him it is sin.

James had just told his readers that their lives needed to be lived in relation to God and His will. People who know this but fail to do it are guilty of sin. However, the principle stated in verse 17 has a broader application than to the issue in verses 13–16. Many people feel self-righteous because they don't commit some of the more obvious sins. This verse is a sober reminder that sin is not just the evil we do and say— it is also the good we left undone and unsaid.

APPLYING THE BIBLE

1. The Beatitudes paraphrased. J. B. Phillips has paraphrased the self-centered person's beatitudes like this:

Happy are the pushers: for they get on in the world.
Happy are the hard-boiled; for they never let life
hurt them.
Happy are they who complain; for they get their own way.
Happy are the blasè: for their sins never worry them.
Happy are the slave drivers; for they get results
Happy are those worldly knowledgeable: for they know
their way around.
Happy are the trouble-makers; for people know them.

2. The curse of unfaithfulness. There is no blight on Christ's church as great as the curse of unfaithfulness. Our church rolls in America are swelled with the names of professing believers who cannot be found, who never attend, and who never give a dime to support God's work. The only time they come to church is Easter Sunday morning or to attend a funeral. What could the church be and do in the world if the unfaithful members really meant business for Jesus? Look at your worship service this morning. How large is your church roll, but how small is the attendance in your services?

Even the Bible lists the names of some of God's servants who were unfaithful to Him in given instances. What would the world be like today if Adam and Eve had been faithful to their Creator? What about Noah, who faithfully built the ark and then made a shamble of things? Would Sodom have been saved if Abraham had prayed more for the city to be spared? Did his stopping with ten righteous people disappoint God (Gen. 18:32–33)? How much did Moses disappoint God with his excuse making? Jonah is another one. King Saul, chosen by the people and permitted by God, was Israel's first king. But at the end of his life he sadly confessed, "I have played a fool" (interpreted: "I have been unfaithful"). James condemns friendship with the world "playing it safe" and unfaithfulness to God (4:4–5).

3. "I just couldn't resist." More than once in my experience as a pastor, a brokenhearted church member has said in the quietness of my office, confessing a sin that was torturing him or her: "I just could not resist. An adulterer, an adulteress, a thief, a bank embezzler, a murderer—we pastors have heard it all.

The excuse, "I just could not resist," won't hold water. It contradicts the Word of God, for James says in 4:7, "Submit yourselves therefore to God. Resist the devil, and he will flee from you." But those who try to resist the devil in their own strength are doomed to fail. Only Christ's strength is sufficient (Phil. 4:13).

4. God has called us to be holy. God's Word for His people is *saints.* It appears about ninety-nine times in Scripture—sixty-two times in the New Testament and thirty-seven times in the Old Testament. *Believers* appears two times, and *Christians* appears three times.

To be holy means to be separated: separated from a sinful life and separated from the world's ways to serve God. Holiness is Christianity put into motion. It is God's love flowing through us and reaching out in love to others. It is faith gone to work. It is love and compassion coined into actions. It is purity of life and piety in prayer (4:8-10). Holiness is the goal Jesus has set for each of us (Col. 1:21–22).

5. The humility of a great tenor. Roland Hayes, an African-American singer, gained international fame as a great tenor. Born in poverty in Georgia in 1877, he never knew his father and had few advantages. But he did have a devout Christian mother. The doors of opportunity were opened for Hayes when a teacher at the Oberlin Conservatory of Music happened to hear Hayes sing. Years later, when he was invited to sing at Buckingham Palace before the king of England, he was nearly overcome with fear and cabled his mother for strength. She cabled back the simple encouragement: "Remember who you are." By that she meant Hayes was a Christian before he was known around the world.

It's good advice. When our pride begins to puff us up, we need to remember we are followers of the humble Galilean in whom there was no pride.

June
30
1996

TEACHING THE BIBLE

▶ *Main Idea:* Living by faith and righteousness will eliminate self-centeredness and strife in our lives.

▶ *Suggested Teaching Aim:* To lead adults to identify three practical applications of the Christian faith, and to choose one application they will accept for their lives.

A TEACHING OUTLINE

1. Introduce the Bible study by sharing an illustration.
2. Use a symposium panel to describe three practical applications of the Christian faith.
3. Challenge members to choose one application they will seek to make a part of their lives.

Introduce the Bible Study

Share the illustration, "The humility of a great tenor" from "Applying the Bible." Point out that this type of humility would eliminate much of the strife in our world.

Search for Biblical Truth

IN ADVANCE, make three strip posters with the following on them:

I. Causes of Strife (James 4:1–5)

PAGE
335

II. Call to Worship (James 4:6–10)

III. Making Plans Without God (James. 4:13–17)

IN ADVANCE, enlist three members to participate in a symposium-forum. Arrange four chairs at the front for you and the participants. Give each participant one of the following assignments. After each presentation, let members ask questions.

Participant 1: Causes of Strife (James 4:1–5)

Study these verses and be prepared to explain difficult words, concepts, and ideas. Keep in mind that the main idea of the lesson is that living by faith and righteousness will eliminate self-centeredness and strife in our lives. Be prepared to answer questions from the class after your presentation. Be sure you cover these specific points:

(1) How self-centeredness causes strife.

(2) The two faults of the prayer life of selfish people: (a) prayerlessness and (b) selfish praying.

(3) Define "adulterers and adulteresses" as spiritual unfaithfulness of God's people.

(4) The worldliness of selfishness, envy, and strife.

Participant 2: Call to Worship (James 4:6–10)

Study these verses and be prepared to explain difficult words, concepts, and ideas. Keep in mind that the main idea of the lesson is that living by faith and righteousness will eliminate self-centeredness and strife in our lives. Be prepared to answer questions from the class after your presentation. Be sure you cover these specific points:

(1) God's gift of grace to humanity.

(2) God's strength allows us to resist the devil.

(3) The need to make proper preparation for worship.

(4) The need for seriousness in our attitudes when we come to worship God.

(5) The part humility plays in our relationship to God and others.

Participant 3: Making Plans Without God 4:13–16)

Study these verses and be prepared to explain difficult words, concepts, and ideas. Keep in mind that the main idea of the lesson is that living by faith and righteousness will eliminate self-centeredness and strife in our lives. Be prepared to answer questions from the class after your presentation. Be sure you cover these specific points:

(1) The proper attitude toward planning for the future.

(2) The fragileness of life.

(3) The danger of assuming that life is under our control.

(4) Life is a gift from God.

(5) The sinfulness of sins of omission.

Give the Truth a Personal Focus

Challenge members to choose one of the areas discussed and decide on one application they will seek to make a part of their lives. Ask them to write one specific step they will take to implement this.

God Is with Us (Psalms)

INTRODUCTION

The Book of Psalms was the hymnbook of the people of Israel. The presence of God is one of the central themes of the psalms. Nearly every psalm is related to the fact that God is present in the world and is lovingly and purposefully involved in the lives of people. The psalms praise God and call for a response to God's presence.

Unit I, "Praising God," shows how the people of God are called to praise: God who creates and sustains (Ps. 104), God who has acted on behalf of His people (Ps. 105), God who delivers from trouble (Ps. 34), and God who knows and cares (Ps. 139).

Unit II, "Responding to God," focuses on the following responses: trusting in God (Ps. 40), obeying God's Word (Ps. 119), repenting and confessing (Ps. 51), and worshiping and witnessing (Ps. 96).

Praising God as Creator and Sustainer

Basic Passage: Psalm 104
Focal Passage: Psalm 104:24–34

P salm 104 is one of the so-called nature psalms. These include Psalms 8; 19; 65; 147; and 148. These psalms deal with the relation of God to His created universe. Psalm 104 is a hymn of praise to God as Creator and Sustainer of the heavens and the earth. The psalm is particularly noted for its descriptions of the interrelations between God and His creation and among the various parts of His creation—animate and inanimate, other forms of life and human life. Thus it may be called the ecology psalm.

▶ ▶ ▶ ▶ ▶ ▶ ▶ ▶ **Study Aim:** *To praise God as Creator and Sustainer of our lives and of all His creations*

STUDYING THE BIBLE

LESSON OUTLINE
   I. Praising God as Creator (Ps. 104:1–9)
      1. A call to praise God (Ps. 104:1)
      2. Creator of the heavens (Ps. 104:2–4)
      3. Creator of earth (Ps. 104:5–9)
   II. Praising God as Sustainer (Ps. 104:10–30)
      1. Sustainer of life (Ps. 104:10–18)
      2. Moon, sun, and time (Ps. 104:19–23)
      3. Praise for the variety and purpose of God's works
         (Ps. 104:24)
      4. The sea and sea life (Ps. 104:25–26)
      5. Preserver of Life (Ps. 104:27–30)
   III. Praise Ye the Lord (Ps. 104:31–35)
      1. God's enduring glory (Ps. 104:31–32)
      2. Praising the Lord (Ps. 104:33–35)

Psalm 104 begins with a call to bless the Lord and with an actual praise to God (v. 1). In figurative language, the psalmist describes how God created the heavens (vv. 2–4). He created the earth by commanding the water to withdraw, thus making mountains and valleys (vv. 5–9). God sustains life by providing springs and sending rains for man and beast, by providing trees for birds, and by making mountains for mountain animals (vv. 10–18). God gives the sun and moon to provide seasons and to provide night for nocturnal animals and day for man to work (vv. 19–23). The psalmist praised God for the variety and purpose of His works (v. 24). God made and sustains a vast variety of large and small sea life, including the mighty sea monsters, which He made for play (vv. 25–26). God gives food with an open hand to all living things; and although God gives and takes away the breath of life, He continues to renew the earth with new life (vv. 27–30). The psalmist declared the enduring glory of God (vv. 31–32). He committed himself to sing praises to God all his life and to continue to find joy in meditation (vv. 33–35).

I. Praising God as Creator (Ps. 104:1–9)

1. A call to praise God (v. 1). The psalmist called himself to praise the Lord, using the same words with which Psalm 103 begins and ends. Then the psalmist responded to his own call with praise directed to the Lord His God for His greatness, honor, and majesty.

2. Creator of the heavens (vv. 2–4). Using figurative language, the psalmist described God's creation of the heavens. God, who was covered with a garment of light, stretched out the heavens like a man pulling a tent over its frame (v. 2). The clouds became God's chariot and the angels His messengers (vv. 3–4).

3. Creator of earth (vv. 5–9). God laid the foundations of the earth and used water to cover it like a garment (vv. 5–6). At God's thunderous command, the waters receded so that the mountains and valleys were formed (vv. 7–8). God set boundaries for the waters (v. 9).

II. Praising God as Sustainer (Ps. 104:10–30)

1. Sustainer of life (vv. 10–18). God gives springs to provide life-sustaining water for animals and birds (vv. 10–12). From His storehouse, God sends rain to water the earth (v. 13). God makes the grass grow for cattle to eat and provides plants for people to cultivate to produce wine, oil, and bread (vv. 14–15). God, not man, planted the huge cedars of Lebanon (v. 16). God provides trees in which the birds build their nests (v. 17). God made the mountains as home for the wild goats and rock badgers (conies, v. 18).

2. Moon, sun, and time (vv. 19–23). God uses the moon to signal the seasons and tells the sun when to set (v. 19). He provides the night for the nocturnal beasts of the forest (v. 20). The roar of the lions is a prayer to God for food (v. 21). At sunrise the lions go to their dens to rest (v. 22). During the day people arise and go about their work until the evening (v. 23).

3. Praise for the variety and purpose of God's works (v. 24)
> 24 O Lord, how manifold are thy works! in wisdom hast thou made them all: the earth is full of thy riches.

As the psalmist thought of the variety of God's creative and sustaining works, he was overwhelmed and moved to praise. As the psalmist looked at the vast creations of God and saw God's sustaining work among His creations, he was moved by the unfathomable wisdom of God. He didn't profess to understand all that God had done and was doing, but he was convinced of God's wise and good purpose back of all His workings.

Believers in every age agree with the psalmist. We look at the grandeur of the natural world and at the amazing beings that we humans are. We see the hand of the Creator in both. Although we cannot explain how God created all things or how He goes about sustaining His creation, we see His wisdom and His goodness in ourselves and in the rest of what God created. Like the psalmist, we lift our hearts and voices in praise to God.

4. The sea and sea life (vv. 25–26)

25 So is this great and wide sea, wherein are things creeping innumerable, both small and great beasts.

26 There go the ships: there is that leviathan, whom thou hast made to play therein.

Among God's creations which He sustains is the great and wide sea. The sea teems with living things, both tiny and huge things. The word "creeping" can be translated "teeming" (NIV). Among the huge sea creatures was "leviathan," a giant sea creature that probably was what we call a whale.

Notice what the psalmist says about the purpose of these giant creatures of the sea. God made them to play in the sea. God made them "to frolic there" (NIV). Some scholars think the word means "play with." Nothing is said here about these creatures as food for the benefit of human beings. Instead the Bible says they were created to play in the sea, perhaps even for God Himself to enjoy as they frolicked in the vast sea. Verse 26 doesn't deny that the same creatures were intended for other uses also, but it states their primary purpose as joyful play.

God created human beings as trustees over the rest of creation (Gen. 1:28). Some people have distorted this divine commission as an excuse to plunder and pollute God's creation without respect for all that God created. Only human beings were created in the divine image, but God loves and cares for all His creation. This is one message that is clear in Psalm 104.

5. Preserver of life (vv. 27–30)

27 These wait all upon thee; that thou mayest give them their meat in due season.

28 That thou givest them they gather: thou openest thine hand, they are filled with good.

The "all" refers to all living things, not just to sea life. All living things wait upon their benevolent Creator to provide food at the proper time. The waiting does not mean passive waiting, for living things themselves must gather their food.

However, the bounty they gather are actually good things provided from the open hand of God.

Jesus taught His followers not to be anxious about food and clothing. He told them how the heavenly Father feeds the birds. Then He said that if God so cared for the birds, how much more would He care for His highest creation (see Matt. 6:25–34)?

29 Thou hidest thy face, they are troubled: thou takest away

their breath, they die, and return to their dust.

30 Thou sendest forth thy spirit, they are created: and thou renewest the face of the earth.

God who created all things sustains all things. He gives the gift of life, and He brings life to an end. Life is described in verse 29 as "breath." The Genesis account of the flood refers to living things as having "the breath of life" (see Gen. 6:17; 7:15, 22). Both the Hebrew and Greek words for "breath" can also be translated "spirit." Thus verse 29 refers to the death that comes to living things when God takes away their breath, and verse 30 refers to God sending His breath or Spirit to give the gift of life to living things. Verse 30 affirms the continuing creative work of God as He gives life to succeeding generations of the offspring of His original creations. Because people are created in God's image, we are capable of relating to God in a way that other living things cannot. However, God is the giver of life and breath to all living things.

III. Praise Ye the Lord (Ps. 104:31–35)
1. God's enduring glory (vv. 31–32)

31 The glory of the Lord shall endure for ever: the Lord shall rejoice in his works.

As the psalmist looked to the future, he predicted that the glory of the Lord would last forever. The psalmist pictured God Himself finding joy in all His works. The verse may be translated as a prayer, "May the glory of the Lord endure forever" (NIV). If it was a prayer, the prayer was prayed with confidence that it would be answered. The psalmist was sure that the eternal Creator and Sustainer's glory would endure forever. He was prophesying and praying that all beings would join in glorifying God.

32 He looketh on the earth, and it trembleth: he toucheth the hills, and they smoke.

The psalmist was aware that God the Creator is also God the Judge. At times He must move with judgment against some of His creatures. The earth trembles at the look of God when He comes in judgment. When He touches the hills, they smoke.

2. Praising the Lord (vv. 33–35)

33 I will sing unto the Lord as long as I live: I will sing praise to my God while I have my being.

This is probably the strongest commitment to praise in Psalm 104, and one of the strongest in the Bible. First of all, it shows that the psalmist committed himself to express his praises to God in song. This makes sense when we remember that the psalms were hymns sung in Hebrew worship. We also know from experience that singing is a natural as well as a spiritual way to express our praises to God. Paul and Silas sang praises to God while they were in the Philippian jail (Acts 16:25). Paul wrote, "Let the word of Christ dwell in you richly in all wisdom; teaching and admonishing one another in psalms and hymns and spiritual songs, singing with grace in your hearts to the Lord" (Col. 3:16).

The other thing to notice about verse 33 is that the psalmist committed himself to sing praises to the Lord as long as he had life and breath. This shows that he considered singing praises to God to be an essential part of life for people of faith.

> **34 My meditation of him shall be sweet: I will be glad in the Lord.**

Singing praises is done openly and often with others. Meditation is more often done silently and alone with God. The psalmist knew that praises to God include both the outward singing of praises and the inner quietness of fellowship with God. Such quiet meditation was sweet to him. It added to the joy and gladness of his life in God.

Verse 35 ends where the psalm began with the psalmist calling himself and others to bless the Lord.

APPLYING THE BIBLE

1. Singing in Sing Sing. B. B. McKinney, a great hymn writer, wrote "Have Faith in God." It is well remembered today. Often he said: "People who can sing and won't sing ought to be sent to Sing Sing and made to sing until they will sing!"

The Book of Psalms was the hymn book of the people of Israel. Singing was a very vital part of their worship experience, and it ought to be a vital part of our worship today. As the psalmist committed himself to be a rejoicing, singing believer all his life, so we should practice the same habit (vv. 33–35).

2. Praise to God. We spend too much time in prayer telling God what we need and too little time praising Him for His goodness and mercy. God wants our praise and rejoices in it. This psalmist knew that well, and opens our lesson today with a strong affirmation of praise to God: "Bless the Lord, O my soul (v. 1), and closes it with the same attitude: "Bless thou the Lord, O my soul. Praise ye the Lord (v. 35).

For a good while, when I was a young pastor, I struggled with the concept of blessing God. How could I possibly bless Him who is everything and has everything? I discovered the answer: by praising His holy name. As God blesses me with manifold blessings, so I can bless Him with manifold praise.

3. The heart of a mouse. There is an old fable about a mouse who was in constant fear of the cat, so a magician turned the mouse into a cat. Then the cat was afraid of the dog, so the magician turned the cat into a dog. Then the dog was afraid of the tiger so the magician turned the dog into a tiger. Immediately, the tiger was afraid of the hunter. Aggravated that he could not satisfy the mouse, the magician said, "Be a mouse again, for you only have the heart of a mouse, and I cannot help you."

The ancient mariners used to pray, "O God, thy sea is so large, and my ship is so small." We have put men on the moon and are now reaching for Mars and outer space. Indeed, how great is God's creation, and how small are we and our ship. But remember that small though we are in a universe with billions upon billions of suns and stars, we are so important that Christ died for us!

4. Animal facts and oddities. Male silkworms have such a keen sense of smell they can detect a female 6 1/2 miles away in the mating season. Flying fish can stay airborne for 1000 feet. Land crabs found in Cuba can run faster than a horse. Tortoises of the Galapagos Islands can live to be 190 years old. Whales weigh 195 tons. Bee humming-birds are so small it takes 18 of them to weigh an ounce. Cobras strike and kill 10,000 people in India alone each year. Gazelles drink no wa-ter. Their chemical processes extract moisture from solid food. Swifts are the world's fastest birds, and can fly up to 200 miles per hour. A human being holds the record for the longest recorded life-span of any known mammal—at least 130 years and perhaps more[1] (according to the Bible many lived much longer). Methuselah lived 969 years (Gen. 5:27), and Noah lived 950 years (Gen. 9:28).

And God not only created them all, but He sustains them (vv. 11–14, 17–18).

5. Facts about the earth. The earth's surface comprises 196,950 square miles, and is the heaviest of all planets, the fifth largest, and the third out from the sun. Its diameter at the equator is 7,926.68 miles, and from pole to pole the diameter is 7,900 miles. Saltwater oceans oc-cupy 72 percent of the earth's surface. Each rotation about its axis re-quires 23 hours, 56 minutes and 4.09 seconds, revolving at a speed of about 17.5 miles per minute. Our earth travels about 18.5 miles per second. The average speed at which our entire solar system is circling within the Milky Way galaxy, of which our earth and solar system are a part, is 180 miles per second. Then why don't we fall off into space in all this movement?[2]

God thought of that, too. One day while Isaac Newton was drinking a cup of tea, he saw an apple fall from a tree. And God told Newton the secret: gravity!

We know far more about the heavens and the earth than did the psalmist. How much more joyously, then, should we shout the benedic-tion, "Praise ye the Lord"?

TEACHING THE BIBLE

▶ *Main Idea:* Praising God as Creator and Sustainer acknowledges our dependence on Him.
▶ *Suggested Teaching Aim:* To lead adults to describe how the psalmist declared his response to God, and to determine how they will praise God.

A TEACHING OUTLINE

1. Use an illustration to introduce the study.
2. Use three listening teams to identify why and how we should praise God.
3. Use brainstorming to list ways members can praise God in their lives.

Introduce the Bible Study

Read "Facts about the earth" from "Applying the Bible" to introduce the lesson. Point out that the Creator of this marvelous earth is worthy of all praise.

Search for Biblical Truth

IN ADVANCE, make a unit poster and include the title of the lesson, the psalms being studied, and the date. Display this each week. Use an arrow cut from brightly colored paper to indicate which lesson is being studied each week.

Enlist two other people to help you introduce the unit. Give one person a copy of the paragraph describing Unit I and give the other person a copy of the paragraph describing Unit II ("Introduction"). Read the first paragraph yourself and then call for the other two readers to read theirs. Point out that for the next two months you will be studying various psalms.

Point out today's lesson on the unit poster. Use "Studying the Bible" to briefly summarize Psalm 104:10–23. Ask a volunteer to read 104:24–32. On a chalkboard or a large sheet of paper, write: Why we should praise the Lord? As the reader reads ask members to listen for reasons the psalmist and we should praise God. Ask a third of the class to be responsible for 104:24–26; a third to be responsible for 104:27–30; and a third to be responsible for 104:31–32.

Ask the first group to share reasons the psalmist gave for praising God. (Their answers may differ but consider: *works, wisdom, riches, sea.*) Write their responses on the chalkboard or large sheet of paper.

Ask the second group to share reasons the psalmist gave for praising God. (Provides food for creation, controls life and death, creates by His Spirit.)

Be prepared to share information from "Studying the Bible" that would help members understand these reasons.

Ask the third group to share reasons the psalmist gave for praising God. (Glory of the Lord, judgment.)

Write on the chalkboard or large sheet of paper: How should we praise the Lord? Ask a volunteer to read 104:33–34. Ask members to list ways the psalmist suggested he would praise the Lord. (Sing as long as he had breath, meditate, be glad.)

Give the Truth a Personal Focus

Ask members to suggest ways this psalm would help them to praise the Lord in a contemporary setting. List all of the ideas on the chalkboard or large sheet of paper. Encourage members to list all ideas that come to their minds. After all the ideas have been listed, go back over the list and ask members silently to choose the two that would appeal most to them. Then ask members to choose one of these two that they will apply to their lives this week. Allow about two or three minutes for members to list some ways they will put this method of praise in practice.

Close by asking members to turn to 104:35 and read the last part of the verse in unison. Even if they have various translations, ask them to read aloud.

1. Adapted from David Wallenchinsky and Irving Wallace, *The People's Almanac* (Garden City, N.Y.: Doubleday and Co., 1975), 695.
   2. Ibid., 678.

Praising God for Mighty Acts

Basic Passage: Psalm 105
Focal Passages: Psalms 105:1-11, 43–45

P salm 105 is one of the hymns that reminded the Hebrews of God's acts in history (see also Pss. 78; 106; and 114). The psalm recited God's past acts of deliverance and guidance in the life of Israel. The remembrance of God's mighty acts moved the people to praise God and bear testimony to Him. The first part of Psalm 105 (vv. 1–15) was sung along with Psalm 96 and part of Psalm 106 when the ark of the covenant was brought to Jerusalem (see 1 Chron. 16; see vv. 8–22).

▶ ▶ ▶ ▶ ▶ ▶ ▶ ▶ **Study Aim:** *To praise God for His mighty acts of deliverance for His people*

STUDYING THE BIBLE

LESSON OUTLINE
  I. Call to Remember, Testify, and Worship (Ps. 105:1–6)
    1. Give thanks, pray, sing praises, and testify (Ps. 105:1–2)
    2. Glory in His name and seek His presence (Ps. 105:3–4)
    3. Remember His mighty acts (Ps. 105:5–6)
  II. Remembering the God Who Remembers (Ps. 105:7–45)
    1. Sovereign Lord over all (Ps. 105:7)
    2. The God who remembers His covenant (Ps. 105:8–11)
    3. Leading and protecting the patriarchs (Ps. 105:12–15)
    4. Bringing good out of evil in the life of Joseph
      (Ps. 105:16–23)
    5. Delivering Israel from Egypt (Ps. 105:24–38)
    6. Guided and fed in the wilderness (Ps. 105:39–41)
    7. Praise the God who remembers His covenant
      (Ps. 105:42–45)

The psalmist called people to give thanks, pray, sing, and testify (vv. 1–2). He called them to glory in God and seek His presence (vv. 3–4). Above all, they were to remember God and His mighty works on their behalf (vv. 5–6). They confessed their faith in the sovereign Lord of all the earth (v. 7). God remembered His covenant with Abraham, Isaac, and Jacob—to bring their descendants into the land of Canaan (vv. 8–11). God guided and protected the patriarchs (vv. 12-15). He brought good out of evil and used Joseph to provide care for his family (vv. 16–23). When the Israelites were mistreated in Egypt, God's mighty power delivered them and blessed them (vv. 24–38). The Lord led Israel and fed them in the wilderness (vv. 39–41). Since God faithfully remembered His promise to give Israel the land, they should obey His laws and praise Him (vv. 42–45).

I. Call to Remember, Testify, and Worship (Ps. 105:1–6)

1. Give thanks, pray, sing praises, and testify (vv. 1–2)

1 O give thanks unto the Lord; call upon His name: make known his deeds among the people.

2 Sing unto him, sing psalms unto him: talk ye of all his wondrous works.

Verses 1–2 provide a call to worship. The people of Israel were called to do four things: (1) give thanks to the Lord for His deliverance and blessings, (2) call on His name in confession and prayer, (3) sing praises to the Lord, and (4) declare and show God's mighty acts among the people of the world. These four aspects of worship form the structure of worship in every generation. When we come together to worship God, we give thanks to God for His blessings, we lift our hearts to Him in prayer, we sing praises to Him, and we proclaim His mighty acts to all.

2. Glory in His name and seek His presence (vv. 3–4)

3 Glory ye in his holy name: let the heart of them rejoice that seek the Lord.

4 Seek the Lord, and his strength: seek his face evermore.

The call to worship continued in verses 3–4. Verse 3 affirms a fact about true worship. Those who worship the Lord glory in Him and His holy character. True worship is a joyful experience of celebration of God's past blessings and abiding presence with His people. Verse 4 is a call for people of faith to seek the Lord in this kind of true worship. These words were used to summon people to join other worshipers on the way to God's sanctuary. They were to join others in seeking God's presence and in drawing fresh strength from His presence.

Even in biblical times, some would-be worshipers were neglecting the assembling of themselves together (see Heb. 10:25). God's Word summons all people of faith not to neglect this essential aspect of life. Our faith needs to be expressed and our spiritual life needs to be renewed in worship.

3. Remember His mighty acts (vv. 5–6)

5 Remember his marvellous works that he hath done; his wonders, and the judgments of his mouth;

6 O ye seed of Abraham his servant, ye children of Jacob his chosen.

The word *remember* is an important word in the Old Testament, the key to Psalm 105, and an essential element in true faith. In the Old Testament, "remember" was used repeatedly to call the people of Israel to remember God and what He had done for His people. Deuteronomy especially emphasizes the need to remember. At the end of the Fourth Commandment are these words, "And remember that thou wast a servant in the land of Egypt, and that the Lord thy God brought thee out thence through a mighty hand and by a stretched out arm" (Deut. 5:15). As the Israelites prepared to enter Canaan, Moses warned them not to forget, but to "remember the Lord thy God" (Deut. 8:18).

Psalm 105:1–6 forms a call to worship by remembering the mighty acts of the Lord. The body of the psalm is a summary of some of these mighty acts of the Lord. Beginning with God's covenant with Abraham, Isaac, and Jacob, the psalmist recited God's acts of deliverance for His people until He led them into the promised land.

People of faith in every generation must know who they are and whose they are. An essential to achieving this is remembering the mighty acts of God in the past—not just our individual pasts, but His past dealings with His people. Some people claim to hate history. Others do their best to ignore history. The Bible, in its divine wisdom, calls us to remember history, because eyes of faith see history as "His story."

People of faith see the hand of God in the events of history. The Bible was written by people of such faith who under the Spirit's direction highlighted the mighty acts of God on our behalf. Psalm 105 ends with the entry into Canaan, but the rest of the Old Testament adds to His story; and the New Testament tells of the coming, life, death, and resurrection of God's Son, Jesus Christ. When we worship, we begin by remembering, thanking God, and proclaiming what God has done, is doing, and will do.

II. Remembering the God Who Remembers (Ps. 105:7–45)

1. Sovereign Lord over all (v. 7)

7 He is the Lord our God: his judgments are in all the earth.

The main section of the psalm begins with a confession of faith. The word translated "Lord" is "Yahweh," the personal name of God as He had revealed Himself to His chosen people. He was their God in a special way, but the psalmist recognized that He was also sovereign Lord over all the earth.

2. The God who remembers His covenant (vv. 8–11)

8 He hath remembered his covenant for ever, the word which he commanded to a thousand generations.

The same word for *remember* is used in verse 5 of Israel's need to remember the Lord and in verse 8 of the Lord's remembering of His covenant with the people of Israel. In other words, Psalm 105 is a call to remember the God who remembers. In both cases, *remember* means more than "having a memory of something." The word includes the meaning of "being faithful to what has been promised." As applied to the Lord, it meant that He would faithfully fulfill His promises to Israel. As applied to Israel, it called on them to remember what God had done for them and remain faithful to Him.

9 Which covenant he made with Abraham, and his oath unto Isaac;

10 And confirmed the same unto Jacob for a law, and to Israel for an everlasting covenant:

11 Saying, Unto thee will I give the land of Canaan, the lot of your inheritance.

Verses 9–11 focus on the covenant God made. He made it with

Abraham (see Gen. 15:18–21). God renewed it with Isaac (see Gen. 26:2–5). The Lord repeated the covenant promise to Jacob (see Gen. 28:13–15). Jacob's name was changed to Israel, and His descendants became the children of Israel. The covenant with Abraham, Isaac, and Jacob thus was a covenant with all Israel. The covenant with Israel was sealed at Mount Sinai (see Ex. 19:1–6). A central feature of the covenant was to give the children of Israel the land of Canaan. The rest of Psalm 105 reminded later generations of Israelites how God faithfully kept that promise.

3. Leading and protecting the patriarchs (vv. 12–15). Having mentioned the patriarchs in verses 9–10, the psalmist described how they were few in number and sojourners in the lands through which they journeyed (vv. 12–13). God preserved and protected them from their powerful enemies (vv. 14–15).

4. Bringing good out of evil in the life of Joseph (vv. 16–23). God used a famine as an indirect blessing (v. 16). He allowed Joseph to pass through severe trials (vv. 17–19) before elevating him and using him to deliver his people (vv. 20–22). As a result, Jacob and all his family moved to Egypt, thus setting the stage for the next act of divine deliverance (v. 23).

5. Delivering Israel from Egypt (vv. 24–38). When the Israelites prospered, the Egyptians grew to hate them (vv. 24–25). God sent Moses and Aaron (v. 26), but the real deliverer was God Himself who sent the plagues on Egypt (vv. 27–36). The enslaved Israelites left Egypt with the wealth of Egypt, and the Egyptians were glad to see them go because of the mighty power of God (vv. 37–38).

6. Guided and fed in the wilderness (vv. 39–41). God led His people by the cloud and pillar of fire (v. 39). He fed them with manna and quail, and gave them water from a rock (vv. 40–41).

7. Praise the God who remembers His covenant (vv. 42–45). The final verses of the chapter tie back in to verses 8–11. God did indeed remember His covenant (v. 42).

43 And he brought forth His people with joy, and his chosen with gladness:

44 And gave them the lands of the heathen: and they inherited the labour of the people.

When God brought His chosen people out of Egypt, they celebrated His deliverance with songs of joy (see Exod. 15:1–22). When the Lord brought the people of Israel into the promised land, He pointed out to them that the land was a gift from Him. They received cities and houses they had not built, wells they had not dug, and crops they had not planted (Deut. 6:9–11).

45 That they might observe his statutes, and keep his laws. Praise ye the Lord.

Verse 45 sums up the twofold response that the people should make as they remembered the God who remembered His covenant with them. First, they should fulfill their covenant responsibilities by keeping the statutes and laws that the Lord gave them. Second, they should continually praise the Lord. This twofold response reminds us that no worship is acceptable to God unless it includes a life that is lived for the Lord. It also should remind us that living for such a God ought not to be a burden. People of faith in the Old Testament spoke of God's law as sweet and joyful (see Ps. 19:7–14).

They didn't separate daily living and times of worship into two compartments. Instead they saw all of life as times of joyful praise to God and testimony to others. In a passage in which Peter addressed Christians as God's New Testament chosen people, he wrote "that ye should shew forth the praises of him who hath called you out of darkness into his marvellous light" (1 Pet. 2:9).

APPLYING THE BIBLE

1. Every day is Thanksgiving Day. In America, we celebrate Thanksgiving Day every November. But for each of us every day ought to be thanksgiving day. Let us begin each day with a prayer of thanksgiving to God, and close each day with a benediction of thanksgiving. This is what the psalmist did. Every day was a day of thanksgiving for this ancient writer.

For what do we have to be thankful? Each of us will have to make an answer. Among these blessings are America, where we are free; our church, where we can worship without fear; our home which shelters us; an abundance of food while millions are starving; medical care which is the best in the world; and loved ones and friends who befriend and encourage us. The list is endless. Above all, we ought to rejoice in our Savior, who forgives our sins and promises a home in heaven for every believer.

The psalmist encourages us to make abundant thanksgiving a daily part of our lives: "O give thanks unto the Lord." How often does the refrain echo in the Psalms?

2. "The Lord He walks here." The late R. L. Middleton once told about a woman who was in Charleston, S. C., with her husband as he waited to sail overseas. It was wartime. Things were so uncertain, and the woman's heart was terribly burdened. She and her husband and three-year-old son walked in the Magnolia Gardens, and although there were hundreds of people walking through the gardens, it was as quiet and reverent as a cathedral.

Coming upon a black gardener down on his knees tending the flowers, the lady thanked him for his careful work in caring for the gardens and then commented on how quiet and reverent the garden was.

Rising slowly from his knees, and with a faraway look in his eyes, the old man put his gnarled hand on the little boy's golden curls and replied: "Yes, ma'am, there is a reason. You see, the Lord—He walks here, too."

The psalmist was recalling in our study today the presence of God with the struggling, wandering patriarchs and with the Israelites from the time of their father Abraham until they settled in Canaan (vv. 5–45). He was reminding them of the spiritual blessings and how Almighty God had walked with them all the way.

Look back over your life. In your greatest joys and severest hardships can you not also say, "He has walked with me all the way"?

3. Walking by faith. The Bible tells us that we walk by faith and not by sight. It also warns us that without faith we cannot please God. But what is faith? One definition of faith that is adequate for me declares that faith is whole-soul trust in God. I use my intelligence, my instincts, my experience in making decisions, but place it all under the faith God has given me. Faith calls the final shot. Faith is not leaping out into the darkness; rather it is walking in the light.

God is the giver of faith. It is not some emotion we work up in ourselves. But faith comes as we pour daily over God's Word and act on what it teaches us (Rom. 10:17, NIV).

As though he were speaking for all the nation and its past history, the psalmist confesses his faith in God. The word *Lord* is the personal name as he revealed Himself to His people. Faith is a personal relationship with God.

4. No mountain too steep for two. Henrik Ibsen (1828–1906) was a noted Norwegian writer and dramatist who is considered the father of modern drama. In one of his books, he describes two people attempting a very dangerous mountain climb in Norway. Friends tried to dissuade them, warning them of the dangers, but the climbers were determined to go. To those trying to discourage them, one of the climbers shouted, "There is no precipice too steep for two."

The psalmist notes this. In Israel's founding as a nation (vv. 5–12), in her slavery in Egypt (vv. 23–36), in her deliverance from Egypt (vv. 37–43), and in her settling in Canaan (vv. 44–45), God was with her all the way. The psalmist now calls on Israel to remember (v. 5) that she was never alone. God was with her all the way. It's worth remembering that none of us walks alone. God walks by our side until the going is too hard for us to bear. Then, as if we were a wounded sheep, He carries us in his arms.

TEACHING THE BIBLE

▶ *Main Idea:* Believers should always praise God for His mighty acts.
▶ *Suggested Teaching Aim:* To lead adults to describe how the psalmist praised God for His mighty acts of deliverance, and to praise God for the way God has delivered them.

A TEACHING OUTLINE

1. *Introduce the Bible study with an illustration.*
2. *Use a responsive reading to present the biblical text.*
3. *Use Scripture examination and group discussion to study the Bible.*
4. *Use listmaking to help members apply the Scripture to their lives.*

Introduce the Bible Study

Use "Every day is Thanksgiving Day" from "Applying the Bible" to begin the session. Read the "Main Idea" and ask members as they study the lesson to be thinking about ways they can praise God for delivering them.

Search for Biblical Truth

IN ADVANCE, enlist two readers to prepare a responsive reading of the Scripture text. The psalms are poetry. Generally, the first line or part of a line will make a statement and the second line or part of a line will make a parallel statement. Have one person read the first statement and the second to read the second. Call for them to read the whole Scripture at this time.

Ask members to open their Bibles to 105:1–2. Ask: What four actions did the psalmist call for Israel to take? (Give thanks, call, sing, declare/talk.)
DISCUSS: How are these four actions still evident in our current worship services?

Ask members to look at 105:3–4. Ask: What should be the attitude of worshipers based on these two verses? (Glory, rejoice, seek God)
DISCUSS: How does seeking the Lord encourage us to worship God regularly? How does regular worship help us in our daily lives?

Ask members to look at 105:5–6. Using the information in "Studying the Bible," lecture briefly on the importance of the word *remember*. Write this definition of *remember* from "Studying the Bible": "Being faithful to what has been promised." In your lecture point out: (1) how the word *remember* is used in the Old Testament; (2) the psalmist calls for Israel to remember God's mighty acts; (3) people of faith need to remember all of God's mighty acts throughout history; (4) the Bible is a record of the remembrance of many people over a long period of time.
DISCUSS: What role has remembering played in your Christian life?

Ask members to look at 105:7–8. Using the information in "Studying the Bible," explain how Psalm 105 is a call to remember the God who remembers.
DISCUSS: Refer to the definition of *remember* and ask: Does the definition support God's remembering more than human remembering?

Ask members to look at 9–11. Ask: What did the covenant with Abraham, Isaac, and Jacob involve? (Covenant with all Israel that God would be their God and give them Canaan.)
DISCUSS: Which features of this covenant were conditional and which were unconditional?

Ask members to look at 105:43–45. Ask: What was the attitude of the people when they left Egypt? (Joy.) What response did God expect the people to make to Him? (Observe statues/keep laws and praise Him.)

Give the Truth a Personal Focus

Read 105:5. Ask members to remember ways God has delivered them. List these on a chalkboard or large sheet of paper. When all have listed the ways God has delivered them, read 105:45. Point out that God's graciousness in delivering us involves our keeping God's laws and praising Him. Share "The doxology" from "Applying the Bible" for next week (July 21). Close by singing or reading the "doxology."

Praising God for Deliverance

Basic Passage: Psalm 34
Focal Passages: Psalm 34:2–10,18–22

salm 34 is one of many psalms that praise God for delivering His people. The writer of Psalm 34 bore testimony to God's goodness and deliverance in times of trouble. The superscription to Psalm 34 attributes the psalm to David, citing one of the many occasions when the Lord delivered David from danger (see 1 Sam. 21:10–15). The psalmist called others to worship using a personal testimony of divine deliverance from troubles (vv. 1–10). He instructed others in the good life and on trusting God in times of trouble (vv. 11–22).

▶ ▶ ▶ ▶ ▶ ▶ ▶ ▶ **Study Aim:** *To bear testimony to God's help in times of trouble*

STUDYING THE BIBLE

LESSON OUTLINE
I. Worship, Testimony, and Invitation (Ps. 34:1–10)
  1. Call to magnify God (Ps. 34:1–3)
  2. Testimony of deliverance (Ps. 34:4–7)
  3. Invitation to experience God's goodness (Ps. 34:8–10)
II. Instructions and Affirmations of Trust (Ps. 34:11–22)
  1. Instructions for the good life (Ps. 34:11–14)
  2. Two views of God (Ps. 34:15–17)
  3. Trust during times of trouble (Ps. 34:18–22)

The psalmist committed himself to praise God and called others to join in magnifying the Lord (vv. 1–3). He testified how God had delivered him and affirmed that the Lord is with His people to deliver them (vv. 4–7). He called others to taste and see that the Lord is good (vv. 8–10). The young were instructed that the good life consists of turning from evil, doing good, and seeking peace (vv. 11–14). The Lord's face is turned toward the righteous to help them, but against the wicked to cut them off (vv. 15–17). The righteous are not immune from trouble but have the assurance of the Lord's deliverance (vv. 18–22).

I. Worship, Testimony, and Invitation (Ps. 34:1–10)

1. Call to magnify God (vv. 1–3). The psalmist declared that he would bless the Lord at all times, not just when his heart was filled with gratitude for a special deliverance (v. 1).

2 My soul shall make her boast in the Lord: the humble shall hear thereof, and be glad.

3 O magnify the Lord with me, and let us exalt his name together.

The Bible often uses the word "boast" to describe selfish, sinful boasting. People boast of their riches (Ps. 49:6), of their sins (Ps. 52:1), of their idols (Ps. 97:7), and of their plans for the future (Prov. 27:1). Psalm 34:2 boldly uses this same word to describe boasting, not of oneself, but in the Lord. The same Hebrew word is sometimes translated "glory in."

When a person of faith boasts in the Lord, other people of humble faith have their hearts warmed by such testimonies. Thus the writer of Psalm 34 called others to join him in magnifying the Lord and in exalting Him together. The psalm thus stresses sharing personal testimonies with one another as an encouragement for all to join in praising the name of the Lord.

2. Testimony of deliverance (vv. 4–7)

4 I sought the Lord, and he heard me, and delivered me from all my fears.

The word for seeking the Lord often was used of seeking the Lord in worship at His sanctuary (Ps. 24:6). Thus the psalmist may have been telling of a prayer for deliverance made at the place of worship. Of course, people of faith know that such prayers can be prayed wherever we are. At any rate, the Lord heard the prayer and delivered the psalmist from all his fears. The word "fears" may refer to the things that he feared, or it may refer to his fear of those things. Sometimes the Lord removes the causes of our fears; when He doesn't, He still provides courage to face our fears (see 2 Tim. 1:7).

5 They looked unto him, and were lightened: and their faces were not ashamed

Verse 5 moved from the psalmist's personal experience to the experience of all those who seek the Lord. "Lightened" means "are radiant." Their lives shined, and they were not ashamed because they received the help they needed.

6 This poor man cried, and the Lord heard him, and saved him out of all his troubles.

Verse 6 is expressed in the third person, but the psalmist was probably using this mode of expression to continue his personal testimony of deliverance. In other words, the "poor man" may have been the writer himself. In any case, the testimony is one that any person of faith can give when the Lord delivers the person from troubles or, more often, delivers him through troubles.

7 The angel of the Lord encampeth round about them that fear him, and delivereth them.

The angel of the Lord is the messenger of God, sometimes a personal manifestation of the Lord (see Judg. 6:11–23). At times, the angel of the Lord revealed Himself in visible form to people of faith. The psalmist was affirming that even when the angel of the Lord was not seen with the physical eyes, people of faith could be aware of His gracious, protecting presence. One such occasion is described in 2 Kings 6:14–17. A Syrian army had surrounded the city of Samaria. Elisha's servant was filled with fear and asked: "'What shall we do?' 'Don't be afraid,' the prophet answered. 'Those who are with us are more than those who are with them.' And Elisha prayed, 'O Lord, open his eyes so he may see.' Then the Lord opened the servant's eyes, and he looked and saw the hills full of horses and chariots of fire all around Elisha" (2 Kings 6:15–17, NIV).

3. Invitation to experience God's goodness (vv. 8–10)

8 O taste and see that the Lord is good: blessed is the man that trusteth in him.

The experience of the psalmist had reinforced his trust in the goodness of God. This is a basic tenet of biblical faith. The child prays, "God is great; God is good." All theology is summed up in this simple affirmation. Some people are overwhelmed at the greatness of God, but lack trust in the goodness of God, whom we call our heavenly Father. We stand in reverence before His greatness; we trust His goodness.

As the psalmist testified to God's goodness, he invited others to experience the goodness of God for themselves. Like someone who had tried a new kind of food and found it delicious, he invited others to taste and see that the Lord is good. Nothing can take the place of personal experience. People can hear from others that God is good, but until they trust Him for themselves, their belief falls short of true faith. When Philip was telling his friend Nathanael about Jesus of Nazareth, Nathanael asked, "Can there any good thing come out of Nazareth?" Philip wisely answered, "Come and see" (John 1:46).

9 O fear the Lord, ye his saints: for there is no want to them that fear him.

No contradiction exists between the calls to trust God and to fear Him. Because of His greatness and holiness, we bow in His presence with reverence and awe.

10 The young lions do lack, and suffer hunger: but they that seek the Lord shall not want any good thing.

Lions have always represented strength; for example, people call the lion the king of the jungle. The psalmist used young lions as symbols of physical strength. Such strength fails to achieve its goals. By contrast, those who seek the Lord find in Him all they want and need. The great and good God does not withhold from His own what they need to do His will (see Matt. 6:33; 7:7–11; Phil. 4:13).

II. Instructions and Affirmations of Trust (Ps. 34:11–22)

1. Instructions for the good life (vv. 11–14). The psalmist moved from testimony to teaching. Based on his experience, he began to teach young people to fear and trust God (v. 11). He asked if they did not want to live the good life (v. 12). Then he instructed them in how to live the good life: by avoiding sins of the tongue (v. 13), by turning from evil and doing good, and by seeking peace (v. 14).

2. Two views of God (vv. 15–17). God's eyes are upon the righteous, and His ears are open to their prayers (v. 15). By contrast, God's face is set against those who persist in their evil (v. 16). Earlier the psalmist had testified of his own experience of divine deliverance (vv. 4, 6) and had affirmed that God delivers His people when they seek Him (vv. 5, 7). In verse 17, he repeated that affirmation.

3. Trust during times of trouble (vv. 18–22)

18 The Lord is nigh unto them that are of a broken heart; and saveth such as be of a contrite spirit.

The word "contrite" may be translated "crushed" (NIV). Thus the psalmist may have been affirming that the Lord helps those whose hearts have been broken and whose spirits have been crushed by troubles. If "contrite" is the correct meaning, his point was that those who pray to God must come with broken hearts and contrite spirits because of their sins. Deciding between these two meanings is hard, because both are clearly taught elsewhere in the Bible. God's concern for the poor and brokenhearted is clear (see Isa. 61:1; Luke 4:18; Matt. 11:28). At the same time, true repentance involves what David called "a broken spirit: a broken and a contrite heart" (Ps. 51:17).

19 Many are the afflictions of the righteous: but the Lord delivereth him out of them all.

Psalm 34 does not teach that the righteous are exempt from troubles; indeed verse 19 acknowledges that they suffer many afflictions. The last part of verse 19 could be taken to mean that the Lord always delivers His people from every evil situation. The personal experiences of people of faith show that sometimes God delivers His people from the hands of evil and evildoers. The experiences of the three Hebrew children and of Daniel are memorable examples of such deliverances (see Dan. 3; 6). The experiences of John the Baptist, Paul, and Jesus Himself show that sometimes God allows people of faith to suffer and to die. However, God always is with His people to deliver them through troubles and from the ultimate power of death itself.

20 He keepeth all his bones: not one of them is broken.

Broken bones in the Old Testament stand for broken health (see Ps. 51:8; Isa. 38:13) or for oppression (see Mic. 3:3). Thus not to have bones broken signified health and security.

21 Evil shall slay the wicked: and they that hate the righteous shall be desolate.

God created a moral and spiritual universe. Those who do evil break the laws of this universe and bring judgment on themselves. Moses said, "Be sure your sin will find you out" (Num. 32:23). Paul warned, "Be not deceived; God is not mocked: for whatsoever a man soweth, that shall he also reap" (Gal. 6:7). In the same way, Psalm 34:21 says that "evil shall slay the wicked." God stands back of such judgment, but the responsibility for spiritual desolation belongs to those who choose the way of evil.

22 The Lord redeemeth the soul of his servants: and none of them that trust in him shall be desolate.

Sinners are to blame for their own desolation; but the righteous cannot take credit for escaping desolation. Rather, they have been redeemed by the Lord. The word *redeem* is a familiar biblical idea. Slaves were redeemed from their plight. The Israelites were redeemed from Egypt. Sinners are redeemed from sin and death through the death of God's Son for us (see Rom. 3:24; Eph. 1:7). The response of God's people to such goodness is to trust their Redeemer.

APPLYING THE BIBLE

1. The doxology. In many churches across the land this morning, the doxology will be sung by thousands of worshipers. It is a hymn of praise to the Holy Trinity: "Praise God from whom all blessing flow; . . . Praise Father, Son, and Holy Ghost."

One night during the Civil War, new Confederate prisoners were being brought into Libby Prison. Among them was a young Baptist minister who almost fainted when he saw the sick, dying, and the filth and squalor. Heartbroken over what he saw, he sat down, put his face in his hands and began to weep. Just then, a lone voice began to sing among the prisoners, "Praise God from whom all blessing flow." Soon, nearly all the prisoners were singing. As the song died away, the young minister stood and sang alone: "Prisons would palaces prove/If Jesus would dwell with me there."

The doxology was written by Rev. Thomas Ken, whom King Charles II made a chaplain to his sister, Mary, Princess of Orange. Ken was so courageous in his preaching that the king often said on his way to chapel, "I must go and hear Ken tell me my faults."

Burdens are lifted, light shines on our pathway, and comfort comes when we focus, not on our problems and trials, but on the goodness of God (vv. 1–3). Practice singing the great hymns of faith, both in public and in private, when your spirits are low. It's good therapy.

2. God's providential care. Each of us, no doubt, can testify to how God has delivered us from some sore trial or from danger. Perhaps He has lifted you out of a deep depression, healed you when all hope was gone, or spared you from a tragic death. Think back, and you will remember some time in your life when the angels of God which, perhaps, you have never considered, delivered you from death (v. 7).

In my last pastorate, a godly mother told me about being awakened deep in the night concerned about her son who was on the highway. She knew something was wrong and began to pray for his safety. Later, he came home and told her about being in an automobile accident that nearly took his life. Another godly saint, who was all but bedfast, related to me that in the quiet of the night she would hear her wooden floors creak. "I knew," she said, "that the angels were surrounding me and watching over me" (Heb. 1:13–14).

This psalm, which is attributed to David, testifies to God's watchcare over and presence with His people at all times, but especially in times of grave crises (vv. 4–7).

3. God is good. Many of us taught our children their first prayer: "God is great/God is good/Let us thank Him for our food." Indeed, God is good as the psalmist stated in vv. 8–10. He then points out that although members of the animal kingdom may suffer from "lack and hunger," God will lavish His love and care upon those who "seek the Lord." They shall "not want any good thing."

Consider the goodness of God poured out upon you: you are well enough to be in church today; you will enjoy a good meal after church in a starving world; you will be sheltered from the July heat in an adequate, air-conditioned home; you will rest safely tonight in your bed— on and on we could go.

With God's goodness so abundantly lavished on us, how foolish we are to complain about things that really matter very little.

4. The need for America to have a "great awakening." There was a period in America's colonial history known as "The Great Awakening" (1740–1745). One of the prime movers of the Great Awakening, which swept through the colonies bringing thousands to Jesus, was Jonathan Edwards, the Congregationalist minister in Northhampton, Massachusetts. His sermon preached there in 1741, "Sinners in the Hands of an Angry God," was used mightily of God to ignite the Great Awakening.

It is recorded that as Edwards preached that now famous sermon, the Holy Spirit swept over the congregation and people held on to the backs of their pews, with white knuckles, crying out to God to save them.

Oh, how America needs that kind of preaching and that kind of awakening. We have lost our fear of God and crime runs rampant across the land!

Billy Graham says that if God does not judge America for her wickedness, then He must apologize to Sodom and Gomorrah! Amen!

TEACHING THE BIBLE

▶ *Main Idea:* Believers who have been delivered will want to praise God.

▶ *Suggested Teaching Aim:* To lead adults to describe how the psalmist said God had delivered him, and to write their own testimony of deliverance.

A TEACHING OUTLINE

1. Use an illustration to begin the session.
2. Use group activity—including paraphrasing and group discussion—to study the Bible.
3. Use a written testimony to help members express their gratitude for God's deliverance in times of trouble.

Introduce the Bible Study

Use "God's providential care" in "Applying the Bible" to introduce the session.

Search for Biblical Truth

IN ADVANCE, print two strip posters with the major points of the lesson: "I. Worship, Testimony, and Invitation (Ps. 34:1–10)" and "II.

Instructions and Affirmations of Trust (Ps. 34:11–22)." Place the first poster on the focal wall at this point.

IN ADVANCE, write the following instructions on a chalkboard or a large sheet of paper (or write them on five small slips of paper to give out individually):

1. Read your assigned Scripture in as many different translations as you can.
2. Read any quarterlies or commentaries you have available.
3. Discuss the verse.
4. Paraphrase the verse.
5. Develop one discussion question to use with the whole class.

To model what you want members to do, ask members to turn to 34:2–3. Ask for as many different translations to be read of the verses as possible. (You may want to bring translations you know your members will not have.) Use the information in "Studying the Bible" to explain what the verses mean. Point out that the psalm stresses sharing personal testimonies with one another as an encouragement for all to join in praising the name of the Lord. Tell them to be thinking of how they can write a personal testimony at the conclusion of the lesson.

Ask members to paraphrase these two verses.

DISCUSS: How can a person "boast" in the Lord? What benefit is it?

Organize the class in five groups and make the following assignments:

> **Group 1**—Psalm 34:4–5
> **Group 2**—Psalm 34:6–7
> **Group 3**—Psalm 34:8–10
> **Group 4**—Psalm 34:18–20
> **Group 5**—Psalm 34:21–22

Allow five to six minutes for study and call for reports of the first three groups.

Place the second strip poster on the wall and call for group 4 and group 5 to report.

Give the Truth a Personal Focus

Distribute paper and pencils to members. Remind them that 34:3 suggests that personal testimonies can be a way of encouraging other believers. Ask members to write their own brief testimony of the way God delivered them in times of trouble. They may begin with something like: "O magnify the Lord with me, and let us exalt his name together for . . ." Allow time for work, and then call on several to read what they have written. Close by giving members an opportunity to offer sentences prayers to express their gratitude for God's deliverance in times of trouble.

Praising God Who Knows and Cares

Basic Passage: Psalm 139
Focal Passages: Psalm 139:1–14, 23–24

With reverent awe, the psalmist meditated on the God who knew him completely, whose presence was with him wherever he was, who shaped him from before birth, and before whom his whole life was lived out. The superscription indicates that the psalm was used in public worship, set to music as part of the Davidic collection.

▶ ▶ ▶ ▶ **Study Aim:** *To evaluate personal experience with God in light of the personal experience reflected in Psalm 139*

STUDYING THE BIBLE

LESSON OUTLINE
  I. God Knows Me (Ps. 139:1–6)
   1. God's knowledge of me (Ps. 139:1–4)
   2. God's hand laid on me (Ps. 139:5)
   3. Beyond human knowledge (Ps. 139:6)
  II. God Is with Me (Ps. 139:7–12
   1. God's inescapable presence (Ps. 139:7–8)
   2. Held by God's hand (Ps. 139:9–10)
   3. With Him in the darkness (Ps. 139:11–12)
  III. God Created Me (Ps. 139:13–18)
   1. Created before birth (Ps. 139:13–16)
   2. God's wondrous ways (Ps. 139:17–18)
  IV. God Hears My Prayers (Ps. 139:19–24)
   1. Condemnation of God's enemies (Ps. 139:19–22)
   2. Prayer for understanding and guidance (Ps. 139:23–24)

The Lord knew the psalmist and everything about him (vv. 1–4). God surrounded him and laid His hand on him (v. 5). God's ways are beyond human understanding (v. 6). Since God is everywhere, His presence is inescapable (vv. 7–8). No matter where the psalmist might travel, the hand of the Lord held him (vv. 9–10). No night was so dark but that God was with the psalmist in the darkness (vv. 11–12). God created him from his mother's womb (vv. 13–16). God's thoughts are precious and as numerous as sand (vv. 17–18). Those who opposed God would be destroyed (vv. 19–22). The psalmist prayed for the Lord's vindication and guidance (vv. 23–24).

I. God Knows Me (Ps. 139:1–6)
1. God's knowledge of me (vv. 1–4)
    1 O Lord, thou hast searched me, and known me.

The psalmist affirmed that the Lord knew him. The fact that he addressed God in prayer shows also that he knew God. He did not know God in so perfect a way as God knew him. He stood in awe before the mystery of God. Still he dared to address God in prayer. The Bible writers did not make impersonal and abstract statements about God. Rather they had a personal faith expressed in prayer and praise to God.

2 Thou knowest my downsitting and mine uprising, thou understandest my thought afar off.

3 Thou compassest my path and my lying down, and art acquainted with all my ways.

4 For there is not a word in my tongue, but, lo, O Lord, thou knowest it altogether.

Not only did the Lord know the psalmist, but He also knew everything about him. God was aware of every detail of his daily routine. For example, God knew when he sat down and when he rose up. God knew the path he took and when he lay down to rest. God knew not only everything he did but also everything he thought. God knew what he would say even before he said it.

2. God's hand laid on me (v. 5)

5 Thou hast beset me behind and before, and laid thine hand upon me.

The word *beset* is used elsewhere in the Old Testament to describe laying siege to a city. Just as an army may lay siege to a city by surrounding it, so God is "all around me on every side" (GNB). Only the context of the entire psalm can determine how the psalmist felt about God surrounding him and laying His hand on him. During his complaints against his sufferings, Job complained of God's hand being laid heavy on him (see Job 10:8). However, later references in Psalm 139 seem to call for a positive interpretation of verse 5. This sees God's hand on him like the hand of a loving father. Sometimes a father's hand is laid on his children to lead or to discipline, but his hand is also to protect, encourage, or help. (See further on v. 10.)

3. Beyond human understanding (v. 6)

6 Such knowledge is too wonderful for me; it is high, I cannot attain unto it.

The psalmist confessed that his awareness of God's knowledge of him left him mentally exhausted. He could not comprehend such knowledge. Fortunately, we do not have to understand God in order to trust Him and His loving care. People who are closest to God are most aware of how little they comprehend of the mystery of God and His ways (see Isa. 55:9; Rom. 11:33).

II. God Is with Me (Ps. 139:7–12)

1. God's inescapable presence (vv. 7–8)

7 Whither shall I go from thy spirit? or whither shall I flee from thy presence?

Like many verses in Hebrew poetry, the two lines of verse 7 repeat the same question using slightly different words. He was asking if he could go any place where God was not present also. Was the psalmist trying to escape from God's presence as Jonah tried to do? The answer to the psalmist's question in verses 8–12 seems to show that the psalmist was not trying to escape from God. He was glorying in the fact that God's presence was with him wherever he was.

8 If I ascend up into heaven, thou art there: if I make my bed in hell, behold, thou art there.

Several words are translated "hell" in the King James Version. This may cause some confusion for the reader. Sometimes "hell" translates a word that refers only to the realm of the dead, as in Psalm 139. At other times, the word refers to the place of punishment. One characteristic of the latter use of "hell" is that God is not there.

The Christian doctrine of eternal life was a matter of divine revelation. During early stages of revelation, people of faith had only a dim awareness of what we know to be the full glory of life after death. Psalm 139:8 is a glint of light as the psalmist dared to believe that God would be with him beyond death itself.

2. Held by God's hand (vv. 9–10)

9 If I take the wings of the morning, and dwell in the uttermost parts of the sea;

10 Even there shall thy hand lead me, and thy right hand shall hold me.

Verse 9 is another vivid example of the Lord's abiding presence. The psalmist imagined going as far as possible toward the east where the sun rose. He also imagined going far to the west beyond the Mediterranean Sea. Most translators think the wording in Hebrew refers to the "far side of the sea" (NIV).

Verse 10 is another reference to God's hand. The reference in verse 5 may be ambiguous, but the meaning of verse 10 is positive. God's hand led him and held him. These are pictures of loving guidance and protection. This testimony is similar to Psalm 73:23–24, "I am continually with thee: thou hast holden me by my right hand. Thou shalt guide me with thy counsel, and afterward receive me to glory."

3. With Him in the darkness (vv. 11–12)

11 If I say, Surely the darkness shall cover me even the night shall be light about me.

12 Yea, the darkness hideth not from thee; but the night shineth as the day: the darkness and the light are both alike to thee.

Some Bible students interpret these verses as if the psalmist was trying to hide from God. If so, the point is that he discovered that no darkness was deep enough to escape the presence of God. More likely, however, the psalmist was using the darkness as a symbol of troubles, which are dark periods of one's life. If that was his meaning, the point in verses 11–12 is that no night is so dark but that the Lord's sustaining presence pierces through the darkness like light.

III. God Created Me (Ps. 139:13–18)

1. Created before birth (vv. 13–16)

13 For thou hast possessed my reins: thou hast covered me in

my mother's womb.

Another translation of verse 13 is, "For you created my inmost be-ing; you knit me together in my mother's womb" (NIV). The reason the Lord knew everything about the psalmist (vv. 1–6) was that God creat-ed him within his mother's womb. By the same token, God whose pres-ence was always with him was with him even before his birth. Verses 13–16 show that the psalmist believed that God's creative work in-cludes the creation of new life within the womb.

14 I will praise thee; for I am fearfully and wonderfully made: marvellous are thy works; and that my soul knoweth right well.

The psalmist's response to this reality was to praise God his Creator and the giver of life. The Old Testament idea of creation makes clear that our whole existence belongs not to ourselves, but to the God who created us for Himself. Apart from God, life has no explanation or pur-pose. When we contemplate God's grace, wisdom, and power in our creation, we bow in praise to Him.

Verse 15 makes the same point as verse 13 except that the heart of the earth signifies the mother's womb. Verse 16 is not easy to translate or understand, but the thought seems to be that God wrote the psalmist's name in the book of the living, even before he was born.

2. God's wondrous ways (vv. 17–18). Verses 17–18 express a similar sentiment to verse 6. The psalmist contemplated the thoughts of God, which seemed as numerous as the sand. As he stood in awe before the infinite wisdom, grace, and power of God, he clung in trust to the assurance that this God of the universe was still with him.

IV. God Hears My Prayers (Ps. 139:19–24)

1. Condemnation of God's enemies (vv. 19–22). Verses 19–22 were not a call for God to take vengeance on the enemies of the psalmist. Instead he was writing of those whose actions showed them to be enemies of God. The psalmist asked that God would deal with them as they deserved.

2. Prayer for understanding and guidance (vv. 23–24)

23 Search me, O God, and know my heart: try me, and know my thoughts:

24 And see if there be any wicked way in me, and lead me in the way everlasting.

The words "wicked way" sometimes denote idolatry. Some Bible students think that the psalmist had been accused of idol worship. This would explain the tone of this prayer. The psalmist was not claiming to be perfect, but he wanted God and others to know that he had not turned from God to idols. In any case, verses 23–24a reflect not arro-gant pride but a humble awareness that God knows all about us. The psalmist threw himself in trust on the loving God who knows but who also understands and forgives. The last part of verse 24 is a prayer that God would guide the steps of the psalmist in the right way, the way that leads to life, even to life everlasting.

1. God knows where we are. Have you ever felt that God has moved off and left no forwarding address? If so, it isn't because He has moved from us but because we have moved from Him. In some "dry spell" of life when the burdens have lain heavily upon you, have you felt God doesn't know your need or, if He does, He just doesn't care? Many of us have felt that way, and so did many of the psalmists. But this psalmist knows full well that God knows all about him and his needs (vv. 1-4) and he isn't a bit uncomfortable with that.

Paul Harvey once told about a criminal who used acid to burn away his fingerprints so that he could carry on his thievery without being caught. But then he was easily caught because he was the only thief who left no fingerprints behind! With or without fingerprints, without dental records, or without any distinguishing marks, God knows us and more—He knows everything about us.

Are you uncomfortable with this?

2. The hands of God. With a good concordance, run the references on the hands of God and the hands of Jesus. God had laid His holy hands on this psalmist and he rejoices in it (v. 5).

We have experienced the same thing. In daily life, or in some acute emergency, we have been aware of His presence with us and of His hands upon us.

One of the best-known preachers of history had such an experience. English preacher George Whitefield (Whit-field) was on his way from America to England in 1731. The trip had been dangerous for months and the crew sensed impending disaster. In his journal Whitefield wrote: "Our allowance of water is just one pint a day, our sails are exceedingly thin, and some of them last night were split. No one knows where we are, but God does and that is sufficient."

3. A pilot's passenger. A young pilot was making his solo flight when he got into serious trouble. Finally, after a difficult struggle, he landed the plane safely. Filling in his log, in the place where it asked for passengers, the young airman wrote "God."[1]

Like the pilot, the psalmist knew that even in the heavens high above the earth, God was still with him.

4. God is with us in the darkness. There can be something fearful about the darkness. Walking on a dark city street, or walking into a darkened home or building, can cause the hair on the back of our necks to bristle.

English Baptist pastor Alexander Maclaren (1826–1910), tells about a frightening experience he had as a teenage boy that left a lasting impression. He took a job in town that required his walking through a thick forest, reported to be haunted, in order to get home. And to compound his fear of the woods, he had to walk through it at night.

One night he entered the woods and, hearing a noise some distance behind him, he picked up the pace. And the sound of feet walking on leaves behind him picked up its pace. In a little while, he began to run, and the noise coming after him sounded as though someone was running. Alexander was nearly scared out of his wits when, suddenly, from behind him he heard someone call, "Alexander! Alexander!" and then he recognized the voice of his father.

Not even the darkness hides us from God, the psalmist says. The darkness of the night, or the black darkness of a personal problem, will not cut us off from God (vv. 11–12). Let us comfort ourselves with the promise, therefore, that "even the night shall be light about me, Yea, the darkness hideth not from Thee."

5. People not numbers. A census taker stopped at a home and asked the mother, "How many children do you have?" She began to name them: "There's Mary, Bob, Jim . . ."

"No, lady, not the names, the numbers." Curtly she replied, "Sir, they do not have numbers, they have names!"

The Bible says that Jesus called His own sheep by name (John 10:3). The psalmist recognized this personal relationship we have with God and states it in verses 13–16. Even in the womb, God knows us and He knows our name. Therein lies the grave sin of abortion.

TEACHING THE BIBLE

▶ *Main Idea:* Understanding that God knows and cares helps us through difficult experiences.
▶ *Suggested Teaching Aim:* To lead adults to describe how the psalmist praised God for knowing and caring about him, and to describe the closeness of our relationship with Him.

A TEACHING OUTLINE

1. Use an illustration to introduce the Bible study.
2. Use a series of questions to guide the Bible study.
3. Use the How to Become a Christian feature to apply the lesson.

Introduce the Bible Study
Use "God knows where we are" from "Applying the Bible" to introduce the session.

Search for Biblical Truth
Down the left side of a chalkboard or a large sheet of paper write: What? How? Where? Why? Ask members to open their Bibles to Psalm 139:1–5. Ask: What do these verses tell us that God knows about us? Let members mention these and list them opposite the word What? (Daily routine, when he sat down and got up, path, and when he rested, everything he thought, surrounded him.) Ask: According to 139:6, what was the psalmist's reaction to this great knowledge? (Too wonderful.)

Ask members to look at 139:7–8. Use the comments on these verses in "Studying the Bible" to explain how *hell* is used in this verse. Ask: How can God be with us in both heaven and hell? Write answers opposite the word *How*? What is the significance of this fact? (Early belief that God was with believers after death.)

Ask members to look at 139:9–12. Ask: According to these verses, where is God's presence with us? (As far east and west as we can go; in deepest darkness.) Write members' answer opposite *Where*?

Ask members to look at 139:13–14. Ask, Why is God with us always? (He created us.) Write this opposite Why?

Explain the meaning of the word reins in 139:13. Ask: What is the significance of this verse in explaining the meaning of life? (Many meanings but consider: Apart from God, life has no purpose.)

Ask a volunteer to read aloud 139:23–24. Using the information in "Studying the Bible," explain the possible reference to idolatry and the psalmist's desire to stand before God and be led to life everlasting.

Give the Truth a Personal Focus

Ask, How many of your activities this past week would you be uncomfortable in sharing with the class? Did you have any thoughts this past week that you would be uncomfortable in sharing with the class?

Assure members that you are not going to ask them to reveal these actions and thoughts, but point out that God knows everything we did and thought this past week. Ask: Does this fact encourage you or frighten you? What did this knowledge do for the psalmist? (Encouraged him because he had been accused of something he had not done.) Point out that the wonderful side of knowing that God understands all about us is that when others accuse us of doing something we did not do, God knows all of the details; He knows we are in the right.

Point out that on the other side, we cannot fool God because He does know if we are genuine in our response to Him.

Ask members to bow their heads and consider how close they are to God as you read 139:23–24. Offer peace and hope to those who have been misunderstood; offer forgiveness to those in whom God does find some "wicked way."

If you have members who are not Christians, you may want to turn to the front of the book and share the "How to Become a Christian" feature.

---

1. Adapted from *Proclaim* (July–September, 1976).

Trust in God

Basic Passage: Psalm 40
Focal Passages: Psalm 40:1–5, 9–11, 16–17

Psalm 40 has two distinct parts. Verses 1–10 constitute a testimony of deliverance and a call for patient trust in God. Verses 11–17 contain a prayer for God's grace and help in a current crisis. Most of Psalm 40:13–17 appears also in Psalm 70.

▶ ▶ ▶ ▶ ▶ ▶ ▶ ▶ ▶ **Study Aim:** *To exercise patient trust in God during times of trouble*

STUDYING THE BIBLE

LESSON OUTLINE
I. A Testimony of Deliverance (Ps. 40:1–10)
    1. Patient trust and divine deliverance (Ps. 40:1–2)
    2. Influencing others to trust in God (Ps. 40:3–5)
    3. Offering joyous obedience (Ps. 40:6–8)
    4. Bearing glad testimony (Ps. 40:9–10)
II. A Prayer for Help (Ps. 40:11–17)
    1. Asking for God's grace and help (Ps. 40:11–13)
    2. Let the wicked be confounded (Ps. 40:14–15)
    3. Let the righteous magnify the Lord (Ps. 40:16)
    4. Humble trust in the Lord (Ps. 40:17)

The psalmist testified how the Lord responded to his patient trust by delivering him from a terrible situation (vv. 1–2). He sang a new song of praise that he expected to lead others to the blessedness of trusting in the Lord, whose deliverances of His people were too many to number (vv. 3–5). The psalmist had learned that the Lord wanted obedience to His will, rather than sacrifices (vv. 6–8). Thus, in the congregation he bore testimony to the righteousness, faithfulness, salvation, lovingkindness, and truth of God (vv. 9–10). He prayed for God's grace and help as he faced a new crisis and his own sins (vv. 11–13). He asked God to confound those who threatened him and mocked him and God (vv. 14–15). He interceded that God's people might magnify His name (v. 16). He expressed his own humble trust as he asked God to hasten to help him (v. 17).

I. A Testimony of Deliverance (Ps. 40:1–10)
1. Patient trust and divine deliverance (vv. 1–2)
    1 I waited patiently for the Lord; and he inclined unto me, and heard my cry.
    2 He brought me up also out of an horrible pit, out of the miry clay, and set my feet upon a rock, and established my goings.
The psalmist testified how God had delivered him from a terrible

situation. Many Bible students think that the "horrible pit" and "miry clay" describe a sickness or situation in which the psalmist was at death's door. He did not go into details about his plight, but it was something that was comparable to being in a horrible pit and miry clay. The "miry clay" was like quicksand, into which he continued to sink ever deeper. Perhaps it is just as well that we don't know exactly what was happening to him. This enables us to identify our own crises with his description in verse 2.

In this situation, the psalmist cried out to the Lord for help. Apparently the deliverance didn't come right away, for the psalmist said that he "waited patiently" for the Lord. Eventually, however, the Lord heard and answered the psalmist's prayer of patient trust. Verse 2 describes both the negative and positive aspects of the Lord's deliverance. The Lord lifted him out of the horrible pit and miry clay. The Lord also set his feet on a rock and thus provided a firm foundation for his life.

Over the years, I have heard many people give a similar testimony. They describe a terrible situation through which they are passing or have passed. They testify that they could not have survived without the Lord's help. Sometimes the help involved removal of the trouble; often the help involved grace and strength to endure the trouble (see comments on v. 17).

2. Influencing others to trust in God (vv. 3–5)

3 And he hath put a new song in my mouth, even praise unto our God: many shall see it, and fear, and shall trust in the Lord.

If we will let Him, God teaches us many lessons in the school of life, especially in the class called "trouble." Going through a time of trouble

Statuette of Baal, the Canaanite weather god, from Minet-el-Beida (15th–14th century B.C.) *Biblical Illustrator* 482/3.

makes any person reflect on life and its meaning. Those of us who believe in God come through trouble with a new appreciation of life as the fragile gift of God. When life and health are threatened and then saved or restored, people of faith have a new awareness of what is important. The psalmist emerged from his trouble with a new song of praise to God. This may mean that he composed this psalm as a new song of praise. Or it may mean that he sang the familiar words of hymns of praise with a new sense of reality and praise to God. His whole life was renewed, and he expressed it in songs of praise to God. He also expected his songs of praise and testimony to be used by God to lead others to see God, themselves, and life in a new way. As a result, they would fear the Lord and trust Him. Thus the psalmist hoped that his testimony of deliverance through patient trust would lead others to trust the Lord for themselves.

4 Blessed is that man that maketh the Lord his trust, and respecteth not the proud, nor such as turn aside to lies.

Using the form of a Beatitude (see Ps. 1:1; Matt. 5:3–12), the psalmist pronounced a blessing on those who trusted in the Lord. He contrasted them with those who put their trust in "lies." Most Bible students think that the "lies" referred to trust in false gods, rather than in the true and living God. Those who put their trust in false gods are seduced by lies. Many people in every generation allow themselves to be deceived into trusting something other than the God who made them.

5 Many, O Lord my God, are thy wonderful works which thou hast done, and thy thoughts which are to us-ward: they cannot be reckoned up in order unto thee: if I would declare and speak of them, they are more than can be numbered.

The psalmist acknowledged that the Lord had blessed and delivered many people, not just him. As he thanked God for his personal deliverance, he also praised God for His wonderful works done on behalf of all His people. These included individual blessings and deliverances, but they also included acts of divine deliverance and blessing on Israel as a whole. Thus verse 5 echoes a typical Old Testament theme: the grateful remembrance of God's mighty acts on behalf of His people. (For example, that is the theme of Ps. 105, which we studied on July 14.) The psalmist was amazed when he tried to recount the many instances of divine deliverance, which were too numerous to count.

3. Offering joyous obedience (vv. 6–8). A typical response to such divine deliverance was to offer a sacrifice in the temple. However, the Lord had opened the psalmist's ears to recognize what so many of the prophets declared: the Lord wants obedience, not sacrifices (v. 6; see 1 Sam. 15:22; Isa. 1:11–17; Hos. 6:6; Amos 5:21–24; Mic. 6:6–8). A book—probably the law of God—called the psalmist to obedience to God (v. 7). Thus the psalmist delighted in doing God's will and obeying the law written within his heart (v. 8).

4. Bearing glad testimony (vv. 9–10)

9 I have preached righteousness in the great congregation: lo, I have not refrained my lips, O Lord, thou knowest.

10 I have not hid thy righteousness within my heart; I have declared thy faithfulness and thy salvation: I have not concealed thy lovingkindness and thy truth from the great congregation.

In his prayer to God, the psalmist noted that he had not kept silent about what God had done for Him and about how great God is. He had spoken boldly in the great congregation, the people who gathered to worship the Lord. The words used in verses 9–10 are the words used in the Old Testament to describe who God is and what He is like. The psalmist bore witness to God's righteousness, faithfulness, salvation, lovingkindness, and truth. Each of these powerful words focuses on some facet of the greatness of our God.

Each believer is a witness of God and His grace. We need to give our testimony of God's grace and help in our own lives. We need to boldly tell all who will hear. Certainly we need to bear witness within our own class and congregation. When others hear such testimonies, many are led to trust and praise God.

II. A Prayer for Help (Ps. 40:11-17)

1. Asking for God's grace and help (vv. 11-13)

11 Withhold not thou thy tender mercies from me, O Lord: let thy lovingkindness and thy truth continually preserve me.

Verse 11 is a transition verse. The psalmist testified to God's deliverance in a past time of trouble in verses 1-10. In verse 11, he asked that the Lord's grace would continually sustain and preserve him. This prayer is linked to a prayer for grace and help in a current crisis, which is described in verse 12. The psalmist declared that he was surrounded by innumerable troubles and overwhelmed by his own iniquities (v. 12). He faced this new crisis as he had faced the earlier one described in verse 2. He prayed for the Lord to come quickly to help him (v. 13).

2. Let the wicked be confounded (vv. 14-15). Very likely, his current crisis involved danger from enemies. At any rate, in verse 14 he asked God to confound those who threatened him. Verse 15 describes their mocking cries against the psalmist and against God. The psalmist prayed that the Lord would put to shame those who sought to shame him.

3. Let the righteous magnify the Lord (v. 16)

16 Let all those that seek thee rejoice and be glad in thee: let such as love thy salvation say continually, The Lord be magnified.

To the psalmist's credit, he focused his prayer beyond his own personal crisis. He interceded on behalf of all God's people. Remembering the lesson he had learned from his earlier deliverance, he prayed that people of faith would find their highest joy in the Lord. Closely related is the prayer that people of faith would praise and testify to the Lord by saying, "Let the Lord be magnified."

4. Humble trust in the Lord (v. 17)

17 But I am poor and needy; yet the Lord thinketh upon me: thou art my help and my deliverer; make no tarrying, O my God.

The psalmist recognized that he was poor and needy in the sight of the Lord. This kind of humble trust is what Jesus meant when He said, "Blessed are the poor in spirit" (Matt. 5:3). The psalmist saw himself as spiritually poverty-stricken. Yet he was encouraged by faith that the Lord knew him and his situation, and cared about him. Thus he affirmed his trust in the Lord as his help and deliverer. He closed with a prayer that the Lord his God would hasten to his aid.

He was in the kind of situation that every believer encounters at times in life. He was in trouble. He had prayed in faith that the Lord would help him. He was waiting for and asking for deliverance. We don't know whether the psalmist was delivered from this trouble as he was from the one described in verses 1-2. We do know that God heard and answered his prayer, which sometimes doesn't include being delivered from a troubling situation but being strengthened to endure with patient trust. Most people of faith can testify of times when the Lord delivered them from bad situations, just as they had asked Him to do. We also can testify how the Lord often provided grace and strength to endure faithfully through a time of trouble.

APPLYING THE BIBLE

1. Easy to trust when all goes well. When everything in our life is moving along pleasantly, it is easy to trust God and have the assurance that all will turn out well. But when the darkness comes and the way is unclear and the burdens are heavy, trusting God is another matter. We want to move against the thing that burdens us rather than wait "patiently for the Lord" (v. 1) as the psalmist instructs us.

It is just at this point that the way Jesus handled trials is in contrast with how we handle them.

When Satan tempted Jesus to turn stones into bread in the wilderness, Jesus refused, saying: "Man shall not live by bread alone." When He sat with the Samaritan woman, tired and weary from His journey, He showed love and compassion for the adulterous woman (John 4). When He was reviled, He did not revile in return. And in the last hours of His life, He forgave and prayed for His tormentors.

This psalmist is learning to trust God patiently and not run ahead of Him (vv. 1–4). In our burdens and cares, we must not run ahead of God.

2. The song of the one delivered. The psalmist had been delivered from some terrible crisis (v. 2). Or perhaps, it was the removal of the guilt of sin he had committed. Anyway, he was safe for he had been delivered, and he sang a song of rejoicing in his heart.

Singing has marked believers in every era of time—singing in times of joy and times of crisis. The magnificent music of the slaves in the Old South developed as an escape vent for their frustrations and sorrows. From them and their singing their way from sadness to joy, we can learn a great lesson.

An anonymous poet has described the trust we should have in our loving Lord in these four simple lines: "Let me like a little sparrow/Trust Him where I cannot see,/In the sunshine or the shadow,/Singing He will care for me."

3. The lost word. George Buttrick, who was an Episcopal rector in New York City, said that *obedience* is a lost word in our culture. Discussing obedience in his book *Don't Sleep Through the Revolution*, Paul S. Rees says that "Christian obedience is surrender to God's will as revealed in Jesus Christ and set out in Holy Scripture."[1]

Rees adds that Christian obedience is not blind acquiescence to blind fate; rather it is joyous, full-heart commitment to our gentle Savior. It is the product of repentance from sin and saving faith in Jesus Christ. It springs to life when our pride is slain with Jesus on the cross and our arrogant will has been submitted to the Lordship of Jesus.

David Livingstone, who spent three decades as a missionary physician in Africa, wrote beautifully about Christian obedience near the end of his life: "Christ is the greatest Master I have ever known. If there is anyone greater, I do not know him. Jesus Christ is the only Master supremely worth serving. He is the only ideal that never loses its inspiration. . . . We go forth in His name, in His power, in His Spirit, to serve Him.[2]

4. The one thing we can't live without. There are many things we think we need, and some are certainly valid needs. But there is one thing without which we cannot live well and joyously: grace! In our lesson the psalmist, knowing this, prayed for grace to cover and surround him (vv. 11–13). What his crisis was we do not know, but we do know that his need for forgiveness was one of them (v. 12).

As a boy, I learned this lesson the hard way, as have most of us. I stole some money from an Indian girl who lived on the Osage reservation near our home and bought a cap pistol for myself. I still have the picture of myself as a ten-year-old boy, with a bandanna around my neck, astride a stick horse, proudly displaying my cap pistol bought with stolen money.

Months went by and the Holy Spirit began to convict me of my sin. One day I stood on the back porch and flung the dreaded thing, that had became like a serpent to me, across the fence and into the field. "I am done with it," I said to myself. When the field was plowed, the pistol was turned under, and I rejoiced. But, lo and behold, when we next plowed the field the pistol was turned up and there it lay on top of the ground hissing at me, "You are not done with me yet!"

I have since tried to find the girl and make restitution to her, as the Scriptures teach, but to no avail. But I did find forgiveness for my sin through the grace of our Lord Jesus.

"It's such a small thing," you say. No, it was a sin, and God does not measure sin as little or big. It is all an act of disobedience, and the only answer to it is the grace of God.

Since that day long ago, I have said and done other things that violate the divine standard. But the answer to them has been the same answer I discovered as a boy: grace!

Have you discovered it to cover your sins?

TEACHING THE BIBLE

▶ *Main Idea*: God's deliverance of us in the past demonstrates that He will care for us in the present.
▶ *Suggested Teaching Aim*: To lead adults to determine how God cared for the psalmist, and to apply His grace to a current crisis they are going through.

A TEACHING OUTLINE

1. Use an illustration to introduce the session.
2. Use a new room arrangement to indicate variety.
3. Use a brief lecture and discussion questions to guide the Bible study through each verse on the Focal Passage.
4. Use reflection to help members apply the lesson.

Introduce the Bible Study
Use "The one thing we can't live without" from "Applying the Bible" to introduce the session.
Search for Biblical Truth

IN ADVANCE, make a poster with the following words from "Studying the Bible:" "If we will let Him, God teaches us many lessons in the school of life, especially in the class called 'trouble.'" Place this on the focal wall.

If possible, place half the chairs on one side of the room and half on the other, facing each other. Leave a space between them. Place one of the following posters over each side: "I. A Testimony of Deliverance (Ps. 40:1–10)"; "II. A Prayer for Help (Ps. 40:11–17)."

IN ADVANCE, copy the eight sentences in the first introductory paragraph under "Studying the Bible" on eight small strips of paper. (Number the strips 1–8 so readers will know what order they are to read.) Tape the four strips that relate to 40:1–10 to chairs on the "Testimony" side; tape the other four to chairs on the "Prayer" side. Ask members to read the strips to survey the chapter.

Call for a volunteer from the "Testimony" side to read 40:1–2. Explain "miry clay" and why the psalmist waited patiently.

DISCUSS: What do you do when deliverance does not come as quickly as you would like for it to come?

Call for a volunteer from the "Testimony" side to read 40:3. Refer to the "Lessons" poster on the wall and explain the reference to "new song."

DISCUSS: What new understanding have you gained as a result of trouble or conflict?

Call for a volunteer from the "Testimony" side to read 40:4-5. Explain *Beatitude* and "lies."

DISCUSS: What wonderful works has God performed in your life? Did you deserve any of them?

Call for a volunteer from the "Testimony" side to read 40:9–10. Explain "great congregation" and "hid thy righteousness." Point out that the psalmist bore witness to God's righteousness, faithfulness, salvation, lovingkindness, and truth.

DISCUSS: How can you witness to God's grace this week?

Call for a volunteer from the "Prayer" side to read 40:11. Point out that the verse is a transition between the testimony and the prayer.

DISCUSS: How does God's past leading help you currently?

Call for a volunteer from the "Prayer" side to read 40:16. Point out that the psalmist prayed for others as he prayed for himself.

DISCUSS: Do we ever have a right to pray just for ourselves in a time of crisis or should our prayers always include those who do not know how to pray for themselves?

Call for a volunteer from the "Prayer" side to read 40:17. Point out the humble trust the psalmist displayed.

DISCUSS: Would you agree with this statement: "God hears and answers all our prayers, but sometimes the answer doesn't include being delivered from a troubling situation but being strengthened to endure with patient trust."

Give the Truth a Personal Focus

Ask members to bow their heads and in a moment of silence identify a current crisis in their lives in which they need to apply God's grace. Read again the "Lesson" poster and urge them to exercise patient trust in God during times of trouble. Close in a prayer that all will know God's loving grace.

---

1. Paul S. Rees, *Don't Sleep Through the Revolution* (Waco, Tex.: Word Books, 1969), 55.
2. Ibid., 57–58.

Obey God's Laws

Basic Passages: Psalm 119:1–16, 45, 105, 129–130
Focal Passages: Psalm 119:1–16, 45, 105, 129–130

P salm 119 is the longest psalm and the longest chapter in the Bible. The form of Psalm 119 is an alphabetic acrostic; that is, each of its stanzas begins with a different letter in the Hebrew alphabet, and each line within a stanza begins with the same letter. For example, each line in verses 1–8 begins with the Hebrew letter *aleph*, which is comparable to the letter *a* in English. Psalm 119 is a prayerful meditation on the law of God. The passages selected for study in this lesson focus on the blessedness and benefits of obeying God's law.

▶ ▶ ▶ ▶ ▶ ▶ ▶ ▶ ▶ **Study Aim:** *To testify of the benefits of studying and following God's Word*

STUDYING THE BIBLE

LESSON OUTLINE
I. Blessedness of Obeying God's Law (Ps. 119:1–8)
    1. The fact of blessedness (Ps. 119:1–3)
    2. Prayer (Ps. 119:4–6)
    3. Commitment (Ps. 119:7–8)
II. Benefits of Obeying God's Law (Ps. 119:9–16, 45, 105, 129–130)
    1. Overcoming temptation (Ps. 119:9–11)
    2. True riches (Ps. 119:12–16)
    3. Freedom (Ps. 119:45)
    4. Guidance (Ps. 119:105)
    5. Understanding (Ps. 119:129–130)

Those who keep God's Word are blessed (vv. 1–3). The psalmist prayed that he might keep God's statutes (vv. 4–6). He committed himself to praise God by obeying God's law (vv. 7–8). He testified that hiding God's Word in our hearts enables us to overcome temptation (vv. 9–11). He found joy in God's Word comparable to the joy of having great riches (vv. 12–16). He found freedom in obeying God's Word (v. 45). He found guidance for knowing and doing God's will, since the Word was like a light on his path (v. 105). He testified that God's Word provided understanding, even for the simple (vv. 129–130).

I. Blessedness of Obeying God's Law (Ps. 119:1–8)
1. The fact of blessedness (vv. 1–3)

    1 Blessed are the undefiled in the way, who walk in the law of the Lord.
    2 Blessed are they that keep his testimonies, and that seek him with the whole heart.

3 They also do no iniquity: they walk in his ways.

The psalm begins like Psalm 1, with a declaration of the blessedness of those who walk in the way of the Lord. Psalm 119 emphasizes that the way of the Lord is expressed in His law. As used here, the word "law" refers to more than a set of rules. It refers to the revealed will of God for how His people are to live: commandments, instructions, examples, and so forth. The Old Testament people of faith did not look on the law as a heavy burden. Those who later made it into a heavy burden by adding their own rigid traditions did not accurately express how writers of the Old Testament felt about God's law (see Matt. 23:4).

One of the characteristics of Psalm 119 is the large number of words that the psalmist used to describe God's law or Word. Verse 1, for example, uses "way"; and verse 2 uses "testimonies." Later in the psalm, a number of other words were used: "commandments," "statutes," "precepts," "word," and "judgments." Each of these has a slightly different emphasis, but the psalmist used all these words to describe God's Word.

Just as the psalm uses a variety of words to describe God's Word, it also uses a variety of expressions to describe how people of faith respond to God's Word. For example, the word "walk" is used in verses 1 and 3 to stress that living by God's Word is a way of life. The words "undefiled" (v. 1) and "no iniquity" (v. 3) describe the difference that obeying God's law makes in one's life. The word "keep" denotes treasuring the Word and obeying it. The clause "seek him with the whole heart" shows that responding to the Word of God is seen as responding to God, whose Word it is. Those who live by the Word of God can do so only as they seek the Lord Himself with all their heart.

2. Prayer (vv. 4–6)

4 Thou hast commanded us to keep thy precepts diligently.

5 O that my ways were directed to keep thy statutes!

6 Then shall I not be ashamed, when I have respect unto all thy commandments.

Beginning with verse 4 and continuing through most of the rest of Psalm 119, the psalmist addressed himself directly to the Lord. This underlines the comments about the words "seek him with the whole heart" in verse 2. The psalmist practiced what he preached. After pronouncing the blessedness of the person who obeys God's Word, he prayed that God would enable him to do just that. Recognizing that God had directed him to keep His precepts diligently (v. 4), he prayed that God would direct his ways to keep God's statutes (v. 5). He realized that he could not do this in his own strength. If God would help him keep His commandments, then he would not be ashamed by failing God (v. 6).

3. Commitment (vv. 7–8)

7 I will praise thee with uprightness of heart, when I shall have learned thy righteous judgments.

8 I will keep thy statutes: O forsake me not utterly.

The psalmist spelled out his twofold commitment. For one thing, he would praise the Lord with a life that had been changed by obedience to God's Word. This shows that our lives as well as our voices are to praise the Lord. The second commitment was to keep God's statutes.

Verse 8 closes with the same kind of prayer we saw in last week's lesson in Psalm 40:17. The psalmist recognized the depth of his need and his inclinations to fail God; therefore, he prayed for the Lord's presence never to forsake him.

II. Benefits of Obeying God's Law (Ps. 119:9–16, 45, 105, 129–130)

1. Overcoming temptation (vv. 9–11)

9 Wherewithal shall a young man cleanse his way? by taking heed thereto according to thy word.

Verse 9 reminds us of the Book of Proverbs, which so often addresses its instructions to young men. Those who are young are still forming their basic outlook and approach to life. Many of the immature young fall prey to ways that are destructive in the long run. Thus the question in verse 9 is answered in the same verse. A young man can cleanse his way by taking heed to live according to God's Word.

10 With my whole heart have I sought thee: O let me not wander from thy commandments.

Verse 10 is a testimony of one whose whole heart was committed to seeking the Lord and His will. The psalmist prayed that God would not let him wander from God's commandments. If we are honest, we must confess to being prone to wander. We need to join the psalmist in praying that the Lord will bind our wandering hearts to Him.

11 Thy word have I hid in mine heart, that I might not sin against thee.

This is one of the most familiar verses in Psalm 119, and rightly so. The psalmist put into words a commitment that each of us—young or old—should have made. One guard against falling into sin is to hide God's Word in our heart. This means to memorize pertinent parts of the Bible and to hide them in our minds and hearts. Then when we face trials and temptations, God will bring to mind the strength and direction of His Word for the situation.

2. True riches (vv. 12–16)

12 Blessed art thou, O Lord: teach me thy statutes.

13 With my lips have I declared all the judgments of thy mouth.

14 I have rejoiced in the way of thy testimonies, as much as in all riches.

15 I will meditate in thy precepts, and have respect unto thy ways.

16 I will delight myself in thy statutes: I will not forget thy word.

Notice the five words used to describe God's Word in verses 12–15: "statutes," "judgments," "testimonies," "precepts," and "ways." Also notice the different words that describe the psalmist's actions: "teach me," "declared," "rejoiced," "meditate," "have respect unto," "delight myself," and "not forget." Notice especially the psalmist's high regard for God's Word. Far from considering God's Word to be a set of burdensome rules, he rejoiced in God's Word.

And he compared the law of God to great riches. He had discovered the secret that all people of true faith eventually realize: that life's highest joy is in knowing and serving God and that the revelation of God and His way is more precious than earthly wealth. The most memorable celebration of joy in the riches of God's Word is in Psalm 19:7–10. The psalmist wrote this about God's judgments: "More to be desired are they than gold, yea, than much fine gold: sweeter also than honey and the honeycomb" (Ps. 19:10).

3. Freedom (v. 45)

45 And I will walk at liberty: for I seek thy precepts.

This verse is reminiscent of Jesus' teaching that sin results in slavery and Christian discipleship leads to freedom (see John 8:31–32, 34). Worldly people believe the exact opposite. They are deceived into thinking that selfish sins lead to freedom because each person is allowed to do his own thing. The writer of Psalm 119 had experienced something of what Jesus was teaching. True freedom comes only when people know the God who made them and walk in the way people were intended to live. Those who walk in the ways of sin join the faceless multitude on its way to destruction. Sin doesn't promote freedom; it leads to a plight from which we are helpless to deliver ourselves.

4. Guidance (v. 105)

105 Thy word is a lamp unto my feet, and a light unto my path.

This is another of the most familiar verses in Psalm 119 or in the Bible itself. The Word of God is like light on the path we walk. Without this light, we stumble through life like a person groping about on a dark, moonless night. The Bible is not a book of magic recipes for each situation, but God uses His Word in each of our lives to provide guidance and direction as we seek to know and do His will. Verse 105 goes well with Proverbs 3:5–6: "Trust in the Lord with all thy heart; and lean not unto thine own understanding. In all thy ways acknowledge him, and he shall direct thy paths."

5. Understanding (vv. 129–130)

129 Thy testimonies are wonderful: therefore doth my soul keep them.

130 The entrance of thy words giveth light; it giveth understanding unto the simple.

This passage is similar to verse 105 in mentioning light. However, verse 105 seems to focus on specific direction as we seek the Lord's will, while verse 130 seems to refer to a more general understanding of what life is all about. Every person needs some sense of meaning and purpose in life. People seek meaning in a variety of ways, most of them wrong. The psalmist had found understanding in the wonderful testimonies of the Lord. The entrance of God's words sheds light on the important issues of life. Thus we are faced with the paradox that some of the world's most intelligent and highly trained people seek but never find out what life is all about, while people of much less intelligence and education have found understanding in God's Word.

1. Some interesting facts about our Bible. Psalm 119 is the longest psalm and the longest chapter in the Bible; the shortest psalm is 117, which is also the middle of the Bible; the middle verse is Psalm 118:8; the longest name in the Bible is "Mahershalalhashbaz" (Isa. 8:1); and the Bible was written using only 6,000 different words, compared to the 20,000 used by Shakespeare.

Also: the shortest verse is John 11:35; all the letters of our English alphabet can be found in Ezra 7:21 except *joy*; the word *and* appears 46,627 times, while the word *Lord* appears 1,855 times; the longest verse is Esther 8:9; and the average word contains but five letters.

The Bible can be read in seventy hours and forty minutes as a minister would read in the pulpit. Reading at an average rate, the Old Testament can be read in fifty-two hours and twenty-two minutes and the New Testament in eighteen hours and twenty minutes. Those who especially love the Psalms can read all one hundred and fifty of them in four hours and twenty-eight minutes. Read the Bible for only twelve minutes a day, and you will read through it in one year.[1]

2. Hitler's comment about the Ten Commandments. Adolph Hitler, the lunatic and dictator who bathed Europe in blood a few decades ago, had no regard for the Scriptures. Hitler once said about the Ten Commandments, "The Ten Commandments have lost their validity. There is no such thing as truth, either in the moral or in the scientific sense." And Hitler gave ample evidence to his belief, murdering millions of innocent people and bringing untold grief to the whole world.

Much to the contrary, the psalmist believed absolutely in God's Word and in the truth it declared. He praised God for His statutes and prayed to be given wisdom to live by them (vv. 1–8).

3. A lesson well learned. When I was a boy, attending Vacation Bible School was a must. Regardless of what had to be done on the farm, we children attended the two-week Bible school year after year.

One of the first verses that I learned, after having learned "God is love" in Sunday School, was verse 11 of this chapter: "Thy word have I hid in mine heart, that I might not sin against Thee." I learned that verse well, and practicing it has kept me from many a sin and moral and spiritual failure.

Thank God for my Sunday School and Vacation Bible School teachers, and especially my parents, who taught me God's Word as a child.

4. Finding great treasure. The Bible is a gold mine of wealth and will endure forever. It is the traveler's map through life; the pilot's compass; the pilgrim's staff; the soldier's sword; and the believer's guide. It contains wisdom to teach us; bread to feed us; honey to sweeten us; living water to refresh us; comfort to console us; fire to warm us; and a bed of hope and grace to rest us. Read it to be wise; believe it to be safe; practice it to be holy; and memorize it to grow spiritually. It is more precious than gold: "More to be desired are they than gold" (Ps. 19:10)[2]

As the psalmist points out in our lesson today, to read and love the Word of God is to find an inestimable treasure (vv. 12–16).

5. Lincoln's comfort. Abraham Lincoln found great comfort in the Word of God during America's greatest national crisis. Often, while president, he would arise long before daylight and pour over the Scriptures seeking heaven's guidance.

Joseph R. Sizoo, who years later was pastor of the New York Avenue Presbyterian Church that Lincoln often attended, once told about holding the Bible Lincoln read. His mother had read from that very Bible when he was a child, and she had taught Lincoln to memorize many verses. It was the only possession Lincoln carried from Pigeon Creek, Kentucky, to the Sangamon River in Illinois, and to the White House.

Sizoo wondered, as he held Lincoln's Bible, what had been his favorite passage—or at least one of his favorites. Putting the Bible on its edge, he let it fall open, and it opened to Psalm 37:1, 7: "Fret not thyself because of evildoers." "Rest in the Lord, and wait patiently for Him." The page was well thumbed, testifying that the great president had often turned there for strength and comfort (v. 105, vv. 129–130).³

TEACHING THE BIBLE

▶ *Main Idea:* Obeying God's Word demonstrates that believers shall experience lasting benefits.

▶ *Suggested Teaching Aim:* To lead adults to describe the psalmist's description of studying God's Word, and to testify of the benefits of studying and following God's Word.

A TEACHING OUTLINE

1. *Use a graffiti wall to introduce the session.*
2. *Use an antiphonal choir to read the Scripture.*
3. *Use lecture and group discussion in the Bible study.*
4. *Use a written testimony to give the Bible truth a personal focus.*

Introduce the Bible Study

Keep last week's room arrangement. Use the two groups to read the Scripture antiphonally or responsively. Ask one side to read the first part of each verse ("Blessed are the undefiled in the way") and the other side to read the last part ("who walk in the law of the Lord").

Place a large sheet of paper on the wall and provide markers. As members arrive, ask them to go to the sheet and write their favorite verse from the Psalms. If they do not know the actual reference or wording, assure them that is all right.

Begin the session by reading some of the verses. If you can recognize any from Psalm 119, read them. Point out that Psalm 119 is a psalm about the importance of God's Word. Share the information in the Facts Box about the psalm.

FACTS BOX

Psalm 119 is the longest psalm and the longest chapter in the Bible.

- Psalm 119 contains 22 separate sections named after the letters of the Hebrew alphabet.
- Each of the 22 sections contains 8 verses.
- Each verse in each section begins with the same letter of the Hebrew alphabet.
- Nearly every verse in the psalm has a word in it that refers to God's Word.

Search for Biblical Truth

Explain that you will be studying the following sections: all of the first two sections—*aleph* (or A) and *beth* (or B), and parts of *waw* (or W), *nun* (or N), and *pe* (or P). Ask if any members have Bibles that show these divisions?

Ask members to read 119:1–8 as suggested above. Ask members to look at 119:1. Ask: Does this verse remind you of the first verse of another psalm? (It is similar to 1:1.) Point out that these verses describe the blessedness of obeying God's law. Ask members to locate as many words as they can in 119:1–8 that refer to God's Word. (Testimonies, law, ways, precepts, statutes, commandments, judgments.)

Point out that just as the psalm uses a variety of words to describe God's Word, it also uses a variety of expressions to describe how people of faith respond to God's Word. Ask members to see how many of these expressions they can find. (Walk, keep, seek, do no iniquity, have respect, learn thy righteous judgments.)

Point out that from verse 4 on that the psalmist addresses himself directly to the Lord.

Ask members to look at 119:7–8. Ask: According to these verses what is the psalmist's twofold commitment? (Praise the Lord and keep God's statutes.)

DISCUSS: What does it mean for you to "walk in the way of the Lord"? Do you need to make any changes in your life to do this? What do you need to know before you can praise God in a particular situation through which you are going (v. 7)?

On a chalkboard or a large sheet of paper, write: Benefits of Obeying God's Laws. Ask members to read 119:9–16, 45, 105, 129–130 as suggested above. Ask members to examine these verses to find the benefits of obeying God's law. (Members may find several but consider these: overcome temptation, true riches, genuine freedom, guidance, understanding.) Write members' suggestions on the chalkboard or a large sheet of paper.

DISCUSS: How does God bind our wandering hearts to Him (v. 10)? Can you cite an example of a time knowing God's Word kept you from sinning? Which benefit of God's Word is more important to you: freedom (v. 45), guidance (v. 105), or understanding (vv. 129–130)? Why? What difference would it make in your life if you achieved this?

Give the Truth a Personal Focus

Distribute paper and pencils and ask members to write how studying and following God's Word has benefited them. Call on several to read their statements.

1. J. B. Fowler, *Illustrating Great Words of the New Testament* (Nashville: Broadman Press, 1991), 161–162 (author unknown).

2. Adapted from *"Faith Prayer and Tract Society League,"* #162 (Grand Rapids, Mich., n.p., n.d.).

3. Adapted from Robert Hastings, *A Word Fitly Spoken* (Nashville: Broadman Press, 1962), 16.

Repent and Confess

Basic Passage: Psalm 51
Focal Passages: Psalm 51:1–13, 17

The superscription to Psalm 51 says that the historical background was David's confession of sins after Nathan confronted him with his guilt concerning Bathsheba (see 2 Sam. 11–12). The psalm fits well David's remorse when the enormity of his guilt finally broke through to awaken his conscience

▶ ▶ ▶ ▶ ▶ ▶ ▶ ▶ **Study Aim:** *To incorporate in personal prayer life the aspects of prayer in Psalm 51.*

STUDYING THE BIBLE

LESSON OUTLINE
I. Praying to God for Forgiveness (Ps. 51:1–12)
   1. Praying to the merciful God (Ps. 51:1–2)
   2. Confessing sins (Ps. 51:3–6)
   3. Seeking cleansing (Ps. 51:7–9)
   4. Asking for renewal (Ps. 51:10–12)
II. Offering a Changed Life (Ps. 51:13–19)
   1. Converting sinners (Ps. 51:13)
   2. Praising God (Ps. 51:14–15)
   3. Offering oneself (Ps. 51:16–17)
   4. Praying for God's blessing (Ps. 51:18–19)

The psalmist prayed to the God of mercy for cleansing from his sins (vv. 1–2). Deeply aware of his sinfulness, he confessed his sin to God, against whom he had sinned (vv. 3-6). He sought cleansing from his sins (vv. 7–9). He asked for a renewal of spirit based on an awareness of God's presence (vv. 10–12). The psalmist committed himself to teach God's ways so sinners could be converted to Him (v. 13). He promised to open his mouth in praise to God (vv. 14–15). He offered the sacrifice of a broken and contrite heart (vv. 16–17). He prayed for God's blessings on people who brought sacrifices of righteousness (vv. 18–19).

Limestone altar. David possibly worshiped at an altar such as this. The real sacrifice God wants is for us to feel sorrow deeply in our hearts for sin. *Biblical Illustrator* 57/26-29.

I. Praying to God for Forgiveness
(Ps. 51:1–12)

1. Praying to the merciful God (vv. 1–2)

1 Have mercy upon me, O God, according to thy lovingkindness: according unto the multitude of thy tender mercies blot out my transgressions.

2 Wash me thoroughly from mine iniquity, and cleanse me from my sin.

Verses 1–2 present the theme of Psalm 51. Notice these three things: (1) words used to describe God, (2) words used to describe sin, and (3) words used to ask for forgiveness.

The words describing God are "mercy," "lovingkindness," and "tender mercies." The psalmist did not base his appeal on his own goodness but on the revealed nature of God as merciful. He did not begin his prayer by reminding God of past good deeds, hoping that this might lessen his guilt. He was too aware of the heavy weight of his own sin and guilt. The broken relationship between him and God completely dominated his thinking. He realized that his only hope lay in God's mercy.

What led the psalmist to dare to expect God to be merciful? The full revelation of God came in Jesus Christ, but God has always been the same. Even in Old Testament times, God sought to make known His mercy and love. The psalmist probably had in mind the revelation of God recorded in Exodus 34:6–7, which is a kind of John 3:16 of the Old Testament. The Lord told Moses His name: "The Lord, The Lord God, merciful and gracious, longsuffering, and abundant in goodness and truth, keeping mercy for thousands, forgiving iniquity and transgression and sin, and that will by no means clear the guilty."

The psalmist used three words to describe his sins. He was not saying that he was guilty of three kinds of sins. His point was that he was a sinner through and through. His sins were a stubborn refusal of God's will ("transgressions"), a perversion of what is right ("iniquity"), and missing the mark ("sin"). He also used three words to describe the forgiveness he sought. He wanted the record of his sins blotted out. He wanted to be washed and cleansed from his sin and guilt.

2. Confessing sins (vv. 3–6)

3 For I acknowledge my transgressions: and my sin is ever before me.

For a long time, David had tried to deceive himself about his sin. He also tried to hide his sin from God and others. When Nathan confronted David with the truth, the structure of his deception collapsed. He realized that he could not hide his sin from God or himself. Thus when he prayed, he said that his sin was ever before him.

4 Against thee, thee only, have I sinned, and done this evil in thy sight: that thou mightest be justified when thou speakest, and be clear when thou judgest.

This verse is sometimes quoted to show that David could not have written Psalm 51. The reason is that David's sins were directly against Bathsheba and Uriah, and his sins had far-reaching deadly effects. How could David write, "Against thee, thee only have I sinned"? However, verse 4 was not intended as a denial of the deadly effects of sin on others. This verse is an exaggerated way of confessing that all sin is ultimately against God. That's what sin is: rebellion against God. Sin has moral and social dimensions, but sin is basically a spiritual matter. Among the worst sins in our world are those directed against people. These sins are wrong because they hurt those whom God loves, and thus they hurt God Himself.

5 Behold, I was shapen in iniquity, and in sin did my mother conceive me.

Verse 5, like verse 4, can be misunderstood. Some have taken it to mean that the sex act by which children are conceived is evil. Others have taken it to mean that sin and guilt are transmitted biologically. The psalmist was not trying to excuse his sins by blaming an inherited sin and guilt. Rather he was using strong language to confess that he was a sinner through and through, and that he lived in a world in which all have sinned against the God who made them.

6 Behold, thou desirest truth in the inward parts: and in the hidden part thou shalt make me to know wisdom.

Verse 6 contrasts with verse 5. Verse 5 is a confession that the psalmist was a sinner through and through. Verse 6 shows what God wanted him to be and indeed what God could make of him. God wants truth, not deception. And God can teach forgiven sinners the wisdom of how to live.

3. Seeking cleansing (vv. 7–9)

7 Purge me with hyssop, and I shall be clean: wash me, and I shall be whiter than snow.

Verses 7–9 continue the prayer for cleansing from verse 2. Hyssop was a plant used in ceremonies of purification and cleansing (see Exod. 12:22). The guilty sinner felt dirty. He yearned for God to cleanse him from the filth of his sins so that he could be whiter than snow (see Isa. 1:18).

8 Make me to hear joy and gladness; that the bones which thou hast broken may rejoice.

During the time when David had tried to hide his sin, he was miserable. Psalm 32:3–4 describes how he felt. He yearned for the joy and gladness of a restored relationship with God (see comments on v. 12).

9 Hide thy face from my sins, and blot out all mine iniquities.

Forgiveness takes place when God sets aside our sin as a barrier to fellowship with Him. Thus, David wanted God to no longer regard his sins as a barrier to such fellowship. As in verse 1, he asked God to blot out the record of his sins.

4. Asking for renewal (vv. 10–12)

10 Create in me a clean heart, O God; and renew a right spirit within me.

The word *create* is the same word used in Genesis 1 of God's creation of all things. The psalmist pleaded for a new heart, something that only God could create. He prayed that God would renew his spirit. He was asking for God to make a profound change in how he thought and felt. He recognized that his own heart and spirit tended to drift from God; he asked for a heart and spirit that could overcome temptation and remain loyal to God.

11 Cast me not away from thy presence; and take not thy holy spirit from me.

The magnitude of his sin caused the psalmist to fear that the joy, comfort, and life-giving presence of God's Spirit might be denied him. He believed the Holy Spirit was still with him; otherwise, he would not have felt divine conviction for his sin. Still he was also aware that sin had interposed a barrier to full fellowship with God. He knew of God's holiness, and he was all too aware of the blackness of his own sin. Therefore, he prayed for God not to withdraw completely from him. In verse 9, he prayed for God to hide His face from his sin; in verse 11, he prayed for God not to hide His face from him—the sinner.

12 Restore unto me the joy of thy salvation; and uphold me with thy free spirit.

When children of God have unconfessed sin in their lives, they lead a joyless existence. This prayer fits well David's experience, but it fits well the experience of any person who allows sin to rob him of the joy of God's salvation. Thus the penitent sinner prayed for a renewal of that joy which flows from communion with God and obedience to His will.

The penitent sinner also asked God to uphold him. The psalmist wanted to serve God with eager willingness and gladness of spirit. But he knew that this did not lie within his own power. Indeed, he lacked motivation, strength, and endurance. Thus, he prayed for God to sustain a willing spirit within him.

II. Offering a Changed Life (Ps. 51:13–19)
1. Converting sinners (v. 13)

13 Then will I teach transgressors thy ways; and sinners shall be converted unto thee.

Up to this point in Psalm 51, the psalmist's full attention was focused on his own relationship with God. Verse 13 shows that he did not practice a self-centered religion. He realized that a right relation with God involved his actions toward others. He was especially sensitive to the plight of those who, like himself, had fallen into sin and needed to turn to God. The penitent sinner vowed that when he was restored to full fellowship with God, he would teach and testify to transgressors so that they might be turned to God.

2. Praising God (vv. 14–15). Asking for deliverance from guilt, the psalmist vowed to sing God's praises (v. 14). Asking God to open his mouth, he promised to lift his voice in praise (v. 15).

3. Offering oneself (vv. 16–17). Verse 16 echoes the prophetic insight of Psalm 40:6 and other passages: God doesn't want burnt offerings.

17 The sacrifices of God are a broken spirit: a broken and a contrite heart, O God, thou wilt not despise.

Before our offerings are acceptable to God, we must first offer ourselves as repentant sinners who become obedient servants of God. David knew that he could go to the house of God and offer all kinds of animal sacrifices. He also knew that none of these sacrifices would please God as long as he was refusing to confess sins. Thus the first sacrifice he had to offer God was a broken spirit and a broken and contrite heart.

4. Praying for God's blessing (vv. 18–19). The psalmist prayed for God's blessing toward Jerusalem (v. 18). He said that God would be pleased with sacrifices when they signified a repentant heart and a righteous life (v. 19).

APPLYING THE BIBLE

1. "Sin had made me crazy." In one of his hymns, Reformer Martin Luther writes:

In devil's dungeon chained I lay
the pangs of death swept o'er me.
My sin devoured me night and day
In which my mother bore me.
My anguish grew more rife,
I took no pleasure in my life
And sin had made me crazy.

An old Testament scholar, the late Kyle Yates, says this psalm we are studying is David's confession of sin with Bathsheba (2 Sam. 11). Yates writes: "For almost a year David endured the lashing of an active conscience. . . . One day Nathan (the prophet) came with the powerful thrust that left the king conscious of his sin and able to sense something of his tragic condition before a just and holy God. His heart was crushed. . . . [and] he readily admitted: 'I have sinned against God.'"[1]

Like Luther, David's sin had almost driven him crazy, but turning to God in repentance, he found God's forgiveness and cleansing (vv. 1–12).

2. The wideness of God's mercy. Frederick W. Faber (1814–1863) was an Anglican clergyman who, in 1846, became a Roman Catholic. After embracing Catholicism, Faber composed many hymns, one hundred and fifty of which are still sung in worship services today. Some are not too well known, but among his most popular hymns are "Faith of Our Fathers" and "There's a Wideness in God's Mercy." Often we have sung both of them, never knowing they were written by a pious Roman Catholic. The latter hymn reads:

There's a wideness in God's mercy,
Like the wideness of the sea;
There's a kindness in His justice,
Which is more than liberty.
There is welcome for the sinner,
And graces from the good;
There is mercy with the Savior;
There is healing in His blood.[2]

With his sin crushing the life and vitality out of him, what was David's greatest need? It was for the mercy of God to cover Him and the grace of God to cleanse him (vv. 1–2). And that is our greatest need, too.

3. Can you relate to David's plea for forgiveness and cleansing? If you can't, your heart is harder than you think. To be led and filled with the Holy Spirit means to be sensitive to sin, sorrowful over it, and to seek cleansing in the blood of Jesus. That is just as true for "respectable sins," such as withholding our tithes from God, as it is for heinous sins such as adultery.

I remember as a child doing a bad thing that was contrary to being a Christian (not the one to which I referred in an earlier lesson). Guilt poured over me and made me feel terrible. But I closed my heart and refused to deal with it in repentance. For months I refused to seek God's forgiveness, but then the day came when I could no longer stand the weight of guilt and made a clean breast of it all. Then the peace of God flooded my heart like a mighty ocean of forgiveness. I learned an invaluable lesson as a child that has served me well, as David learned the same lesson as a king: the only answer to sin and guilt is confession and forgiveness (vv. 2–10).

4. God is present. Carolus Linnaeus (1707–1778) was a renowned authority on plants who developed the modern, scientific method of naming plants and animals. Given $50 by the Royal Society of Science, he spent five months in 1732 collecting plants in Lapland, traveling 4,800 miles and walking nearly 1,000 miles.

Over the entrance to his laboratory, Linnaeus had carved his motto. Translated from Latin, it read: "Do not sully hand and heart today. Deity is present." When the king's lust for Bathsheba was so fierce it led to adultery and murder, the memory that God is always present with us would have saved him a world of grief (v. 11). And when we are tempted to sin, let us, too, remember that God is a witness to our every word, thought, and deed.

TEACHING THE BIBLE

▶ *Main Idea:* David's prayer of confession and repentance demonstrates that we must confess and repent of our sin.

▶ *Suggested Teaching Aim:* To lead adults to examine David's prayer of confession and repentance, and to determine how God wants them to respond to Him

A TEACHING OUTLINE

1. *Use an illustration to introduce the session.*
2. *Use a lesson poster to guide the Bible study.*
3. *Use a creative writing assignment to apply the Scripture.*

Introduce the Bible Study

Use "Sin had made me crazy" from "Applying the Bible" to introduce the session.

Search for Biblical Truth

IN ADVANCE, make a lesson poster with the following headings. Leave space for writing four points under the first heading and two points under the second heading.

Repent and Confess

I. Praying to God for Forgiveness (Ps. 51:1–12)
II. Offering a Changed Life (Ps. 51:13–19)

Place this poster on the focal wall for all to see.

Call attention to the first point on the poster. Ask members to open their Bibles to Psalm 51:1–2. Ask: In these two verses, what words did David use to describe God? (Mercy, lovingkindness, and tender mercies.) Use the information in "Studying the Bible" to explain the significance of each of these words.

Ask: What three words did David use in 51:1–2 to describe his sins? (Transgressions, iniquity, sin.) Use the information in "Studying the Bible" to explain the variation of meaning in these three words. Ask: What three words or phrases did David use to describe the forgiveness he sought? (Sins blotted out, washed, cleansed.)

Point out that David described at least four steps that he went through to pray for forgiveness. Write the following phrases on the lesson poster under the first heading and ask members to suggest which verses would support these statements. The suggested answers are in parentheses.

1. Praying to the merciful God (51–12)
2. Confessing sins (51:3–6)
3. Seeking cleansing (51:7–9)
4. Asking for renewal (51:10–12)

DISCUSS: How could David say his sin was against God when he committed adultery with Bathsheba? How does God create a clean heart in us? What do you need to do to have the joy of your salvation restored?

Point out the second statement on the lesson poster. Ask members to read silently 51:13,17. Write the following phrases on the chalkboard or a large sheet of paper and ask members to suggest which verses would support these statements. The suggested answers are in parentheses.

1. Converting sinners (51:13)
2. Offering oneself (51:17)

Ask: In addition to these two evidences of forgiveness, what other evidences would you suggest? Add them to your list.

DISCUSS: If we do not want to share our faith with others, is our faith genuine? If we do not tell others who have fallen into sin that they can find forgiveness, who will? What kind of sacrifices does God want you to offer?

Give the Truth a Personal Focus

Call attention to the two points on the lesson poster. Ask: Which area—seeking forgiveness or showing you have been forgiven—is the greatest need of your life? Ask members to determine how God wants them to respond to Him. Distribute paper and pencils. Ask members to write a psalm of their own in which they ask God for forgiveness that incorporates the elements of this psalm. Ask for volunteers to read theirs to the class but do not force anyone.

---

1. Kyle Yates, *Preaching from the Psalms* (Nashville: Broadman Press, 1948), 3.
2. *Broadman Hymnal* (Nashville: Convention Press, 1975 edition), 171.

Worship and Witness

Basic Passage: Psalm 96
Focal Passage: Psalm 96

P salm 96 is preserved in slightly different words in 1 Chronicles 16:23–33. Psalm 96, along with Psalm 105:1–15 and parts of other psalms, was sung when the ark of the covenant was brought to Jerusalem. Psalm 96 is an invitation for all people and all creation to join in praise to God as Creator, King, and Judge.

▶ ▶ ▶ ▶ ▶ ▶ ▶ ▶ ▶ **Study Aim:** *To explain why worship and witness are inseparable*

STUDYING THE BIBLE

LESSON OUTLINE
I. **Sing Unto the Lord, All the Earth (Ps. 96:1–6)**
   1. Call to sing praises to the Lord (Ps. 96:1–3)
   2. The greatness of the Lord (Ps. 96:4–6)
II. **Call to Worship the Lord as King (Ps. 96:7–13)**
   1. Give God the glory due His name (Ps. 96:7–9)
   2. God as King and Judge (Ps. 96:10–13)

The psalmist invited all the earth to join in singing unto the Lord and called people of faith to bear witness to Him (vv. 1–3). The psalmist proclaimed the greatness of the Creator over all idols (vv. 4–6). He called all people to give the Lord the glory due His name (vv. 7–9). He called on all people and things to recognize God as reigning and coming King and Judge (vv. 10–13).

I. Sing unto the Lord, All the Earth (Ps. 96:1–6)
1. Call to sing praises to the Lord (vv. 1–3)
   1 O sing unto the Lord a new song: sing unto the Lord, all the earth.
   2 Sing unto the Lord, bless his name; shew forth his salvation from day to day.
   3 Declare his glory among the heathen, his wonders among all people.

Verses 1–3 show several aspects of true worship. One is that worship includes singing. The word *sing* is found throughout the Book of Psalms because these were hymns designed to be sung. Throughout history, singing has been an essential part of worship. Singing, with its melody and poetic wording, is ideal for expressing the feelings of true worship. Such singing is not just sung to and for one another, but "unto the Lord." Singing in worship is praise directed to the Lord Himself.

Another aspect of true worship is that it is inseparable from witness. The word translated "shew forth" in verse 2 literally means "to tell good tidings." The worshipers were called to bless the name of the Lord and to tell the good news of His salvation. Verse 3 uses the word "declare" to make the same point. Witness is part of worship, and worship leads to witness in daily life. After Isaiah had a tremendous experience of worship, he heard the call of God and volunteered to bear God's message (see Isa. 6:1–8). Worship without witness would fall short of true worship. Witness with worship would be shallow and lifeless.

The recipients of the witness were not only the people of God but also all people. The call to sing unto the Lord was issued to "all the earth." The worshipers were to declare God's glory "among the heathen" and to tell of His mighty works "among all people." During this year, we have studied Old Testament passages that stressed the universal nature of Israel's faith. Among these were the final chapters of Isaiah, the Book of Jonah, and the Book of Ruth. This theme appears not only in verses 1 and 3 of Psalm 96, but also in many of the other verses.

Another aspect of true worship is that it must be renewed. The "new song" of verse 1 is mentioned in other psalms (see 33:3; 40:3; 98:1; 149:1). At some point, of course, each of these was a new song in the sense of having been newly composed. However, each of them continued to be a new song in the sense of expressing the renewal of worship. Just as God's mercies are new every day (Lam. 3:22–23), so singing His praises should be new every day. Notice also the words "from day to day" in verse 2. Both worship and witness should be part of our daily living.

2. The greatness of the Lord (vv. 4–6)

4 For the Lord is great, and greatly to be praised: he is to be feared above all gods.

Many people claim to believe in God, but they do not respond to God the way the Bible says that people respond to the true and living God. They believe in an impersonal god, an abstract god, not in the great and good Lord. One of the acid tests of true faith is whether one's professed faith results in praise to God. Some people use the right words to describe the god in whom they believe. Many would affirm with the psalmist that the Lord is great; however, their actions show they don't respond by praising Him greatly.

5 For all the gods of the nations are idols: but the Lord made the heavens.

Idolatry was widely practiced in ancient times, as indeed it still is, although often in different forms than the images of ancient people. The Old Testament contains some scathing denunciations of idolatry. Isaiah 44, for example, describes how images of gods were created by human hands. People took a piece of wood. With part of it they built various items for their own use. Part of it was burned to make a fire on which they cooked. Part of it was shaped into an image before which they bowed in worship (see vv. 9–20).

Over against idols, created by men, the psalmist set the only true and living God, who is the Creator of all things. God created the heavens and the earth and all that is in them. What folly to put our trust and give our allegiance to other objects of worship, which are our own creations, subject to the failings of their human creators and totally unable to help us in our needs.

> **6 Honour and majesty are before him: strength and beauty are in his sanctuary.**

The psalmist sought words that were worthy of describing this great God, who created all things and whom we worship. He used "honour and majesty," which were words used to describe the royal dignity of earthly kings. The psalmist used these words of the King over all things and all people.

He also used "strength and beauty" to describe God in His sanctuary. An increasing number of people profess to believe that public worship is unimportant in their lives. Some of these are people who claim to be able to worship God just as well in nature as with the congregation in the house of the Lord. I often wonder if such excuse-makers worship God anywhere. People of faith worship God in nature, in the quietness of their place of prayer, and within the congregation of other people of faith.

II. Call to Worship the Lord as King (Ps. 96:7–13)

1. **Give God the glory due His name (vv. 7–9)**

> **7 Give unto the Lord, O ye kindreds of the people, give unto the Lord glory and strength.**
>
> **8 Give unto the Lord the glory due unto his name: bring an offering, and come into his courts.**

Verses 7–9 continue the call for all people to worship the Lord. "Kindreds of the people" can be translated "families of nations" (NIV). The call is to "all the earth."

The word *glory* is a key word in the Bible. The basic meaning of the Hebrew word is heavy in weight. The verb came to be used of giving weight or honor to something. To glorify God is to recognize the essential being of God that gives Him importance and weight in relationship with the people who are worshiping Him. To put it another way, to give glory to God means to give Him the kind of honor that matches His true weight or character.

God's reputation is often far short of His true character. People do not see God as He truly is; as a result, they don't give Him the love, honor, and obedience He deserves. This is what the psalmist meant by giving God "the glory due unto his name." God's name is the character of God as He truly is, not as sinful, unbelieving people think He is. The purpose of worship and witness is to give God the glory due His name.

The last part of verse 8 mentions another aspect of worship. People show their faith and love by bringing offerings to God as part of their worship. In our study of the psalms, we have noted that God doesn't want offerings that are made as substitutes for repentance and obedience (see Pss. 51:16–17; 40:6–8). On the other hand, when we have first of all offered ourselves to the Lord, offerings are expressions of our faith and love to the Lord. In Christian churches, offerings also support witness to the people of the world who are called to know and glorify God.

9 O worship the Lord in the beauty of holiness: fear before him, all the earth.

Worship involves coming into the presence of the holy God. Although through Christ we are encouraged to come boldly to the throne of grace (Heb. 4:16), we are also told to come with a sense of reverence and awe.

2. God as King and Judge (vv. 10–13)

10 Say among the heathen that the Lord reigneth: the world also shall be established that it shall not be moved: he shall judge the people righteously.

11 Let the heavens rejoice, and let the earth be glad; let the sea roar, and the fulness thereof.

12 Let the field be joyful, and all that is therein: then shall all the trees of the wood rejoice

13 Before the Lord: for he cometh, for he cometh to judge the earth: he shall judge the world with righteousness, and the people with his truth.

Verse 10 contains the clearest statement of the call to witness to all people. God's people were to declare to the heathen that the Lord reigns. In other words, the people of Israel were called to declare that their God was King and Judge over all the earth, not just over their people and land. Such Old Testament passages foreshadowed the time in God's plan when Spirit-led followers of Jesus Christ would receive the Great Commission (see Matt. 28:18–20; see also Acts 1:8). The people of Israel were chosen not just for their own blessings but in order to be channels of blessings to all nations (see Gen. 12:1–3).

Psalm 96 proclaims the reality of God as reigning King and functioning Judge over all the earth; however, verse 13 recognized that the full revelation of His rule and judgment lay in the future. When Jesus came, He came declaring that the kingdom or reign of God had come (see Mark 1:15); yet He also taught His followers to pray, "Thy kingdom come" (Matt. 6:10). Even we who live in light of God's new covenant are still living in a world that doesn't recognize the eternal King and Judge. Only people of faith dare to believe that God's righteousness and truth will have the final word. The world in which we live is much like the world of the psalmist. Injustice and evil often seem to be the only realities. We need to heed the words of verses 10 and 13. We must tell the world that the Lord already reigns and they can acknowledge Him by faith. We also need to share the word that His kingdom will come. This is a word of judgment to some and a word of encouragement to others.

Verses 11–12 are a call to all God's creation to join in praising Him. These verses show that all the earth means more than all the people of the earth. These verses call all of nature to praise God. The sea is to praise Him with its roar. The fields and everything in them are to be jubilant. The trees are called to sing for joy.

1. Ira Sankey's life saved by singing. America's best-known preacher during the last century was evangelist Dwight L. Moody. And Moody's singer who sang to the thousands who attended Moody's services was Ira D. Sankey.

One Christmas Eve, Sankey was asked to sing as he traveled up the Delaware River. After the song had ended, a man came up to Sankey and asked him if he had served in the Union Army, and if he were standing guard on a clear, moonlight night in the spring of 1861. When Sankey said he had, the man, a Confederate veteran, told Sankey: "I had you in my sights and was about to pull the trigger when you began to sing the hymn: 'We are thine, do thou befriend us,/Be the guardian of our way.' I waited for you to finish singing, saying to myself, 'I'll kill him when he finishes.' But the hymn brought back memories of my mother singing it to me as a child long ago, and I couldn't pull the trigger."

Knowing the power of singing hymns to lift the spirit and to praise God, the psalmist encourages us to sing (vv. 1–3).

2. Bearing witness to Jesus. In one of his books Paul Powell, president of the Southern Baptist Annuity Board, tells about a sign he saw in a Colorado motel: "There ain't hardly no business here that ain't been gone after!"

God is not only concerned about what we believe, but also about the faithfulness with which we serve. A Quaker service was just breaking up when a late member rushed up, asking, "Is the service over?" "Yes," said a friend, "the meeting is over, but the service has only begun!"

He hit the nail right on the head! We worship to replenish our spiritual strength in order to serve God in our communities. Worship is to be followed by witnessing, as the psalmist practiced in his day (vv. 1–11). We must remember in witnessing to the unsaved, "there ain't hardly no business here that ain't been gone after." We are to go after them and bring them in (vv. 3–10).

3. Who or what is your God? Each of us worships a god of some kind. Perhaps it is the God of creation who has fully revealed Himself in Jesus Christ. Perhaps not. The priority in our life is our god. To what do you give the most attention? On what do you spend your money? What most occupies your mind and thoughts? Perhaps it is family, or your business, or your savings accounts, or your stocks and bonds. Each of us must search our heart and let God speak to us and show us if we have any other gods before Him (Exod. 20:3). There is no rest for the soul until it forsakes all man-made gods and bows before the true God in repentance and faith. Well did Augustine, the fourth-century church father, put it when he said: "My soul is restless until it can rest in Thee, O God."

This is what the psalmist of our lesson says to us today in verses 4–6.

4. Giving glory to God. With a good concordance, check to see how many times the word *glory* appears in the Bible. You will be amazed. Above all things, God wants to be glorified in His people and in His creation. And more is said about the glory of God in the Book of Psalms than in any other book of the Bible. The word in the Old Testament refers to "the weighty importance and shining majesty which accompany God's presence. . . . The New Testament uses 'doxa' [doxology] to express glory and limits the meaning to God's glory. . . . [and the] New Testament carries forth the Old Testament meaning of divine power and majesty. The New Testament extends this to Christ as having divine glory (Luke 9:32; John 1:14; 1 Cor. 2:8)."[1]

5. The King is coming. When I was a boy, I remember how I felt in turning the last corner in the road that led home from school. The days often were very cold and, most of the winter, snow lay on the ground. I would often see in the near distance my mother's face framed by the kitchen window, and I knew the house was warm and smelled of good things such as sugar cookies.

Why did my mother keep her daily vigil so faithfully? It was because she knew her son was coming home and she wanted to see him, hug him, and welcome him home.

With that same kind of joy and anticipation, we who are followers of Christ must expect His coming and be ready when He comes for us (vv. 10–13).

TEACHING THE BIBLE

▶ *Main Idea:* The relationship of worship and witness point out that the two are inseparable.

▶ *Suggested Teaching Aim*: To lead adults to examine the relationship between worship and witness, and to identify ways their worship can be a witness.

A TEACHING OUTLINE

1. Use an illustration to begin the session.
2. Use a research project to involve a member.
3. Use Scripture search to identify elements of true worship.
4. Use a group project to identify how your worship services can be a witness to nonbelievers.

Introduce the Bible Study

Use "Ira Sankey's life saved by singing" from "Applying the Bible" to begin the session. Point out that our psalm today—Psalm 96—encourages singing to the Lord.

Search for Biblical Truth

IN ADVANCE, enlist a member to read "Hymn" in the *Holman Bible Dictionary* or another dictionary and report on how singing was used in the Old Testament.

On a chalkboard or a large sheet of paper write, True Worship. Ask:

What elements should be present in true worship? Ask members to open their Bibles to Psalm 96 and call for a volunteer to read these verses. Ask members to provide answers from these verses. Be sure the following elements are listed. Share the suggested information and use the discussion questions.

Singing (vv. 1–2). (1) Psalms were designed to be sung; (2) Singing should be "unto the Lord" and is praise directed to the Lord Himself. Call for the report on "Hymns" in the Old Testament at this point.
DISCUSS: What is the purpose of singing? Is it to make us feel good or to honor God? Why? How can we know the difference? When is singing not "unto the Lord"?

Witness (vv. 2,10–13). Witness is part of worship, and worship should lead to witness in daily life.
DISCUSS: Are we engaging in true worship if our worship does not lead us to witness to the whole world?

Renewed (v. 3). Worship should be new and fresh; we should be willing to sing "new songs."
DISCUSS: How can we balance remembering God's mighty acts of deliverance (Ps. 105:5) and singing a new song?

Praising and magnifying God (vv. 4–6). Our actions in magnifying God must back up our words. God alone has "honor and majesty" and "strength and beauty."
DISCUSS: What false gods can we honor in our worship services? What elements of our worship do not praise God?

Offering (v. 8). God doesn't want offerings as a substitute for repentance and obedience; He wants them as an expression of our faith and love.
DISCUSS: What purposes does bringing an offering serve in our worship today?

Accountability (v. 13). God will have the final word. This will be a word of judgment to some and a word of encouragement to others.
DISCUSS: Why would you fear or welcome God's judgment? After you have listed all of the elements of worship members can find in these verses, ask: Do all worship experiences have to have these elements in them? Which ones could be left out and still be true worship?

Give the Truth a Personal Focus

Use a church bulletin and ask members to examine the elements of worship. Which parts of the service are designed for members only? Which parts would appeal to nonbelievers? Which parts would make nonbelievers feel uncomfortable?

Ask members to list ways your worship services could be a witness. Suggest they approach this question by pretending they are complete pagans and have never been in a Christian worship service before. What would make them feel uncomfortable? at home? welcomed?

Share your list with those who plan your worship.

---

1. *Holman's Bible Dictionary* (Nashville: Holman Bible Publishers, 1991), 557.

Sexual Purity

Basic Passages: Matthew 19:4–6; 1 Corinthians 6:13b,18–20;
Romans 12:1–2
Focal Passages: Matthew 19:4–6; 1 Corinthians 6:13b,18–20;
Romans 12:1–2

Many problems in today's society result from sexual immorality.
The rising tide of abortions is one of the problems. In this special
lesson for Sanctity of Human Life Sunday, we will look at biblical teachings about sexual purity. If biblical teachings about sex were
observed, one of the main causes of abortions would be removed. Each
of us can be responsible only for our own actions; but as Christians, we
should teach and promote the Christian way of sex and marriage.

▶ ▶ ▶ ▶ **Study Aim:** *To practice and promote Christian teachings about
sex and marriage to counteract abortion and other problems
arising from sexual immorality*

STUDYING THE BIBLE

LESSON OUTLINE
I. Sexuality—Part of God's Creation Plan (Matt. 19:4–6)
1. God's plan for sex and marriage (Matt. 19:4–5)
2. Marriage as a lifetime one-flesh union (Matt. 19:6)
**II. Flee Fornication—God's Plan for Escape
(1 Cor. 6:13b,18–20)**
1. Sexual immorality (1 Cor. 6:13b)
2. Flee fornication (1 Cor. 6:18–20)
III. Total Commitment—What God Requires (Rom. 12:1–2)
1. Living sacrifices (Rom. 12:1)
2. Not conformed, but transformed (Rom. 12:2)

In answering the Pharisees' question about divorce, Jesus referred to
Genesis 1:27 and quoted Genesis 2:24 (Matt. 19:4–5). Jesus emphasized that marriage partners are one flesh and that no person is to separate what God has joined together (Matt. 19:6). Paul stressed that the
body is not to be used for fornication but for the Lord (1 Cor. 6:13b).
Paul urged the Corinthian Christians to flee fornication because fornication is a sin against a person's body, because a believer's body is the
temple of the Holy Spirit, and because we belong to God, not ourselves
(1 Cor. 6:18–20). Paul pleaded with the Roman Christians to present
their bodies as living sacrifices to God (Rom. 12:1). Paul urged them
not to be conformed to the world but to be transformed by the renewal
of their minds (Rom. 12:2).

I. Sexuality—Part of God's Creation Plan (Matt. 19:4–6)
1. God's plan for sex and marriage (vv. 4–5)

4 And he answered and said unto them, Have ye not read, that he which made them at the beginning made them male and female,

5 And said, For this cause shall a man leave father and mother, and shall cleave to his wife: and they twain shall be one flesh?

Jesus asked this question to the Pharisees after they had posed a question to Him about divorce. The Pharisees were trying to trap Jesus when they asked, "Is it lawful for a man to put away his wife for every cause?" (Matt. 19:3). Deuteronomy 24:1 allowed a man to divorce his wife if "it come to pass that she find no favour in his eyes, because he hath found some uncleanness in her." The grounds for divorce had become a subject of debate among the Pharisees. One school of thought, led by Rabbi Shammai, taught that only adultery was a valid reason for divorce. Another view, championed by Rabbi Hillel, said that a man could divorce his wife for almost any reason.

Rather than becoming entangled in this debate, Jesus responded to their question by quoting Scripture. First, He referred to the statement in Genesis 1:27 that God had created human beings as male and female (v. 4). Then He quoted Genesis 2:24, which contains the basic biblical teaching about sex and marriage (v. 5). Genesis 2:24 is so crucial that Paul also quoted it when presenting the Christian view of marriage and sexuality (see 1 Cor. 6:16; Eph. 5:31).

For one thing, Genesis 2:24 shows that the marriage relation of husband and wife takes precedence over all other human relations. Married people still have obligations to their parents, but their primary responsibility is to their spouse.

2. Marriage as a lifetime one-flesh union (v. 6)

6 Wherefore they are no more twain, but one flesh. What therefore God hath joined together, let not man put asunder.

Jesus' explanation in verse 6 was His own interpretation of the meaning of Genesis 2:24. Jesus emphasized that marriage is a one-flesh union of a man and a woman. A husband and a wife become one in many aspects of their lives, but the primary biblical meaning of "one flesh" is the consummation of their relationship in sexual union. Thus Genesis 2:24 is the basic Bible text about God's purpose in making us sexual beings. God's purpose in sex was to provide the means for a man and a woman to make a total commitment to each other in responsible love.

Procreation is one purpose of sex within marriage (see Gen. 1:28), but not the only purpose. Passages like 1 Corinthians 7:3–5 mention the sexual union of husband and wife without mentioning procreation. Instead the focus is on the mutual claim of a married couple on each other's body. The sexual act is the most intimate expression of love and trust; thus it is only for a husband and a wife who have a relationship of total love and trust. Some people say that marriage is only a sheet of paper, but it is God's way for a man and a woman publicly and legally to accept full responsibility for their relationship and its consequences. Only in such a relationship should people make themselves vulnerable to the total intimacy and trust for which sex is designed. Thus so-called "casual sex" is a contradiction in terms.

Jesus stressed that such a relationship was intended by God to last a lifetime. A man and woman who become husband and wife enter into a relationship that only death can sever. They have been joined not just by the law but by God; and "what therefore God hath joined together, let not man put asunder."

II. Flee Fornication—God's Plan for Escape (1 Cor. 6:13b,18–20)

1. Sexual immorality (v. 13b)

13 Now the body is not for fornication, but for the Lord; and the Lord for the body.

Ancient society was a sexual wilderness, much like our society is becoming. Corinth was especially noted for its sexual immorality and permissiveness. Paul addressed the problem in 1 Corinthians 6:12–20, the classic biblical passage about why sex outside marriage is sinful. Paul was dealing directly with sexual relations with prostitutes (see v. 15), but the word "fornication" can refer to any sexual relations outside marriage.

The Corinthians tried to claim that sex was not a moral issue. They said that having sex did not break any law (v. 12). They also claimed that sex is just a physical drive like eating (see v. 13a). Thus satisfying sexual desires was no different from satisfying physical hunger by eating. By contrast, Paul insisted that sex is a moral and spiritual issue because it affects our essential being and our relation with God and others.

2. Flee fornication (vv. 18–20)

18 Flee fornication. Every sin that a man doeth is without the body; but he that committeth fornication sinneth against his own body.

19 What? know ye not that your body is the temple of the Holy Ghost which is in you, which ye have of God, and ye are not your own?

20 For ye are bought with a price: therefore glorify God in your body, and in your spirit, which are God's.

Paul used the word "body" in much the same way we use the word "personality." The Corinthians argued that sex is just a physical thing done with a body that will perish at death. Paul insisted that although the flesh-and-blood body returns to the dust, the body or human personality is eternal. Sex is an act of the human personality or body, not just a physical drive. How we use sex is a moral act. It involves the most intimate human relations with others and affects our relation with God. God intended sex for the one-flesh union of total love, trust, and responsibility. Using sex apart from this purpose is to pervert and distort God's will. It also hurts other people, some directly and some indirectly. Among the results, for example, are unexpected pregnancies, which are often dealt with by abortions.

Christians know that their bodies are not just flesh-and-blood collections of organic matter. Our bodies are ourselves and thus are temples of the Holy Spirit. Because God sent His Son to redeem us, we have been bought with a price. This means that we belong to God in a special way. We are not our own to misuse ourselves as we please. The purpose of our lives is to glorify God. In this context, glorifying God means two things: one negative and one positive. We are to flee fornication as Joseph literally ran from the sexual advances of Potiphar's wife (see Gen. 39:7–13). We are to glorify God by practicing God's plan for the one-flesh union of marriage. This means sexual purity if we are unmarried, and it means total commitment and faithfulness within marriage.

III. Total Commitment—What God Requires (Rom. 12:1-2)

1. Living sacrifices (v. 1)

1 I beseech you therefore, brethren, by the mercies of God, that ye present your bodies a living sacrifice, holy, acceptable unto God, which is your reasonable service.

Paul was not writing specifically about sexual issues in Romans 12:1–2, but the principles apply to this and every area of Christian living. The word "therefore" shows that Paul was beginning to draw practical applications from his impressive description of the "mercies of God" in Romans 1–11. Because of our experience of God's saving grace, we ought to present our bodies or ourselves as living sacrifices. Paul used the language of the temple. Believers are like priests, but what we offer are not animal sacrifices. Instead we offer ourselves. And we don't offer ourselves as dead but as living sacrifices. Sometimes faithfulness to Christ calls for us to offer ourselves to death for His sake, but Paul was thinking here of the call to every Christian to offer himself as a living sacrifice. Such sacrifices are holy and acceptable to God. "Reasonable service" may be translated "spiritual act of worship" (NIV). In other words, "this is the true worship that you should offer" (GNB).

2. Not conformed, but transformed (v. 2)

2 And be not conformed to this world: but be ye transformed by the renewing of your mind, that ye may prove what is that good, and acceptable, and perfect, will of God.

Offering ourselves as living sacrifices involves living differently from the world in which we live. It means being transformed by the kind of renewal that is possible as we walk with the Lord and live in the power of His Spirit. Such transformed living results in living in a way that pleases God and fulfills His will.

First-century believers were under tremendous pressure to conform their thoughts and actions to those of the unbelieving world in which they lived. In spite of almost twenty centuries of Christian influence, we live in a world that promotes different standards and values from the values and standards of God's eternal kingdom. In no area is this difference so apparent as in attitudes and actions about sex. Our culture promotes the same distorted views that Paul refuted in 1 Corinthians 6:12–20. We can live transformed lives in such a world only as we allow God's Word to be our guide and His Spirit to be our power.

APPLYING THE BIBLE

1. **"Trial marriages."** *USA Today* reported about "trial marriages" in 1991: thirty-seven percent of live-in partners broke up, ten percent still live together, thirteen percent had their marriages later "dissolved," and forty percent had successful marriages. The article reported that about one-fourth of those who eventually married are now divorced, and the forty percent of live-in couples who reported "successful marriages" is below the national average of about fifty percent.[1] Americans who live together before marriage separate in significantly greater numbers than couples who go directly to the altar.

God's plan for sex and marriage is sacred. It does not include some sort of "trial marriage" to see if it works before a lifelong commitment is made (Matt. 19:4–5).

2. **Making marriage work.** Making a marriage work is a 24-hour-a-day assignment that must be worked at 365 days for life! Author Charles M. Crowe gives some steps which, if practiced, would help a great deal: (1) realize that some conflict is inevitable; (2) don't try to reform your mate; (3) don't bury your grievances; (4) stick to the issues while quarreling and don't go off on tangents; (5) be quick to apologize even if you are right; (6) let your mate be difficult occasionally; (7) be patient; (8) consult a counselor if quarrels become chronic.[2] And I would add: Always make up; have special, romantic times together, such as dinner out and a night in a nice hotel; and say, "I love you" often (Matt. 19:5–6).

3. **The Bible speaks out on sex.** Our lesson today focuses on sexual immorality, perhaps the greatest curse of our day with all its attending problems. But it is not new, unfortunately (1 Cor. 6:12-20). The Bible provides clear guidance for us in our sex-saturated society:

- Sex is a part of God's creation.—(Gen. 1:27; 1:31);
- Immorality is a manifestation of sin.—(Rom. 1:24–25);
- Christ's redemption makes sexual purity possible.—(Phil. 4:13; 2 Pet. 1:4–7);
- Sexual intercourse creates a "one-flesh" union.—(Matt. 19:4–6);
- Sexual intercourse provides profoundly meaningful communication between a husband and a wife.—(Gen. 4:1);
- Sexual intercourse provides mutual pleasure of husband and wife.—(Prov. 5:18–19);
- Premarital and extramarital sexual intercourse are condemned.— (1 Cor. 6:13,15,18; Exod. 20:14; Matt. 5:27–28);
- Homosexuality is a sin and is condemned by a holy God.—(Rom. 1:26–27; 1 Cor. 6:9–11);
- Sexual lust is also a sin.—(Matt. 5:27);
- But God is eager and willing to forgive all sexual offenders upon the conditions of repentance and faith (1 John 1:9; 1 Cor. 6:9–11). And Christians must control their sexual behavior.[3]

4. Why adultery is wrong. In the Ten Commandments, and elsewhere in the Bible, God condemns the sins of immorality among all people, especially believers. But adultery is not wrong just because the Bible condemns it, the Bible condemns it because it is wrong! And why is immorality, either among married or unmarried Christians wrong? Because a holy God says it is; because it destroys character; because it makes of one a thief, taking something from another, that is not his or hers; because it destroys the home which is the very foundation of society; because it brings a flood of unwanted, unwelcome babies into the home of a single parent who cannot care for herself much less another mouth to feed; because it destroys other worthy programs of society, pouring millions of tax dollars into our welfare system that could be better used; because for believers it is a mockery of the great price Jesus has paid to redeem (1 Cor. 6:20); and because the believer's body is the temple in which Jesus through His Holy Spirit, dwells with us. (1 Cor. 6:18–20).

TEACHING THE BIBLE

▶ *Main Idea:* The Bible's pleas for sexual purity demands that all Christians practice and promote sexual purity.
▶ *Suggested Teaching Aim:* To lead adults to describe the Bible's standards of sexual purity, and to commit themselves to that standard.

A TEACHING OUTLINE

1. Use an illustration to begin the session.
2. Use three small groups to examine the focal passage.
3. Use discussion questions to examine the relationship of these passages to abortion.
4. Use brainstorming to identify ways adults can maintain sexual purity.
5. Use a time of commitment to challenge members to a new level of commitment.

Introduce the Bible Study
Use "Trial marriages" in "Applying the Bible" to introduce the session. Point out that anything that violates God's standards of sexual purity is wrong.

Search for Biblical Truth
Make a lesson poster with the following headings:
I. Sexuality—Part of God's Creation Plan (Matt. 19:4–6)
II. Flee Fornication—God's Plan for Escape (1 Cor. 6:13b,18–20)
III. Total Commitment—What God Requires (Rom. 12:1–2)
Place this poster on the focal wall. Use it in making the group assignments below.
Organize the class into three groups. Assign each group one of the three points on the poster. Give each group one of the following assign-

ments. (If you prefer not to organize groups, you can do these assignments as a whole class.)

Group 1—Study Matthew 19:4–6 and be prepared to present to the class how these verses describe sexuality as a part of God's creation plan. In your presentation cover the following: (1) What is Jesus' plan for marriage? (2) What Jesus meant by "one flesh"; (3) What claim does a husband or wife have on the body of the other? (See 1 Cor. 7:3–5.) (4) What happens when God's plan for "one-flesh" marriage is broken? What should be our response?

Group 2—Study 1 Corinthians 6:13b,18–20 and be prepared to present to the class how fleeing fornication fits in God's plan for escaping sexual immorality. In your presentation cover the following: (1) how sexual immorality is a sin against one's own body; (2) what it means for our bodies to be the temple of the Holy Spirit; (3) how the price Christ paid for us should spur us to holy living.

Group 3—Study Romans 12:1–2 and be prepared to present to the class how these verses describe the total commitment that God requires of believers' lives. In your presentation cover the following: (1) how we are like priests in offering our bodies as living sacrifices; (2) what our reasonable service is; (3) what it means to offer our bodies as living sacrifices.

Allow approximately six to eight minutes for study and then call for reports. After each group's report, ask: What do these verses have to say about abortion?

Give the Truth a Personal Focus

On a chalkboard or a large sheet of paper, write Sexual Purity. Ask members to suggest actions they can take that will lead to sexual purity. Write these beneath Sexual Purity.

Suggest that members look over this list and compare their actions and thoughts to it. Do they need to make any changes in their thoughts or actions? Ask them to commit themselves to a new level of commitment in this area. Close with a time of reflection and prayer that all members will achieve a new level of commitment in this area.

---

1. Bob Laird, "How live-in partners fared," *USA Today* (August 9, 1991, D-1); reported by Dale L. Rowley in *Proclaim* (July, August, September, 1993), 28.

2. Adapted from Charles M. Crowe, *Sermons from the Mount* (New York, Nashville: Abingdon Press, 1954), 51-52.

3. Adapted from a pamphlet by J. Clark Hensley, *Christian Action Committee,* Mississippi Baptist Convention, Box 530, Jackson, Miss. 39205.

INDEX

The following index gives the lesson date on which a particular passage of Scripture has been treated in *Broadman Comments* from September 1990 through August 1996. Since the International Bible Lessons, Uniform Series, are planned in six-year cycles, the lessons during any six consecutive years include the better-known books and passages on central teachings. Thus, anyone who has access to the 1990–96 volumes of *Comments* can use this index to find a discussion of almost any part of the Bible he or she may be interested in studying.

Genesis

1:1–15	9–5–93
1:26–28	9–12–93
1:28a	1–15–95
2:18–25	9–12–93
3:1–13	9–19–93
3:22–24	9–26–93
6:5–8	9–26–93
9:8–13	9–26–93
15:1–16	10–3–93
16:1–4,11–16	10–10–93
17:1–14	10–17–93
21:1–14	10–24–93
25:19–34	10–31–93
27:6–8, 15–27	1–7–93
29:15–30	11–14–93
33:1–14	11–21–93
48:9–19	11–28–93

Exodus

1:8–11	6–5–94
2:1–9a, 23–25	6–5–94
3:1–7, 10–14	6–12–94
3:10–15a	6–12–94
4:1–5, 10–12	6–12–94
6:5–7	6–19–94
11:1	6–19–94
12:29–33	6–19–94
14:21–31	6–26–94
15:1–10,13	12–1–91
16:2–7, 13–18	7–3–94
18:13–25	7–10–94
19:4–6a	7–17–94

20:2–4, 7–17	7–17–94
25:1–8	7–31–94
29:42–46	7–31–94
32:15–19, 30–34	7–24–94
34:4–6	7–24–94
40:33c–38	7–31–94

Leviticus

25:8–10, 23–28, 39–42	8–7–94

Numbers

13:25–28, 30–31	8–14–94
14:6–10a, 28–30	8–14–94

Deuteronomy

6:1–13	8–21–94
18:10a	1–15–95
28:1–6, 15–19, 64–66	8–28–94

Joshua

1:11	9–20–92
2:1, 8–14, 22–24	9–4–94
3:7–17	9–11–94
6:1–5, 15–20	9–18–94
24:1–2a, 11–16, 22–25	9–25–94

Judges

2:11–19	10–2–94
7:2–7, 19–21	10–9–94

Ruth

1:1–8, 16–18 2–18–96
2:1, 8–12 2–25–96
4:13–17 2–25–96

1 Samuel

2:1–5 12–22–91
7:15, 8:9, 19–22 10–4–92
8:4–9, 19 10–16–94
9:15–17 10–23–94
10:1a, 20–24 10–23–94
10:17–25 9–2–90
12:19–25 10–16–94
13:5–14 10–30–94
16:1,6–7, 11–13 10–11–94

2 Samuel

1:17–27 12–15–91
5:1–5 10–11–92
7:4–16 9–9–90
7:18–29 11–6–94
12:1–10, 13 11–13–94
12:1–10, 13 9–16–90

1 Kings

2:1–4 10–18–92
3:5–12 10–18–92
9:1–3 11–20–94
10:1–7, 23–24 11–20–94
11:1–13 11–27–94
12:6–11, 16–17 6–4–95
18:17, 20–24, 36–39 11–1–92
18:30–39 6–11–95
21:1–4, 15–20 6–18–95
21:4–11a,17–19............9–23–90
22:13–16, 19–23, 26–29 9–30–90

2 Kings

7:1–9 6–25–95
9:1–12 10–7–90
17:6–14 8–27–95
19:14–20, 32–34 10–28–90
22:12–20a....................11–4–90

2 Chronicles

34:2, 8, 14b–16a,
   19, 21, 30–32 10–25–92

Ezra

1:1–8, 11 6–2–91
3:1,6–8, 10–12 6–9–91
5:1–11 6–16–91
7:11–16, 25–28 6–23–91
9:2–3, 10–11 6–30–91
10:9–13 6–30–91

Nehemiah

1:5–6 7–7–91
2:2-5, 15–18.....................7–7–91
4:6–12, 15–20 7–14–91
5:1–12 7–21–91
6:1–9, 15–16 7–28–91
8:1–3, 6-9, 14,17 8–4–91
9:1–3, 32–37 8–11–91
13:1, 3, 10–12, 15–19.....8–25–91

Psalms

8:1–9 12–29–91
34:2–10, 18–22 7–21–96
40:1–5, 9–11, 16b–17 8–4–96
51:1–13, 17 8–18–96
84:1–12 1–5–92
96 8–25–96
103:1–17 1–12–92
104:24–34 7–7–96
105:1–11, 43–45 7–14–96
119:1–16, 45, 105,
   129–130 8–11–96
139:1–14, 23–24 7–28–96

Song of Solomon

2:8–17 1–19–92

Isaiah

1:14–17	8–6–95
5:1–7	1–26–92
5:8–12, 18–23	8–20–95
6:1–8	8–6–95
7:2–6, 10–17	8–13–95
9:1–7	12–17–95
11:1–6	12–24–95
40:1–11a	12–3–95
42:1–9	1–7–96
49:1–6	1–14–96
50:4–11	1–21–96
51:1–6	12–10–95
53:1–6, 10–11	1–28–96
60:1–4	12–31–95
61:1–4	12–31–95

Jeremiah

1:9–10	11–29–92
20:7–11	11–29–92
26:1–6, 12–16	11–11–90
34:4–8, 27–31	11–18–90

Ezekiel

34:1–12	11–25–90

Hosea

1:1–3	11–15–92
1:2–9	7–16–95
3:1–2	7–16–95
3:1–5	7–16–95
6:4–6	11–15–92
11:1–4a	1–15–92
11:1–9	7–23–95

Amos

2:4–8	7–2–95
2:6–12	11–8–92
3:1–2	7–2–95
3:2	11–8–92
4:4–5	7–9–95
5:18–24	7–9–95
7:8–17	10–14–90

Obadiah

1–4, 10–11, 15, 17, 21	6–7–92

Jonah

1:1–4, 10–15, 17	2–4–96
1:1–9, 15–17	6–14–92
2:1, 10	2–4–96
3:1–5, 10	6–21–92; 2–11–96
4:1–4, 10–11	6–21–92
4:1–5, 11	2–11–96

Micah

3:5–12	7–30–95
6:1–8	11–22–92

Nahum

1:2–3, 6–9, 12–13, 15	6–28–92

Habakkuk

1:1–7	7–5–92
2:1–4	7–5–92

Zephaniah

1:1–3, 7, 12	7–12–92
2:1–3	7–12–92
3:12, 14–20	7–19–92

Matthew

1:18–25	12–18–94
2:1–12	12–25–94
3:1–15	12–4–94
3:16–4:11	12–27–92
5:1–12	5–5–96
5:38–48	5–12–96
6:5–15	5–26–96
6:7–15	2–2–92
6:19–21, 24–34	5–19–96
8:28–34	1–1–95
9:1–8	1–1–95
11:2–15	12–1–94
12:9–23	1–8–95

13:1-9, 18-23......1–6–91; 3–3–96
15:21–31 1–15–95
17:1–13 1–22–95
18:10, 4 1–15–95
18:21–34 2–17–91
18:21–35 3–10–96
19:14–15a......................1–15–95
20:1–16........12–30–90; 3–17–96
21:1–11, 14–16 1–29–95
25:1–13 1–1–91
25:14–30 3–24–96
25:31–46 2–24–91
26:20–30 2–5–95
26:57–68 2–12–95
27:27–44 2–19–95
28:1–10, 16–20 2–26–95

14:15–25 3–31–96
15:1–10 4–14–96
15:11–24 1–30–94
16:19–31 1–20–91
18:9–14 12–9–90
18:15–30 2–6–94
19:11–27 1–27–91
20:9–19 2–13–94
22:14–30 2–20–94
23:32–46 2–27–94
24:1–11 4–16–95
24:13–27 4–7–96
24:33–34 2–27–94
24:36–53 2–7–93

Mark

1:1–15 3–1–92
2:23–3:6 3–8–92
6:1–13 3–15–92
7:24–37 3–22–92
8:27–9:1 3–29–92
12:28–37 4–5–92
15:22–39 4–12–92
15:42–16:8 4–19–92
16:1–8 4–3–92

Luke

1:5–17 12–13–92
1:26–38 12–12–93
1:46–55 12–22–91
2:1–7, 22–32 12–20–92
2:4–20 12–19–93
2:8–12 12–23–90
2:10–14 12–24–95
3:2b–4, 7–17 12–5–93
4:1–15 12–26–93
4:16–28 1–2–94
4:31–43 1–9–94
6:20b–36 1–16–94
9:57–62 1–23–94
10:1–12 1–23–94
10:25–37 2–3–91
11:5–13 2–10–91
14:12–24 12–16–90

John

1:1–18 3–7–93
1:19–34 5–2–93
1:35–51 5–9–93
3:1–17 3–14–93
4:7–15, 20–26 5–16–93
6:35–51 4–25–93
7:37–52 5–23–93
9:1–12, 35–41 3–21–93
10:1–18 4–21–96
10:11–18 12–23–90
11:1–4, 21–27, 38–44 3–28–93
13:1–16 4–4–93
14:15–27 2–25–90
15:1–7 4–28–96
17:1–11, 20–21 2–9–92
20:1–16 4–11–93
21:12–22 ....4:18–93

Acts

1:1–14 9–3–95
2:1–4, 14a, 29–33, 37–39,
    44–45 9–10–95
2:1–7, 12–17a 1–3–93
3:1–8 9–17–95
4:5–12 9–17–95
5:17–32 9–24–95
6:1–14 10–1–95
8:5–6, 26–38................10–8–95
9:1–6, 10–20................10–15–95
9:1–16 9–1–91

9:26–30 9–8–91
10:30–39a, 44–48 10–22–95
11:1–18 1–17–93
11:19–30 10–29–95
11:19–26, 29–30 9–8–91
12:24–25 10–29–95
13:1–5 11–5–95
13:26–39 9–15–91
14:1–7, 24–27 11–5–95
14:8–18 9–22–91
15:1–2, 6–18 11–12–95
15:1–12 9–29–91
16:9–12, 16–23 10–6–91
16:9–10, 13–15,
   25–34 11–19–95
16:25–39 10–13–91
17:22–34 10–20–91
18:24–19:6 10–27–91
19:1–6, 11–20 11–26–95
20:17–31 11–3–91
21:26–33, 37–39a 11–10–91
26:1–8, 22–23, 27–29 ..11–17–91
28:21–31 11–24–91

8:1–13 4–23–95
8:8–9:14 3–24–91
9:1–7, 19–27 5–7–95
9:19–23 3–24–91
10:1–17 3–9–95
11:17–29 4–7–91
12:4–7, 12–26 4–14–91
12:4–20, 26 4–2–95
12:17–13:13 4–21–91
13:1–13 5–28–95
14:20–33a.....................4–9–95
15:12–17, 56–58 4–16–95
15:12–22, 53–58 3–31–91

2 Corinthians

1:1–11 4–28–91
1:3–14 4–30–95
1:23–2:11, 14–17 5–5–91
4:1–2, 7–18 5–12–91
5:6–20 5–19–91
5:11–21 5–14–95
8:1–15 7–29–91
9:1–8, 10–15 5–21–95
12:19–21 3–26–95
13:5–13 3–26–95

Romans

1:1, 3–17 3–6–94
4:13–25 3–13–94
5:6–17 3–20–94
6:3–14, 20–23 3–27–94
8:1–11 4–10–94
8:12–17 4–3–94
10:5–17 2–14–94
12:1–18 4–17–94
14:7–19 4–24–94
15:1–13 7–21–94

Galatians

1:6–7 5–1–94
2:11–21 5–1–94
3:1–5, 23–29 5–8–94
4:1–7 5–8–94
4:8–20 5–15–94
5:1, 13–26.....................5–22–94
6:1–10, 14–18 5–29–94

Ephesians

1:3–14 12–6–92
2:1–10 8–1–93
2:11–22 8–8–93
3:14–19 8–1–93
4:1–16 1–31–93
5:1–20 8–15–93
5:21–6:4 8–22–93
6:10–20 8–29–93

1 Corinthians

1:10–17 3–3–94
1:18–31 1–24–93
2:1–13 3–5–95
4:1–2, 6–16 3–12–95
6:9–20 3–10–91
7:3–16 3–17–91

Philippians

1:3–14, 27–30 6–6–93

2:1–11 2–16–92
2:1–16 6–13–93
3:1–16 6–20–93
4:4–20 6–27–93

Colossians

1:3–5a, 11–23 7–4–93
2:5–19 7–11–93
3:1–17 7–18–93

1 Timothy

1:3–11, 18–20................7–26–92
4:1–16 8–2–92
6:6–14, 17–21 8–9–92

2 Timothy

2:1–15 8–16–92
2:14–26 2–28–93
3:10–17 8–23–92
4:1–5 8–23–92

Titus

2:7–8, 11–14 8–30–92
3:1–8 8–30–92

Philemon

4–21 7–25–93

Hebrews

1:14 12–6–92

James

1:2–4, 12–15, 19–27 6–2–96
1:5–8 6–23–96
2:1–13 6–9–96
2:14–26 6–16–96
3:1–5a, 13–18 6–23–96
4:1–10, 13–17 6–30–96
4:11–12 6–9–96
5:13–16 6–16–96

1 Peter

1:3–9, 13–21 4–26–92
1:13–25 1–10–93
2:1–10 5–3–92
3:13–18 5–10–92
4:1–2, 7–11 5–10–92
5:1–11 5–17–92

2 Peter

2:1–14 5–24–92
3:3–14 5–31–92

Revelation

15:2–4 2–23–92
19:4–8 2–23–92